# Bringing the Plague

# Bringing the Plague

## Toward a
## Postmodern Psychoanalysis

Edited by
### Susan Fairfield
### Lynne Layton
### Carolyn Stack

OTHER

OTHER PRESS
*New York*

Permission to reprint the following is gratefully acknowledged:
Chapter 1: "Toward a Social-Constructivist View of the Psychoanalytic Situation." Permission from The Analytic Press to reprint *Ritual and Spontaneity in the Psychoanalytic Process*, pp. 133–162 (1998).
Chapter 2: "Analyzing Multiplicity: A Postmodern Perspective on Some Current Psychoanalytic Theories of Subjectivity." Permission from The Analytic Press to reprint *Psychoanalytic Dialogues* 11:221–251 (2001).
Chapter 2a: "The Treatment of Choice: A Response to Susan Fairfield." Permission from The Analytic Press to reprint *Psychoanalytic Dialogues* 11:283–291 (2001).
Chapter 2b: "In Our Consciousness, in Our Conscience, in Our Backyard: A Reply to Mitchell." Permission from The Analytic Press to reprint excerpts from "Reply to Crastnopol, Goldman, and Mitchell," *Psychoanalytic Dialogues* 11(5):807–822.
Chapter 5: "What You Know First: Construction and Deconstruction in Relational Psychoanalysis." Permission from The Analytic Press to reprint *Psychoanalytic Dialogues* 4:441–471 (1994).
Chapter 6: "Cultural Hierarchies, Splitting, and the Dynamic Unconscious." Permission from Ohio State University Press to reprint an earlier version of *Journal for the Psychoanalysis of Culture & Society* 5:65–71 (2000). Also permission from The Analytic Press to reprint excerpts from an earlier version of "What's Disclosed in Self-Disclosures? Gender, Sexuality, and the Analyst's Subjectivity. Commentary." *Psychoanalytic Dialogues* 8:731–739 (1998).
Chapter 7: "A Dialogue on Racial Melancholia." Permission from The Analytic Press to reprint *Psychoanalytic Dialogues* 10:667–700 (2000).
Chapter 9: "The Analyst's Participation: A New Look." Permission to reprint *Journal of the American Psychoanalytic Association* 49:359–381 (2001).

Copyright © 2002 Susan Fairfield, Lynne Layton, Carolyn Stack

Production Editor: Robert D. Hack

This book was set in 11 pt. Goudy by Alpha Graphics of Pittsfield, New Hampshire

10 9 8 7 6 5 4 3 2 1

Library of Congress Cataloging-in-Publication Data

Bringing the plague : toward a postmodern psychoanalysis / edited by Susan
    Fairfield, Lynne Layton, and Carolyn Stack.
        p. cm.
    Includes bibliographical references and index.
    ISBN 1-892746-85-9
    1. Psychoanalysis and culture.   2. Postmodernism—Psychological aspects.   3.
Psychoanalysis—Social aspects.   I. Fairfield, Susan.   II. Layton, Lynne, 1950–   III. Stack,
Carolyn.
BF 175.4.C84 B75 2002
150.19'5—dc21

                                                                    2001050013

*Bringing the Plague* is dedicated to one of our contributors, Stephen A. Mitchell, who died during the production of the book. His work has been an exceptionally important influence on our approach to psychoanalysis.

# Contents

# Acknowledgments

For several years the editors were part of a group that met regularly to explore the intersection of postmodernism and psychoanalysis. We would like to thank the other members of that group: Jill Bloom, Joel Greifinger, and Richard Nasser, for their contribution to the thinking that led to this volume.

# Contributors

**Michael Bronski** is a journalist, cultural critic, and political commentator who has been involved in gay liberation as a political organizer, writer, editor, publisher, theorist, and public speaker since 1969. He is the author of *Culture Clash: The Making of Gay Sensibility* (1984) and *The Pleasure Principle: Sex, Backlash, and the Struggle for Gay Freedom* (1998). He has edited two books of gay men's essays and has published in numerous journals, newspapers, and anthologies.

**Steven H. Cooper** is a Training and Supervising Analyst at The Boston Psychoanalytic Society and Institute and the Massachusetts Institute for Psychoanalysis. He is Clinical Associate Professor of Psychology, Harvard Medical School at Beth Israel Deaconess Medical Center.

**Muriel Dimen** is Associate Editor of *Psychoanalytic Dialogues* and *Studies in Gender and Sexuality*, and Professor of Clinical Psychology in the New York University Postdoctoral Program in Psychotherapy and Psychoanalysis. She is the author of *Surviving Sexual Contradictions* and *The Anthropological Imagination* and coeditor of *Regional Variation in Modern Greece and Cyprus* (with Ernestine Friedl), *Storms in Her Head: Freud and the Construction of Hysteria* (with Adrienne Harris), and *Gender in Psychoanalytic Space* (with Virginia Goldner). She is in private practice in New York City.

**David L. Eng** is an Assistant Professor of English and Comparative Literature at Columbia University, where he is also an affiliate member of the Asian American Studies Program. He is author of *Racial Castration: Managing Masculinity in Asian America* (forthcoming) and coeditor (with Alice Y. Hom) of *Q&A: Queer in Asian America* (1998). His current project is a coedited collection (with David Kazanjian) entitled *Loss: Mourning and Melancholia in the Twentieth Century*.

**Susan Fairfield** is in private practice in Cambridge, Massachusetts. A graduate of the Massachusetts Institute for Psychoanalysis, she is also an editor and translator of psychoanalytic books. Her articles have appeared in *The International Journal of Psycho-Analysis* and *Psychoanalytic Dialogues*, as well as journals of literary studies.

**Virginia Goldner** is Editor of the journal *Studies in Gender and Sexuality* and is on the editorial board of *Psychoanalytic Dialogues*. She is also Faculty and Supervisor at the Derner Institute of Advanced Psychological Studies at Adelphi University.

**Jay Greenberg** is a psychoanalyst in private practice in New York City. He is a Training and Supervising Analyst at the William Alanson White Institute of Psychiatry, Psychoanalysis, and Psychology and a Clinical Associate Professor of Psychology at New York University. He is the author of *Oedipus and Beyond* (1991) and, with Stephen A. Mitchell, of *Object Relations in Psychoanalytic Theory* (1983).

**Shinhee Han** is a psychotherapist at the Counseling and Psychological Services of Columbia University. She is a doctoral candidate in the Shirley M. Ehrenkranz School of Social Work at New York University and maintains a private practice in New York City.

**Irwin Z. Hoffman** is a Supervising Analyst and faculty member at the Chicago Center for Psychoanalysis and a Lecturer in Psychiatry at the University of Illinois College of Medicine. He has served on the editorial boards of *Psychoanalytic Dialogues* and *The International Journal of Psycho-Analysis* and is an editorial reader for *The Psychoanalytic Quarterly*. He is the author of *Ritual and Spontaneity in the Psychoanalytic Process* (1998) and coauthor (with Merton M. Gill) of *Analysis of Transference, Vol. II: Studies of Nine Audio-Recorded Psychoanalytic Sessions* (1982). He is in private practice in Chicago.

**Lynne Layton** is Assistant Clinical Professor of Psychology, Harvard Medical School at Beth Israel Deaconess Medical Center. She teaches popular culture for the Committee on Degrees in Social Studies, Harvard University. Currently an advanced candidate and a faculty member of the Massachusetts Institute for Psychoanalysis, she is in private practice in Brookline, Massachusetts. She is the author of *Who's That Girl? Who's That Boy?: Clinical Practice Meets Postmodern Gender Theory* (1998) and coeditor (with Barbara Schapiro) of *Narcissism and the Text: Studies in Literature and the Psychology of Self* (1986).

**Kimberlyn Leary** is Associate Director of the University of Michigan Psychological Clinic, Adjunct Assistant Professor of Psychology at the University of Michigan, and a Visiting Scholar at the Program on Negotiation at Harvard Law School. She is also a candidate at the Michigan Psychoanalytic Institute.

**Ronnie C. Lesser** is coeditor with Erica Schoenberg of *That Obscure Object of Desire: Freud's Female Homosexual Revisited* (1999) and with Tom Domenici of *Disorienting Sexuality: Psychoanalytic Reappraisals of Sexual Identities* (1995). She is Editor of *The Psychoanalytic Activist*, the newsletter of Psychoanalysts for Social Responsibility, and is on the editorial boards of *Studies in Gender and Sexuality* and *The Journal of Gay and Lesbian Psychotherapy*. She maintains private practices in Westchester and New York City.

**Stephen A. Mitchell** was the Founding and Associate Editor of *Psychoanalytic Dialogues*; Training and Supervising Analyst, William Alanson

White Institute, New York; and Faculty and Supervisor, New York University Postdoctoral Program. He was the author of *Object Relations in Psychoanalytic Theory* (with Jay Greenberg; 1983), *Relational Concepts in Psychoanalysis: An Integration* (1988), *Influence and Autonomy in Psychoanalysis* (1997), and *Relationality: From Attachment to Intersubjectivity* (2000).

**David Schwartz** is a psychoanalyst in private practice in Manhattan and Westchester County, New York. He is on the editorial boards of *Studies in Gender and Sexuality* and *The Journal of Gay and Lesbian Psychotherapy*. His articles have appeared in *Psychoanalytic Dialogues*, *Psychoanalytic Psychology*, and *Gender and Psychoanalysis*.

**Carolyn Stack** is a member of the faculty and the board of directors of the Massachusetts Institute for Psychoanalysis, where she is also an Advanced Training Candidate. She is on the board of *Gender and Psychoanalysis*. Her papers have appeared in numerous psychoanalytic anthologies and journals. She is in private practice in Cambridge, Massachusetts.

**Donnel B. Stern** is Editor, *Contemporary Psychoanalysis*; Faculty, Training, and Supervising Analyst, William Alanson White Institute, New York; and Faculty, New York University Postdoctoral Program in Psychotherapy and Psychoanalysis. He is the author of *Unformulated Experience: From Dissociation to Imagination in Psychoanalysis* (1997), coeditor of *Handbook of Interpersonal Psychoanalysis* and *Pioneers of Interpersonal Psychoanalysis* (both 1995), and a member of the editorial boards of *Psychoanalytic Dialogues*, *Psychoanalytic Inquiry*, and *Psychoanalytic Psychology*.

# Introduction: Culture and Couch

*Susan Fairfield, Lynne Layton,*
*and Carolyn Stack*

## "DEFINING" POSTMODERNISM

The anecdote has it that in 1909, as Freud and Jung were crossing the Atlantic for the United States, the two great men stood conversing on deck. In response to Jung's enthusiasm about bringing psychoanalysis to America, Freud replied, "Little do they know we are bringing the plague." Revolutionary changes in contemporary psychoanalysis are perhaps the second plague. Shifts into both relational and social constructivist models over the past decade have been greeted by some analysts with enthusiasm, by others with horror. The Freud of the above anecdote well understood that his ideas were revolutionary, that they would spread across the nation and have profound effects on the culture, whether the people of the United States liked it or not. So it is with the assimilation of postmodern ideas and language into psychoanalysis. Because we already live in an era of postmodernity, psychoanalysis cannot ignore the consequences of contemporary culture that show up in our perpetually changing theories and consulting rooms (Elliott and Spezzano 1996). For example, the quality and nature of interpersonal relationships and modes of subjectivity—topics with which psychoanalysis is deeply concerned—are increasingly affected by massive contemporary technological advances.

Because the notion of a unified postmodern theory or a set of coherent positions goes against the very tenets of postmodernism, we need to spell out how we understand that concept and why we believe it is a useful, indeed a necessary, lens in our understanding of psychoanalytic theories and practices. Although we are using the broad term *postmodernism* because of its familiarity, it would be more accurate to say that our project is part of the movement within postmodernism known as *poststructuralism*.

Best known in this country through the work of Jacques Derrida as well as through queer theory and much of feminist theory, poststructuralism represents a reaction to the theoretical school known as structuralism, which claims that it is possible not only to discern but also to describe with scientific rigor the underlying structures that systematically produce the meaning of a text or other cultural formation. For the poststructuralists, however, any attempt to fix meaning is subverted by ambiguities both within the object of study and within the interpreter herself or himself: ambiguities such as the internal haunting of closed systems by what they attempt to define as external to them, as well as the multiplicities, paradoxes, and irreducible inconsistencies that undermine foundational theories and preclude definition and closure. Thus any attempt at rational ordering, at rule-bound structuring, can only lead to a critical impasse, or, much more seriously, to abuses of power when human attributes or experiences that do not fit within the master system are rendered invisible or forcibly suppressed. Poststructuralists analyze the assumptions that produce and reproduce what are intended to be fixed categories of meaning. But, unlike structuralists, they recognize at the same time that they can never stand fully outside the very conceptual frameworks that they are attempting to explain.

Postmodernism offers a critique of the conventional notions of truth and reason that were championed by modernity as the source of social and scientific progress. Its adherents argue that "reality" and "subjective experience" are always co-constructed events and, as such, are open to sociopolitical analysis. Thus what are held to be our soundest theories, the very foundations of our knowledge, are more accurately spoken of as beliefs, and, importantly, as beliefs that carry specific culturally bound values and meanings.

Poststructuralism puts in question all binary classifications, and so, on the principle that we cannot exempt our own thinking from the same critical procedures that we apply to what we are discussing, we propose no rigid definition of poststructuralism as opposed to structuralism (see Culler 1982 for a nuanced account of differences and similarities between the two orientations), nor, on the larger scale, a rigid definition of postmodernism as opposed to modernism. In different ways, Irwin Z. Hoffman, Carolyn Stack, Steven H. Cooper, and Susan Fairfield discuss the persistence of modernist (objectivist, positivist) patterns of thought at the heart of psychoanalytic theories and clinical practices that claim to belong to the postmodern paradigm.* But clearly, along with the larger culture, psychoanalysis is undergoing a sea change. Stephen A. Mitchell sees this change as one from a monistic to a more pluralistic concept of self. Fairfield, however, discusses ways in which a pluralistic model of subjectivity, often held to be a hallmark of a postmodern turn in psychoanalysis, can in itself be entirely compatible with a modernist sensibility. More consistent with a postmodern perspective is Hoffman's account of the vanguard of psychoanalytic thinking not as a shift from drive theory to relational theory but, more radically, from a positivist to a constructivist model. While we are aware of the dangers of simplification, our goal is to explore what this shift involves. Thus we begin our anthology with Hoffman's important contribution to current theory, "Toward a Social-Constructivist View of the Psychoanalytic Situation."

## PSYCHOANALYSIS AND POSTMODERNISM

Though discussions of psychoanalysis and postmodernism draw on a variety of twentieth-century psychoanalytic theories (cf. Elliott and Spezzano 1999), we have restricted our investigation to relational psy-

---

*Where no date is given after an author's name, the reference is to a chapter in the present volume.

choanalysis, with a special emphasis, in many of the papers presented here, on the challenges that academic postmodern theory may pose to clinical practice, and vice versa. (Readers unfamiliar with the tenets of two-person relational psychoanalysis will find them briefly summarized in Jay Greenberg's paper and further described and illustrated in many of the other contributions to this volume.) More specifically, our focus is what we shall go on to describe as a social-constructivist or perspectival approach to theory and practice. Numerous classical one-person theorists, however, have utilized postmodern ideas in interesting ways. Barnaby Barratt (1993), for example, views the process of free association as subversively deconstructive. And narrative approaches such as those of Spence (1982) and Schafer (1992) make clear that the analyst's theoretical biases affect the patient's life story. For example, according to Schafer (1992) the analyst who uses the theory and language of defense and resistance is contributing to the construction of a military narrative. Classical theory has been embraced by multi-disciplinary academics precisely because it lends itself to postmodern readings and because the ambiguity of much of Freudian theory, and its paradoxical and subversive nature, are consistent with the work of a deconstructive critique. The very idea of unconscious processes, for example, supplants the modernist valorization of reason. The papers by Greenberg, David Schwartz, and Fairfield discuss elements of the complex relationship of classical psychoanalysis to postmodernism.

Some contemporary analytic theorists, such as Teicholz (1999), view all two-person models—models that understand that treatment takes place in the transitional space between two subjects, patient and analyst—as intrinsically postmodern. In contrast to this perspective, we believe that there is a wide and significant variation in the usage and the reach of postmodern concepts among two-person psychoanalysts. Only those two-person models that put their own assumptions into question can be said to belong to the postmodern episteme. As Mitchell notes, "If psychoanalysis is viewed, as it increasingly has been, as an intersubjective encounter, the clinician needs to understand all features of his participation, including his belief that psychoanalysis is usefully understood as an intersubjective encounter, as one among many possible ways of organizing experience." (A dyed-in-the-wool psychoanalytic poststructuralist might add that what constitutes "experience" in the first place is an intersubjective and culturally mediated formation.)

Just as a pluralistic concept of subjectivity does not automatically imply a postmodern as opposed to a modern approach, neither does a two-person theory. Mitchell is hesitant about where to locate self psychology with respect to a one-person or a two-person model. But Hoffman argues that the older relational models and the postmodern model of social constructivism differ in that object relations theory, self psychology, and interpersonal and intersubjectivity theories have remained largely within the positivist framework in ways that he spells out, whereas, in the perspectivist epistemology he advocates, "the personal participation of the analyst in the process is considered to have a continuous effect on what he or she understands about himself or herself and about the patient in the interaction."

## PSYCHOANALYSIS AND SOCIOPOLITICS

In developing our approaches to postmodernism, we were strongly influenced by two landmark books that preceded the postmodern turn in psychoanalysis: Stephen A. Mitchell's (1988) delineation of the relational-conflict theory of psychoanalysis and Jessica Benjamin's (1988) theory of intersubjectivity, and then, as the postmodern influence began to be felt in our field, by the constructivist model developed by Hoffman (this volume and 1998). For our purposes, it is important to distinguish between relational theories that, as Hoffman (chapter 1) puts it, see the psychoanalytic process as "a world of mutual influence and constructed meaning" and those maintaining that, to a greater or lesser degree, analysts are "able to assess accurately what they and their patients are doing and experiencing." This distinction marks how far a particular theorist or theory affords the kind of sociopolitical analysis that we champion in this project.

Postmodernism has influenced psychoanalytic relational theories and techniques in a number of different ways. This influence has in turn produced a backlash, hostile responses that account for why our title likens postmodernism to the psychoanalytic plague that Freud envisioned en route to the United States. The relational theorists who are interested in postmodern concepts have been particularly attuned to the ways in which traditional notions of reality, truth, and knowledge are thrown into question by the postmodern critique. Hoffman's (1998) use of social constructivism, more than any other relationalist body of work, takes seriously the notion that reality is co-constructed moment to moment between patient and analyst. His injunction that the analyst always maintain a position of uncertainty vis-à-vis her own convictions suggests an openness to a sociopolitical interpretation of theory. Unfortunately, Hoffman does not extend his analysis into the cultural domain, and, in fact, has moved further away from this possibility by renaming his theory of social constructivism *dialectical constructivism*, a more narrow focus that does not take into account the sociopolitical factors that shape the patient–analyst interaction. In contrast, most of the contributions to *Bringing the Plague* explore ways in which the theorizations and clinical practices of psychoanalysis are pervaded by strongly entrenched categories of race, ethnicity, class, gender, and sexuality, as well as by more transient ideas that may capture the popular imagination from time to time.

As part of an extensive discussion of the influence of politics and culture on the ways in which psychotherapy is theorized and practiced, Cushman (1995) draws on Gadamer to argue that, on both the societal and the psychic levels, a cultural clearing and horizon of understanding determine what elements are intelligible. He, too, is critical of object-relational theories and self psychology for their neglect of sociocultural factors, and he therefore calls for a "three-person psychology," one in which the political context and its moral implications shape the interactions of the therapeutic dyad. His constructivist position, however, is almost the diametric opposite of Hoffman's, in that sociocultural factors are emphasized to the point where there is little attention to the moment-to-moment interactions of patient and therapist. Yet surely the very subtlety of these interactions, often exerting considerable influence out of awareness, must be taken into account by any theory of what patient and analyst can claim to know.

## KNOWLEDGE, MEMORY, AND AUTHORITY IN A POSTMODERN PARADIGM

What the analyst can claim to know is addressed by numerous analytic thinkers. Mitchell (1993) speaks of the contemporary revolution in theory in which "it now sometimes appears that the capacity to contain the dread of not knowing is a measure of analytic virtue: the fewer convictions, the better and the braver!" (p. 43). Steven H. Cooper (1993) suggests that our epistemological positions must be understood as an aspect of countertransference. To complicate matters, Hoffman's paper in this volume raises the issue of whether the term *countertransference* is still usable in a constructivist model (cf. McLaughlin 1981). Replacing classical analytic language that emphasizes insight and certainty, the relationalists' language tends to underscore uncertainty, ambiguity, paradox, and ambivalence. The goals of treatment become less about genetic insight and finding the underlying truth of symptomatology. Instead, treatment aims at helping patients bear uncertainty and develop the capacity for critical reflection on how their reality is constructed both historically and in the moment. Thus Cooper argues that traditional notions of "cure" are no longer relevant to psychoanalysis, which is, instead, about helping to "expand meaning systems, sometimes including those associated with symptomatic relief." Relationalists speak of tolerating in contrast to knowing (Bollas 1992, D. B. Stern 1997), bearing dialectically opposed thoughts and affects (Aron 1996, Bromberg 1998, Hoffman 1998, Pizer 1998), and developing more relativistic perspectives on life (Hoffman 1998, cf. also Schafer 1992).

The meaning of the concept of interpretation also changes radically under the postmodern gaze. We no longer seek a single definitive story of a patient's symptomatology. Rather, we understand that there must be multiple interpretations, each with its own valence, each in dialectical relation with other interpretations. Following Merton Gill (1983), Aron (1996) argues that there are always plausible perspectives other than one's own. Analytic neutrality now refers to the therapist's capacity to be open to alternate readings. This is not to say that any interpretation is as good as any other, but that the postmodern lens opens up the psychic space to allow a wider arena of possible perspectives (Elliott and Spezzano 1996).

For some, a postmodern psychoanalysis becomes an aesthetic endeavor (Flax 1990, Geha 1993), where the analyst turns her interpretive gaze to that which enriches, develops, and furthers the patient's life stories. And Spezzano (1993) argues that when we are no longer talking about which interpretation is right or wrong, the question becomes more about what is "conversationally useful." We must now ask what work a particular interpretation does and does not do. But how could we determine this? As Greenberg importantly reminds us, therapeutic effectiveness tends to be retrodictively defined by the reporting analyst, without consideration of what another kind of intervention (including remaining silent) might have achieved. Cautious about postmodern relational models on the grounds that they do not take into account what he considers to be non-relational, "uniquely private and personal dimensions of the patient's experience," Greenberg also notes that relationalists claiming to be in the vanguard of psychoanalysis do not always avoid the dangers of causal explanation. Just like their traditional, rule-bound predecessors, he points out, relational theorists who advocate spontaneity tend to generalize and prescribe their own clinical approach despite the fact that a postmodern theory cannot "assert the benefit of any technical intervention a priori." In "On Thinking We Know What We're Doing," his commentary on Greenberg, Schwartz agrees that, from a postmodern perspective, "any claims by an analyst that he or she has had an experience that shows why a patient did what he or she did, or, even more improbably, shows us what the best way to do psychoanalysis is, is first of all false, and, perhaps more important, likely to be part of a larger political project, explicit or not and conscious or not."

The related question of memory is problematized under postmodern scrutiny. Nowadays we believe that our experiences and those of others can never be known in some essential form. All events are experienced, interpreted, remembered, narrated, and retold from particular perspectives and in specific contexts that carry social, emotional, psychological, political, and historical meanings. This is not to say that external events do not happen, but that we organize our experiences of these events, and the data of others' experiences, in specific ways to give them coherence and narrative meaning, and to sustain personal and sociocultural meaning systems that are important to our self-definitions. While the notion that realities, and therefore memories, are always constructed within a relational context is central to all two-person psychoanalytic models, the theoretical and clinical applications of this idea vary. For some theorists, all memories are perceived as fictive constructs—not within the fiction/reality binary but in the sense that fictions are the only reality (Geha 1993). Others may theorize the co-constructed nature of memory, and yet their clinical illustrations suggest that patients enact preexisting memories in treatment. Carolyn

Stack's paper, "(Ir)reconcilable Differences," notes that anxieties about "reality" are especially acute in patients' claims of childhood abuse. In the context of a case discussion in which her patient urgently demanded validation of a memory of ritual torture for which there seemed to be no objective basis, Stack found that her postmodern commitment to openness, uncertainty, and paradox posed a serious threat to the therapeutic relationship. Seeking to "delineate a mode of treatment that relies less on linking current symptoms to past events and more on mining the imaginative space created between patient and analyst," she describes how she took the major theoretical and clinical risk of conceptualizing the claim of ritual abuse in terms of a set of victimhood narratives available in the culture to encode, and serve as projective screens for, acute subjective distress and cultural hysteria.

In his discussion of this paper, Steven H. Cooper agrees with the importance of considering "multiplicity of meaning, ambiguity, compromise, and paradox" within a "dialectics of difference," but he argues for the assumption of a "working stance" that inevitably entails a belief in "the truth of the matter" when it comes to understanding a patient. Like other contributions to this volume that pay attention to how the authority of the analyst is unsettled in postmodern models, the exchange between Stack and Cooper raises the issue of who gets to define whatever it is that we mean by the patient's reality, or, for that matter, the analyst's reality. In refusing to accept her patient's account of ritual abuse, Stack felt her own belief system becoming undermined; moreover—and here is where postmodern clinicians face a compelling challenge that postmodern academicians do not—she recognized that the well-being of this very fragile patient was profoundly threatened by the unwillingness of the analyst, who is in a position of power, to confirm a particular, strongly invested version of the truth.

For a number of relational theorists, the analyst is no longer the same kind of "expert" as the classical analyst who knew what the patient did not (Mitchell 1993). The patient's interpretations are as valid and plausible as the analyst's (Aron 1996, Gill 1983, Hoffman 1998), and the analyst must be prepared to believe that the patient at times may know more about the analyst than he or she knows (Russell 1999, Stack 1998). The distinction that Aron (1996) makes between mutuality (in which both patient and analyst generate the data of the work, and each recognizes the other as a separate subject) and asymmetry (the "differences between patient and analyst in their roles, functions, power, and responsibilities" [p. 124]) ensures that the patient remains the primary subject of investigation.

Postmodernism's most fervent critics argue that the dismantling of objectivist claims to knowledge, truth, and reality dooms this method to an endless, nihilistic intellectual exercise. Mitchell, for example, describes his uneasiness with what he finds to be the "aggressive edge" of deconstruction, its "body slam" or "gotcha" quality. While we agree that poststructuralist critique can be, and sometimes is, used in this manner, we also believe that the capacity to keep questioning one's own positions, as well as those of others, is an act of courage that is a highly moral endeavor. As Goldner points out, "Instead of the judgmental, never-satisfied Mother or Father Confessor to whom [analysts] have traditionally been beholden, theories of . . . social constructivism and the postmodern turn are permission-giving and responsibility-enhancing. They generate a collective voice of authority that encourages us to question authority and yet to recognize how embedded in its matrix we will always be." In other words, relational psychoanalysis inflected by postmodern concerns about subject positions and power inequities has a therapeutics that is tied to an ethics. Thus Fairfield's reply to Mitchell details the ways in which the extensive and explicit ethical underpinnings of deconstruction can open the psychoanalytic encounter to the wider sociopolitical domain. She notes that "postmodern theories are not explanatory systems but a set of techniques precisely for putting explanatory systems into question," for discovering areas of "give" in what had seemed to be immutable "givens."

In a similar vein, Kimberlyn Leary writes that "it is useful to remember that postmodern discourses are not theories in and of themselves. Rather, they involve critiques that are meant to destabilize existing constructs. In finding the tensions and inconsistencies in an idea previously assumed to represent an essential truth, a new conceptual space opens—one that reveals the ambiguity of lived human experience." A postmodern perspective, then, unsettles fixed explanatory systems that delimit the visibility of whole reaches of human life, from the prevalence of racism, sexism, and homophobia in the larger culture to the idiosyncratic rigidities that constrain individual creativity and intersubjective understanding. In so doing, postmodernism performs the work of ethics, honoring the irreducible complexity of human experience within each of us and between us and others. Its goal is to open pathways toward change, within us and between us.

Contrary to the arguments of some critics, we believe that a post-modernist cannot avoid taking specific positions at any given moment. As Cooper points out in what he calls "the return of the repressed positivistic," even postmodernists are obliged to adopt a working stance in the clinical situation. For a postmodernist, however, these positions must always be open to scrutiny of their inevitable sociopolitical underpinnings, a process that, as many of the contributors to *Bringing the Plague* describe it, extends the traditional injunction to monitor one's "countertransference" to include consideration of the ways in which the analyst's tacit assumptions about sexuality, gender, class, ethnicity, race, and the nature of the psyche constantly inform clinical work. Thus, in both the theoretical and clinical arenas, the postmodern psychoanalyst might be passionately (or not so passionately) committed to a particular belief, but an essential aspect of the very work of psychoanalysis would be a deconstructive understanding of that belief.

## POWER/KNOWLEDGE: THE AUTHORITY
## TO DEFINE WHAT IS NORMAL

As we have mentioned, one of the primary reasons we are sympathetic to a postmodern critique of psychoanalysis is that it assumes that power relations infuse all claims to knowledge. Though few psychoanalysts fully incorporate this concept into their theories and practices, notable exceptions are a number of feminist and queer-theory analysts working particularly in the arenas of sexual subjectivities and gender relations. The ethical imperative of relational perspectives such as those of Benjamin (1988) involves not only a stake in the individual coming to know his or her desire (a potentially individualistic goal) but also the evolution of new forms of relating. In particular, and drawing on the work of Daniel Stern (1985), Benjamin elaborates the difference between subject–object (or doer–done to) relating and subject–subject relating. Certainly not all relational theorists would agree with Benjamin's implicit suggestion that a psychoanalytic treatment might be incomplete if the patient still is not largely living in the realm of subject–subject relating. And not all theorists who see their own work on gender and sexuality as more consistently postmodern would follow Benjamin in all respects (cf. Lesser 1997 and Schwartz 1992). But we want to draw attention to the fact that a relational psychoanalysis inflected by post-modern concerns about subject positions and power inequities ties a therapeutics to an ethics.

Relevant to this ethical project is deconstructionism's assertion that binary identity categories such as masculinity and femininity, black-ness and whiteness, are in fact not dichotomous but rather are inextri-cably co-defining and take on their meaning in a context of power in-equities. They are pairs in hierarchical relation, and the valued member of the pair defines itself primarily by excluding unwanted characteris-tics from its self-definition. These in turn become the defining char-acteristics of the devalued member of the pair. The deconstruction of identity categories both influenced and resonated with the work of re-lational analytic feminists (Benjamin 1988, Dimen 1991, Flax 1990, Goldner 1991, Layton 2000), who were beginning to understand gen-der as a product of splitting. At the same time, postmodern assertions of gender fluidity and critiques of core gender identity (e.g., Butler 1990a,b) also influenced relational analytic models of gender develop-ment. Theorists such as Harris (1991), Benjamin (1996), and Layton (1998) incorporated gender fluidity into their models in diverse ways. Questions of race, ethnicity, and class, while still the marginalized ter-rains of psychoanalysis, are beginning to be deconstructed by specific relational theorists as well (Altman 1995, Leary 1997, Moskowitz 1996, Whitson 1996). In this volume, the unsettling of binary oppositions is most extensively illustrated by Layton's discussion of gender categories and Fairfield's analysis (in reply to Mitchell) of what is involved in being "American."

Psychoanalysts drawing upon postmodern queer theory have launched an attack both on traditional developmental models and on models of sexual identity (see Jagose 1996 for further explication of the queer-theory movement). Analysts such as Dimen (1996), Lesser (1997), Coates (1997), Stack (1999), and Schwartz (1999) argue that linear models of development inevitably construct norms of health and disease along dominant cultural lines. Coates (1997) argues that the contemporary developmental theorists founder in their conflation of developmental lines and the sequential phenomena of physiological maturation. Thus she agrees that children develop biologically along similar lines (infants crawl before they walk; they babble before they produce words), but she argues that children's understanding of their sexed bodies and of gender is always a complexly determined, contextually driven, individual process. And Stack (in press) argues that no matter how Freudian constructs of the sexed body are revised to attempt to incorporate a feminist perspective, the stamp of traditional developmental markings always remains. In her contributions to this volume, she discusses the sociopolitical implications of developmental stories in psychoanalysis and argues that reaching for such stories may be a way that patients and analysts avoid turmoil in the analytic encounter. Discussing Stack's chapter, Cooper refers to the great clinical utility of developmental accounts, even if we recognize them to be "metaphors" or "mythologies." Similarly, in addressing the question of whether developmental narratives are essential to psychoanalytic theory and practice, Fairfield notes that, although they would have no place in a strictly postmodern psychoanalysis, "the pull of the modernist need for causal narratives may be so strong that clinical psychoanalysis, right now, cannot do without some version of them." (Once again, poststructuralist academicians need to be aware of complexities that must be dealt with by their counterparts who are practicing analysts.)

The larger issue here, of course, is the positivistic strain, backed by infant research, that has traditionally seen psychoanalysis as compatible with a science of human development. Among our contributors, Schwartz, Donnel B. Stern, and Fairfield are most explicit in presenting the poststructuralist case against scientism, but the assumption that psychoanalysis is a hermeneutic or constructivist enterprise is also shared by a number of other contributors to this volume.

Theorists in the various academic domains of cultural studies use poststructuralist techniques to analyze categories of race, class, and ethnicity. The insights of feminist perspectives and queer theory into the social construction of sexuality and gender have been of major importance not just within the fields of their primary focus, but, given the imbrication of sexuality and gender with concepts of race, class, and ethnicity, also far beyond them. Nevertheless, gender studies are only one strand in academic poststructuralism. But perhaps because psychoanalysis began by positing a key role for psychosexual challenges in the formation of subjectivity, gender studies have been the most widely felt influence in unsettling traditional psychoanalytic assumptions; even those analysts who are resistant to anything that smacks of constructivism are increasingly willing to rethink some of the normativizing constructs of gender and sexuality that carried over from the earliest decades of our discipline. Only a relatively small set of analysts have made use of poststructuralist feminisms and, more recently, queer theory. Among our contributors, these movements are most extensively represented by the papers of the theorist-clinicians Layton and Dimen, as well as by other works of Goldner, Lesser, Schwartz, and Stack referred to in this Introduction.

The growing influence of queer theory on psychoanalysis has radically changed notions of sexual identity. Queer theory asserts that the binary of heterosexuality and homosexuality, like the binaries of race and gender, is a social construct that maintains a hierarchy of sexual norms. Queer analytic relationalists argue for a more fluid and liberatory appreciation of sexual identities, desires, and behaviors (Dimen 1995, Domenici and Lesser 1995, Schwartz 1995, Stack 1999). Schwartz (1995), for example, contests the dominant notion that sexual desire is based primarily on the gender of the object choice. Surely, he argues, our desires might be, and are, as easily aroused by other factors such as dominance and submission, physical place, or specific personality characteristics of the other.

However, despite the growing acceptance among analysts of some aspects of gender studies, clinicians and theorists who believe in the biological necessity of the division into male and female, masculine and feminine, heterosexual and homosexual have been severely critical of postmodern influences on psychoanalysis. To them, nothing could be more objectionable than Butler's (1990a) assertion that the division into male and female is a social decision and not a biological fact, a social decision meant to inaugurate and legitimate the dominance of heterosexuality. Equally unacceptable to them is her idea that heterosexuality is haunted by split-off same-sex desire, although she grounds her analysis in the best of psychoanalytic authorities, Freud himself (Butler 1995). Those who believe in the psychological or biological necessity of the division into male and female, homosexual and heterosexual, come from camps as disparate as evolutionary psychology, gay and lesbian theory, and Lacanian theory.

In order to complicate notions of gender and genre, we have included in what is otherwise a collection of papers on psychoanalysis

Michael Bronski's ambiguously genred piece on erotic cutting among gay men. "Dr. Fell" provokes questions about the ways in which gender and sexuality are deeply involved in issues of—we shall put them in poststructuralist scarequotes—"truthfulness" and "psychopathology." In her discussion, Muriel Dimen sees all sexuality, not just what are deemed perversions, as intrinsically deceptive, the domain par excellence of the irony, ambiguity, and paradox she and other postmodern psychoanalysts broadly champion in theory and in clinical practice. In contrast, Bronski's reply insists on the specificities of a variety of cultural influences—pervasive homophobia, the AIDS crisis, the erotization of suffering and death in Roman Catholicism—as shaping the deliberate ambiguities in his essay. Irony, in his view, is not primarily important as a general theoretical or therapeutic stance to be cultivated toward traditional notions of certainty in matters of sexuality. On the contrary, it is a crucial survival skill of persons marginalized and endangered by a culture that pathologizes certain gendered subject positions and sexual practices.

To what extent, then, do postmodern psychoanalytic theory and practice need to take concrete political and cultural formations into account? Contributors to this volume offer a range of approaches to this question. With a focus on sexuality, but extending to other areas in which the dominant culture asserts its power, Layton's paper discusses what she calls the heterosexist unconscious, showing how it operates out of awareness to enforce processes of splitting that result in the culturally dominant categories of sexuality and gender. Offering extensive examples from her own clinical work and that of others, Layton demonstrates how easy it is for even the most well intentioned of analysts to replicate the prejudices of the heterosexual majority norm. For example, "the tendency to build theory around white, middle-class heterosexual women and call it a theory of women is one thing that reveals the operation of a heterosexist unconscious." As this passage indicates, because sexuality and gender are inseparable from other identity assignments the heterosexist unconscious also reinforces the power relations dictated by racism and classism, likewise the result of culturally sanctioned processes of splitting. Layton uses the general term *normative unconscious* "to account for a range of clinical theories and practices that replicate rather than challenge the splits demanded by dominant identity categories, by the racism, sexism, classism, and homophobia in which these categories are forged." Thus she argues that "political realities dictate what counts and what doesn't, and clinicians, along with other cultural experts, enforce particular views of normalcy."

The notion that psychoanalysis must be understood in terms of power relations has drawn hostility from those who claim that postmodernism is "politicizing" the psychoanalytic field. These critics blame feminism and queer theory for this, and to some extent they are correct, for, as noted above, it is largely feminist and queer clinicians who are drawn to postmodern theories, and for obvious reasons. (When Stern wonders why women seem to be more inclined toward postmodernism and men toward hermeneutics, we would answer that this is so precisely because feminists and queer theorists have more at stake in challenging the status quo.) These theories, strongly influenced by Foucault, depathologize homosexuality and various other non-normative practices, question the way our field has prescribed what is normal and what is deviant with regard to gender and sexuality, and make power inequities central to an understanding of cultural practices—cultural practices that include psychotherapy and psychoanalytic theory. Jane Flax (1990, 1993), for example, uses Foucault's work to engage psychoanalysis more fully at the sociopolitical level. From a Foucauldian perspective, hierarchical systems of power operate unconsciously and unreflexively in all discourse. By considering psychoanalysis as a discursive formation, Flax argues that disciplinary forms of power structure our theories and practice through, for example, the attention that is paid and is not paid to all the issues enumerated above: race, class, gender, sexual identity, notions of health and disease, and authority. Many of the contributors to this volume, mindful of the power differential in the analytic relationship, discuss the dangers of remaining unaware of our prejudices. Thus, supplementing Layton's examples concerning the unconscious heterosexism of many analytic treatments, Leary points to what she calls racial enactments in clinical practice, "interactive sequences that embody the actualization . . . of cultural attitudes toward race and racial difference."

Relational analytic theorists influenced by Foucault have tried to make his work on power and subject positions relevant to clinical practice. In addition to Layton's chapter, Goldner's contribution explicitly refers to Foucault, arguing that, in itself, a constructivist or hermeneutic approach "cannot frame or contain the combustible questions of power and its claims on the subject that relational psychoanalysis must also engage with"; her special concern is what she sees as the failure of constructivism to make gender and sexuality "ground zero" concepts. Schwartz sees Foucault's contention that "all regimes of knowledge, no matter how tried and true, are first and foremost instruments of power" as consistent with Freud's emphasis on the operation of unconscious processes behind the scenes of conscious discourse. Though recognizing the major influence of Foucault, Fairfield's papers view the workings of power in psychoanalytic theory and practice primarily through a Derridean lens, while Stern, acknowledging the signal contributions of Foucault and Derrida, also appeals to the hermeneutic school of philosophy, particularly to Gadamer's investigation of ways in which a dialogic understanding of the other's particular frame of reference can counter the operations of power in the analyst's relationship to the patient.

In his debate with Goldner, Stern offers a personal example of the ways in which it is not adequation to objective truth but, instead, multiply determined subjective factors that shape our theoretical orientations. He describes how his own development as an analyst—importantly including culturally gendered assumptions—led him to his preference for a hermeneutic/narrative or constructivist approach. In contrast, the power/knowledge orientation favored by Goldner and many other feminists emphasizes identity categories or subject positions (gender, class, etc.) as having greater explanatory value in thinking about unconscious meaning and its interpretation. Each of these two theorists acknowledges the value of the other's position; nevertheless, Goldner argues that what matters most is not just the dialogic co-creation of meaning but "the discursive formations and cultural narratives that determine what is possible for the dialogical participants to think and to know," whereas Stern claims a larger role for the insights of hermeneutic theory into the interpretive traditions that promote or hinder dialogic understanding and the co-construction of therapeutic narratives. Although, Stern concludes, there is an irreducible tension between the two orientations, "the power/knowledge position needs the mutuality of the constructivist position if [it] is to be a clinical theory, and the constructivist approach needs the doubt and skepticism of the power/knowledge position if it is to preserve the precious awareness that important parts of ourselves will always be strange, incomprehensible, and even destructive."

Thus, while defending his preference for the constructivist theory to which he (1997) is a major psychoanalytic contributor, Stern agrees that it is crucial to understand the ways in which power can operate out of awareness to shape our subject positions. From a poststructuralist standpoint, the classical psychoanalytic notion of a psychic apparatus wholly or largely unformed by the multiple contingencies of a specific place, time, and society serves to naturalize and reinforce the privilege of those who hold power in the dominant culture of the West. Several contributors to this volume discuss psychic processes in terms of particular cultural mythologies or concrete historical events. Stack, for example, notes the current availability of narratives of satanic abuse and alien abduction to contain persecutory anxieties, and Bronski explores the ways in which the Vietnam War and the AIDS crisis contributed to the shaping of particular sexual practices through which the most intimate of private relationships were expressed.

Observing that race has been largely neglected in the psychoanalytic literature, David Eng and Shinhee Han discuss the sociocultural trauma that marks racial identity as a melancholic structure. (The symposium on race to which *Psychoanalytic Dialogues* 10.4 [2000] is devoted, and in which their paper originally appeared, is an important contribution to what we hope will be an ongoing attempt to redress this inattention.) Eng and Han develop the concept of racial melancholia in the context of the Asian-American immigrant experience. This non-pathological form of melancholia, the authors explain, is not simply an intrapsychic process of individuals as in the Kleinian model of the depressive position. Instead, it is an effect of the losses and sacrifices exacted by the unattainable ideal of the white dominant society, and by its racist and colonialist structures, on the subjectivity of Asian Americans and other racial and sexual minority groups. The history and ongoing presence of discriminatory practices coexisting with "democratic myths of liberty, individualism, and inclusion force a misremembering of these exclusions, an enforced psychic amnesia that can only return as a type of repetitive national haunting" for Asian immigrants to the United States and their children. In addition to its discussion of minority subjectivities and the experience of first- and second-generation immigrants from other cultures, Eng and Han's paper is particularly important in calling attention to Asian Americans, a group insufficiently studied in most discussions of racism in the United States.

In her commentary on this paper by a Chinese-American academician and a Korean-American psychotherapist, Ronnie C. Lesser begins with what has become an obligatory part of any intervention by a poststructuralist as she marks her positionality: "I join this discourse from various subject positions, some of which differ from Eng and Han's in significant ways: Eastern-European Jewish, middle-class, baby boomer, lesbian, psychoanalyst." For a poststructuralist, identity categories such as these can never be self-explanatory, internally consistent, or exhaustive. But the statement of positionality acknowledges the inescapably perspectival framework of any human encounter, the limitations on one's ability to grasp the experience of the other, all the more so of the culturally different other. Lesser's most radical contribution in this piece may be her raising of questions posed by the new academic discipline known as Critical White Studies (cf., for example, Delgado and Stefancic 1997). Noting that "whiteness contaminates not only non-white people but also so-called white people," Lesser provocatively urges us to examine this unmarked but powerful form of racism in the standard course of analytic treatment of white patients, and, further, to examine clinically not only whiteness but another form of the invisible power that, Lesser argues, shapes the psyches of our patients: capitalism, nowadays especially global capitalism. The need to decide whether to introduce material recognized by the analyst to be politically urgent but not brought up—or even seen as problematical—by the patient is yet another situation in which the task of the postmodern clinician is more complex than that of the scholar.

## THE POSTMODERN SUBJECT: CLINICAL DILEMMAS

Like Lesser, many other contributors to *Bringing the Plague* explore the relation between culture and psyche and the ways in which the emergence of new models of treatment reflects changing views of subjectivity. Thus, in her reply to Mitchell, Fairfield draws a parallel between the task of negotiating a multiplicity of diverse and competing interests in the global economy and new psychoanalytic models of the mind and of treatment. Here and in her primary paper, Fairfield is concerned to show how a thoroughgoing postmodern approach would denaturalize all models of subjectivity, locating within particular socio-cultural and political contexts theories that psychoanalysts tend to put forth as universal, objective accounts of the psyche.

Thus the challenge for clinicians of the relational schools is to deal with postmodern notions of subject, self, and agency that are sometimes very different from their own views (Layton 1998), different not only because of the diversity of our culture but because, once we discard a scientistic standpoint, it becomes impossible to make firm truth claims about the subjectivity of any patient, any analyst. As Schwartz observes, the dilemma of the postmodern analyst is "to foster treatment without much in the way of a road map." Relational theorists who take a con-structivist approach have had no problem adapting to clinical theory the postmodern critique of the modernist self—that univocal, coher-ent, immutable psychic structure that has given way to a notion of multiplicity of self, mutable and flexible according to context. They seem fairly comfortable with the idea that one's sense of identity is, as Jeffrey Weeks (1991) claims, "a necessary fiction": necessary for psy-chological and political functioning, but a fictional construction none-theless. What relational clinicians (and all clinicians perhaps) have more trouble with are those forms of postmodernism that celebrate frag-mentation and disdain any striving for coherence (these are the forms clinicians have in fact critiqued; see Bader 1998, Flax 1990, Layton 1998, chapter 5, and Leary 1994; for a non-clinical critique of this ver-sion of postmodernism, see Jameson 1983). Therapists who treat pa-tients suffering from the fragmenting effects of cultural and familial traumas tend to see this version of postmodernism as a symptom of current social life, hardly as a cure.

Clinicians are also skeptical of poststructuralism's anti-humanist foundations. In particular, many clinicians are sympathetic to aspects of poststructuralism yet cannot accept its view that individuals are not agents and that human action is an effect of, alternately, language, regu-latory discourses, repetitive performances of norms, or some diffuse notion of power (for a critique of postmodern views of agency, see Layton 1998, McCarroll 1999). Mouffe (1979) summarizes the anti-humanist position articulated by Althusser (whose Marxism was influ-enced by Lacan) as follows: "The subject is not the originating source of consciousness, the expression of the irruption of a subjective prin-ciple into objective historical processes, but the product of a specific practice operating through the mechanism of interpellation." Explaining interpellation, she continues: "The social agent . . . is hailed (interpellated) as the member of either sex, of a family, of a social class, of a nation, of a race or as an aesthetic onlooker etc., and he lives these different subjectivities in which he is constituted in a relation of mutual implication" (p. 171). The debate is reflected in this volume, as Mitchell (more conservatively, though with caveats) and Fairfield (more radically, suspicious of the need to multiply caveats) discuss whether terms such as *agency* and *authenticity* continue to be theoretically and clinically viable nowadays. With regard to the concept of *authenticity*, especially controversial in view of injunctions that the analyst be more "real" in relating to the patient, Goldner observes that, for postmodernists, the ideal of clinical authenticity is "no longer an ad hoc statement of interpersonal humanism or personal self-expression." Necessarily used only within scarequotes, "'authenticity' has been recast, paradoxically, as an ironic position, a philosophically derived implication of the demise of certainty."

As we have noted, Bronski and Dimen, too, offer differing perspectives on the relation between truth and ambiguity, honesty and irony, in the formation of complex subject positions vis-à-vis sexuality. Is a radically nonnormative practice like erotic cutting to be seen as a symptom, a pointer toward a deep psychic wound within the narrator of Bronski's piece, a wound that he hides in reticence and ambiguity, as Dimen suggests? Or, as she also notes, is the causal concept of a symptom meaningful only in terms of the pragmatic "truth" of the clinical act of healing distress? Alternatively, as Bronski argues, is it important to distinguish between the narrator of "Dr. Fell" and Bronski himself as its author, or, some might add, between a patient's report and the patient herself, or between what the Lacanians call the "said," the content of an utterance, and the "saying," the subject's communicative act?

Inevitably, such debates about the grounding of subjectivity raise the issue of a possible challenge posed by postmodernisms to psychoanalytic theories of the unconscious. Foucault, whose work influences many forms of social constructivist thinking, was no fan of psychoanalysis. A common criticism of Foucault and Foucauldian social constructivism is that it holds no place for the unconscious, another reason clinicians are skeptical toward this variety of poststructuralism. Indeed, Lacanians tend to feel that the turn toward Foucault and historicism has inaugurated yet another abandonment of the unconscious. Foucault locates agency and resistance in places that transcend individual motivation: in discourses that reverse hierarchical binary assumptions (such as "black is beautiful") and in unforeseen possibilities for subverting norms that open up when different discursive regimes inadvertently converge. Whereas for certain Lacanians (e.g., Rose 1987) resistance to identity norms such as femininity or blackness originates in the unconscious, Foucauldians understand resistance to norms to come from the possibilities inherent in symbolic systems and discursive regimes themselves, "and these subversions are unanticipated effects of symbolic interpellations," as Butler (1997) says with reference to Foucault (p. 99), or, further on in the same text, "Disciplinary apparatus fails to repress sexuality precisely because the apparatus is itself eroticized, becoming the occasion of the incitement of sexuality and, therefore, undoing its own repressive aims" (p. 101).

While Anglo-American psychoanalytic practice certainly takes as foundational the notion that agency is complicated by the force of unconscious motivation, most clinicians hold the humanist assumption that agency emanates from individuals, not cultural subject positions, norms, or apparatuses. Indeed, few North American clinicians in the relational tradition (as opposed to, perhaps, Kleinians) operate under the assumption held by poststructuralists such as Foucault, Butler, Lacan, and Althusser that "subjection" is a universal condition of subject formation; perhaps what this says regarding U.S. optimism about the human condition is precisely what led Freud to postulate in the first place that he was bringing the plague. Relational clinicians are more likely to account for such effects of subjection as sadism and masochism by appealing to relational failures in the subject's history and to feel that poststructuralists and Lacanians alike ignore those failures in favor of tragic assumptions about the human condition.

As mentioned above, many Lacanians express skepticism, if not outrage, about what they see as a travesty inherent in some schools of postmodernism and relational analytic theory: that both do away with the unconscious. One charge is that relational theory is dyadic, missing the third term that takes an analysis out of the realm of narcissistic relating (Bernstein 1999). Another is that relational theory influenced by postmodernism collapses subjectivity and social subject positions, and does so because it has no understanding of the Lacanian Real, a realm beyond social construction (Dyess and Dean 2000). Ironically, Lacanians have been among those who have most interestingly elaborated on Althusser's discussion of interpellation, and so they have contributed greatly to the theory that subject positions are central to understanding the relation between the social and the individual (e.g., Smith 1988, Bhabha 1994). Nonetheless, the position that subjectivity is constructed from all three Lacanian registers—the Real, the Symbolic, and the Imaginary—makes Lacanians question both a relational analytic theory that ignores cultural subject positions (collapsing the social into the psychic), and one that centers on these positions (collapsing the psychic into the social).

While it is true that some relational clinical practice does its work in realms that are not unconscious in the traditional drive-theory sense, it nonetheless continues to elaborate expanded views of the unconscious. Some Lacanians seem to worry that relational notions of cure suggest that everything unconscious can be rendered conscious, or that relationalists provide a transference cure based on love and idealization, bypassing the gradual coming into awareness of unconscious material. If this is so, they argue, then nothing remains of a subjectivity structured by an irreducible otherness: the social and the individual are one. This scary prospect is one that these Lacanians see as implicit in both postmodern and relational theories. But there is perhaps a difference between what constitutes the subject and what the subject suffers from. Relational theorists would never say that a therapeutic outcome eliminates unconscious processes; rather, one of the therapeutic outcomes might be to make enough of that part of the unconscious that is invested in suffering conscious, allowing both for awareness of how one sets one's own traps and for a new freedom to be creative, playful, and more fully related. In particular, relationalists who are influenced by poststructuralism are skeptical about claims to know a priori what type of material is to be found in the unconscious (for example, agonizing psychosexual or early relational conflicts, or primitive aggression, or anxiety regarding sexual difference, or needs for mirroring and idealization or for the refinding of the lost primary object). Hence they are skeptical about what processes are involved in bringing this material into consciousness or keeping it out. Such analysts might favor as therapeutic outcomes holding incompatibilities in awareness instead of seeking to resolve them, and being able to bear knowing that we are not masters in our own house, that much of who we are and what motivates us is unconscious and may always be so.

Unconscious conflict is perhaps not all there is to the unconscious, or perhaps not all unconscious conflict or processes cause suffering: the postmodern analyst does not feel a need to make these kinds of determinations and is wary, as Schwartz puts it, of falling into "the modernist trap of making inferences and claims in a realm that really only permits speculation." Despite their areas of strong disagreement, Schwartz and Greenberg concur in their view that there can be no "royal roads" to the unconscious. In ways of which some Lacanians may be unaware, a number of postmodern relational theorists make a distinction between repressed material, that is, material that was at one time symbolically encoded before being banished from awareness, and material that never reached awareness because it was unformulated (D. B. Stern 1997; cf. Bollas 1987, Elliott and Spezzano 1996). As operationalized in a clinical treatment influenced by perspectivism, this theory sees the articulation of previously unformulated unconscious contents not as the result of an archeological dig unearthing pregiven material, but as a construction evolving within a particular patient–analyst dyad at a particular moment or set of moments in their relationship. If the analyst is interested in cultural influences on the formation of the psyche, such an approach can include discussion of those sociopolitical processes that affect subjectivity but remain unrecognized, for many of the causes of suffering (and of creativity) are explicitly and implicitly imbricated with social inequities of all kinds.

It has not been easy for clinicians who are proponents of postmodernism to make it clear to their audiences how such abstract theoretical ideas might be translated into clinical practice. Several of the chapters in this book address this dilemma. Leary, Goldner, and Fairfield observe that postmodern analysis is in danger of setting itself up as the very sort of orthodoxy and regulatory practice that it decries, but it is Greenberg, examining a clinical report by Hoffman, who makes this point at greatest length. Discussing Greenberg's observations about the definitional impossibility of establishing standards of technique for a constructivist relational psychoanalysis, Schwartz recognizes "how difficult a relinquishment it is that the postmodern framework asks of psychoanalysis" but remains confident that this relinquishment can be made. Greenberg retorts that if it were true, as Schwartz suggests, that we have no certain way to theorize what takes place in the psychoanalytic encounter, then clinical psychoanalysis would be undermined. We must inevitably form judgments, he argues, and, though he steps outside the modernist framework to the extent that he calls his judgments facilitative hypotheses as opposed to truth claims, he argues that postmodern theory, if taken to its limits, would silence us. Referring to the anxiety aroused by putting all models of subjectivity in question, Fairfield likewise wonders whether a thoroughgoing postmodern clinical psychoanalysis is possible at the present time.

In *The Social Construction of What?* (1999), the philosopher Ian Hacking repeats the usual complaint made by clinicians about postmodern views: Even if we know that anorexia, for example, is a socially constructed disease, how does that knowledge help an anorexic get well? What is a clinician to do with the knowledge that most pathologies are social constructs? Fraser (1997) and many others note that poststructuralist critiques of the binary identity categories within which most of us live are often not psychologically convincing, for the very reason that the critiques do not take into account the fact that the binaries are simultaneously constructed fictions and, as Butler, speaking of her lesbianism, once put it, "deeply lived" (1991). Chodorow (1995), Benjamin (1998), and several other clinicians counter the narrow poststructuralist focus on the determinism of subject positions with a view that individuals always also make something personal and idiosyncratic of identity categories such as gender. Agency is located in these idiosyncratic constructions. But many are led to wonder how sociohistorical subject positions and idiosyncratic elaborations are related. William Simon (1996) outlines a model of the production of human behavior and experience that includes the ongoing negotiation among the intrapsychic, the interpersonal, and the cultural. Simon's thesis brings us closer to a model of "dynamic nominalism" (Hacking 1995), which explicates a continuous relation among intrapsychic self-experience (presumably including unconscious processes), interpersonal experience, and culturally available representations of identity.

With models such as Simon's in mind, we are not as certain as Hacking that a knowledge of anorexia as a social construct will not help those who suffer from it. Bartky (1990), for example, talks about the way that a feeling such as shame can only be understood when we define the social context within which we speak of it. In particular, she notes that there are some subordinate social groups for whom the feeling of inferiority that manifests as shame is a condition of daily life. She cites a group of female teachers in a class she taught, women who, though academically superior to the male teachers in her class, always apologized for their work and seemed to feel ashamed of their self-perceived defects. She traces these feelings to years of subtle subordination in classrooms, empirical documentation for which she amply provides. When she looks at how shame is usually discussed in academic treatises, she finds that the definition does not fit these women. It fits those in more dominant cultural positions, for whom shame can be understood as arising from individual acts and failures. Indeed, the more one thinks about the relation among poststructuralism, social constructivism, and clinical work, the more clear it is that gender, race, class, sexuality, and their intersections are not secondary to such staples of analytic thinking as dependency and autonomy, affects, affect regulation, and defenses, but rather are inextricably interwoven with them (see Benjamin 1988, Goldner 1991 and this volume, and Layton, this volume). Subjectivity and subject positions, then, are not reducible to one another, but they are imbricated with one another, and clinicians need to be schooled in their possible connections if they do not wish inadvertently to keep current unequal power relations in place.

## CONCLUSION

As we have noted, many psychoanalysts still see their discipline as separate from culture; they feel that what are held to be psychoanalytic facts, such as the Oedipus complex, are impervious to historical or societal changes. These clinicians worry that postmodernists are politicizing what they imagine to be a non-political field. But those influenced by the Foucauldian claim that psychoanalysis is a sociohistorical normative practice counter that there is something terribly distorting about the charge that feminists and queers are polluting with politics a non-political field, whose innocent goal is to expand people's options and enrich their lives. Postmodernists maintain, as did Marxists before them, that all positions are political. The fact is that those who feel that only poststructuralists are political speak from a position of power called "the mainstream," a place whose power consists in its ability to deny that its theories and practices contain all kinds of politics, for example, the power to co-define, with other mainstream discourses, what is normal and what is not. Those influenced by Foucault and Derrida do indeed see the psychoanalytic field as political; many believe that Butler (1990b), Irigaray (1985), and a multitude of other poststructuralist theorists are correct that, for example, psychoanalytic narratives of human development, subjectivity, and unconscious processes do not simply describe what goes on in the world but prescribe what goes on. Such descriptions/prescriptions bring about particular kinds of subjectivities that tend to legitimate and replicate the sexist, racist, classist, and heterosexist status quo.

The claim made by poststructuralist theorists, then, is that the field of psychoanalysis is and always has been political; it is the privilege of the dominant to be able to get away with failing to see this or with actively denying it, while participating in promoting certain versions of subjectivity and pathologizing others. One of the major privileges of privilege is to remain invisible as such, to view itself—often unthinkingly and accompanied by good intentions—as the norm instead of as an accomplice in systems of injustice (cf. Wildman 1996). As editors of *Bringing the Plague*, we have assembled papers on the challenges psychoanalysis will confront as it enters its second century and a new millennium. It is our hope that readers who are academicians will go beyond Freud, Lacan, Winnicott, and Klein to recognize the postmodern theorists of United States psychoanalysis as important allies in their projects of denaturalizing hegemonic meaning systems and encouraging reflexivity in theory-making so as to unsettle privilege. And we hope that readers who are clinicians will come to appreciate the ways in which poststructuralist theories can promote a more ethical practice of psychoanalysis, one that is more aware of the ways in which culture and power thread through our work.

## REFERENCES

Altman, N. (1995). *The Analyst in the Inner City. Race, Class, and Culture through a Psychoanalytic Lens.* Hillsdale, NJ: Analytic Press.

Aron, L. (1996). *A Meeting of Minds: Mutuality in Psychoanalysis.* Hillsdale, NJ: Analytic Press.

Bader, M. J. (1998). Postmodern epistemology: the problem of validation and the retreat from therapeutics in psychoanalysis. *Psychoanalytic Dialogues* 8:1–32.

Barratt, B. (1993). *Psychoanalysis and the Postmodern Impulse. Knowing and Being since Freud's Psychology.* Baltimore: Johns Hopkins University Press.

Bartky, S. (1990). *Femininity and Domination. Studies in the Phenomenology of Oppression.* Baltimore: Johns Hopkins University Press.

Benjamin, J. (1988). *The Bonds of Love.* New York: Pantheon.

———— (1996). In defense of gender ambiguity. *Gender and Psychoanalysis* 1:27–43.

———— (1998). *Shadow of the Other: Intersubjectivity and Gender in Psychoanalysis.* New York: Routledge.

Bernstein, J. W. (1999). Countertransference: Our new royal road to the unconscious? *Psychoanalytic Dialogues* 9:275–299.

Bhabha, H. (1994). *The Location of Culture.* London and New York: Routledge.

Bollas, C. (1987). *The Shadow of the Object: Psychoanalysis of the Unthought Known.* New York: Columbia University Press.

———— (1992). *Being a Character.* New York: Hill and Wang.

Bromberg, P. M. (1998). *Standing in the Spaces.* Hillsdale, NJ: Analytic Press.

Butler, J. (1990a). *Gender Trouble: Feminism and the Subversion of Identity.* New York: Routledge.

———— (1990b). Gender trouble, feminist theory, and psychoanalytic discourse. In *Feminism/Postmodernism*, ed. L. J. Nicholson, pp. 324–340. New York: Routledge.

———— (1991). Imitation and gender subordination. In *Inside/Out: Lesbian Theories, Gay Theories*, ed. D. Fuss, pp. 13–31. New York and London: Routledge.

———— (1995). Melancholy gender—refused identification. *Psychoanalytic Dialogues* 5:165–180.

———— (1997). *The Psychic Life of Power: Theories in Subjection.* Stanford, CA: Stanford University Press.

Chodorow, N. J. (1995). Gender as a personal and cultural construction. *Signs* 20:516–544.

Coates, S. (1997). Is it time to jettison the concept of developmental lines? Commentary on de Marneffe's paper "Bodies and Words." *Gender and Psychoanalysis* 2:35–53.

Cooper, S. (1993). Introduction: hermeneutics and you. *Psychoanalytic Dialogues* 3:169–176.

Culler, J. (1982). *On Deconstruction.* Ithaca, NY: Cornell University Press.

Cushman, P. (1995). *Constructing the Self, Constructing America: A Cultural History of Psychotherapy.* Reading, MA: Addison Wesley.

Delgado, R., and Stefancic, J. (1997). Imposition. In *Critical White Studies: Looking behind the Mirror*, ed. R. Delgado and J. Stefancic, pp. 98–105. Philadelphia: Temple University Press.

Dimen, M. (1991). Deconstructing difference: gender, splitting, and transitional space. *Psychoanalytic Dialogues* 1:335–352.

——— (1995). On "our nature": prolegomenon to a relational theory of sexuality. In *Disorienting Sexuality: Psychoanalytic Reappraisals of Sexual Identities*, ed. T. Domenici and R. Lesser, pp. 133–156. New York: Routledge.

——— (1996). Bodytalk. *Gender and Psychoanalysis* 1:385–401.

Domenici, T., and Lesser, R., eds. (1995). *Disorienting Sexuality: Psychoanalytic Reappraisals of Sexual Identities*. New York: Routledge.

Dyess, C., and Dean, T. (2000). Gender: the impossibility of meaning. *Psychoanalytic Dialogues* 10:735–756.

Elliott, A., and Spezzano, C. (1996). Psychoanalysis at its limits: navigating the postmodern turn. *Psychoanalytic Quarterly* 65:52–83.

———, eds. (1999). *Psychoanalysis at Its Limits: Navigating the Postmodern Turn*. London: Free Association.

Flax, J. (1990). *Thinking Fragments. Psychoanalysis, Feminism, and Postmodernism in the Contemporary West*. Berkeley: University of California Press.

——— (1993). *Disputed Subjects. Essays on Psychoanalysis, Politics, and Philosophy*. New York: Routledge.

Foucault, M. (1980). *The History of Sexuality*, vol. 1, trans. R. Hurley. New York: Vintage.

Fraser, N. (1997). *Justice Interruptus: Critical Reflections on the "Postsocialist" Condition*. New York: Routledge.

Geha, R. (1993). Transferred fictions. Symposium: "What does the analyst know?," part 2. *Psychoanalytic Dialogues* 3:177–208.

Gill, M. (1983). The interpersonal paradigm and the degree of the therapist's involvement. *Contemporary Psychoanalysis* 19:200–237.

Goldner, V. (1991). Toward a critical relational theory of gender. *Psychoanalytic Dialogues* 1:249–272.

Hacking, I. (1995). *Rewriting the Soul: Multiple Personality and the Sciences of Memory*. Princeton, NJ: Princeton University Press.

——— (1999). *The Social Construction of What?* Cambridge, MA: Harvard University Press.

Harris, A. (1991). Gender as contradiction. *Psychoanalytic Dialogues* 1:197–224.

Hoffman, I. Z. (1998). *Ritual and Spontaneity in the Psychoanalytic Process: A Dialectical Constructivist View*. Hillsdale, NJ: Analytic Press.

Irigaray, L. (1985). The blind spot in an old dream of symmetry. In *Speculum of the Other Woman*, trans. G. Gill, pp. 13–129. Ithaca, NY: Cornell University Press.

Jagose, A. (1996). *Queer Theory. An Introduction*. New York: New York University Press.

Jameson, F. (1983). Postmodernism and consumer society. In *The Anti-Aesthetic*, ed. H. Foster, pp. 111–125. Seattle, WA: Bay Press.

Layton, L. (1998). *Who's That Girl? Who's That Boy?: Clinical Practice Meets Postmodern Gender Theory*. Northvale, NJ: Jason Aronson.

——— (2000). The psychopolitics of bisexuality. *Studies in Gender and Sexuality* 1:41–60.

Leary, K. (1994). Psychoanalytic "problems" and postmodern "solutions." *Psychoanalytic Quarterly* 63:433–465.

——— (1997). Race, self-disclosure, and "forbidden talk": race and ethnicity in contemporary clinical practice. *Psychoanalytic Quarterly* 66:163–189.

Lesser, R. (1997). A plea for throwing development out with the bathwater: discussion. *Gender and Psychoanalysis* 2:379–388.

McCarroll, J. (1999). Performativity, transsexualism, and benevolent psychopathology: some psychoanalytic reflections on postmodernist views of sexuality. *Psychoanalytic Dialogues* 9:505–530.

McLaughlin, J. T. (1981). Transference, psychic reality, and countertransference. *Psychoanalytic Quarterly* 50:639–664.

Mitchell, S. A. (1988). *Relational Concepts in Psychoanalysis*. Cambridge, MA: Harvard University Press.

——— (1993). *Hope and Dread in Psychoanalysis*. New York: Basic Books.

Moskowitz, M. (1996). The social conscience of psychoanalysis. In *Reaching Across Boundaries of Culture and Class*, ed. R. Perez Foster, M. Moskowitz, and R. A. Javier, pp. 66–79. Northvale, NJ: Jason Aronson.

Mouffe, C. (1979). Hegemony and ideology in Gramsci. In *Gramsci and Marxist Theory*, ed. C. Mouffe, pp. 168–204. London: Routledge and Kegan Paul.

Pizer, S. A. (1998). *Building Bridges*. Hillsdale, NJ: Analytic Press.

Rose, J. (1987). *Sexuality in the Field of Vision*. London: Verso.

Russell, P. (1999). *Trauma, Repetition, and Affect Regulation: The Work of Paul Russell*, ed. J. Teicholz and D. Kriegman. New York: Other Press.

Schafer, R. (1992). *Retelling a Life: Narration and Dialogue in Psychoanalysis*. New York: Basic Books.

Schwartz, D. (1992). Commentary on Jessica Benjamin's "Father and Daughter: Identification with Difference." A contribution to gender heterodoxy. *Psychoanalytic Dialogues* 2:411–416.

——— (1995). Current psychoanalytic discourses on sexuality: tripping over the body. In *Disorienting Sexuality: Psychoanalytic Reappraisals of Sexual Identities*, ed. T. Domenici and R. Lesser, pp. 115–126. New York: Routledge.

——— (1999). The temptations of normality: reappraising psychoanalytic theories of sexual development. *Psychoanalytic Psychology* 16:554–564.

Simon, W. (1996). *Postmodern Sexualities*. New York: Routledge.

Smith, P. (1988). *Discerning the Subject*. Minneapolis: University of Minnesota Press.

Spence, D. (1982). *Narrative Truth and Historical Truth: Meaning and Interpretation in Psychoanalysis*. New York: Norton.

Spezzano, C. (1993). A relational model of inquiry and truth: the place of psychoanalysis in the human conversation. *Psychoanalytic Dialogues* 3: 177–208.

Stack, C. (1998). The analyst's new clothes: the impact of the therapist's unconscious conflicts on the treatment process. *Contemporary Psychoanalysis* 34:273–287.

———— (1999). Psychoanalysis meets queer theory: an encounter with the terrifying other. *Gender and Psychoanalysis* 4:71–87.

———— (in press). Does psychoanalysis need Oedipus? In *Unconventional Couples, Uncoupling Conventions: Reappraisals and Revolutions in Psychoanalytic Theory and Practice*, ed. A. D'Ercole. New York: Analytic Press.

Stern, D. B. (1997). *Unformulated Experience. From Dissociation to Imagination in Psychoanalysis*. Hillsdale, NJ: Analytic Press.

Stern, D. N. (1985). *The Interpersonal World of the Infant*. New York: Basic Books.

Teicholz, J. G. (1999). *Kohut, Loewald, and the Postmoderns: A Comparative Study of Self and Relationship*. Hillsdale, NJ: Analytic Press.

Weeks, J. (1991). *Against Nature: Essays on History, Sexuality, and Identity*. London: Rivers Oram.

Whitson, G. (1996). Working-class issues. In *Reaching Across Boundaries of Culture and Class*, ed. R. Perez Foster, M. Moskowitz, and R. A. Javier, pp. 143–157. Northvale, NJ: Jason Aronson.

Wildman, S. M. (1996). *Privilege Revealed: How Invisible Preference Undermines America*. New York: New York University Press.

# Toward a Social-Constructivist View of the Psychoanalytic Situation

*Irwin Z. Hoffman*

## COMMON THEMES: TOWARD A NEW PARADIGM?

A common theme in papers by Aron (1991), Greenberg (1991), and Modell (1991), appearing in the inaugural issue of the journal *Psychoanalytic Dialogues*,[1] is an emphasis on the importance of the personal presence and participation of the analyst in the psychoanalytic process. A real, personal relationship of some kind is thought to develop inevitably. The only options have to do with whether or how the patient and the analyst attend to it, choices that will, in turn, affect the quality of the experience for both participants. These articles suggest that exploring the patient's perceptions of the analyst's immediate experience in the analytic situation, as well as perceptions of the analyst's general attributes, is at least in keeping with the value of bringing resisted aspects of the patient's experience to consciousness. More boldly, there is the suggestion that such exploration, which entails an overcoming of reciprocal resistance, creates the opportunity for a special kind of affective contact with the analyst that is thought to have therapeutic potential.

All three authors recognize that increased attention to the patient's experience of the analyst's personal qualities must occur in a context in which the patient's mental life remains the supraordinate focus. Both Aron and Modell stress the importance of integrating the "asymmetrical" requirements of the process with the principles of "mutuality" (Aron) or "egalitarianism" (Modell). Greenberg seeks an integration framed in terms of exploring, in a balanced way, endogenous sources of the patient's desire and the patient's perceptions of the external world and of the analyst in particular. We can discern a rough parallel between Aron's and Modell's dual principles and Greenberg's view in that the asymmetrical aspect of the analytic situation can be thought of as promoting the emergence and understanding of repressed, endogenous wishes, whereas the mutual aspect can be considered as more conducive to illumination of denied or disavowed perceptions of the analyst.

Each author locates his ideas in the context of a movement that he identifies within psychoanalysis and/or related fields of inquiry. Modell feels that his idea of paradox is in keeping with contemporary developments in the physical sciences. Moreover, he believes that there are broad social changes, including "critical consumerism," underlying the increased emphasis on the analyst's participation as a "real," fallible person (pp. 19–20). Aron sees his position as consistent with a broad movement in psychoanalytic theory that has been catalyzed recently by feminist social theory and by ideas emerging from research on mother–infant interaction. Greenberg regards his ideas as consistent with "a shift in the theoretical winds" (p. 58). He traces a movement in the direction of increased appreciation of the nuances of the influence of the environment to relatively late developments in Freud's thinking. In these developments, arising from Freud's ego psychology, the role of defense against anxiety-laden perception gains in importance. Greenberg feels that this emphasis has been further developed in the work of a variety of contemporary theorists.

Do these authors have in mind the same theoretical movement or different aspects of the same movement? If so, what are its essential features? Does it amount to a new paradigm? If it does, to what extent has it taken hold as the prevailing model that is guiding contemporary practice and theory building, including the ideas presented in these papers?

My own conviction is that there is a new paradigm struggling to emerge in the field, but it has not yet fully "arrived," much less been firmly established. These articles, and much of the theoretical work that the authors cite as consistent with their own positions, can be viewed as transitional from the old to the new paradigm. Because they are transitional, residues of the old paradigm are mixed together with indications of the new. In this discussion I take the liberty of regarding the authors of these three papers as "aiming" for the new paradigm. This view is my own construction, of course, and is open to debate. The authors themselves may not subscribe to my view of the nature of the new paradigm, not to mention its current status relative to their own work.[2]

Let me begin by immediately saying that the paradigm shift I have in mind is not the shift from the drive model to the relational model that Greenberg and Mitchell (1983) and Eagle (1984) have identified as central in the field. Put succinctly, the change that I regard as fundamental and still germinal in psychoanalytic theory and practice is from a positivist model for understanding the psychoanalytic situation to a constructivist model (Berger and Luckmann 1967, Gergen 1985, Gill 1983, Hoffman 1987, chapter 4, Protter 1985, Schön 1983, Stern 1985). Moreover, the confounding of the two axes, drive-relational and positivist-constructivist, leads to a great deal of inconsistency and confusion. The move to the relational perspective may be conducive in some respects to the more basic change in epistemology, but it is not equivalent to it. In fact, there are aspects of classical theory that are also conducive to a shift to a constructivist point of view. One could even argue that they seem to just about pave the way for its emergence, a point that is hinted at in Greenberg's article. Unfortunately, for the most part, post-Freudian theories, whether relational or not according to the criteria of Greenberg and Mitchell (1983), have not taken that path. Instead, ego psychology, object relations theory, self psychology, and interpersonal theory, despite their varied and rich contributions, have perpetuated the positivist aspect of Freudian theory, even while, in many instances, disclaiming it (see Hirsch 1987 and Hoffman 1998, chapter 4).

What I have called the "social paradigm" (Hoffman 1998, chapter 4), cited by Aron and Greenberg as influential in their thinking, is not, despite the apparently similar terms, the same as the relational model. It does more than emphasize the importance of the patient's awareness of the analyst as a person. Its features are not fully or perhaps even accurately described in terms of a move from a view of the transference as illusory to a view of it as also real (Modell), a move from a view of analysts as objects of their patients' desires to a view of them as also desiring subjects (Aron), or a move from exploration of endogenously based fantasy to exploration also of realistic perceptions of the analyst (Greenberg).

A different step is required, one that has to do specifically with the kind of knowledge that the participants are thought to have of themselves and of each other. The paradigm changes, in my view, only when the idea of the analyst's personal involvement is wedded to a constructivist or perspectivist epistemological position. Only in effecting that integration is the idea of the analyst's participation in the process taken fully into account. By this I mean, very specifically, that the personal participation of the analyst in the process is considered to have a continuous effect on what he or she understands about him- or herself and about the patient in the interaction. The general assumption in this model is that the analyst's understanding is always a function of his or her perspective at the moment. Moreover, because the participation of the analyst implicates all levels of the analyst's personality, it must include unconscious as well as conscious factors. Therefore, what the analyst seems to understand about his or her own experience and behavior as well as the patient's is always suspect, always susceptible to the vicissitudes of the analyst's own resistance, and always prone to being superseded by another point of view that may emerge.

A version of these principles applies to the patient, of course, just as much as one applies to the analyst. In the constructivist model, a proportion of the patient's perceptions of the analyst do not suddenly become simply objective or realistic in a reversal of the classical view that they merely reflect fantasies divorced from reality. I think Langs and Levenson are notable examples of theorists who, in very different ways, have fallen into this reversal (see Gill 1984 and Hoffman 1998 on Langs, Greenberg 1987 and Hoffman 1990 on Levenson). The idea is not that fantasy and reality have been redistributed but that we have moved into a world of mutual influence and constructed meaning. Experience is understood to be continually in the process of being formulated or explicated. Although not amorphous, unformulated experience is understood to be intrinsically ambiguous and open to a range of compelling interpretations and explications (Fourcher 1975, Gendlin 1962, 1964, Stern 1983, 1989).

Finding a good term for the new paradigm is problematic. The term *constructivism* sometimes connotes the interpretation of reality, but not necessarily the shaping of it through reciprocal, interpersonal influence. This connotation of constructivism, often modeled upon the reading of texts (e.g., Hare-Mustin and Marecek 1988), does not adequately take account of the fact that there is no pre-established text in the evolving interaction and dialogue between two people. Not only is the patient's life story a matter of historical reconstruction, it is also a piece of new history being made or constructed right now in the immediate interaction. The term *social* has the connotation of participation and interpersonal influence, but it does not necessarily have the additional connotation of giving particular meaning to an ambiguous reality. To capture both meanings and to avoid confusion with the relational model, the term *social-constructivist paradigm* seems useful. Also, although unwieldy, the term *participant-constructivist* might well describe the role of the analyst in this paradigm.[3]

Although psychoanalysis may be lagging behind developments in contemporary physics, philosophy, and literary theory with regard to the paradigm issue, it is not out of step within the world of professional practice. Schön (1983) argues persuasively that even when it is disclaimed, positivism[4] continues to be the dominant epistemology across a wide range of professions. The expression of positivism in these disciplines (ranging from architecture to city planning to psychotherapy) is an approach Schön calls "Technical Rationality." In this model, "professional activity consists in instrumental problem solving made rigorous by the application of scientific theory and technique" (p. 21). In the contrasting paradigm, which Schön calls "reflection-in-action," the practitioner engages in "reflective conversation with a situation that he treats as unique and uncertain. Through his transaction with the situation he shapes it and makes himself a part of it. Hence, the sense he makes of the situation must include his own contribution to it" (p. 163). I would add that analysts working in this model would assume not only that their contributions could be described and interpreted in various ways, but also that their own particular ways of understanding their contributions would be skewed in keeping with their personal participation in the process.

## WHOLLY AND PARTIALLY INCOMPATIBLE
## BEDFELLOWS FOR THE NEW PARADIGM

Although it may seem like a departure from my primary task of discussing the substantive points of these papers, I want to take a critical look at a sample of the literature cited by the authors as contributing to their own views and to the movement that they discern in the field. With respect to the paradigm issue, a good deal of confusion can result from grouping various theorists together as implicitly or explicitly constructivist when their positions vary considerably in terms of their adherence to that point of view.

In general, because the relational model is often loosely and incorrectly thought of as constructivist, theorists often overestimate the extent to which the positivist tradition in psychoanalysis is a dead relic of the past. Modell speaks as though the view of the transference as simple distortion and of the analyst as the arbiter of reality is virtually extinct. I think the reports of the death of this notion are highly exaggerated. On the contrary, I agree with Greenberg that the asocial view of transference is "alive and well in contemporary psychoanalytic practice" (p. 60). Although Greenberg has elsewhere recognized the extent to which certain relational theorists, especially the interpersonalists, have been infected by some form of objectivism (e.g., Greenberg 1981, pp. 251–252 on Sullivan and Thompson, Greenberg 1987 on Levenson), in this paper he continues to leave the impression that classical drive theory is the primary, if not the only, culprit with regard to this issue. Some of the theorists whom he identifies here as sympathetic to the new paradigm are relational, but they are also positivist in one way or another. Thompson (1964a), for example, whom both Aron and Greenberg mention as an important contributor to the social paradigm, wrote: "Transference consists entirely of irrational attitudes toward another person" (p. 14), and "In psychoanalysis, the therapist has a different attitude toward the irrational trends in the patient from that of all other therapists. By persistently indicating to the patient that he does not wish to dominate, that he is not angry, that he does not feel contempt, nor, on the other hand, is he a paragon of all virtues, he aims at eventually destroying his unique position in the patient's eyes" (p. 17). In the same article, Thompson, like Greenson (1971) and other theorists, pays due respect to the patient's allegedly "realistic" perceptions of the analyst, but these are unequivocally distinguished from the patient's irrational ideas, and it is the analyst who decides which is which (see Hoffman 1998, chapter 4).[5] Greenberg (1981) previously termed the idea of in-evitable, partially blinding entanglement "a friendly and compatible extension of the interpersonal approach" (p. 254). I believe that, on the contrary, the idea that the analyst inevitably gets caught up in this way is a radical departure from that approach. Moreover, the idea is an es-sential aspect of the social-constructivist paradigm.

Similarly, Weiss and Sampson and their colleagues (1986) are cited by Greenberg because of the emphasis on perception in their theory. Consistent with the model of technical rationality, however, there is something remarkably formulaic and "prescriptive" (cf. Green-berg 1981) about the way in which these theorists go about identify-ing "pathogenic beliefs" and the attitudes and behaviors that the ana-lyst can adopt in order to disconfirm them. The control-mastery theory developed by Weiss and Sampson does not encourage the analyst to expect to be caught up in complex patterns of interaction involving ambiguous integrations of repetition and new experience. Similarly, it does not encourage analysts to expect that their own understanding will inevitably be skewed by their personal participation in the process (see Hoffman and Gill 1988 for further discussion of Weiss and Sampson).

Schafer's work is especially interesting with respect to the para-digm issue because he has written so much about psychoanalysis from a constructivist point of view. Greenberg is particularly interested in Schafer's view of danger situations. It is noteworthy, however, that with respect to the psychoanalytic situation, Schafer's constructivism is fo-cused primarily on the way the analyst's theoretical bias affects the patient's life story as it emerges in the process. With respect to the issue of personal participation, the analyst remains quite detached and ob-jective. Schafer's "analytic attitude" (1983) is essentially purified of the analyst's personal influence through "*continuous* scrutiny of counter-transferences" (p. 221, italics added). The intrusion of countertransfer-ence "results in analytic incoherence" (p. 228). The whole tenor of Schafer's book *The Analytic Attitude* is consistent with the classical view of countertransference as occasional, as undesirable, and as something to be overcome when it does intrude. There is no latitude in many of Schafer's statements, any more than there is in the statements quoted from Thompson, for the idea of an inevitable interplay of transference and countertransference with concomitant effects on understanding, including the inevitable undiscovered blind spots that Greenberg mentions. The very fact that Schafer seems to believe that "continuous scrutiny" of the countertransference is possible, not to mention what he implies such scrutiny can accomplish, gives his view of the process the stamp of positivism rather than constructivism.

Since the concept of intersubjectivity that Aron is trying to develop has been grounded at least partly in self psychology, it is important to underscore the extent to which that point of view in particular departs from the social-constructivist paradigm. In the first place, as Aron says, although there is a focus in self psychology on the analyst's subjectivity as a source of understanding, in another sense, in relation to the needs of the patient, the emphasis is entirely on the analyst as an object, as a person whose subjectivity is decidedly not "recognized" (Benjamin 1988). If anything, the selfobject transference is associated with a need that I discuss later for a relatively selfless, idealized other, a need that conflicts with the patient's interest in discovering and exploring the analyst's subjectivity. In the second place, even the focus on the analyst's subjectivity in the process of "introspection and empathy" is of such a nature as to locate it outside the paradigm in which the analyst is a participant-constructivist. The discrepancy from that paradigm is evident from the fact that the self psychologist, as Eagle (1984, pp. 64–65), Mitchell (1988, p. 296), and Black (1987) have pointed out, ultimately lays no less claim to the possibility of an objective or accurate reading of the patient's experience than does the classical analyst. Such a view of the analyst's position is perpetuated in some instances by neo-self psychologists. Even Stolorow, a leading exponent of the theory of intersubjectivity, despite his determination to reject the positivist tradition (see especially Stolorow 1988), seems, at times, to end up squarely within it. Atwood and Stolorow (1984), for example, have written the following: "Whether or not . . . intersubjective situations facilitate or obstruct the progress of analysis depends in large part on the extent of the analyst's reflective self-awareness and capacity to decenter [citing Piaget] from the organizing principles of his own subjective world and thereby to grasp empathically the *actual meaning* of the patient's experiences" (p. 47, italics added). This is old wine in new bottles, yet another search for an apprehension of the reality of the patient's inner life that is uncontaminated by countertransference (especially by potentially useful complementary countertransference) or any kind of perspective that the analyst may have. The idea of the analyst's participation is not taken seriously in this account.[6]

For the theory of intersubjectivity to be consistent with the social-constructivist paradigm, it must encompass interaction on multiple levels of psychological organization and consciousness. Any divorcing of the intrapsychic and the interpersonal is unacceptable in this model. Thus, for example, Benjamin (1988), who Aron believes influenced his own view of intersubjectivity, takes a position that is contrary, in one respect, to the social-constructivist viewpoint. Her strategy is to put aside the realm of the intrapsychic while developing theory addressed to what she feels is the relatively neglected realm of the intersubjective. To some extent, this strategy is a temporary expedient. She recognizes that intersubjectivity theory is "unidimensional" when separated from intrapsychic considerations and that the two domains are "interdependent" (p. 21). The strategy itself, however, as well as some of her specific statements, creates the impression that she is prepared to accept the meanings of the terms without the redefinitions that their synthesis would require. She writes, for example: "The intersubjective foundation of erotic life . . . emphasizes the tension *between interacting individuals* rather than that within the individual. . . . [T]hese rival perspectives seem to me not so much mutually exclusive as concerned simply with different issues" (p. 29, italics in original). This approach effectively succumbs to the traditional polarization of the intrapsychic and the interpersonal. I think of intersubjectivity as the interaction at all levels of two hierarchically organized psychological systems.[7] The notion of interaction on multiple levels gives full meaning to the idea of participation in the analytic situation. Moreover, we certainly are not starting from scratch when we attempt to integrate the interpersonal and intrapsychic domains. Racker (1968), in a paper published originally in *The Psychoanalytic Quarterly* in 1957, was ahead of his time, and perhaps our own, when he wrote:

> The first distortion of truth in "the myth of the analytic situation" is that it is an interaction between a sick person and a healthy one. The truth is that it is an interaction between two personalities, in both of which the ego is under pressure from the id, the superego, and the external world; each personality has its internal and external dependencies, anxieties and

pathological defenses; each is also a child with his internal parents; and each of these whole personalities—that of the analysand and that of the analyst—responds to every event of the analytic situation. [p. 132]

Racker's concept of the countertransference goes a long way toward synthesizing the idea of the analyst's subjectivity, considered in depth, with the idea of his responsiveness in the analytic situation. The countertransference for Racker is not simply reactive, the connotation of the term to which Aron objects.

I cannot discuss all the theorists who are cited in these articles as contributing to the "shift in the theoretical winds" (p. 58) that Greenberg detects. I agree with Aron, who, following Hirsch (1987) and me (1998, chapter 4), points out that a variety of theorists, including Sullivan, Winnicott, and Kohut, continue to suggest that analysts can somehow manage to keep their own subjective experience from "contaminating" their patients' transferences. A corollary of this view is that analysts are in a position to assess accurately what they and their patients are doing and experiencing. That there is no advance here beyond Freud's positivism is obscured by Aron's emphasis on the progression from drive theory to relational perspectives. In fact, the most that could be said is that some of the internally contradictory features of the positions taken by some of these theorists lend themselves to a constructivist resolution. But, in the end, I am not sure that the gulf that separates Kohut, Winnicott, and Sullivan from the social-constructivist point of view is less wide than the gulf that separates Freud from that perspective.

## BACK TO AND BEYOND FREUD: ON THE VERGE OF SOCIAL CONSTRUCTIVISM

Returning to Greenberg, I want to examine his analysis of the historical origins of the tendency to focus on "endogenous" determinants of the transference at the expense of perceptions of external reality. Greenberg takes us back to Freud, a laudable approach, I think, because it so often yields either a rediscovery of lost insights or an awareness of obsolete foundations for aspects of current practice or theory that should be discarded or modified. I find his review of Freud's theorizing illuminating, although I missed reference to a few of Freud's writings that are especially relevant to the issue of Freud's recognition of the importance of unconscious perception. I am thinking, for example, of the "Postscript to Dora" (1905), in which Freud says he regrets having failed to inquire as to whether there was anything about himself that reminded Dora of Herr K (pp. 118–119). It is remarkable that this kind of inquiry and its theoretical implications are never developed further in Freud's writings. In addition, the paper on fetishism (1927) is pertinent as Freud's paradigmatic example of nonpsychotic disavowal and splitting. It is interesting, too, that Freud (1940) seems inadvertently to illustrate his own "splitting of the ego in the process of defense" when he opens the paper with that very title by remarking, "I find myself for a moment in the interesting position of not knowing whether what I have to say should be regarded as something long familiar and obvious or as something entirely new and puzzling. But I am inclined to think the latter" (p. 275). In light of the writings just mentioned, as well as other works (Freud 1940, Strachey's introductory note, pp. 273–274), Freud's musing here seems like an intriguing indication of his disavowal of the significance of disavowal in his own thinking!

These points, however, are merely in support of Greenberg's thesis that Freud failed to develop the idea of defense against perception of external reality and to give it the theoretical status of repression of impulses. More important for the purposes of this discussion, Greenberg's critique of Freud stops with this point and thereby implicitly accepts the dichotomy of endogenous instinctual pressures and perception of the external world. I recognize that Greenberg is interested in getting away from this dichotomy. He refers to the seemingly paradoxical dimension of Freud's thought with respect to the interdependence of drive and external danger. He writes that "at our best, we listen to our patients from a perspective that emphasizes the mutually interdependent matrix of their needs and the circumstances in which they live," and he speaks of "the elegant ambiguity" (p. 55) of this posture. In much of the paper, however, he seems to accept the classical notion of a tension between the two sources of influence, each of which seems to retain its integrity. By not thoroughly challenging Freud's dichotomy of realistic perception and drive-determined fantasy, Greenberg fails to identify a major additional impediment in Freudian thought to the development of a constructivist view of the analytic situation.

Freud's view of perception is consistent with naive realism rather than constructivism. As Holt (1989) has written, "Like his contemporaries in psychology and psychiatry alike, Freud assumed as a matter of course that perception is a simple matter of coming into contact with reality" (p. 285). And Schimek (1975), in a detailed discussion of this issue, writes the following:

> Freud seems to have been hampered by his belief in the originally veridical nature of the contents of perception and memory and the dichotomy between factual and psychical reality. He retained the concept of immaculate perception rather than assuming that perception always involves the interaction between the "objective" features of the external stimuli and the "subjective" drive or schemata of the individual which selectively organize and give meaning to immediate experience. [p. 180]

I have discussed this issue myself (1998, chapter 2) in connection with Freud's failure to consider death anxiety as an emergent, irreducible danger situation. Freud (1926) lamely argues that death cannot have psychodynamic significance because it cannot be "pictured" like "faeces being separated from the body" (pp. 129–130). Hartmann and Kris (1945, pp. 21–22) noted that Freud felt impelled to resort to phylogenetic explanations of castration anxiety, insofar as a boy may not encounter literal threats to his penis as he is growing up. They suggest that Freud failed to consider the possibility that the boy might construe and react to possible latent meanings of the parents' behavior rather than to its manifest content alone. In Freud's thought, the swing of the pendulum from literal seduction in childhood to drive-determined fantasy (complemented by phylogenetic memory) in the etiology of the neuroses seems like a thesis and an antithesis that are just begging for the synthesis that constructivism could offer. But Freud's return to consideration of perception and defenses against it within the ego does not translate into a constructivist paradigm, even though it may seem on the verge of doing so. Throughout his paper, Greenberg himself seems too comfortable with the polarity of internal and external influence. For example, he says "not only *impulses* but *observations*, too, become subject to repression" (p. 59); he objects to the lack of evidence for Arlow's claim that his patient is "*wishing* rather than *seeing*" (p. 61); he says that "patients often try to protect us from the less palatable aspects of what they see" (p. 63); and he says that the patient and the analyst each brings to the analytic situation "a unique and *observable* personality" (p. 63, italics added).

I recognize that to some extent this is just a manner of speaking; that is, one could hold a perspectivist view and still speak of "seeing" and "observing" another person's qualities, with the understanding that what is meant is not simple observation, but rather a certain degree of inference or speculation regarding behavior that is ambiguous in meaning. In fact, I think that for most purposes it would be too confining to have to watch every word and too cumbersome continually to be putting one's terms in quotation marks. Also, at the extreme there are categories of experience that are so accepted as part of our consensually validated world that the sense in which they are "constructions" becomes somewhat academic. Greenberg, moreover, feels that "some of [the patient's] conclusions [about the analyst] may be elaborations of the most obvious, concrete observations that can be made" (p. 64). Nevertheless, in attempting to develop theory, I believe there is reason to try to be more rigorous about terminology, especially if there is an interest in shifting from one paradigm to another when the paradigm that is supposedly being superseded is still very entrenched. To speak of "observable personality" in this climate, and to organize an argument around the question of the relative weights of endogenous pressure and the influence of the external world without fully addressing the extent to which such terms and polarities are problematic, gives just too much fuel to the positivist fire, assuming, of course, that one has some interest in putting it out.[8]

Despite the residues of Freud's positivist dichotomies, there is a clear contribution in Greenberg's paper to the development of the social-constructivist paradigm. In bringing out the disequilibrium in Freud's theorizing, in particular the failure to integrate the importance of perception into the theory, Greenberg implicitly demonstrates the way in which Freud's model is virtually poised for a transformation that would not simply accommodate perception but would change its meaning. Similarly, in his insistence that transference is penetrated by reality, Greenberg separates himself from all the "conservative critics" of the blank-screen fallacy who emphasize the real relationship, but only as something apart from the transference (see Hoffman 1998, chapter 4).

Greenberg's own valuable clinical vignettes illustrate the practical application of a perspectivist or constructivist attitude. He does not ask the patient who claimed to know nothing about him to report his "fantasies," nor does he simply ask for factual observations. Instead, he encourages the patient to "speculate" about him, and he listens with a sense of openness to the patient's conjectures (pp. 62–63). Not only is he interested in establishing that a patient noticed his messy waiting room, a perception he regards as important as a starting point, but he wants to go further by asking what the patient "thought about the messiness" (p. 71). With the financially successful patient who "has every reason to assume, correctly as it happens, that [Greenberg's] net worth is considerably less" (p. 64), Greenberg is interested not only in this "observation" by the patient, but also in what conclusions the patient might draw from this as to how he should handle his own success in the therapist's presence, conclusions that would be guided in part by other impressions of the analyst and in part by common sense.

Common sense is a very important factor in this process. It is often common sense that tells patients that their own behavior is likely to have elicited some kind of inner reaction from the analyst, so that perceptual confirmation may be of secondary importance. In the instance cited by Greenberg, the patient may plausibly imagine that the analyst would be envious or annoyed if the patient allowed himself to gloat. Greenberg says that "it will be a long time before [the patient] will be able to express an emotion like gleefulness about having more money than I do" (p. 64). Although he does not spell it out in this example, it would be in the spirit of Greenberg's paper to add that this "long time" may be partly associated with the period that the analyst would require to struggle with his feelings about the matter and to come to terms with whatever resentful envy he may be experiencing.

In general, might we not actually secretly appreciate the fact that patients are considerate enough to give us the opportunity to interpret their inhibitions about touching on our points of vulnerability? If that is so, and if we interpret the inhibition with the implication that it has not been necessary at all, we are being subtly dishonest. Grappling with what we are experiencing and with our personal attributes as they impinge on the patient is an important implication of the social-constructivist position. But just how our experiences are formulated and understood is a function of perspectives that are themselves more or less formulated and that are subject to change. Moreover, the analyst struggles not only with anxiety and defense (as in Levenson 1990, p. 300), but also with the intrinsic ambiguity of experience.

## ON CALLING ATTENTION TO ONESELF

Both Greenberg and Aron want the analyst to work to overcome the reciprocal resistance that interferes with exploration of what the patient discerns about the analyst. One of the ideas that emerges from Aron's application of the theory of intersubjectivity is that patients are not only responsive to their impressions of their analysts' mental lives, but are also actively interested in exploring their analysts' personal qualities as part of a basic tendency that has roots in the infant's interest in the subjectivity of the mother. This idea is challenging and opens the door to a very different orientation toward the patient's curiosity. Now, instead of viewing that curiosity only as an expression of a forbidden or unrealistic wish in the transference, we are invited to consider it also as a relatively healthy search for meaningful contact with the analyst. Aron gives us a sense of the way in which he actively encourages his patients to overcome their resistance to this exploration, an exploration that might lead the analyst to discover something new about himself. I do not think the importance of this point can be overestimated. I would add that if this discovery is not something completely new, it might be something familiar from one's private life that one never dreamed would be apparent to any of one's patients. The attitude Aron recommends entails a radical kind of openness. In working in this way, Aron, courageously I think, removes or reduces that component of the patient's resistance that is accommodating to what the patient might otherwise plausibly attribute to him, namely, a wish to remain hidden or invisible, or at least a wish not to have his prevailing self-image as an analyst disturbed.

Greenberg and Aron, following some of my own suggestions on this issue in 1983 (now 1998, chapter 4), articulate some of the arguments against analysts actually disclosing their experience. Assuming that, in keeping with the principle of asymmetry, analysts are going to listen much more than they talk and focus on their patients much more than on themselves, there is a danger that whatever they do disclose will be taken to imply that they, unlike their patients, have relatively easy access to their own experience. Nevertheless, I agree with Aron that there are often times when it makes sense for analysts to reveal some aspects of their experience to patients, including, when it seems pertinent, reference to their reservations about doing so. In that connection, when the patient asks a direct question, there can be much honest self-disclosure, paradoxically, in the process of struggling out loud with one's conflict about answering it. In fact, what might be a need on the patient's part for more personal contact with the analyst may be partially satisfied by such frankness, and the original question itself may become less pressing. However the analyst responds, such exchanges should be explored retrospectively to understand better the nature of the patient's need or wish and feelings about the analyst's response.[9]

It is important to recognize, however, that exploring our patients' perceptions of us frequently does make necessary some struggle with the issue of self-disclosure. Greenberg does not address this issue in the context of any of his vignettes, but it seems likely that inviting patients to formulate and speak of their impressions of the analyst would sometimes generate new dilemmas for the participants. Aron says that "once analysts express interest in the patient's perceptions of their subjectivity, they have tantalized the patient and will surely be pressured to disclose more of what is going on inside themselves" (p. 40). Although I prefer that this warning be restated in more qualified, perspectivist terms (e.g., "may be experienced as tantalizing" and "may feel pressured to disclose") it is, nevertheless, useful and raises important questions. I think, however, it is a mistake to add immediately that "self-revelation is not an option; it is an inevitability" (p. 40) because—contrary, perhaps, to Aron's intention—this view minimizes the likely differences among three possibilities: betraying something about ourselves without exploring the patient's perceptions, exploring the patient's perceptions, and deliberate self-disclosure. Just as showing interest in the patient's perceptions is an option, so is deliberate self-disclosure an option. In each case, in different ways, we are making a point of inviting attention to our subjectivity, and the repercussions for the patient's experience and our own have to be considered. Those repercussions are not fully predictable. Ferenczi (1931) found that his principles of "relaxation" and "indulgence" eventually led his patients to relive childhood traumas at a level of intensity far greater than what had been promoted by the principles of abstinence and frustration. Unfortunately, he died before he could give us a fuller sense of how things worked out for those patients. These were people, one might say, who felt seduced by the element of mutuality in their relationships with their analyst and abandoned when the principle of asymmetry was reasserted. Notwithstanding Ferenczi's conviction that such reliving of childhood traumas could serve the purposes of the analysis, the fact is that sometimes our patients may feel more drawn in by our accessibility and then more hurt or traumatized by the limits of the relationship than seems optimal. We ourselves may end up feeling more involved, exposed, or vulnerable than we had anticipated. Aron and Greenberg are talking about opening themselves up in a certain way, not about some kind of fully controllable, technical maneuver. The challenge is to recognize fully the complexities and problems of this approach and yet not shrink back into positions in which our own subjectivity is denied and in which any kind of spontaneous, personal participation is prohibited.[10]

The underlying paradigm is decisive with regard to this issue. If exploring the patient's perceptions is thought of as merely getting at something that is "there" anyway, so that the only choice is whether it is made conscious or left unconscious, then, assuming the value of self-awareness for the patient, there is generally only one reasonable course to take. Also, its consequences from this positivist viewpoint should not be especially problematic. The analyst, as a reader of the patient's unconscious, rather complacently feels sure that he or she is not going to be as disturbed by the patient's impressions as the patient might fear. If, instead, we think of such exploration, in the first place, as frequently explicating something that had never been formulated before and, in the second place, as affecting the experiences of the participants in ways that may be surprising, then we have to recognize that there is more risk and more responsibility involved than is connoted by the idea of merely making unconscious perceptions conscious. Instead, we are contributing to shaping the relationship in a particular way among many ways that are possible. Both the process of explication and the moment of interpersonal influence entail creation of meaning, not merely its discovery. And whatever is explicated by the patient and the analyst about themselves or about each other, out loud or in their private thoughts, affects what happens next within and between the two people in ways that were not known before that moment.

I think that in the past, Gill and I (e.g., Gill and Hoffman 1982a,b) failed to take adequate account of this aspect of the analysis of transference. Although we wrote about the transference repercussions of transference interpretations, especially, in fact, about the effects of interpretations that refer to the analyst's contributions to the patient's experience, I do not think we fully grappled with this issue of opening up something that is not entirely captured through extensions of the "technique" of analysis of transference. The term *technique* itself suggests a degree of control that does not fit the fluid movement of the process (cf. Schafer 1983, p. 291). A more open and flexible attitude is called for. The baseline to which the analyst continually returns remains that of critical reflection on the way the immediate interaction is being shaped by the participants, but a deeper appreciation is required of the fact that the unformulated aspects of the process necessarily and continually elude analytic closure. Gill and I might have progressed further had we considered more fully the unexpected *countertransference* repercussions of exploring the patient's experience of the relationship. That consideration would have helped to free us of the particular kind of technical rationality to which the analysis of the transference is prone.

In addition to the importance of the asymmetrical arrangement as a means of ensuring that the patient's experience remains the center of attention and as a means of reducing the chances that the analyst's involvement could become excessive and ultimately traumatic for the patient, I want to suggest one other important source of conflict and legitimate reciprocal resistance to the emergence of the analyst's subjectivity in the process. Could it not be argued that the whole ritual of psychoanalysis is designed, in part, to cultivate and protect a certain aura or mystique that accompanies the role of the analyst, and is there not a residue of this aura that remains even after we have analyzed it in many ways? I think this question touches on a fundamental conflict, both sides of which need to be both respected and questioned as they emerge in the process: on the one hand, the interest in the emergence of the analyst as a subject and, on the other hand, the interest in the submergence of the analyst's subjectivity. This conflict undoubtedly has its precursors in childhood. The primal scene, both literally and as metaphor for the parents' private experience, is aversive as well as magnetic, and the aversiveness is surely not merely a defense to be overcome. In the analytic situation there is an important tension between the desire *to know* and the desire *not to know* more about the analyst's personal experience.[11] Moreover, I would argue that it is against the backdrop of idealization, promoted by the ritualized asymmetry of the psychoanalytic situation, that the analyst's willingness to participate in the spirit of mutuality can become so meaningful for the patient and so powerful.

## CONSTRUCTIVISM AND PARADOX IN THE PSYCHOANALYTIC SITUATION

Modell's paradox points to a central dimension of the analytic experience for both the patient and the analyst. From the point of view of the analyst it can be thought of as a tension between a relatively methodical clinical perspective and one that is relatively personal, spontaneous, and affectively responsive. Of course, what is, in the foreground, a part of psychoanalytic technique is also, in the background, personally expressive and vice versa. But with this caveat, the notion of a dialectic between these two ways of participating in the interaction is clinically useful. If the patient who has slighted or depreciated the analyst asks, "Did I annoy you or upset you?," the analyst's inner response, whether or not it is revealed, usually is more complex than even an elaboration of a "yes" or a "no" would capture. Even if the patient has reached the analyst in a very personal way, the analyst's experience usually includes a clinical perspective on this very interaction. Thus, in keeping with Modell's paradox, a relatively full answer would often include elaborations of both "yes" and "no." There is a good chance that the affective response that the patient is asking about, even if it is intense, will have been mitigated by the analyst's interest in its meanings in the context of the interplay of the transference and the countertransference. An awareness of the amalgam of personal and clinical-technical responses may be more likely in therapists who work implicitly or explicitly in accord with the social-constructivist paradigm, in which this mix is not only expected but welcomed.

The premise of such a direct question often denies that the analyst may have some personal experience associated with the role-determined aspects of the relationship. In some instances, analysts may buy into the implicit disallowing of this aspect of their experience so that they may have a vague sense that the only legitimate choices are to "confess" or to refuse to reply. In fact, the question itself may have aggressive connotations, in that it may be designed to "knock the analyst off his perch," as Modell puts it (p. 24). So if the analyst decided to respond directly, the reply might well include some account of his or her experience of the question itself.

Regardless of the emotional aspect, the clinical perspective is usually an organic part of the analyst's experience. It is not merely tacked on in a superficial way, nor is it necessarily defensive. In this regard, I think Modell is wrong to say that "one feels angry, guilty, sexually aroused, and so forth in *precisely* the same way as one does in everyday life" (p. 24, italics added). To say that the feeling is "precisely" the same and that "mental labor is required in order to transpose this experience back into the therapeutic frame" is to compartmentalize the personal and the technical aspects of the analyst's experience and to underestimate its immediate complexity.

Modell is somewhat inconsistent in the way that he refers to the role-related and the more idiosyncratically personal dimensions of the analytic exchange for both participants. He usually speaks in terms of "two levels of reality," but he sometimes refers to the affective aspect as illusory and to the role-determined aspect as real. Speaking of more disturbed patients, he says that "[the therapist] may be forced to remind the patient that this relationship is, after all, a treatment" (p. 23). What are the implications of the phrase "after all"? Could one not argue just as well that the situation is, "after all," a personal relationship between two people? The notion of paradox implies a contradiction, but the contradiction is too easily resolved if we slip into regarding the emotional connection between the patient and the analyst as somehow less real than the technical aspects of the relationship. The converse is also true. When Modell says that we respond affectively precisely as we do in everyday life and then have to work to bring back the relevance of the frame, he comes close to resolving the paradox in the opposite direction, that is, one that grants the personal exchange more "reality" than artificially imposed analytic discipline. In this regard, he speaks of "real affects within an 'unreal' context" (p. 24).

Modell's idea of the paradox of the therapeutic relationship is limited in that it is not clear how the paradox is representative of a general phenomenon in human experience. Modell does refer to it as an instance of "acceptance of contradictory phenomena without striving for a synthesis" (p. 14), and he refers to various thinkers, such as William James and Winnicott, who have discussed the issue in other contexts. However, the emphasis is so much on the peculiar nature of the therapeutic situation that more general implications are either missed or understated. In fact, Modell seems unclear as to why tolerance of the specific paradox of the analytic situation should be desirable in the long term. He says, rather vaguely, "It would seem that the acceptance of paradox may in some way be connected to mental health" (p. 23).

What is missing from Modell's conceptualization in this article is the universal relevance of the insight that, however real and inevitable the forms of an individual's social life may seem, they can generally be shown to be constructions that reflect the capacities and potentialities of the human organism but are not necessary or inevitable in terms of their specific features. Social reality is neither externally given nor created out of whole cloth by the individual. As Berger and Luckmann (1967) put it, with emphasis, "*Society is a human product. Society is an objective reality. Man is a social product*" (p. 61). The patient's "ordinary life," in Modell's terms, corresponds to what Berger and Luckmann refer to as the "taken-for-granted world." This world is itself a social construction. Mitchell (1988) has discussed the importance of the interplay of "narcissistic illusion" and more realistic appraisals of the worth of self and others. But these appraisals are themselves constructions that could be regarded as narcissistic illusions. The fact is that people, against a threatening and omnipresent, preconscious awareness of the potential meaninglessness of their existence, forge and sustain a sense that their lives do matter. All social realities are "sandcastles" (Mitchell 1988, p. 195), jeopardized by awareness of mortality. In the terms of Berger and Luckmann (1967):

> The experience of the death of others and, subsequently, the anticipation of one's own death posit the marginal situation par excellence for the individual. Needless to elaborate, death also posits the most terrifying threat to the taken-for-granted realities of everyday life. . . . All legitimations of death must carry out the same essential task—they must enable the individual to go on living in society after the death of significant others and to anticipate his own death with, at the very least, terror sufficiently mitigated so as not to paralyze the continued performance of

the routines of everyday life. . . . All social reality is precarious. All societies are constructions in the face of chaos. The constant possibility of
anomic terror is actualized whenever legitimations that obscure the pre-
cariousness are threatened or collapse. [pp. 101–103]

We all live in innumerable, concentric worlds within worlds. At
the outer limits there is the sense of our mortality in the context of
infinite time and space. Moving rapidly inward, we find human history,
the cultures and subcultures to which we belong, and then our family
and individual histories. The psychoanalytic situation can be thought
of as a special kind of interaction designed to expose the dialectic between the activity of patients in constructing certain problematic aspects of their lives, past and present, and the preestablished givens with
which they have had to live and with which they have to live now in
the immediacy of the relationship with the analyst.

On the one hand, this project has a very narrow focus. Only a
minuscule proportion of the multiplicity of realities in which the
patient's life is embedded and in which the patient is implicated is lifted
out for exploration and critical reflection. The rest are likely to be
unexamined, taken-for-granted values and conventions, many of which
the patient and the analyst may share. On the other hand, the project
is ambitious in two ways. First, the aim is to affect some of the most
longstanding and deeply rooted ways in which patients experience
themselves and others. For example, the attempt may be to affect even
central aspects of the patient's sense of worth, established originally in
childhood before there was any possibility of questioning the authority of caretakers. Second, the recognition of the ways in which the patient and the analyst are implicated in the repetitive patterns of the
transference and the countertransference can generalize so that patients
become aware, not only that these patterns are relative rather than
absolute and inevitable, but also that all aspects of their lives can, in
principle, be subject to the same analysis. In other words, patients are
encouraged to develop an implicitly constructivist attitude toward their
own experience (Protter 1985, Schafer 1983, pp. 125–127). One effect
of such an attitude is to take oneself a little less seriously, to cultivate
a sense of humor about oneself. Yet this attitude does not preclude living with passion and commitment. Modell begins his article by distinguishing between the love relation of the analyst and the patient and

other love relations, on the grounds that in the case of the former, "the partners will inevitably separate when the aim of the treatment has been realized [and] this separation is a fact that neither participant can forget" (p. 13). But this separation is analogous to the final and ultimate separation. In the context of the latter, the paradoxical effect is simultaneously to divest life of meaning and to promote people's responsibility for making their lives as meaningful and as rich as possible (see Hoffman 1998, chapters 1 and 2).

The authority of the analyst plays an important role in the process by which the patient's fixed ways of experiencing himself or herself and the world are affected in analysis. The analytic situation is a setup, not only for deconstructing the sense of necessity that underlies the transference, but also for constructing an alternative social reality involving modifications in the patient's sense of self and of others. The "ritualized arrangements," as Modell calls them, which include the ritualized asymmetry of the process, are likely to promote the sense of the relationship as hierarchical. The authority of analysts rests not only on their professional expertise and not only on the fact that the situation tends to elicit, in relatively concentrated form, their capacity to offer a special kind of attentive presence, what Schafer (1983) refers to as an analytic "second self" (p. 291). I believe it usually also draws upon the power generated by the asymmetrical arrangement combined with the special, regular time and place. The frequency of meetings adds to the emotional intensity and to the transformative potential of the process. Psychoanalysis can be viewed as a psychologically complex kind of relearning, in which a major objective is to promote critical reflection on the way the patient's reality has been constructed in the past and is being constructed interactively right now, with whatever amalgams of repetition and new experience the current construction entails. Embedded in this process of critical reflection, however, there is something going on that is affirming to the patient in a general way. The analyst's attitude conveys a variety of messages to the patient, including, for example: "Your subjective experience matters. Your responsibility for your life is mitigated by these aspects of your history and current circumstances that have not been in your control. You have the power to significantly affect the quality of your life." The magical component in the analyst's authority, an extension of Freud's "unobjectionable positive transference" with, undoubtedly, close connections to the "idealizing transference" of self psychology, may be explored and partially understood, but it is not likely to be completely undone. Moreover, that outcome would not necessarily be desirable.

If, as Greenberg and Aron suggest, there is a need on the part of both participants to protect the analyst from exposure, the need cannot be dismissed entirely as an irrational clinging to an unnecessary idealization. Some aspect of the idealization may be a necessary, jointly created and sustained construction. Here is an example of actions speaking louder than words. The fact is that from the beginning to the end, despite the possibility of temporary departures and modifications, basic ritual features of the analytic situation—the regular visits, the fee, the asymmetry of personal expression—generally remain intact. Indeed, they are likely to promote the special power that the analyst has in the patient's mental life even beyond the point of termination of the analysis.

## FIGURE–GROUND RELATIONSHIPS, SIMULTANEITY, AND TERMINOLOGICAL ISSUES

Turning to a terminological issue that is also important theoretically, let us look at the suggestion by Aron that the term *countertransference* be discarded because of the connotation that the patient is responsible for the analyst's experience. When we try to develop a new model, it is very difficult to escape from the polarities that characterized the old ones that we are used to. And one of the most tempting and deceptive avenues of escape is always the one that reverses who has what while still retaining the old terms of discourse (or their equivalents). What happens, then, is a dramatic but superficial change. The difficulties of the old model will invariably come back to haunt us, a little like the return of the repressed. On the other hand, bringing in new terms like *constructivism* or *intersubjectivity* is not a panacea. These terms also usually require some sort of tailoring or redefinition.

With regard to the term *countertransference*, I would agree with Aron that it is stretched beyond recognition when used to refer to all aspects of the analyst's character to which the patient may be responsive in the analytic situation. To say, however, that the term necessarily implies that the analyst's experience is "reactive rather than subjective, emanating from the center of the analyst's psychic self" (p. 33) is implicitly to accept the very polarization of responsiveness and subjectivity that I think Aron wants to reject. We want a model in which responsiveness is understood to be simultaneously self-expressive, just as self-expressive initiative is understood to be simultaneously responsive to the other person in the interaction. Aron and the classical analyst do not mean the same thing, even when they both speak of wanting to emphasize the "subjective" component in the analyst's experience of the countertransference. Aron suggests that what is essential in the new model is to recognize that both patient and analyst are simultaneously both subject and object. But that which is simultaneously both subject and object is, in a certain sense, neither, because the meanings of those terms have been established primarily in the context of their polarization. So we have to consider that we have moved into new territory where the boundaries among various categories have been altered. In effect, we have new terms of discourse, even if we continue to use the old ones. As noted earlier in connection with the polarity of endogenous pressures and perception, if it would not make our writing and speaking ridiculously cumbersome, we would and should be saying or writing "quote, unquote" all the time, for example, in conjunction with the terms *transference, countertransference, reality, fantasy, intrapsychic, interpersonal, subject, object, individual,* and *social.*

My own preference would be to hold on to many of the traditional terms and try to redefine them (or assimilate redefinitions of them that have been offered) rather than change them. This is what Gill and I, in fact, tried to do with the term *transference,* and it is what I would suggest we try to do with the term *countertransference.*[12] In fact—and this is the substantive issue that is at stake—the redefinition of the terms is crucial. Without redefinition—if, for example, we call the analyst's experience "transference," as McLaughlin (1981) suggests—we are in danger of making the same mistake that is associated with the use of that term for the patient. In this case, in our zeal to recognize the analyst as an agent, we might neglect the extent to which the analyst is responsive to what the patient is doing. Also, as Aron suggests, this strategy would put us well on the road toward mind-boggling terminological confusion. There is, in fact, just as much reason to call the patient's experience "countertransference" to emphasize responsiveness to the analyst as there is to call the analyst's experience "transference" to emphasize the extent to which the analyst is "the initiator of interactional sequences." In the interest of preserving our sanity, in light of the fact that the terms have to be redefined anyway, and perhaps most importantly, in deference to the principle of asymmetry that governs the analytic situation, I think keeping the terms *transference* and *countertransference* for the patient and the analyst, respectively, is by far the least of the various evils among which we have to choose.

In the model to which Aron is objecting, although the analyst is seen as participating in a sequence of interactional events, the claim would be that it was the patient who "started it." The whole tenor of the evolving interaction would essentially reflect the patient's influence, with analysts only playing out roles or positions (presumably experienced as foreign to themselves) into which they are cast by the patient. This model is the one to which both Aron and Greenberg object, correctly I think, to the extent that it understates the analyst's responsibility for what is going on and the way in which the personality of the analyst affects the nature of the interactions and the transferences that emerge.

I do think, however, that there is much to be said for a modified version of this model, one that does not make this error. In this modified version, the two directions of influence are understood to be simultaneous (although usually unequal) from the beginning. As Benjamin (1988, p. 26) points out, simultaneity is much more difficult to grasp than sequences of events. If, for example, we try to look at the origins of the interaction between a patient and a therapist, it may seem obvious that the patient made the first move when he or she called for an appointment. But one could argue that, at the same time, the patient is responding to the fact that analysts have advertised themselves as available for this kind of relationship, a version, one might say, of "creation of consumer demand." From that point of view, it is the analyst (as a representative of the whole culture or institution of psychotherapy) who "started it." Racker (1968) makes this point in a hyperbolic way when he says:

The analyst communicates certain associations of a personal nature even when he does not seem to do so. These communications begin, one might say, with the plate on the front door that says "Psychoanalyst" or "Doctor." What motive (in terms of the unconscious) would the analyst have for wanting to cure if it were not he who made the patient ill? In this way the patient is already, simply by being a patient, the creditor, the accuser, the "superego" of the analyst; and the analyst is his debtor. [p. 146]

So the analyst is calling the patient in to ask for the opportunity to atone for past crimes and failures. Here we have the basis for a redefinition of the "presenting complaint"!

Nevertheless, as I have said, I believe there is still wisdom to the traditional allocation of the terms. As a participant-constructivist, the analyst sets himself or herself up to be, not the detached observer, but the relatively malleable one, whereas the patient comes with a story to tell and to enact. But we can capture the asymmetrical nature of the process by speaking in terms of the patient's transference and the analyst's countertransference, even while recognizing that by reversing figure and ground we can find a current in the process in which it is the patient who is responding to the impact of the analyst's influence.

The notion of figure–ground relationships is central to the transition to the social-constructivist paradigm. Often the change in the way things are viewed has the general form that what had been polarized between analyst and patient is now understood in terms of multiple, fluctuating, complementary figure–ground relationships within each of the participants. For example, when we reverse figure and ground, the patient's associations become interpretations, and the analyst's interpretations become personally expressive associations. Searles (1975) reverses figure and ground when he writes about "the patient as therapist to the analyst." We name our professional conferences as gatherings of psychoanalytic therapists and psychoanalysts. That aspect is in the foreground. But in the background, the fact is that there are few, if any, places where one could find a greater concentration of psychoanalytic patients. In general, it is a good idea to call things by whatever aspects are usually in the foreground, with the understanding that the resulting terms often connote complementary aspects that are in the background.

## CONCLUSION:
## ONE-PERSON AND TWO-PERSON THEORIES
## IN THE SOCIAL-CONSTRUCTIVIST PARADIGM

The paradigm issue is independent of questions regarding the content of the primary issues in human development and the specific needs, wishes, and conflicts that are central in governing human experience and behavior. To be sure, a constructivist position is, by definition, wary of overly confident assertions about human nature. There is, however, no obstacle to theory building if framed in terms of heuristic working assumptions and corollary propositions and hypotheses.[13]

Although the terms *social-constructivist* and *participant-constructivist* refer to the continuous interaction in the psychoanalytic situation, they do not preclude consideration of aspects of experience and motivation that are not primarily social, even though they inevitably take on additional meanings in a social context. In each of the articles discussed, despite what I regard as the misleading status given to the shift from drive theory to relational theory or from a one-person to a two-person perspective, there is an emphasis on not losing sight of the patient as an individual. Modell underscores the requirement of asymmetry in the analytic situation in order to allow for the emergence of the patient's desire. Aron also writes about this asymmetry and about the importance of the analyst's finding the right balance between being responsive and giving patients the "space" they need for self-expression. Greenberg is emphatic about the importance of not discarding attention to "endogenous" factors, even while exploring the patient's perceptions of the analyst.

The constructivist paradigm actually demands taking account of both relatively social aspects of experience and relatively individual aspects. Berger and Luckmann (1967) take pains to emphasize that "subjective biography is not fully social" (p. 134), and they discuss the dialectic between the individual and the social in experience (cf. Ghent 1989 and, since the first appearance of this essay in 1991, Benjamin 1995, Seligman and Shanook 1995). Whichever aspect is in the foreground can be understood only in the context of its complement in the background. Neither has to be conceptualized exclusively as a derivative of the other. Sexuality can have primary autoerotic as well as primary object-related facets. The experience of love has both a self-centered, narcissistic dimension and a dimension that recognizes the other as a subject. The exercise of motor or cognitive functions can be understood in terms of the immediate intrinsic gratification that it affords as well as in terms of the social meanings and rewards that become attached to it. Even if we think of language as necessarily social, so that no symbolic experience as such can be considered as purely individual, experience that is not yet formulated, whether in the molar sense of the preverbal life of the child or the molecular sense of moment-to-moment implicit experiencing, can be thought of as having a relatively nonsocial aspect that is not merely reducible to biology. An integrative theory would take account of both sources of the quality of experience, recognizing that neither will be manifested in pure form but that both will be reflected in a continuous dialectical interplay of figure and ground in human experience (Flax 1996, Fourcher 1975, 1978, Ghent 1989, Gill 1994, Greenberg and Mitchell 1983, pp. 400–408, Slavin and Kriegman 1992, Stern 1983, 1989).

With respect to the issues that are the focus of these papers, the interest that the patient has in making fuller contact with the analyst as a person places the two-person, relational aspect of motivation in the foreground while the one-person, individual aspect recedes to the background. But the interest patients have in denying or ignoring their analysts as desiring subjects, as people like themselves, does just the opposite. It highlights the individual, one-person dimension of experience while throwing the relational dimension into the background. The meaning and power of whichever aspect is in the foreground are partly dependent on the aspect that is in the background. In our zeal to correct the overemphasis in classical psychoanalytic theory on the individual dimension, it is important that we not swing to an overemphasis on the relational dimension, thereby isolating each from the other. The shift to a social-constructivist paradigm for understanding the psychoanalytic situation certainly does not require such a reversal. If anything, it requires a synthesis of the two perspectives with appropriate redefinitions of each in the light of their interdependence.

## NOTES

1. Although it appeared originally as a discussion of these three papers, I believe this essay can stand on its own. Throughout, unless indicated other-

wise, references to Aron, Greenberg, and Modell are to the papers in that in-augural issue, which were followed by this discussion.

2. Since this paper's original publication, Greenberg (1995), in his re-sponse to my review (Hoffman 1995) of his book *Oedipus and Beyond*, has taken exception to having his ideas evaluated in terms of their consistency with some kind of constructivist ideal that is not his own. I believe, however, that iden-tifying apparent internal inconsistencies in any theory can be useful and can lead to important clarifications.

3. If it were not for their common connotations, either of these terms, *social* or *constructivist*, might be conceptually sufficient. No thoroughgoing application of the idea of social participation could omit taking account of the factor of selective construction of meaning, and no thoroughgoing applica-tion of constructivism to the analytic situation could omit taking account of the social factor as it relates to the past and the present. Accordingly, depend-ing on the context, in this essay (originally published in 1991) I sometimes use the terms *social* and *constructivist* as shorthand for social-constructivist paradigm. For a debate about the relative merits of the terms *constructivism* and *perspectivism* or *perspectival realism* see Donna Orange's (1992) commen-tary on this discussion and my reply (Hoffman 1992). Partly in light of the connotation of radical relativism that some, like Orange, associate with *social constructivism*, I now believe that *critical constructivism* or *dialectical constructivism* may be less misleading and convey more of my intent.

4. Schön uses the term *positivism* in a broad sense. See Hoffman 1998, chapter 6, note 2 on "objectivism" versus "positivism."

5. In some later, less formal statements, Thompson's (1964b) descrip-tion of the process has more the flavor of constructivism or "reflection-in-action." Such inconsistency is in keeping with Schön's (1983) observation that the way practitioners actually work, at least some of the time, may put them into conflict with their own theories.

6. Stolorow and his collaborators have identified their viewpoint with a "perspectivalist" epistemological position (Stolorow and Atwood 1992, p. 123). Although the tendency toward objectivism in their thought is reflected in the centrality of key concepts such as "sustained empathic inquiry" (see, for ex-ample, Brandchaft and Stolorow 1990, reprinted with revisions in Stolorow and Atwood 1992, pp. 87–102), they have also struggled to extricate their intersubjective view from that paradigm, as reflected, for example, in their formulation of the stance of "empathic-introspective inquiry," which "does not seek to avert, minimize, or disavow the impact of the analyst's psychological organization on the patient's experience" (Stolorow and Atwood 1997, p. 441).

7. Actually, Benjamin herself, despite her stated strategy, deals with patterns of interaction in terms that combine the intrapsychic and the inter-

subjective. For example, the dominated person, in her theory, is understood to be unconsciously identified with the dominating one, and vice versa. For a discussion of intersubjectivity in Benjamin's perspective compared to my own see Benjamin's (1991) commentary on this discussion and my reply (Hoffman 1991).

8. It should be noted that even "the most obvious, concrete observations that can be made" are selectively lifted out of the "chaos" of "unformulated experience" (Stern 1983, 1989, cf. Gendlin 1962, 1964). In another individual, in another culture, in another time, these "facts" might not matter in the same way or might not matter enough to be noticed at all.

9. The traditional idea that it is always better to explore the patient's wishes in this regard under conditions of abstinence and deprivation is another reflection of positivist thinking. The implication is that the "true" nature of the wish or need will be exposed if the analyst does not "contaminate" the field by yielding to the patient's pressures. In the constructivist model, whatever way the analyst responds is likely to affect what is then "found out" about the intensity and quality of the patient's desire (cf. Greenberg 1986, Mitchell 1991).

10. It is important to remember that keeping our subjectivity in the background is also a choice that has repercussions that are not fully predictable, even though it may be more conducive to an illusion of control over the process.

11. Since the time of the symposium that included the paper by Aron (1991) and this discussion, Aron (1996) has proposed that we distinguish between the dialectics of mutuality and autonomy on the one hand, and symmetry and asymmetry on the other. With respect to analyst and analysand, he has emphasized the inevitability of their mutual influence as well as the importance of the asymmetry of the role requirements. His book (1996) explores in depth the theoretical and clinical issues associated with these dimensions of the process.

12. Racker (1968) made a great advance in the 1950s in reconceptualizing countertransference, combining the notion of externalization of internal object relations with appreciation of the personal involvement of the analyst on multiple levels. A number of authors, particularly the "radical critics" of the blank-screen fallacy (Hoffman 1998, chapter 4), have taken a similar position in conceptualizing countertransference without the implication that it is merely reactive. And yet Racker himself may fall short of the social-constructivist paradigm because of the kind of certainty that he has about the nature of the countertransference and what it indicates about the patient's experience.

13. I would amend this now to say that dialectical constructivism has its own theoretical implications regarding human development as it applies

to the adult analysand as well as the child. In a nutshell—always a risky condensation—it points to a fundamental need for balance between freedom to shape one's own experience on the one hand, and responsiveness to external influence on the other. See the conclusion of Hoffman 1998, chapter 8 for an attempt to articulate these implications more fully (also see Hoffman 1995).

## REFERENCES

Aron, L. (1991). The patient's experience of the analyst's subjectivity. *Psychoanalytic Dialogues* 1:29–51.

———— (1996). *A Meeting of Minds: Mutuality in Psychoanalysis*. Hillsdale, NJ: Analytic Press.

Atwood, G., and Stolorow, R. (1984). *Structures of Subjectivity: Explorations in Psychoanalytic Phenomenology*. Hillsdale, NJ: Analytic Press.

Benjamin, J. (1988). *The Bonds of Love: Psychoanalysis, Feminism, and the Problem of Domination*. New York: Pantheon.

———— (1991). Commentary on Irwin Z. Hoffman's discussion: "Toward a Social-Constructivist View of the Psychoanalytic Situation." *Psychoanalytic Dialogues* 1:525–533.

———— (1995). *Like Subjects, Love Objects: Essays on Recognition and Sexual Difference*. New Haven, CT: Yale University Press.

Berger, P., and Luckmann, T. (1967). *The Social Construction of Reality: A Treatise in the Sociology of Knowledge*. Garden City, NY: Anchor.

Black, M. (1987). The analyst's stance: transferential implications of technical orientation. *The Annual of Psychoanalysis* 15:127–172. New York: International Universities Press.

Eagle, M. (1984). *Recent Developments in Psychoanalysis*. New York: McGraw-Hill.

Ferenczi, S. (1931). Child analysis in the analysis of adults. In *Final Contributions to the Problems and Methods of Psycho-Analysis*, ed. M. Balint, pp. 126–142. New York: Brunner/Mazel.

Flax, J. (1996). Taking multiplicity seriously: some consequences for psychoanalytic theorizing and practice. *Contemporary Psychoanalysis* 32:577–593.

Fourcher, L. A. (1975). Psychological pathology and social reciprocity. *Human Development* 18:405–429.

———— (1978). A view of subjectivity in the evolution of human behavior. *Journal of Social and Biological Structures* 1:387–400.

Freud, S. (1905). Fragment of an analysis of a case of hysteria. *Standard Edition* 7:7–122.

—— (1926). Inhibitions, symptoms, and anxiety. *Standard Edition* 20:77–175.

—— (1927). Fetishism. *Standard Edition* 21:149–157.

—— (1940). Splitting of the ego in the process of defense. *Standard Edition* 23:275–278.

Gendlin, E. T. (1962). *Experiencing and the Creation of Meaning: A Philosophical and Psychological Approach to the Subjective*. New York: Macmillan.

—— (1964). A theory of personality change. In *Personality Change*, ed. P. Worchel and D. Byrne, pp. 100–148. New York: Wiley.

Gergen, K. (1985). The social constructionist movement in modern psychology. *American Psychologist* 40:266–275.

Ghent, E. (1989). Credo: the dialectics of one-person and two-person psychologies. *Contemporary Psychoanalysis* 25:169–211.

Gill, M. M. (1983). The distinction between the interpersonal paradigm and the degree of the therapist's involvement. *Contemporary Psychoanalysis* 19:200–237.

—— (1984). Robert Langs on technique: a critique. In *Listening and Interpreting: The Challenge of the Work of Robert Langs*, ed. J. Raney, pp. 395–413. New York: Jason Aronson.

—— (1994). *Psychoanalysis in Transition: A Personal View*. Hillsdale, NJ: Analytic Press.

Gill, M. M., and Hoffman, I. Z. (1982a). *Analysis of Transference II: Studies of Nine Audio-Recorded Psychoanalytic Sessions*. New York: International Universities Press.

—— (1982b). A method for studying the analysis of aspects of the patient's experience of the relationship in psychoanalysis and psychotherapy. *Journal of the American Psychoanalytic Association* 30:137–167.

Greenberg, J. R. (1981). Prescription or description: the therapeutic action of psychoanalysis. *Contemporary Psychoanalysis* 17:239–257.

—— (1986). Theoretical models and the analyst's neutrality. *Contemporary Psychoanalysis* 22:87–106.

—— (1987). Of mystery and motive: a review of *The Ambiguity of Change* by Edgar Levenson. *Contemporary Psychoanalysis* 23:689–704.

—— (1991). Countertransference and reality. *Psychoanalytic Dialogues* 1:52–73.

—— (1995). Reply to discussions of *Oedipus and Beyond*. *Psychoanalytic Dialogues* 5:317–324.

Greenberg, J. R., and Mitchell, S. (1983). *Object Relations in Psychoanalytic Theory*. Cambridge, MA: Harvard University Press.

Greenson, R. (1971). The real relationship between the patient and the psychoanalyst. In *The Unconscious Today*, ed. M. Kanzer, pp. 213–232. New York: International Universities Press.

Hare-Mustin, R., and Maracek, J. (1988). The meaning of difference: gender theory, postmodernism, and psychology. *American Psychologist* 43:455–464.

Hartmann, H., and Kris, E. (1945). The genetic approach in psychoanalysis. *Psychoanalytic Study of the Child* 1:11–30. New York: International Universities Press.

Hirsch, I. (1987). Varying modes of analytic participation. *Journal of the American Academy of Psychoanalysis* 15:205–222.

Hoffman, I. Z. (1987). The value of certainty in psychoanalytic practice. (Discussion of paper by E. Witenberg.) *Contemporary Psychoanalysis* 23:205–215.

——— (1990). In the eye of the beholder: a reply to Levenson. *Contemporary Psychoanalysis* 26:291–299.

——— (1991). Reply to Benjamin. *Psychoanalytic Dialogues* 1:535–544.

——— (1992). Reply to Orange. *Psychoanalytic Dialogues* 2:567–570.

——— (1995). Review of *Oedipus and Beyond* by J. Greenberg. *Psychoanalytic Dialogues* 5:93–112.

——— (1998). *Ritual and Spontaneity in the Psychoanalytic Process. A Dialectical-Constructivist View.* Hillsdale, NJ: Analytic Press.

Hoffman, I. Z., and Gill, M. M. (1988). Critical reflections on a coding scheme. *International Journal of Psycho-Analysis* 69:55–64.

Holt, R. R. (1989). *Freud Reappraised.* New York: Guilford.

Levenson, E. A. (1990). Reply to Hoffman. *Contemporary Psychoanalysis* 26:299–304.

McLaughlin, J. T. (1981). Transference, psychic reality, and countertransference. *Psychoanalytic Quarterly* 50:639–664.

Mitchell, S. A. (1988). *Relational Concepts in Psychoanalysis: An Integration.* Cambridge, MA: Harvard University Press.

——— (1991). Wishes, needs, and interpersonal negotiations. *Psychoanalytic Inquiry* 11:147–170.

Modell, A. H. (1991). The therapeutic relationship as a paradoxical experience. *Psychoanalytic Dialogues* 1:13–28.

Orange, D. M. (1992). Perspectival realism and social constructivism: commentary on Irwin Hoffman's "Discussion: Toward a Social-Constructivist View of the Psychoanalytic Situation." *Psychoanalytic Dialogues* 2:561–565.

Protter, B. (1985). Toward an emergent psychoanalytic epistemology. *Contemporary Psychoanalysis* 21:208–227.

Racker, H. (1968). *Transference and Countertransference.* New York: International Universities Press.

Schafer, R. (1983). *The Analytic Attitude.* New York: Basic Books.

Schimek, J. G. (1975). A critical re-examination of Freud's concept of unconscious mental representation. *International Review of Psycho-Analysis* 2:171–187.

Schön, D. (1983). *The Reflective Practitioner: How Professionals Think in Action.* New York: Basic Books.

Searles, H. F. (1975). The patient as therapist to his analyst. In *Tactics and Techniques in Psychoanalytic Therapy*, vol. 2: *Countertransference*, ed. P. Giovacchini, pp. 95–151. New York: Jason Aronson.

Seligman, S., and Shanook, R. S. (1995). Subjectivity, complexity, and the social world: Erikson's identity concept and contemporary relational theories. *Psychoanalytic Dialogues* 5:537–565.

Slavin, M. O., and Kriegman, D. (1992). *The Adaptive Design of the Human Psyche.* New York: Guilford.

Stern, D. B. (1983). Unformulated experience. *Contemporary Psychoanalysis.* 19:71–99.

——— (1985). Some controversies regarding constructivism and psychoanalysis. *Contemporary Psychoanalysis* 21:201–208.

——— (1989). The analyst's unformulated experience of the patient. *Contemporary Psychoanalysis* 25:1–33.

Stolorow, R. D. (1988). Intersubjectivity, psychoanalytic knowing, and reality. *Contemporary Psychoanalysis* 24:331–338.

Stolorow, R. D., and Atwood, G. E. (1992). *Contexts of Being: The Intersubjective Foundations of Psychological Life.* Hillsdale, NJ: Analytic Press.

——— (1997). Deconstructing the myth of the neutral analyst: an alternative from intersubjective systems theory. *Psychoanalytic Quarterly* 66:431–449.

Thompson, C. (1964a). Transference as a therapeutic instrument. In *Interpersonal Psychoanalysis*, ed. M. Green, pp. 13–21. New York: Basic Books.

——— (1964b). The role of the analyst's personality in therapy. In *Interpersonal Psychoanalysis*, ed. M. Green, pp. 168–178. New York: Basic Books.

Weiss, J., Sampson, H., and the Mount Zion Psychotherapy Research Group (1986). *The Psychoanalytic Process: Theory, Clinical Observations, and Empirical Research.* New York: Guilford.

# 2

# Analyzing Multiplicity: A Postmodern Perspective on Some Current Psychoanalytic Theories of Subjectivity*

*Susan Fairfield*

## INTRODUCTION

What comes to mind when you hear the term *postmodern psychoanalysis*? Is it a tautology? A contradiction in terms? A puzzle, a threat, a banner to rally around, a passing fad that will go away if ignored? At a time when analysts are increasingly finding that they have to take a position regarding postmodernism, I think we might want to stand back and consider the extent to which psychoanalysis can coexist with the postmodern way of looking at the world. The present paper, which will offer some thoughts on current psychoanalytic theorizing of subjectivity, is a small contribution to what I hope will become a larger, more general debate.

*For their comments on an earlier version of this paper, I would like to thank Joel Greifinger, Lynne Layton, Richard Nasser, and Carolyn Stack, with whom it has been a challenge and a joy to discuss our differing views on modernism and postmodernism in an atmosphere of mutual respect.

*Postmodernism* is an ambiguous term. As its name indicates, it defines itself with reference to modernism and exists in constant tension with it.[1] Zygmunt Bauman (1990), a major theorist of the movement, puts it this way: "Postmodernity does not necessarily mean the end, the discreditation, or the rejection of modernity. Postmodernity is no more (but no less either) than the modern mind taking a long, attentive, and sober look at itself, at its condition and its past works, not fully liking what it sees and sensing the need to change" (p. 272). It is, he says, what you get when a non-naive modernity psychoanalyzes itself. Can we go on to ask what would it be like for a non-naive psychoanalysis to psychoanalyze itself, to address the tensions between modernism and post-modernism in its own theory and practice?

Consider, if you're inclined to jump on the postmodern band-wagon, not only that we postmodernists regard with suspicion such terms as *Enlightenment* and *humanism* (and hence such concepts as *identity*, *empathy*, and—one I'll be mentioning below—*authenticity*). You might well come to agree philosophically once you saw how that suspicion stems from a respect for difference. And you would not, by any means, have to forego the depth, intensity, and devotion of your engagement with your patients. But you would find yourself asking some profoundly unsettling questions. Then again, perhaps you'd choose not to; after all, postmodernists are for the most part academicians and creative artists, and only the relatively few who also have clinical training realize that the way things look when you're sitting behind the analytic couch is very different indeed from the way they look when you're sitting around a seminar table with a group of graduate students.[2] Still, can psychoanalysts, of all people, honestly refuse the challenge to analyze their own practice and theory from a postmodern perspective?

As a way of setting forth some of the problems confronting those of us who are interested in the new paradigm, I'll be discussing an issue that is often taken to divide analysts who consider themselves post-modernists from those who don't: whether subjectivity is unified (what I'll call the monist view) or multiplex (the pluralist view). I'll be suggesting that, contrary to what seems to be a common assumption, while all monists are modernists, not all pluralists are postmodernists. Are *any* psychoanalytic pluralists postmodernists? Is a thoroughgoing postmodern pluralism consistent with psychoanalysis as it's currently theorized and practiced? With the aim of suggesting a typology of pluralisms in the psychoanalytic theorizing of subjectivity, I'll be distinguishing between two sets of pluralists, modern and postmodern, and, for the sake of argument, affiliating with the latter set, though I'm not at all sure that it in fact has any members.[3] It's my hope that this discussion will help to clarify what postmodernism implies, and, in particular, to locate psychoanalytic pluralisms in relation to postmodernism.

A word in advance: postmodernists often prefer to speak of *subjectivity* instead of *self* (cf. Flax 1996). Subjectivity is the more general term, referring as loosely as possible to a person's experience of being in the world. It may or may not coalesce into something as bounded as a self, and it is unspecified as to interiority, agency, homogeneity, degree of consciousness, and any relation to the body, the physical and social environment, or a supernatural realm. Its modalities vary widely across time and cultures,[4] and that brings us right to the unity/multiplicity issue.

## SUBJECTIVITY IS . . . NOT OBJECTIVE

By way of a loose analogy, I'll begin by asking a question about food. Is food appetizers or desserts? The question probably leaves you perplexed at the category error and the narrowing of options: after all, appetizers and desserts are kinds of food, and why mention only those two? Yet, in a similar move, a number of psychoanalysts are currently involved in a debate, sometimes a heated one, about whether subjectivity is unitary or multiple.[5] But consider: you cannot find food as such; it's a purely generic term. It occurs out in the world only in specific instances of things considered suitable for eating, and (in the case of human beings) normally for eating in a certain, often highly patterned, way. And so it is with subjectivity. It has no ontological status and no essence. There is no "as suchness" about it; there are only highly patterned ways of experiencing oneself in particular cultural and subcultural contexts. This means that there is no objective, noncontextual vantage point outside subjectivity from which we could walk around it, look it up and down, peer into it, and say, for example, "Hmm, seems to be multiple! And what's this over here? Why, it's a function that keeps integration and unintegration in balance" (or whatever your model happens to be).

Wait a minute, a modernist might protest, aren't *unity* and *multiplicity* abstract categories that can be applied to any specific subjective contents whatsoever? To which a postmodernist would reply: yes indeed, in our Eurocentric terms, but while all cultures, presumably, distinguish between "one" and "more than one," subjectivity refers to experience as it is lived in a particular context, and not all cultures would consider unity and multiplicity salient categories in which to describe their mode of being in the world. Our Western notions could be explained, but they might be remote from lived experience in another culture, just as "appetizers" and "desserts" would be intelligible but alien terms where a meal is a bowl of rice or doesn't come in separate courses. To a postmodernist, it makes no more sense to ask whether subjectivity is unitary or multiple than it does to ask whether food is appetizers or desserts.

We Westerners nowadays readily describe ourselves as being "all over the place and needing to get it together," or "too tightly wound and needing to loosen up a bit," or feeling "too one-sided and needing to get in touch with other parts of myself." In other words, binary terms like unity and multiplicity, integration and unintegration, apply to the way people in our culture actually express concerns with the way we are in the world. In contrast, to take just one set of examples, Geertz (1983) studied a semirural Javanese population that he describes as quite sophisticated when it came to discussing their view of subjectivity; these people defined subjectivity in terms of two polarities, inside/outside and refined/vulgar, and held as an ideal a flat, uninterrupted inner state and correspondingly smooth outward behavior. Two other groups—Balinese and Moroccan—had elaborate theories of subjectivity that differed greatly from one another and were not conceptualized in terms of binary distinctions. The Balinese experienced themselves as occupying generic social positions (e.g., "grandmother," "third-born"), and they viewed life as the public, ceremonial performance of these roles. The Moroccans saw themselves not as separate psychic entities but as representing a highly complex set of attributions specifying their origins, descent, religion, occupation, and the like, any personal characteristics being expressed from within these categories. As a postmodernist would see it, to overlay on these societies the binary concepts *unity* and *multiplicity* as descriptive of subjective experience would be to replicate the procrustean and imperialist act of imposing Western thought patterns on other cultures.

For a postmodernist, a theory of subjectivity does not *describe* anything. It *produces a version* of subjectivity from elements available in the culture, projects it out onto the world, and seeks to establish it through one or more of the legitimating discourses accepted by that culture, for example science, religion, or psychology (cf. Foucault 1980). If insisted on by people with power, the theory enforces its tenets—perhaps subtly, perhaps not so subtly—often with the cooperation, even the gratitude, of those on whom the power is exerted, since in many ways life is indeed easier if one conforms to dominant belief systems.

A postmodernist would view psychoanalytic monism and pluralism in this light. For example, pluralists often describe the unitary self as a necessary fiction or necessary illusion, sometimes even a "healthy" one (Bromberg 1998): we are unable, in this view, to experience our essentially divided nature without occasionally resorting to a false sense of coherence. But to say that the cohesive self is a fiction or illusion is to assume that a multiplex subjectivity is *not* this. From a postmodern perspective, however, there just is no objective, essential "human nature." The meaning of experience is constituted in particular discursive frameworks, and each such framework has legitimating and normativizing strategies for creating (and enforcing) effects such as "necessity," "illusion," "psychological health," or "nature," as well as "self," "individual," and many others. Thus any description we give of subjectivity is no more and no less a story than any other.

Each culture, then, and within it each subculture, makes certain modes of subjectivity possible and renders others difficult to maintain or even invisible. The modes of subjectivity available to members of the dominant culture nowadays in the West—unsurprisingly, since psychoanalysis has helped to shape these modes and has been shaped by them in turn—roughly correspond to psychoanalytic monism and pluralism. Nevertheless, despite the fact that there is room for choice, the psychoanalytic community seems to feel a growing need to take sides. For example, Malcolm Owen Slavin (1996), discussing a paper by Frank Lachmann (1996a) that is entitled "How Many Selves Make a Person?" and that argues for a unitary, continuous self, asks pointedly, "Is one self enough?" To which Lachmann (1996b) firmly replies, "Yes, one self is enough!"

To which I, in turn, would like to ask: Enough *for what*? What work do we want a theory of subjectivity to do? There are two possibilities, two criteria for the adequacy of monism or pluralism, namely the representational and the therapeutic. We want our model to reflect the true nature of subjectivity, and/or we want it to be clinically useful. The first option—the "and" part of the "and/or"—links clinical practice to an essentialist view of subjectivity, as in Adrienne Harris' (1996) claim that there is a tension between separateness and unity "at the heart of the human mind and personality and simultaneously at the heart of healing" (pp. 538–539). A postmodernist would reply that there is no external reality to subjectivity, no "heart" or essence of it apart from particular discursive systems, to which we could compare our model and assess the degree of its correspondence. A clinician cannot hope to succeed by holding a mirror up to nature (cf. Rorty 1979). But, the postmodernist would go on to say, she'd have a better chance with the "or" option, the purely pragmatic criterion, trying somehow to match up her clinical practice to the way people in our culture would like to experience themselves, since this is something she *can* know a bit about. (I say "a bit" because we are each limited by what our familial, ethnic, professional, and other reference groups have made available to us and by our idiosyncratic assimilation of those meanings.) And in that regard, I would say that right now the dominant culture, the culture from which, for better or worse, the psychoanalytic patient population is drawn, will support both therapeutic models, monist and pluralist, equally well.

If we imagine a continuum extending from a monolithic, rigid, and undifferentiated subjectivity to sheer random dispersion,[6] it turns out that every psychoanalytic theorist has a mixed model (cf. Mitchell 1993), with the center of gravity located closer to one or the other end of the continuum but well short of the extremes. So well short, in fact, so clustered near the center, that subjectivity as a "mosaic" in the theorizing of the monist Lachmann (1996a) is formally difficult to distinguish from subjectivity as a "kaleidoscope" in that of the pluralist Davies (1996, 1998). And compare the monist position that the "fluidity [of] divergent and conflicting states, wishes, affects, and ideas . . . is tolerable and sustainable when a sense of self-unity provides the background" (Lachmann 1996a, pp. 596–597) with the pluralist account of "a central consciousness that can handle the contradictions of the different voices and different desires within one person [and that represents] the growing ability to call all these voices 'I,' to disidentify from any one of them as the whole story" (Benjamin 1998, p. 106, quoting Rivera).

Is there any substantive difference between the two? Monists object to what they see as the pluralists' caricature: monist advocacy of static undifferentiation. And pluralists bristle at what they see as their opponents' caricature: pluralist advocacy of fragmented incoherence. But, I would argue, as these two positions are actually set forth by their proponents, they differ only in moving the center of gravity somewhat more toward the forest or toward the trees, toward cohesion or toward heterogeneity, within the model of the superordinate, integrated "self" of modernism. As I'll be suggesting in the rest of this paper, the radical difference is not the one between psychoanalytic monism and the modern school of psychoanalytic pluralism; it's the one between the modern and the postmodern sensibilities. The categories we'll be working with, then, are monism and modern pluralism on the modern side, in contrast to a (largely hypothetical) postmodern psychoanalytic pluralism.

But my concern for the moment is to propose that the majority culture in the United States at this time will support both models, that is, any of the subject positions advocated by psychoanalytic monism or current psychoanalytic pluralism. People can feel reasonably comfortable anywhere in, say, the two middle quartiles of our imaginary continuum and, in congenial subgroups (a fundamentalist religious community, a troupe of experimental performance artists), even somewhat further out toward one or the other extreme. But, given the availability of options, what makes people—patients, analysts—choose, and often cling fiercely to, a particular position on the continuum or a certain limited range beyond which they do not stray? It remains for us to reflect on the nature of our investment in our choice.

## IT'S ABOUT US

In psychoanalytic case presentations, unsparing self-examination is now the order of the day. With heightened sensitivity to what they may be bringing to the clinical situation, analysts reveal the ways in which their own empathic failures, family secrets, childhood sufferings, even their state of sexual arousal, influenced the conduct of a treatment. Amid all these candid confessions, however, the literature on countertransference and enactment does not discuss the author's model of subjectivity as a possible source of bias. Yet as soon as we give up a pretense to positivism when it comes to the psyche, it becomes clear—well, it becomes clear to a postmodernist, anyway—that our model of subjectivity is a complex set of personal and cultural biases, conscious and unconscious, that affect clinical practice in the same way as do our views on gender, sexuality, class, ethnicity, and religion (all of which are, of course, involved in our notions of subjectivity).

For a deconstructionist, theory, process, and content are inter-implicated. A psychoanalytic theory and its clinical implementation are not *about* a certain kind of subjectivity. They enact it, reiterate it performatively, within a cultural setting that allows for the legibility of that construct, and this legibility makes the enactment one in which the patient can learn to join. Metapsychology, clinical description, and subjectivity—that is, the discourses and their ostensible object—are thus on the same level, the two former employing the rhetoric of legitimation and objective referentiality so as to seem to be *accounts* of the latter as opposed to *examples* of it. Any pluralist theory of subjectivity that presents itself as a superordinate referential discourse and does not allow for its own reflexivity, its active participation in what it describes, remains to that extent within the modern paradigm. It is not, as Bauman would put it, psychoanalyzing itself.

From a postmodern perspective, the unity/multiplicity debate is not about some fact out there that certain analysts obtusely refuse to acknowledge. It's about us. It's about strong investments by individual theorists in our choice from among the models, predominantly monist or predominantly pluralist, made available in the culture. A monist or a pluralist analysis is the treatment of choice only in the sense that it's the treatment a given analyst has chosen in order to pursue his personal mode of engagement with issues of subjectivity. Thus the choice of either of these theories is as overdetermined, and requires as much analytic scrutiny, as what used to be called the choice of neurosis. A postmodernist would have a much broader view of what determines an inclination toward a particular subjective modality, but for the moment let's play a modern game of psychoanalytic reductionism and put the choice of multiplicity on the couch.

What fantasies emerge as we pluralists contemplate experiencing ourselves as more bounded or more open, more cohesive or more fragmented? (Grossman [1991] interestingly notes that our concept of subjectivity may be less important than our fantasies about it.) What feels liberating or empowering, what arouses feelings of helplessness, or object loss, or sexual anxiety? The very categories in which we frame such questions are themselves cultural artifacts, but let's ignore that in order to play the game.

Pluralism can provide a whole host of benefits. If we believe that unity is an illusion, however necessary, whereas a multiple subjectivity is the genuine article (a belief I've called into question above), we can enjoy taking pity on monists for needing to cling to a comforting falsehood and can congratulate ourselves for being able to withstand the rigorous truths of heterogeneity. If our pluralism is of the modern variety in other ways as well, we can frame these differences in a developmental context. We can get together with other developmentalists and lament the immaturity of the monists; after all, a need for boundedness and cohesion is infantile, if not downright fetal, whereas a need for multiplicity is . . . no, our theory is not a need, but simply the expression of a higher stage in the development of subjectivity. We can also enjoy deploring the defensiveness of the monists and (with a stunning lack of self-observation on our part that we'll ignore) their inability to tolerate otherness.

We can also set ourselves up as guardians of the treasure. When faced with the inconvenient fact that monists and those who have been analyzed by them seem to lead as full, happy, and ethical lives as pluralists and their patients, we can assert that this is the result of transference cure or of a supportive psychotherapy that leaves the patient with the kind of consolidated self-structure that we, offering the unalloyed gold of pluralist psychoanalysis, would then proceed to deconstruct.

Though I'm using the term, postmodern psychoanalytic pluralism does not exist in anything like pure form. Still, if we're oriented toward postmodernism, we can claim that our Freud ("the I is not master in its own house") is bigger and stronger than the monists' Freud ("where It was, there I shall come into being"), though this may lose us some allies among modern pluralists, who also tend to hold the latter view.

If we see ourselves as being in the plague-bringing business as opposed to the adaptationist business, we can use the postmodern version of pluralism, with its disruptive potential, as part of a commitment to radical social change. But, to keep the issue on the intrapsychic level, this challenge can also serve unconscious transgressive and aggressive aims. For pluralism can be tinged with a subversive excitement, its polymorphousness temptingly erotized: no gender position is denied one, and the postmodern—"postconventional"—destabilization of boundaries can promote unconscious fantasies of strange couplings, forbidden liaisons. Moreover, as psychoanalysis and postmodernism are alike in pointing out, the anxious thrill of transgressing a boundary actually affirms the boundary. It thus provides for a highly gratifying cycle of defiance and reassurance; this is especially true if ours is the standard pluralist model of a dialectical tension between disintegration and wholeness.

In its potential transgressivity, pluralism's cool intellectual questioning of unities can be driven by unconscious fantasies of tearing asunder stable entities, of aggressive rupture. Are we not on the "cutting edge" of theory and "pushing the envelope"? Harris (1996) forthrightly speaks of the "conceptual power" of multiplicity.[7] But since, in its openness to alterity, pluralism can view itself as the least harmful theory of subjectivity (Flax 1996), we pluralists can tell ourselves that we are the least power-seeking, the most open and receptive, of theorists. After all, we preach negotiation, holding in tension, and accepting difference when it comes to subjectivity, and we can manage not to look too hard at the fact that we don't often preach accepting difference when it comes to theories of subjectivity. Like any theory, pluralism can become a hegemonic discourse—rigid, a phallus, a mantra, a fetish—and a regulatory practice, determining what is taught in institutes and who graduates from them, what gets published, and who is invited to speak at conferences, disempowering other theories not in any crude sense, but in terms of what Foucault (1980) calls the establishment of a regime of power/knowledge.[8] For a given analyst, pluralism can represent a reaction formation, an unconscious iron hand in a conscious velvet glove, a means of foreclosing dissent while seeming to welcome it.

If we aim to be postmodern pluralists, we acknowledge our constructivist role (cf. Hoffman 1991, 1998, Schwartz 1995, 1996). Aware of the power we wield as analysts, we do not (like monists and modern pluralists) conceal that power from ourselves or others by claiming that we're merely bringing about the natural and universal state of the human psyche, facilitating a normal developmental process. But not to worry: postmodern pluralism offers us other opportunities for sublimating aggression. We can claim to be more postmodern than some "thou" with whom we feel competitive, searching the papers of theorists who claim to be postmodern pluralists for signs of essentialism and objectivist referentiality (which we'll always find, since it's impossible to do without them) and implying that these colleagues should turn in their badges or shape up. After all, if we don't have firm ground under our feet, why should anyone else? And since postmodern pluralism is likely to be a painful approach, bringing warded-off agonies into awareness and then keeping them there, instead of striving for the resolution of dissonance, it may offer some analysts more scope for sadistic and masochistic fantasies, not to mention enactments, than does monism.

But this is not all that pluralism can do for us. A celebration of multiplicity can be a counterphobic attempt to master a fear of fragmentation. In a related move, we can project onto the world our own felt incoherence, naturalizing the state of unintegration and thereby calming the personal anxiety that it evokes.

Postmodern philosophy isn't a paralyzing relativism that makes it impossible to take a position or offer an intervention; like psychoanalysis, what it does is offer ways to think about our complex investments. Nevertheless, if our pluralism is of the postmodern variety, we can use the theory's emphasis on provisionality and uncertainty to mask obsessional doubt or to serve a paranoid need to be a moving target and thus avoid attack.

And pluralists can feel good about being in the vanguard of psychoanalytic theory, especially if we want to consort with academicians and can ignore the fact that, while we're congratulating ourselves, many of them will be wondering why (if we're postmodernists) it took us so very long to "get it," or why (if we're modernists) we still don't.

The list could continue. Having used psychoanalytic reductionism to put the pluralist disposition on the couch, a postmodernist would now insist that psychoanalytic reductionism itself be put on the couch. But let's set that aside, important though it is, and think some more about what's involved in holding a particular pluralist theory of subjectivity.

## PLURALISM AND THE SCIENTIFIC "VIEW FROM NOWHERE"

Psychoanalysis helped to shape the postmodern outlook, and so it's not coincidental that one defining characteristic postmodernism shares with psychoanalysis is a suspicion of any attempt to cordon something off from scrutiny: to deny, or fail to see, that it can be put in question. Whenever it's claimed that some aspect of the way people behave or make meanings is simply the way things are, a fact about the world and not about the propounder of the claim, we're pretty sure that we're dealing with a fear of losing control, be it in a political regime, a culturally privileged group, or their intrapsychic analogues in a patient. Yet, while it's occasionally acknowledged that psychoanalytic theories are not neutral, for the most part analysts tend to confer objective validity on them.

As I've been trying to argue, a deconstructionist would hold that a metapsychology of subjectivity is subjectivity carried on by other means, and that the wish to put it "meta," "beyond," is grist for the mill. Deconstruction joins Freudian psychoanalysis in examining the ways in which we are inhabited by what we attempt to put outside us. Nevertheless, the modernist tendency to claim a "view from nowhere," in Nagel's (1986) felicitous phrase, has characterized psychoanalysis from its beginnings, right alongside the development of conceptual tools with which to deconstruct that very tendency. The objectivist position persists among some pluralists (e.g., Bromberg 1998, Pizer 1996, 1998, Slavin 1996), who turn to science—neurobiology, evolutionary biology, cognitive science, ethology, infant research, or artificial intelligence—as a foundational discourse, a metasubjective warrant for claims about a universal, precultural human subjectivity, and, more specifically, for their particular version of pluralism.

Now, even for a postmodernist there are certain givens about human life. Every person comes into the world as a helpless infant, with a unique set of congenital attributes, needing to be cared for and to be socialized into the meaning-making systems of its particular reference groups. Every human being must struggle somehow or other with relationships, with sexuality, and with the materiality of the world and the materiality of the body, its vulnerability to illness and death. But, precisely because we are socialized into meaning-making systems, all of these elements are so thoroughly saturated with culturally assigned import that we simply cannot recover any prediscursive subjectivity. There is no such thing. To put it another way, while hard wiring and the necessity of dealing with other people, the body, and the nonhuman surround are of course acknowledged, any meanings assigned to them, or experienced through them, are embedded in a relational context so pervasive that any prerelational features are impossible to specify for human beings in general or for any one person.

Just as not all pluralists are postmodernists, neither are all relational analysts. But postmodernists are the most relational of relationalists, since for us all experience occurs in a context. While we do not deny that on some level physiology, neurochemistry, and the like affect subjectivity, we see the human psyche (which includes, among other things, all motivations for explaining the human psyche and all particular explanations offered) as formed in a highly dense, complex web of relations. We do not, therefore, believe that it is possible to isolate any extrarelational factor in pure form, and we consider the leaps from the brain to the mind to the psyche to be fraught with problems. And postmodernists are aware that the power to declare what is "natural" to human beings—because we were divinely created that way, because our primitive ancestors were that way, because our cognitive apparatus works that way, and so forth—has historically been used to legitimate regulatory practices that stigmatize those declared "unnatural" as inferior, deviant, criminal, sick.

Mitchell's (1997) critique of scientism is one that United States psychoanalytic theory will have to reckon with. Instead of seeking a foundation in science, postmodern psychoanalytic pluralists will find analogies in hermeneutic theory proper (cf. Messer et al. 1988, Spence 1993, Stern 1997), and, more generally, in disciplines like critical legal theory, literary criticism, and cultural studies, disciplines that are concerned with interpretation, with meanings as opposed to causes. Since postmodern theories are not explanatory systems but a set of techniques precisely for putting explanatory systems into question, we value these disciplines not as foundational but as having developed ways of investigating the sorts of human situations that concern us. We believe that, where human behavior and its motivations are concerned, science yields the conclusions favored by the "observer." What we "discover" in scientific investigation is determined by the questions we ask, the domain of observation that we isolate, and the types of outcomes that, even if unanticipated, are intelligible in our discursive system and compatible with our personal needs. In the case of subjectivity, science offers only self-fulfilling prophecies, dependent on the kind of self we need to fulfill.

For postmodernists, then, an epistemology in which an objectively real external phenomenon can be observed in an unmediated fashion by a neutral researcher is not suitable when it comes to the psyche.[9] As Nietzsche said, we cannot leap beyond our own shadow. From this perspective, there is no universal human nature that is subsequently configured in various ways by different cultures. Quick to deconstruct the nature/culture binary, postmodernists see modernists as working back from what they consider to be a culturally desirable trait to a scientific "cause" that retrodictively naturalizes and universalizes it. But since the "cause" follows upon, and is shaped by, the desire for validation, it is actually its effect. Cause and effect, origin and sequel, are interchanged: what counts as nature is seen to be an effect of culture, not its cause or prior state.

It is for similar reasons that, as psychoanalytic pluralists continue to negotiate with modernism and postmodernism, those who hold to a developmental theory will encounter some challenges (cf. Wolff 1998 on the inadequacies of a "scientific" developmentalism, Cushman 1991, 1995 and Kirschner 1996 on the cultural construction of psychoanalytic developmental models). Each psychoanalytic theory of subjectivity traditionally comes packaged with its own developmental story—usually presented in terms of "observational data" and often with underpinnings in one or the other science—that purports to explain the normative unfolding of subjectivity as linear (according to monists) or as multifocal and nonlinear (according to modern pluralists). A consistently postmodern psychoanalytic theory, if there were such a thing, would be the exception. For starters, the linear teleologies of modernism will no longer serve if we see subjectivity as multiplex (e.g., Coates 1997). An even further shift from the traditional psychoanalytic position is Chodorow's (1996) argument that objectivist views of the patient's past are becoming increasingly difficult to maintain; nevertheless, she goes on to say, we do seem to need developmental narratives and should choose from infant research those that are compatible with current views of fluid subjectivity. For pragmatic purposes, I would agree. The pull of the modernist need for causal narratives may be so strong that clinical psychoanalysis, right now, can't do without some version of them. Where I would disagree, still in the clinical context, is that I believe many patients and analysts will continue to be quite satisfied with a model of a unified, cohesive and/or true "self" for some years to come. But from the theoretical point of view, Chodorow's recommendation that pluralists turn to infant research coexists uneasily with the postmodern position she takes at the beginning of her paper.

Can we go further in the direction of a postmodern pluralism? To put it bluntly, a postmodern psychoanalyst would have no need whatsoever of a developmental theory, much less of any infant "observation" to back it up. Why? Because, when it comes to subjectivity, there are no raw data of observation; because postmodern eyes would simply see a postmodern baby; and because, while agreeing that early experience in some way influences what comes afterward, postmodernists believe that any specific causal account is likely to be a retrodictive construct. The only purpose such a theory might serve is the pragmatic one of relieving the (modern) anxiety many patients and analysts still feel at the thought of doing without a fairly detailed story of psychological origins. This is a compelling purpose, and that anxiety must be respected in the consulting room, where it abounds. For a postmodern pluralist, however, it would ultimately have to be deconstructed, with the components of the patient's subjectivity left to shapeless dispersion and the very notion of a multiplex subjectivity denaturalized and relativized. The question with which I began this paragraph is not a rhetorical one. I would venture to say that no psychoanalyst who talks the postmodern talk can actually walk the walk. Not yet? Not ever?

## PLURALISMS: MODERN, POSTMODERN, MIXED

At any rate, pluralism is as close as we can comfortably get right now to a postmodern clinical practice of psychoanalysis. I would propose that we develop a flexible, open-ended typology of pluralisms, so that we can articulate and examine the way we position ourselves within (or outside) this approach. Here are some of the questions those of us who are pluralists might ask with regard to one of the issues I've been looking at, namely whether our particular version of pluralism (which is likely to be a mixed model) leans more toward modernism or toward postmodernism.

Is your pluralism confined to psychoanalysis, or is it informed by a sociopolitical ideal of openness to alterity (e.g., in matters of gender orientation or minority cultural practices)? Do you see it as part of a project of sociocultural critique in which persisting unitary categories are disrupted and subverted or, instead, in terms of adaptation to an increasingly tolerant and inclusive mainstream culture? Or some of each? Do you consciously or unconsciously code multiple subjectivity in gendered terms? As at all influenced by class and ethnicity? In our culture, women (especially non-WASP women), children, gay and bisexual men, dark-skinned people, and the poor have generally been permitted, even expected, to "go to pieces" or "fall apart" under stress, whereas people who do not belong to those groups—that is, those who hold power—are expected to "pull themselves together" and "get a firm grip on themselves." In the way you describe multiplicity and unity, and the relative importance you assign to them, do you intend to consolidate or, alternatively, to undermine prevailing gender and status categories? A postmodern psychoanalytic pluralism is more likely than the modern kind to be part of a larger set of sociocultural concerns, to have a subversive edge, and to examine the conventional coding of the terms it employs.

Do you (as a modern pluralist) envision the dissociated elements of your patients' subjectivity as sitting off in some dark corner, fully formed and waiting to have the light of consciousness beamed upon them, or do you (as a postmodernist) conceptualize them as being at least partially unformulated until they are symbolized and contextualized, that is, given a particular name in the discourse of a particular patient and analyst at a particular time? (On the latter view, cf. Fourcher 1992 and Stern 1997; this is also a tenet in one aspect of Lacanian theory.)

Is your clinical work as a pluralist aimed at helping the patient to achieve a greater sense of authenticity (e.g., Bromberg 1998, Mitchell 1997)? If so, would you also agree with Aron (1998) that there is a "reciprocal induction or mutual regulation of therapeutic dissociations" (p. 210) as patient and analyst, in the context of their relatedness, bring to the fore various elements of subjectivity in one another? In that case, there is a confusion of modern and postmodern tendencies here, since authenticity is a modern concept difficult to reconcile with a thoroughgoing two-person or constructivist approach.

For, a postmodernist would ask, how in the world could you possibly know which of the patient's subjective components are "authentic" ones—know this, that is, despite your own overdetermined subjective biases, the patient's conscious and unconscious strategies of concealment, and the shaping of the patient's material by the analytic situation itself? With which of *your* subjective components do you discern "authenticity," and on what basis do you grant this component the privileged status of objective judge? Why is the need, often felt with existential urgency, to exclude a thought or feeling from awareness any less "authentic" than the excluded element itself? After all, if dissociation or disavowal has been a patient's chief psychic operation over a lifetime, the dominant influence on the way he experiences himself and relates to others, why isn't *this* what is "authentic" about him?

If it isn't, then "authenticity" is code for "what I, as this patient's analyst, believe to be psychological normality." The normativizing view currently held by most pluralists, and some monists as well, seems to be that the hallmark of authenticity is the acknowledgment of dissociated elements of the "self," in other words, the recovery of a fuller and hence (in this view) more natural state of subjectivity (cf. Bromberg 1998, Mitchell 1997). I'll be returning for a closer look at this position further on, but for now I'll just note that, while postmodernists welcome greater awareness, we bridle at essentialist or identitarian claims. We would not arrest the play of difference by saying that any element or process of subjectivity is more "authentic" than any other, or that there is a true, natural, normal, "authentic" subjectivity that is capacious or multiplex (or unified, or anything else). We may run into aporias, or out of time or acumen, but we never reach bedrock.

The problem for postmodern theorists who are also analysts, however, is bedrock envy. Given a subjectivity formed in a modern culture, there remains a profound residual longing for authenticity in all of us and a profound unwillingness to deconstruct that longing beyond a certain point, if at all.

But let's continue. Assuming that, as an analyst, you work within a range, a comfort zone, on the imaginary continuum between total invariance and total dispersion of subjectivity, do you keep track of when you find yourself moving toward the monadic end? The disintegration end? With which patients? What material? If so, do you locate the temporary need for that more extreme position, or the anxious slide into it, in the patient (the modernist position) or in the intersubjective field (the postmodern view)? And how far does a patient have to move out of your particular comfort zone toward one or the other end of the continuum before you start thinking in terms of psychopathology? A

postmodern pluralist, averse to the devaluation or exclusion of otherness, would have a strong *theoretical* bias against pathologizing difference. But can *clinical* psychoanalysis do without normativizing constructs, that is, without seeing some forms of subjectivity as in need of
remediation? And who makes that decision? These questions are starting to trouble psychoanalysis from the direction of queer theory, but
there are still other "others" waiting in the postmodern wings.

Do you see multiplicity as leading to greater acceptance and understanding of otherness, and hence as adaptive intrapsychically and
interpersonally, or, alternatively, as the result of a tragic splitting of
subjectivity leading to irremediable self-estrangement and an inability
ever truly to understand the other? Both views are compatible with
versions of postmodernism, but there's a cultural difference: if you're
happy with the former position, you're likely to be shrugged off in French
postmodern circles as a naive United States meliorist and crypto-
modernist, a prospect that may or may not cause you to lose sleep. (I'll
be saying more about this difference below.)

Do you theorize pluralism as part of a binary distinction in which
it is contrasted with monism, or in some non-binary schema, such as
Lacan's (1972–1973) complex entwining of the Real, the Symbolic, and
the Imaginary or Ogden's (1989, 1994) model of a shifting among the
autistic-contiguous, paranoid-schizoid, and depressive positions? Postmodernists deconstruct binary divisions, showing the ways in which
apparent opposites are interimplicated. For that matter, we mistrust any
rigid distinctions and would thus look askance at a map of the mind
drawn with clear boundary lines.

This notion of mapping calls for further examination. To draw the
map of another person's subjectivity is to exercise great power, and a
postmodernist will ask how, and in whose interest, that power is exer-
cised. On what basis does the analyst—who has much more power than
the patient in this matter—configure the welter of the patient's verbal
and nonverbal material, deciding what are islands and what are the spaces
between them that we bridge (Pizer 1996) or in which we stand (Bromberg 1998), or what are the kaleidoscopic pieces and patterns (Davies
1996), or whatever imagery we favor for the components of subjectivity? After all, these components aren't real entities; they're our metaphors,
both as to their being units in the first place and as to their being units
of a particular nature, related to one another in a particular way.

Postmodernism, exquisitely sensitive to the power wielded by those with the right to map and to name, interrogates the drawing of boundaries (e.g., of gender, sexuality, race, psychopathology) and reflects on the interests served by decisions about what counts and what doesn't, about what is inside and what is outside the domain of normativity— or the domain of visibility altogether. Whenever you, as an analyst, name a component or a pattern in a patient's subjectivity, what might you be leaving unnamed, and why? When you draw the map of a patient's psyche, what is relegated to the margins, or falls off the edge of the map altogether, and why? When you conceptualize "identity" and "difference" in a particular patient, on what basis do you decide what counts as ongoing selfsameness and what counts as otherness or mutability? From a postmodern perspective, every act of mapping and naming is an enactment on the part of the analyst: inevitable, often joined by the patient, often highly therapeutic for both parties, but an enactment nonetheless.

Theoretical writings occasionally make use of visual maps of subjectivity, but the maps drawn in clinical psychoanalysis are verbal. As I've noted, postmodern pluralists, unbeguiled by any notion of representing an objective state of things, will take a critical interest in the language with which they think and speak of subjectivity. Like any theory, each version of pluralism is an allegory with its own favored metaphors; these metaphors inform the analyst's work even when they're not made explicit in talking to the patient, and problems can arise if analysts are not aware of their choices or the motivations underlying them. When a pluralist's patient comes in as a monist, or as a pluralist with a different unconscious allegory, he has to learn the terms in which the analyst needs to reconfigure his, the patient's, subjectivity. Because the reconfiguration is carried out in the guise of a discussion of the patient's material, for the most part this process goes on out of awareness for both parties. Patients are usually eager to be taught a language through which to sustain a relationship with the analyst, and this need makes them vulnerable; much work in postmodern literary criticism, philosophy, gender studies, and cultural studies has been devoted to revealing the ways in which another person's separate subjectivity can be violated by a tacit metaphorics.

For postmodern pluralists, there just is no non-metaphorical way of describing the psyche (cf. Derrida 1971). Once we discard a representational theory, thereby distinguishing ourselves from monists and modern pluralists, it becomes clear—to us, at least—that our choice of metaphors says something about us that we would do well to examine. How do we imagine the components of the manifold psyche? What particular images come to mind (islands, braid, kaleidoscope, etc.), and why? Are the components static or in flux, separate or intertwined? Each of us will have a host of idiosyncratic motives for our choices, but I'd like to suggest, as one possibility among many, that the components are often represented in terms that are conventionally gendered. Stereotypically coded female are openness; non-hierarchical juxtaposition; images of flowing, continuity, or interweaving; and containment as shelter. Coded masculine are discrete, static, bounded entities linked by a superordinate function (bridging, overarching, straddling), and containment as control.

Historically, in this culture, women have been socialized to think of themselves as being on the receiving end of straddling and over-arching. A "feminine" description of multiplicity will use terms of passive-organic receptivity, entwining, amorphousness, and unpredicta-bility, not those of the agentic mastery of mounting or bestriding, for stereotypically it is men who get out and erect bridges between discon-nected islands. A postmodernist, needless to say, would see these as cultural constructs, not essentialisms. But all of us have been strongly indoctrinated with these metaphors, and they may affect the way ana-lysts and patients theorize and experience subjectivity, whether one way all the time (why?) or shifting as mood and material change in private musings or in an analytic hour (when? why?).

## PLURALISMS AS CULTURAL CONSTRUCTS

Gender is not the only domain in which a postmodernist would see psychoanalytic pluralisms as socially constructed. Those post-modernists who are investigating the ways in which modern culture was formed in the age of imperialist expansion and capitalist appropriation[10] would regard as examples of that culture current psychoanalytic alle-gories of enlarging the dominion of the "I" over internal otherness. Bromberg (1998), for example, states that "[m]ultiple versions of the self exist within an overarching, synthetic structure of identity" (p. 274, quoting Slavin and Kriegman), a structure he describes as "a broadening experience of 'me-ness'" (p. 289). In the same vein, Mitchell (1997) sees a pluralist analysis as serving to "help people expand and enrich themselves" (p. 213). Sometimes the story of psychic expansion and enrichment is a modernist variation on the age-old narrative pattern of the return to the lost paradise of a pre-dissociated state, to a primary fullness of being. Thus we find allegories such as Benjamin's (1998), in which the "I" encompasses internal otherness and recovers an originary plenitude in which available gender positions are not limited.

In contrast to these narratives of the expansion and enrichment of the "me" or "I," think of those Eastern and earlier Western religious traditions in which aspects of subjectivity—thoughts, feelings, desires—that are considered extraneous to a small set of ultimate truths, or to the achievement of a state of non-awareness, are banished from consciousness through asceticism and meditation. This is a *via negativa*, a path of dispossession, a disciplined narrowing of mental focus, an emptying of the mind, a silencing of disturbing voices, a surrender of ego, and a correspondingly minimalist way of life. It is a therapeutic practice that could not be more different from our project of encompassing, mastering, and acquiring. Yet, as we know, the mode of subjectivity to which it leads can be deeply meaningful to those who cultivate it.

When it comes to subjectivity in *our* culture, though, we can't have too much of a good thing. More is more, and the United States pluralist model tends to be an additive one. We hold as much as possible (even if we're holding opposites in tension), contain as much as possible (even if what we're containing is paradoxical), and seek to include and recuperate instead of letting go or doing without. In its totalizing impulse, this type of pluralism is consistent with the modern sensibility and thus folds a monist element into its pluralist intent.

There are a variety of other ways in which the unity/multiplicity binary, like the modern/postmodern binary, can get complicated in the pluralist approach. For example, a metanarrative constructed by patient and analyst of the process by which they gradually came to deal with paradox, irresolution, and heterogeneity in the patient's psyche, and/or in the analytic relationship, can harmonize its dissonant contents by means of its own formal coherence and the mutuality of its creation. For deconstructionists, always wary of claims to superordinacy and objectivist referentiality, a metanarrative is not "meta"; it is on the same level as its contents. It is not about something external to itself but constitutes part of the reality (in terms of meaningfulness) of what it is ostensibly just describing. A unifying narrative of a pluralist treatment brings that treatment into the modern domain.

In Barbara Johnson's (1980) articulation of a central tenet of deconstruction, a difference *between* opposites is always a difference *within* them; they reciprocally define each other. It is not just the patient's psyche that holds selfsameness and difference in tension: a pluralist theory and practice of multiplicity, of internal otherness, must make room for their own internal otherness, and that is unity. However, while there can be no pluralism that is not inhabited by unity, I've been suggesting that the characteristically unitarian cast of much modern pluralist theorizing may be a reflection of United States culture.

For, to generalize very loosely, a postmodern pluralism might look more European (that is, continental). It would be not an additive model but a subtractive one, a vision not of plenitude but, as Harris (1996) characterizes the Lacanian position, of "a fundamental experience of alienation and loss" (p. 545), one in which, as Flax (1996) says, the patient learns "to tolerate the absence of meaning, the limits of narrative organization, and the ineradicable persistence of unintelligibility" (p. 589).[11] It would not resemble the pluralism indigenous to the United States, with our abiding national myths of a limitless frontier and abundant resources, there for the taking if we can just get to them. We are, after all, the country that not only opens McDonald's franchises in Beijing but actually planted our flag on the moon: there is no otherness that we cannot bring within our I- or me-sphere. Where United States analysts see a cornucopia, Europeans tend to see the death's head at the feast; where we strive to integrate previously unavailable elements of subjectivity into a richer, fuller whole, they tend to resign themselves to a degree of irreducible lack and unknowing. Modern pluralists, seeing the goal of analysis as the ability to tolerate both/and, normativize an optimistic plenitude, however difficult it may be to achieve in actual clinical practice.[12] In contrast, a European postmodern view might be more likely to see in the inclusive both/and a denial of loss, lack, helplessness, and finitude, a need for omnipotentiality if not omnipotence, a manic defense against both/and's sinister shadow, neither/nor.

I mentioned above the value modernists place on authenticity. In the present context of expansive possibility for the "individual," we can add agency to the list of modern concepts found in some versions of pluralism. For example, Mitchell (1997) says that "[t]he analysand leaving treatment experiences himself, to a greater or lesser extent, as the agent of much more of his experience, perpetually generating and reshaping both his outer and inner worlds, as the author of his own story" (pp. 213–214). In contrast, Derrida (1982), writing from the postmodernist's thoroughgoing relational perspective, argues that we are not the authors of our own stories; as he puts it, the other must countersign my autobiography.

For, in postmodern narratives, the "individual" has become "divid-ual," inhabited by others and otherness beyond its awareness or control. You may, however, prefer to write a modern psychoanalytic autobiog-raphy, delineating a finite set of components that you posit as consti-tuting your alterity and bringing them under at least some degree of surveillance by the "I." Then you can hope that you'll never be taken unawares by the emergence of an otherness in yourself that could dis-turb the equilibrium you've established between unity and multiplicity. Hence Bromberg (1998) advocates "a broadening experience of 'me-ness'" (p. 289) precisely because it safeguards us from unexpected irruptions of alterity. If our "me-ness" is commodious enough, nothing can surprise or traumatize us from without (or from the internal "with-out," in the sense of loss and lack). Similarly, Pizer (1996) cites the United States poet Whitman: "I contain multitudes." Yes, a postmodern pluralist would reply, but what of the multitudes I don't contain? These are the multitudes that, even after an optimal analysis, will never reach consciousness because they're still unformulated or repressed, or because they aren't legible in the belief system I share with my analyst. As Flax (1996) puts it, writing from a postmodern perspective, some experiences "cannot be incorporated into or contained within liveable meaning systems. We can only register their existence and some of their effects on us" (p. 589).

Helping the patient to contain multitudes may well be a clinically pragmatic strategy for those patients and analysts whose conscious psy-chic repertoire is theorized or experienced as meager, and hence in need of enhancement through the introduction into awareness of disavowed elements of subjectivity, or for those patients and analysts whose suffer-ing is attributed to excessive identity diffusion. But, a deconstructionist would say from a theoretical standpoint, the component of subjectivity that is able to reflect on its multiplicity, tolerating or containing it, for example, is on the same level as what it contemplates. If reflexivity is just one of many aspects of a manifold subjectivity, one that can come to the fore at times while non-reflexive states predominate at other times, then (*pace* Descartes) there is no warrant for privileging the former as "I." The postmodern sensibility will continue to probe what is involved in the construction of even a capacious container, one that holds in a unitary personality the dynamism of unresolvable differences—in other words, one that resembles the monists' construct in significant ways.

This construct is not really an oscillation or holding in tension of sameness and difference. It is rather the reining in of alterity, of the constant play and dissemination of unconscious meaning and affective experience, by a Hegelian (not to mention imperialist) process of sublating the dissociated not-me back into an increasingly spacious and variegated me, an analogue, in the intrapsychic microcosm, of the British Empire on which the sun never set. Until, of course, it did. We are not the masters of all we survey. Are we the masters of any of it? According to Derrida (1987), a degree of narcissism is inevitable: "What is called non-narcissism is in general but the economy of a much more welcoming, hospitable narcissism, one that is much more open to the experience of the other as other." But, he goes on to say, "there are little narcissisms, [and] there are big narcissisms" (p. 199). Pluralists have to decide which kind we want to argue for. A postmodern pluralist will wonder whether the "overarching cognitive and experiential state felt as 'me'" (Bromberg 1998, p. 273), the ego whose role is to "master" dissociated experience and bring it under "omnipotent control" (p. 133, quoting Winnicott), the superordinate function that, in many pluralist theories, organizes the heterogeneity of subjective experience, may be just the latest avatar of the executive, synthesizing ego that has been so characteristic of modernist psychoanalysis in the United States, the heir to the ego that, for Freud, is the colonizer of the dark(-skinned?) territory of the id: the I that is to come into being where It was.[13]

For a postmodernist, there will always be an It at work off beyond what the I can see. A postmodern pluralism would accept that beyond the named lie the unnamed and the unnamable, that beyond paradox lies enigma. The unconscious will never be made fully conscious, we can never go beyond the navel of the dream, not all alpha elements will become beta elements, vast tracts of the Real will remain unsymbolized.

Derrida (1981) says that he has to laugh when he finds himself speaking of "his" unconscious. Yet the rhetoric of ownership and control of one's otherness pervades modern pluralist theorizing. For a postmodern pluralist, in contrast, my otherness is mine not in the sense that it belongs to me, but in the sense that it pertains to me; that is to say, it is not lodged in other people, nor is it something I want to go on disavowing in order to shore up a precarious psychic unity. I own it not in the sense that I possess it but in the sense that I accept responsibility for dealing with the distress it may arouse, and I will not place that responsibility on others (my spouse or partner, my family of origin, people of other races or sexual orientations, etc.). Even if I, as a member of a disadvantaged or oppressed group, can point to the malign influence of societal prejudices and may want to work to change them, I will acknowledge and address the ways in which I have contributed to my unhappiness. But I will do so in the realization that my account of my subjectivity is itself an aspect of my subjectivity, the realization that, while I can never stand fully within myself, I can never stand fully outside myself either. I don't deny my painful otherness, but I also don't overarch, contain, control it.

For not only is the postmodern "I" not master in its own house, but its house isn't even its own. That's why a postmodern subjectivity may have something not just paradoxical but uncanny to it, something *unheimlich*, in the literal sense that one is not quite at home in it. There's a strangeness in the familiar, and an unsettling familiarity about what would seem not to pertain to us. Lacan's neologism "extimacy" (*extimité*) captures the tone of this inner alienness that is at the same time intensely compelling (cf. Miller 1994). Similarly, Lacan (1966), echoing Heidegger, describes the subject as "ex-sisting," always eluding identitarian stability. He quotes Rimbaud's statement to the effect that "I is an other" (1954–1955, p. 7), where the tension between the first-person pronoun and the third-person verb disconcerts us even before we get to the noun, a tension Derrida (1991) expresses in more abstract terms when he speaks of the subject's "non-identity to self" (p. 103). In contrast to this decentered subject of postmodern thought,[14] we have some United States pluralists' vision of progress toward coinciding with oneself, toward the assimilation to an I-system of even the most recalcitrant inner otherness. The paradoxes in much United States pluralists' theory (cf. Pizer 1998) can be bridged, negotiated, and tolerated; those of European postmodernism are irremediably disorienting.

## CONCLUSION

Before I began psychoanalytic training, I taught comparative literature. In order to relieve the tedium of paper marking, literature professors sometimes circulate student "howlers," egregious blunders made on papers and exams, and one venerable instance, often cited when we needed an example of a mixed metaphor for class, was that of the hapless student who wrote: "Dante had one foot in the grave of the Middle Ages, while with the other he saluted the rising sun of the Renaissance." Well, we too live in a period of mixed metaphor, a paradigm shift in which we have one foot in the grave of the Renaissance and the period of modernity that it ushered in, while with the other we salute (or, as the case may be, kick in the pants) the new postmodern era. The raised foot is the more mobile, vitally responsive one. But the other foot, though stuck and sinking, is the one that holds us up.

Most of us who were raised in this culture learned that *to be* was to be a cohesive self. At this time we can't easily do without monism, either as the sole experiential modality or as a major component in a variegated subjective repertoire. My suggestion, however, is that we not try to gerrymander authenticity, autonomy, a superordinate ego, scientific validation, developmental theory, and the like into postmodernism, where they fit only as that concept's others. I would hope that we can instead live with the awkwardness and uncertainty of a hybrid model while we take the time to think about what we are willing and able to change as psychoanalysis enters its second century. Postmodernists are the last people to insist on narrow definitional boundaries and the purity and consistency of historical periodization and theoretical constructs, but many of us would prefer to label the moments in clinical work when there arises a need (on whose part?) for a sense of ownership, or mastery of difference, or authenticity, or an integrative function, not as postmodernism-because-that's-what-I-want-to-call-it, but as the continuing hold of modernist thinking on all of us. To do so is to acknowledge difference, not to smooth it over it by the same sort of assimilationist fiat that we would want to analyze in a patient.

The challenge for an evolving psychoanalytic pluralism, as I see it, is to respect otherness within and among theories: to decenter so as to see pluralism as an other to its internal and external theoretical others, and to do so without devaluing these others, or "encompassing" them, "overarching" them, or "calling them all 'I.'" Because all we have are subjectivities, not subjectivity, I would hope that, as the debate continues, monists and pluralists, modernists and postmodernists, can treat one another with what William Connolly (1991) calls agonistic respect. This is an attitude in which one argues for one's position while making space for differences of opinion, in which otherness is not obliterated by a need for dominance or even for consensus, "in which one of the ways of belonging together involves strife, and in which one of the democratizing ingredients in strife is the cultivation of care for the ways opponents respond to the mysteries of existence" (p. 33).

## NOTES

1. It's important to note that there's tension within postmodernism, as well; we disagree about all sorts of things, and we therefore sometimes prefer to use the plural *postmodernisms* to signal our differences and to avoid narrowing the definition of our enterprise. In what follows, I'll often be referring to deconstruction in particular, since this has been among the major influences on my particular version of postmodern thought. (For general introductions to Derrida and deconstruction, see Spivak 1976, Culler 1982, and Norris 1986.)

2. See Bader 1998, Flax 1990, Layton 1998, Leary 1994, and Stein 1995 for a variety of concerns about the clinical issues raised by postmodernism.

3. The exception might be the late French analyst Félix Guattari (Deleuze and Guattari 1977). Among United States analysts, the thinking of Jane Flax (1993, 1996), Donnel B. Stern (1997), and Stephen A. Mitchell (1997) comes closest to what a postmodern pluralism might look like, but a glance at Guattari will show why the plural *postmodernisms* is needed.

4. See Bock 1988, Cushman 1991, 1995, Geertz 1983, Kleinman 1988, Rosaldo 1984, Sass 1988, Shotter and Gergen 1989, and Shweder and Bourne 1984 on subjectivity or "the self" as culturally constructed. Flax 1996, Mitchell 1997, and Roland 1988 are among the few psychoanalytic theorists who make this point.

5. In addition to an ever-increasing set of papers, an entire symposium has been devoted to this topic. Entitled "The Multiplicity of the Self and Analytic Technique," the symposium was sponsored by the Massachusetts Institute for Psychoanalysis in 1995; the contributions were published in *Contemporary Psychoanalysis* 32.4 (1996). For discussions of multiplex subjectivity in psychoanalytic theory of the 1990s, see in addition Aron 1995, 1996, Benjamin 1998, Davies 1998, Elliott 1996, Elliott and Spezzano 1996, Flax 1993, Mills 1998, Mitchell 1993, 1997, and Stern 1997.

6. This is a purely heuristic image. Hacking (1995) points out the problems of a linear model of dissociation.

7. Here, as in the later discussion of figurative language, I'm not suggesting that authors who use particular terms necessarily intend the implications I'm drawing.

8. Flax (1993, 1996) discusses the bearing of Foucauldian thought on the unity/multiplicity debate.

9. In response to postmodernism, new views of science are emerging in which perspectivist and constructivist biases are acknowledged, and in which it is accepted that much is not only unknown but unknowable (cf. Barrow 1998). In contrast, science as invoked by psychoanalysis tends to be of the positivist variety.

10. I'm referring here especially to postmodernists from the field of postcolonial studies (e.g., Bhabha 1994). And Jameson's now classic 1991 study considers from a Marxist perspective the relation between late capitalism and what he sees as the salient features of postmodernism. I trust it is unnecessary for me to state that I am not accusing modern pluralists of supporting geopolitical exploitation. But our discourses are not innocent, and I think we need to be aware of their complicity with larger cultural attitudes.

11. An alternative way to describe this difference would be in terms of Schafer's (1976) contrast between the comic/romantic and the tragic/ironic visions in psychoanalysis. For representative European views of postmodern subjectivity, see Cadava and colleagues (1991). While the European postmodern subject is sometimes said to occupy multiple sites, these are theorized as discursive positions, not (or not only) as modalities of inner experience. Thus Dean (1997) reminds us of the important Lacanian distinction between the imaginary other (the other-of-the-same) that constitutes the ego and the symbolic other that constitutes the subject divided by language. The Lacanian subject is split between the different signifying systems of conscious and unconscious discourse, alienated in the gaze, the language, and the desire of these others, its longed-for plenitude always out of reach. While not all aspects of Lacanian metapsychology are compatible with postmodernism (and—though limitations of space preclude a fuller discussion of this point—Lacanian clinical

theory is even less so), United States analysts interested in postmodernism must somehow come to terms with the concept of the discursively split subject.

12. Layton (1997) argues that "to seek completeness is not to seek plenitude . . . as Lacanians suggest; rather, it is to seek recognition for parts of the self that have been rendered illegitimate" by "sexism, racism, homophobia, and other cultural and relational traumas [that] leave everyone narcissistically vulnerable" (p. 523). A postmodern pluralism will need to articulate further this important distinction between legitimation and a fantasy of plenitude.

13. The dark continent is, of course, also feminine. With regard to the passages quoted from Bromberg, though Bromberg (1998) asserts that the observing self of his theory is not the observing ego of conflict psychology, the distinction is not entirely persuasive to me. Current pluralist theory in the modern mode might benefit from assessing itself over against critiques of ego psychology from within that tradition; compare for example Schafer (1976, 1992) on the problems of theorizing a superordinate mental function and Pruyser (1975) on splitting. (The more things change . . . .)

14. As the quote from Rimbaud indicates, the decentered or multiple subject associated with postmodernity has its roots in late-nineteenth-century Europe. The notion of the split or decentered subject needs to be refined, since it is not wholly intelligible given the ongoing modernist influences on conceptualizing, and hence on being, a subject. Here deconstruction, working as it does simultaneously inside a paradigm and outside it, is typically more cautious than other postmodern theories. According to Spivak (1989), for example, "deconstruction considers that the subject is always centered, [but it] looks at the mechanisms of centering" (p. 134).

## REFERENCES

Aron, L. (1995). The internalized primal scene. *Psychoanalytic Dialogues* 5:195–237.

———— (1996). *A Meeting of Minds: Mutuality in Psychoanalysis.* Hillsdale, NJ: Analytic Press.

———— (1998). Clinical choices and theory of psychoanalytic technique: commentary on papers by Mitchell and by Davies. *Psychoanalytic Dialogues* 8:207–216.

Bader, M. J. (1998). Postmodern epistemology: the problem of validation and the retreat from therapeutics in psychoanalysis. *Psychoanalytic Dialogues* 8:1–32.

Barrow, J. D. (1998). *Impossibility: The Limits of Science and the Science of Limits.* New York: Oxford University Press.

98 / *Bringing the Plague*

Bauman, Z. (1990). *Modernity and Ambivalence*. Cambridge, UK: Polity.
Benjamin, J. (1998). *Shadow of the Other*. New York and London: Routledge.
Bhabha, H. (1994). *The Location of Culture*. London and New York: Routledge.
Bock, P. K. (1988). *Rethinking Psychological Anthropology*. New York: Freeman.
Bromberg, P. M. (1998). *Standing in the Spaces*. Hillsdale, NJ: Analytic Press.
Cadava, E., Connor, P., and Nancy, J.-L., eds. (1991). *Who Comes after the Subject?* New York and London: Routledge.
Chodorow, N. J. (1996). Reflections on the authority of the past in psychoanalytic thinking. *Psychoanalytic Quarterly* 65:23–51.
Coates, S. (1997). Is it time to jettison the concept of developmental lines? Commentary on de Marneffe's paper "Bodies and Words." *Gender & Psychoanalysis* 2:35–53.
Connolly, W. E. (1991). *Identity/Difference*. Ithaca, NY: Cornell University Press.
Culler, J. (1982). *On Deconstruction*. Ithaca, NY: Cornell University Press.
Cushman, P. (1991). Ideology obscured: political uses of the self in Daniel Stern's infant. *American Psychologist* 46:206–219.
——— (1995). *Constructing the Self, Constructing America*. Reading, MA: Addison Wesley.
Davies, J. M. (1996). Linking the "pre-analytic" with the postclassical: integration, dissociation, and the multiplicity of unconscious processes. *Contemporary Psychoanalysis* 32:553–576.
——— (1998). Multiple perspectives on multiplicity. *Psychoanalytic Dialogues* 8:195–206.
Dean, T. (1997). Two kinds of other and their consequences. *Critical Inquiry* 23:910–920.
Deleuze, G., and Guattari, F. (1977). *Capitalism and Schizophrenia*, vol. 1, *Anti-Oedipus*. trans. R. Hurley, M. Seem, and H. R. Lane. New York: Viking.
Derrida, J. (1971). White mythology: metaphor in the text of philosophy. In *Margins of Philosophy*, trans. A. Bass, pp. 207–272. Chicago: University of Chicago Press.
——— (1981). Telepathy, trans. N. Royle. *Oxford Literary Review* 10:3–41, 1988.
——— (1982). Otobiographies. In *The Ear of the Other*, ed. C. McDonald, trans. P. Kamuf, pp. 1–38. Lincoln, NB: University of Nebraska Press.
——— (1987). "There is no *one* narcissism." In *Points . . . . Interviews, 1974–1994*, ed. E. Weber, pp. 196–215. Stanford, CA: Stanford University Press.
——— (1991). "Eating well," or the calculation of the subject. In *Who Comes after the Subject?*, ed. E. Cadava, P. Connor, and J.-L. Nancy, pp. 96–119. New York and London: Routledge.

Elliott, A. (1996). *Subject to Ourselves*. Cambridge, UK: Polity.

Elliott, A., and Spezzano, C. (1996). Psychoanalysis at its limits: navigating the postmodern turn. *Psychoanalytic Quarterly* 65:52–83.

Flax, J. (1990). *Thinking Fragments*. Berkeley: University of California Press.

———— (1993). *Disputed Subjects*. New York and London: Routledge.

———— (1996). Taking multiplicity seriously: some implications for psychoanalytic theorizing and practice. *Contemporary Psychoanalysis* 32:577–593.

Foucault, M. (1980). *Power/Knowledge: Selected Interviews and Other Writings, 1972–1977*. New York: Pantheon.

Fourcher, L. A. (1992). Interpreting the relative and absolute unconscious. *Psychoanalytic Dialogues* 2:317–329.

Geertz, C. (1983). *Local Knowledge*. New York: Basic Books.

Grossman, W. I. (1991). Discussion of "Contemporary Perspectives on Self: Toward an Integration." *Psychoanalytic Dialogues* 1:149–160.

Hacking, I. (1995). *Rewriting the Soul: Multiple Personality and the Sciences of Memory*. Princeton, NJ: Princeton University Press.

Harris, A. (1996). The conceptual power of multiplicity. *Contemporary Psychoanalysis* 32:537–552.

Hoffman, I. Z. (1991). Discussion: toward a social-constructivist view of the psychoanalytic situation. *Psychoanalytic Dialogues* 1:74–105.

———— (1998). *Ritual and Spontaneity in the Psychoanalytic Process*. Hillsdale, NJ: Analytic Press.

Jameson, F. (1991). *Postmodernism, or the Cultural Logic of Late Capitalism*. Durham, NC: Duke University Press.

Johnson, B. (1980). *The Critical Difference*. Baltimore and London: Johns Hopkins University Press.

Kirschner, S. (1996). *The Religious and Romantic Origins of Psychoanalysis*. Cambridge, UK: Cambridge University Press.

Kleinman, A. (1988). *Rethinking Psychiatry*. New York: Free Press.

Lacan, J. (1954–1955). *The Seminar of Jacques Lacan. Book II*, ed. J.-A. Miller, trans. S. Tomaselli. New York and London: Norton.

———— (1966). *Ecrits*. Paris: Seuil.

———— (1972–1973). *The Seminar of Jacques Lacan: Book XX*, ed. J.-A. Miller, trans. B. Fink. New York and London: Norton.

Lachmann, F. M. (1996a). How many selves make a person? *Contemporary Psychoanalysis* 32:595–614.

———— (1996b). Yes, one self is enough! *Contemporary Psychoanalysis* 32:627–630.

Layton, L. (1997). Reply to Judith Butler. *Gender & Psychoanalysis* 2:521–524.

———— (1998). *Who's That Girl? Who's That Boy?: Clinical Practice Meets Postmodern Gender Theory*. Northvale, NJ: Jason Aronson.

Leary, K. (1994). Psychoanalytic "problems" and postmodern "solutions." *Psychoanalytic Quarterly* 63:433–465.

Messer, S. B., Sass, L. A., and Woolfolk, R. L., eds. (1988). *Hermeneutics and Psychological Theory*. New Brunswick, NJ and London: Rutgers University Press.

Miller, J.-A. (1994). Extimité. In *Lacanian Theory of Discourse*, ed. M. Bracher et al., pp. 74–87. New York: New York University Press.

Mills, J. (1998). Multiplicity, essentialism, and the dialectical nature of the soul. *Contemporary Psychoanalysis* 34:157–169.

Mitchell, S. A. (1993). *Hope and Dread in Psychoanalysis*. New York: Basic Books.

——— (1997). *Influence and Autonomy in Psychoanalysis*. Hillsdale, NJ: Analytic Press.

Nagel, T. (1986). *The View from Nowhere*. New York: Oxford University Press.

Norris, C. (1986). *Deconstruction*. London: Routledge.

Ogden, T. (1989). *The Primitive Edge of Experience*. Northvale, NJ: Jason Aronson.

——— (1994). *Subjects of Analysis*. Northvale, NJ: Jason Aronson.

Pizer, S. A. (1996). The distributed self: introduction to symposium on "The Multiplicity of Self and Analytic Technique." *Contemporary Psychoanalysis* 32:499–507.

——— (1998). *Building Bridges*. Hillsdale, NJ: Analytic Press.

Pruyser, P. W. (1975). What splits in "splitting"? *Bulletin of the Menninger Clinic* 39:1–47.

Roland, A. (1988). *In Search of the Self in India and Japan*. Princeton, NJ: Princeton University Press.

Rorty, R. (1979). *Philosophy and the Mirror of Nature*. Princeton, NJ: Princeton University Press.

Rosaldo, M. Z. (1984). Toward an anthropology of self and feeling. In *Culture Theory*, ed. R. A. Shweder and R. A. LeVine, pp. 137–157. Cambridge, UK: Cambridge University Press.

Sass, L. A. (1988). The self and its vicissitudes: an "archeological" study of the psychoanalytic avant-garde. *Social Research* 55:551–607.

Schafer, R. (1976). *A New Language for Psychoanalysis*. New Haven, CT and London: Yale University Press.

——— (1992). *Retelling a Life*. New York: Basic Books.

Schwartz, D. (1995). Retaining classical concepts—hidden costs: commentary on Lewis Aron's "The Internalized Primal Scene." *Psychoanalytic Dialogues* 5:239–248.

——— (1996). Questioning the social construction of gender and sexual orientation. *Gender & Psychoanalysis* 1:249–260.

Shotter, J., and Gergen, K. J., eds. (1989). *Texts of Identity*. London: Sage.

Shweder, R. A., and Bourne, E. J. (1984). Does the concept of the person vary across cultures? In *Culture Theory*, ed. R. A. Shweder and R. A. LeVine, pp. 158–200. Cambridge, UK: Cambridge University Press.

Slavin, M. O. (1996). Is one self enough? Multiplicity in self-organization and the capacity to negotiate relational conflict. *Contemporary Psychoanalysis* 32:615–625.

Spence, D. P. (1993). The hermeneutic turn: Soft science or loyal opposition? *Psychoanalytic Dialogues* 3:1–10.

Spivak, G. C. (1976). Translator's preface. In Derrida, J., *Of Grammatology*, pp. ix–lxxxvii. Baltimore: Johns Hopkins University Press.

——— (1989). In a word: interview. *Differences* 1:124–156.

Stein, R. (1995). Reply to Chodorow. *Psychoanalytic Dialogues* 5:301–310.

Stern, D. B. (1997). *Unformulated Experience: From Dissociation to Imagination in Psychoanalysis*. Hillsdale, NJ: Analytic Press.

Wolff, P. H. (1998). Response to Silverman and Nahum. *Journal of the American Psychoanalytic Association* 46:274–278.

# The Treatment of Choice:
# A Response to Susan Fairfield

*Stephen A. Mitchell*

I found Susan Fairfield's paper fun and illuminating to read. Although I am interested in literary theory and philosophy, I haven't been formally trained in those fields; there is quite a bit of the postmodern literature that I haven't read and don't fully understand. I am a psychoanalytic theorist and clinician, and developments in literary theory and philosophy are of interest to me partly because writers in those disciplines deal with many of the same issues with which psychoanalysts struggle, both in theory and in clinical practice. So I am grateful for the way in which Fairfield so vividly brings to life the complex issues addressed by postmodern authors and their distinct sensibility and relates them to psychoanalytic concerns; I would call what I have to offer here a clinician's response to her paper.

Fairfield's argument revolves around the exploration of two different distinctions: monism versus pluralism and modernist pluralism versus postmodern pluralism. Fairfield is more interested in the second distinction, but her take on modernism versus postmodernism derives from her analysis of the ways in which the debate between monists and pluralists has been conducted.

I've been part of the audience and sometimes a participant at discussions and debates by adherents on both sides of the first distinction: monists versus pluralists. Human beings are singular: there is a superordinate motivational need for the establishment and maintenance of an integrated, cohesive self, say the monists. Human beings are multiplicitous: self-states and self-organizations are multiple and discontinuous, say the pluralists. It didn't take me too long to realize that it is futile to argue about which of these understandings is correct, and this is one of Fairfield's most important points. Is the self singular or plural? How could we possibly decide? There are continuities and discontinuities to human experience. If you are more impressed with the continuities, you think of the self as monadic and see discontinuities as "facets" of a singular self. If you are more impressed with the discontinuities, you think of the self as multiplicitous and see continuities as subjective illusions. This is not a resolvable argument; it is a question of preference. To remain interesting, the question really needs to be reframed. The issue is not, is the self singular or plural, but rather: What are the implications of thinking about it one way or the other?

However, by putting it this way, I am not at all suggesting that this issue is unimportant. In fact, by characterizing the different positions as merely differences in "center of gravity," I believe that Fairfield underplays the enormous clinical implications of the broad shift from a monistic to a more pluralistic view of the self; it has been, in my view, one of the most important changes in psychoanalytic thought over the past several decades.

It is a question of ideals of mental health or, more broadly, the good life. American psychoanalysis from the 1950s through the 1970s was dominated by the ego psychological ideal of integration. The hallmark of psychopathology was fragmentation and splitting; health was integrative and synthetic. Ambivalence was the highest form of emotional maturity—intense love and intense hatred were blended together into modulated shades of gray; ideal and despised objects converged together into "whole" objects.

The concept of multiplicity has brought with it a very different ideal of mental health. For many of us now, psychopathology comes in two forms: excessive fragmentation and excessive uniformity. Mental health is understood in terms of the capacity to sustain and tolerate discontinuous shifts among self-states and self-organizations, oscillations between passionate feelings of different sorts, and a tolerance for surprises from unconscious sources. In this view, ambivalence can sometimes be understood as a defense against passion and commitment.

The clinical implications of this shift in assumptions about the ideal form of the richest human experience are enormous. The ego psychological model and the contemporary model[1] are not completely dichotomous, but they often lend themselves to very different clinical responses. What in the patient's experience is considered symptomatic in one model might be encouraged in the other. And pluralistic theory leads to a very different way of thinking about not just the patient's experience but the analyst's experience as well. The type of listening and self-monitoring in the ego psychological model, an evenly hovering neutrality, is very different from the type of listening and self-monitoring in the contemporary model, a receptivity to intense countertransferential reactions and enactments. Thus, although no one can claim to know whether subjectivity, in some essential sense, *is* singular or multiplicitous, whether you tend to think of it one way or the other is enormously important for the clinical practice of psychoanalysis. For example, these differences have had a great deal to do with the decline in the influence of Freudian ego psychology over recent decades in favor of the much more multiplicitous vision in Kleinian theory, despite the latter's anachronistic epistemology.

Let us return to the binary that Fairfield regards as much more important: the distinction between modernist pluralism and postmodern pluralism. Metapsychology does not legitimize or house subjective choices in theory, Fairfield shows us; metapsychology itself is an expression of subjectivity. With great wit and incisiveness, she demonstrates precisely why the pluralistic model of subjectivity is not objective reality but itself a subjective preference by showing us all the ways in which we pluralists can get extra mileage out of our pluralism, all sorts of narcissistic gratifications. Fairfield's discussion of the hidden smugness and appropriativeness of certain forms of pluralism is brilliant, and her political analogies are very thought-provoking. Fairfield's account of the complacency of the pluralists reminded me of the grandiose claim of Dr. Seuss's Cat in the Hat. "But that is not all," claims Fairfield's benighted pluralist: "I can do more, much more!" The modernist-pluralist, because he regards multiplicity as the truth rather than his own preferred organization, is opaque to himself and misses the opportunity to understand and reflect upon all these fringe benefits provided by his belief.

Fairfield identifies herself with the pluralism she is examining and calls her exploration of these potential narcissistic perks of pluralism putting the choice of multiplicity on the couch. Yet there is a tone here that I find problematic, and I believe this accounts for why I don't find the term *deconstructionism* quite so appealing as she does. For me, the most important and constructive response to her argument for the persuasiveness of the postmodern challenge is the need for a kind of self-reflectiveness. Multiplicity, like all theories, is one among many possible ways of organizing experience. If we take it as *the* way in which experience is really, naturally, organized, we fall into the modernist trap.

This is more than a problem of political incorrectness, especially for clinicians. If psychoanalysis is viewed, as it increasingly has been, as an intersubjective encounter, the clinician needs to understand all features of his participation, including his belief that psychoanalysis is usefully understood as an intersubjective encounter, as one among many possibilities of organizing experience. This is important because, in this model, the clinician needs to be alert to the ways in which his own metapsychology influences the process, is apprehended by the patient, and might usefully become in itself a subject for investigation with the patient. One can never avoid influence, but if the analyst's preferences, especially her metapsychology, are made part of the inquiry at appropriate points, influence operates collaboratively and self-reflectively rather than through indoctrination. So it is crucial for the analyst never to mistake any aspects of the way things seem to him to be the way things are.

Is deconstructionism, as Fairfield claims, the antidote to the narcissisms of pluralism, its tendency to slide into a latent modernism? For me, deconstructionism has always seemed to have an aggressive edge. One generally deconstructs someone else's point of view. "Putting multiplicity on the couch" conveys some of this tone, as if the subject arrives on the couch via a wrestler's body-slam. This "gotcha" quality (see Goldner 1994, p. 585) seems like the wrong attitude. To be honest, deconstructionism would have to apply at least as much to the deconstructor as to the deconstructee and the act of deconstruction itself. But its methodology often conveys the sense of exposure, as if one is catching the subject in something embarrassing. Further, in the way Fairfield uses deconstructionism in this paper, there is that characteristic touch of French anti-Americanism, both imperious and defensive. I am not sure whether it is a "little narcissism" or a "big narcissism," but there is a one-upsmanship in this game that distracts from the importance of the issue. For this reason, I prefer the term *constructivism* to *deconstructivism*, because it implies that there is no way not to be constructive in organizing the world. The point is to take responsibility for one's constructions, their advantages, and their foreclosures.

Being more deconstructionist than thou (like being more pluralistic than thou) seems to me to be no protection against the kind of narcissism Fairfield is warning us against. I once came across a quote from the artist Fairfield Porter during the time in which artists of the New York abstract expressionist school were trying to decide whether the tradition of signing one's paintings was vain or not. Porter captured something really crucial by saying, "If you are vain, it is vain to sign your paintings; if you are not vain, it is not vain to sign your paintings, and it is not vain not to sign your paintings." Similarly, I don't find the deconstructionist strain of postmodern ideology much of a safeguard against the narcissism of modernism. If you are narcissistic ("My ideology/country/language/theory is much better than those of the other guys/patients"), you are narcissistic whether you are postmodern or not postmodern.

I think it is because I am not so sanguine as she is about deconstructionist ideology that I disagree on some of the positions Fairfield takes in this paper.

Fairfield dismisses "authenticity" as a hopelessly modernist concept. I think it actually comes in both modernist and postmodernist forms. If you think authenticity involves approximating some sort of structural "true self," you are being modernist. But for me, authenticity involves issues of honesty and dishonesty, and self-expression versus mimicry of others. Aren't I being more authentic when I am telling what I believe is the truth than when I am deliberately lying? (Of course, we need to presume an ambiguous, postmodern notion of truth rather than Truth.) And is there not preconscious and unconscious lying as well? Am I not being more authentic when I am presenting what I think (of course, we need to presume an ambiguous and complex notion of

*I*) rather than mimicking what I believe someone else thinks? Isn't Derrida himself struggling to be more authentic by sharing ownership over *his* unconscious? So I don't agree with Fairfield that authenticity is a necessarily modernist concept. She argues that, if we feel we need a concept of authenticity because of the way we were raised in this culture, we should preserve a hybrid modernist/postmodernist model rather than try to force it into a postmodern frame. I think we do better deciding which of these concepts are still usable and reconceptualizing them along postmodern lines.

The concept of agency is another case in point. Fairfield, apparently following Derrida, regards agency as hopelessly Enlightenment-based and modernist. If unconscious experience is saturated with alterity, it is argued, how can we claim authorship over it? Surely this is an important (Freud-inspired) challenge to the early modern notion of an omnipotent agent boasting a Victorian willpower over his psychic dominions. But unless we present ourselves as completely passive, determined foils of otherness, do we not assume at least co-authorship? Isn't Derrida's pride in granting otherness within his experience its due a form of taking responsibility (as in the ability to respond) for what goes on in his mind? I think there is a false dichotomy at work here, and, as with authenticity, it is possible and very useful to rework and complicate the concept of agency both to take account of the destabilizations of postmodernism as well as to preserve a way of addressing individual responsibility, which, I believe, is crucial in clinical work.

Some of Fairfield's most breathtaking rhetorical flourishes are in her analogies between the psychological and the political, for example in her comparison between the ego's/self's assimilation of alterity and the West's colonization of the third world. She is pointing to a very real and interesting difference around the issue of how knowable one assumes one's experience to be. I think there is a fascinating contrast between a European tragic pessimism and an American optimism that clearly reflects different cultural histories. Are parts of the self always incommunicado, as Winnicott suggested, even unknowable to oneself? But I think Fairfield goes too far in conflating the otherness of world politics with the "other" in oneself. Ultimately, in a clinical sense, the presence of others in my unconscious experience *is* me and *will become* me in a way in which the third world *is not* and never will be European or American. Clinically, my experience is enhanced, my options broadened (not omnipotently), my self-understanding more informed by the (never-complete) extent to which I can explore and understand the selectivity through which I internalized and came to unwittingly use others.

I also disagree with Fairfield's characterization of the views of Bromberg and Pizer. I read them as pluralists, not monists. I think what Bromberg means by a sense of "me-ness" and what Pizer means by bridging and negotiating paradoxes is not at all equivalent to the observing, synthetic ego of Freudian ego psychology. Language gets very tricky here, and they may be inconsistent at times, but I read the thrust of their work to be emphasizing precisely the qualities embraced by Fairfield under the banner of "deconstructionism": discontinuities, surprises, alterity. I think what Derrida means by an openness to alterity—for example, the otherness of the unconscious—is precisely what Bromberg and Pizer mean when they describe a capacity to "own" or identify with or assume responsibility for discontinuities within one's experience. There is no continuity of content implied here. There is, rather, an assumption of responsibility for (as in the ability to respond to) all one's experiences, including the most surprising and alien. Fairfield suggests that there is no fully postmodern psychoanalysis. I was surprised to find no discussion of the work of Barnaby Barratt,[2] because he claims to be offering just that. Barratt, like Fairfield, embraces a deconstructionist program and reinterprets Freud's methodology of free association in deconstructionist terms. The intent is to continually break up the patient's limited and limiting secondary-process, socially conventional organizations to allow the power and creativity of the unconscious to break in and break out. Lynne Layton and Louis Sass, both of whom are very appreciative of postmodern contributions, point to ways in which the banner of "deconstructionism" allows Barratt to palm his own commitments, appearing to have a view from, in fact, no place at all. As Layton (1998) puts it, "So what is liberating? If, like Barratt, we are looking for a 'left-minded' psychoanalysis, we cannot assume that the process of free association itself will liberate; we also need to interpret the content that free association produces and interpret it in the context of a culture built on structural inequalities of all kinds" (pp. 46–47). And as Sass (1995) notes,

There seems . . . to be something contradictory about Barratt's attack on systematizers, with their "models of the mind," given that Barratt himself seems very committed indeed to a particular view of human consciousness. To assume that human existence is characterized by constant, utterly uncategorizable change is, after all, to adopt a conception of the human mind, and a rather specific one at that, a view that is no less essentialist for its being Heraclitean at its core. . . . Surely truth-claims are being asserted (or presupposed) here; surely these imply acts of ideological positioning not so very different from those of the psychoanalytic schools. [p. 133]

Of course, one could claim that in deconstructing Barratt's deconstructionism, Layton and Sass expose him as a smuggler of essentialisms and therefore not really postmodern at all. But this is where it seems more useful to me to regard postmodernism and deconstructionism as themselves types of constructions. The point is not to keep exposing someone else's constructions, in an infinite regress of "gotchas," but to build in self-reflection and an assumption of responsibility (yes, even in an old-fashioned agentic sense) for one's own constructions. Discovering one's own constructions should not be an embarrassment but an opportunity for growth.

Nietzsche, the grandfather of postmodernism, wrote about philosophizing "with a hammer." I've always loved the emancipatory quality of his writing and the freedom of thought and experience it made possible. But, ultimately, one also needs a pen to philosophize. It is easy to hammer the pens of others; the trick is to build a critical self-reflectiveness into one's own thought. Fairfield very much helps us pluralists in this regard; I wish she were a bit less sanguine about deconstructionists. For a clinician, self-reflective constructionism is crucial to my sense of what today is compelling, useful, and responsible analytic work. At least (he said with an eye toward his hammer) it is for me.

## NOTES

1. The question as to where to place Kohut and self psychology with respect to this dichotomy has become more complicated recently. Kohut's work grew out of ego psychology, and I always understood his perspective on the self as clearly monistic. This is certainly reinforced by current self-psychological writers like Lachmann (in the argument with Slavin discussed by Fairfield). However, Judith Teicholz (1999) has recently offered an interesting reading

of Kohut as much more of a transitional figure on the way to relational theory and postmodernism; she understands Kohut's vision of subjectivity, despite the language of "coherence," as fluid and pluralistic. Kohut, like all major theorists, was inconsistent and can be read in different ways.

2. At one point Edgar Levenson also embraced deconstructionism and linked it to his clinical methodology of a continual analysis and therefore transformation of transference–countertransference enactments.

## REFERENCES

Goldner, V. (1994). Theoretical metaphors in psychoanalysis. *Psychoanalytic Dialogues* 4:583–594.

Layton, L. (1998). *Who's That Girl? Who's That Boy?: Clinical Practice Meets Postmodern Gender Theory.* Northvale, NJ: Jason Aronson.

Sass, L. (1995). Review of *Psychoanalysis and the Postmodern Impulse* by Barnaby Barratt. *Psychoanalytic Dialogues* 5:124–136.

Teicholz, J. G. (1999). *Kohut, Loewald, and the Postmoderns: A Comparative Study of Self and Relationship.* Hillsdale, NJ: Analytic Press.

# In Our Consciousness, in Our Conscience, in Our Backyard: A Reply to Mitchell

*Susan Fairfield*

*Preliminary note*: Stephen Mitchell's death was a loss to the entire psychoanalytic community, but I felt it all the more keenly because it occurred in the course of our dialogue on "Analyzing Multiplicity." The following reply was written as part of a conversation that I hoped would continue.

I am, of course, pleased that Stephen Mitchell found things to like in "Analyzing Multiplicity." But I'm even more pleased that he disagrees with me on several points, since this gives me the chance to refine my own thinking in dialogue with a theorist who has been crucially influential in the formation of my approach to psychoanalysis. "Analyzing Multiplicity" questions the possibility, at this time, of a consistently postmodern clinical psychoanalysis. Mitchell addresses aspects of this central concern, but he also raises other issues, less emphasized in the paper, that I'm glad to have the opportunity to discuss at greater length.

He opens his discussion with the disclaimer that he is not fully conversant with postmodern thought. As those of us who have learned so much from his work can attest, he is being far too modest here about his profound grasp of the issues that confront psychoanalysis as it enters its second century. Nevertheless, I do want to maintain a view of deconstruction that is much more benign than his.

While I draw a great deal on a variety of other postmodern theories, in particular Foucauldian and postcolonial perspectives, it is true that I turn most often to deconstruction. But, though Mitchell suggests indirectly that this orientation carries over from my previous academic career, it happens that I came to deconstruction, and to poststructuralism and postmodernism in general, not as a literary critic but only after I had started my psychoanalytic training. The intense and intimate encounter with the suffering other in clinical work brought me up against ethical problems in a way that teaching had not done. And, as I gradually found a home base in relational psychoanalysis, it became important to me to integrate this approach with my political concerns—that is, with the challenges of complex human relationships on a larger scale. Deconstruction, particularly in Derrida's engagement with the thought of the philosopher Emmanuel Levinas, offers a theory of justice and of openness to the other that I found impressive, even moving (see, e.g., Cornell 1992, Critchley 1992, Handelman 1991, and Kearney 1993).

Yet for many people the notion of an ethics of deconstruction is an oxymoron. Thus Mitchell says that, for him, "deconstructionism has always seemed to have an aggressive edge," a "body-slam" or "gotcha" quality. And, though "Analyzing Multiplicity" stresses how little claim any of us can have to certainty, and though it ends with a plea that we respect our opponents' views, he seems to see its deconstructionist author as in league with those who wield the hammer, who smite down instead of building up, constructing.

This view of deconstruction is a very common misunderstanding. It seems to have two causes. The first applies to postmodernisms in general, and it is that all of us feel threatened when doubt is cast on our familiar modes of being in the world. The second, amplifying the first, is peculiar to deconstruction, namely that the word sounds so much like "destruction." Derrida has often lamented this and regretted that the name for the set of techniques he founded has become

so entrenched that it can't be changed to avoid the unwanted negative tonality. But, in fact, "deconstruction," both etymologically and
as it is deployed by its practitioners, is virtually synonymous with "analysis," as Freud used the term. Both deconstruction and analysis take rigid
structures and break them down into their components, loosening up
what had seemed fixed, natural, and inevitable. Derrida (e.g., 1966)
speaks of opening a space for play, in the sense of the play or "give" in
a mechanism that allows enough freedom of movement for the mechanism to function well. It is in this play space opened up within a formerly inflexible structure that deconstruction, like psychoanalysis, does
its creative, liberating work.

If some who call themselves deconstructionists (mainly literary
critics in the United States) have proceeded with a recklessness that gave
the theory a bad name, that is no fault of the theory itself; there is wild
deconstruction just as there is wild analysis. If anything, deconstruction
as defined and practiced by its proponents outside the domain of literary
criticism actually tends to be more cautious than other poststructuralist
approaches. Far from being the "gotcha" that Mitchell is right to deplore,
deconstruction is concerned to demonstrate a thorough and respectful
understanding of the concept or practice that it is putting in question,
and to do so from within the set of assumptions, the world-view, in
which that concept or practice presents itself. As it goes about its task
of loosening and complicating, a deconstructive interpretation also
leaves room for the questioning of its own presuppositions and methodology; as Mitchell puts it in the more positively toned terms he understandably prefers, in so doing one "take[s] responsibility for one's own constructions, their advantages and their foreclosures."

The psychoanalytic relationship is unique, and so no exact analogies can be drawn. But don't many of us, as analysts, try to do something very similar to the deconstructionist's double gesture of affirma-
tion and questioning? We seek a detailed and empathic understanding
of the patient's subjective experience, but we also provide a relational
space for the emergence of some "give" in the patient's "givens," thereby
promoting openness, movement, and the awareness and tolerance of
complexities. At the same time, and as an intrinsic part of the process,
we try to be mindful of biases on our part that may be influencing not
only our hearing of the patient's material but the nature of that material itself.

Deconstruction's central ethical concern is for the separate subjectivity of the other *as* other, sometimes expressed as offering hospitality or saying "yes" to her—no hammers here! It thus offers compelling ways to extend similar lines of thought in psychoanalytic theory (e.g., Benjamin 1995) beyond the consulting room to the wider domain of sociopolitical relations. Of course, not all of those who use deconstruction are interested in its ethical import. And literary critics, in particular, have mostly moved on in other directions. But many thinkers in such fields as critical legal, critical race, queer, and feminist theories, postcolonial theories, technology studies, sociology, anthropology, and history continue to find in deconstruction a crucial set of techniques for analyzing human relations and a way to think about the problems of bridging the gap between the abstractions of poststructuralist theorizing and intervention in concrete social practices. As is true of certain elements of Foucauldian thought, deconstruction has often become so much a part of the way ideas are formulated in these fields that it no longer has to announce its pedigree. Like Molière's gentleman who was surprised to learn that he had been speaking prose, if you've questioned essentialist presuppositions in your own or a patient's thinking, or tried to unsettle a rigid male/female, me/not-me, or patient/analyst binary in your theory and practice of psychoanalysis, you've been speaking deconstruction.

The deconstructionist's concern to question binary structures and to open a space for alterity shapes my perplexed reaction to another issue on which Mitchell and I seem to disagree, namely what it means to be "American." Mitchell finds in my use of deconstruction "that characteristic touch of French anti-Americanism, both imperious and defensive." It would be easier to know what to make of this comment if I knew just what it is that Mitchell finds anti-American in my approach. I do critique some aspects of the dominant culture in the United States, but in terms that are used by many thousands of people in this country and in foreign countries other than France (though the French do have a way of being especially acerb in this regard). On what grounds is it anti-American to express concerns about, for example, some aspects of the global capitalism that is transforming the world under our leadership? It seems to me that one of the most valuable contributions the United States has made is its extensive legal protection of the

right—some might even say the duty—of its citizens to offer responsible criticism of national policy.

Mitchell would probably agree with me on this last point. But if,
as he cogently argues, we must take responsibility for our own constructions, then surely this applies to what he might call the construction,
and I the deconstruction, of the term *American*. Such a project might
be especially relevant in view of the fact that nearly all relational analysts of a postmodern bent are from the United States. Here Mitchell
offers a clue as to what he might mean by *American* when he says that
my paper "[goes] too far in conflating the otherness of world politics
with the 'other' in oneself." And, he continues, "Ultimately, in a clinical sense, the presence of others in my unconscious experience is me
and will become me in a way in which the third world is not and never
will be European or American."

One of the tenets of deconstruction that has been most extensively
utilized by theorists of race, ethnicity, class, gender, sexuality, and their
role in colonial and postcolonial experiences is that a privileged term is
defined by what it excludes. Such a term is identified through what it puts
outside itself so as to show forth as the dominant member of a binary
pairing that both devalues the other member and precludes any intermediate categories.[1] Consider man/woman, white/nonwhite, straight/gay.
What is the "other" of the term *America*? Mitchell links "Europe and
America" over against an eternally other "third world."

Historically, Western Europe and the United States have defined
themselves as white; Christian (in the U.S. and U.K., preferably Protestant); heterosexual; preferably male; and, in recent times, as promoting
free enterprise and a more or less democratic system of government. All
this stands in self-defining contrast to everyone who does not fit into those
categories, which includes everyone in the so-called third world along with
a great many individuals, citizens of Europe and the United States, who
are defined as internal others within the master culture of the West itself.
These others must be kept subordinate in order to shore up the dominance
of the privileged member of the binary structure us/them.

Each of us in this country has his or her own notion of what it
means to be a citizen of the United States, a notion that can be formed
only *in contrast to* the way things are done elsewhere, even in the liberal democracies of Western Europe. For example, my personal aware-

ness of being a citizen of this country includes such elements as (for better) that our criminal-justice system offers the presumption of innocence and that we do not have an established church, and (for worse) that there is a sizable disparity between the richest and the poorest segments of our population and that we do not have universal health care. Many of us find ourselves becoming aware of valued but hitherto unmarked features of our United States culture only when we encounter a different way of life in traveling abroad. In other words, while each of us has her or his own conscious, preconscious, and unconscious notions of what it means to be from the United States, the elements of this composite definition will tend to coalesce into a binary distinction U.S./not-U.S., that is, us/not-us, "us" and "those others."

As a poststructuralist would see it, saying that the otherness of world politics is not akin to the other in oneself, and that "the third world is not and never will be European or American," has a number of implications with regard to one's subjectivity. For example, one may wish not to look too closely at one's participation in the historical constitution of "European or American" identity as white, Christian, characteristically male, heterosexual, and so forth, and at the effect of this participation on one's dealings with that identity's others. And let's look at the possessive construction, "that identity's others." I need otherness to be my constitutive outside, that is, to define the boundary of any selfsameness, of any coherent identity in the modernist mode that I organize for myself. These others are thus "my" others in two senses: they are constitutive of me, and, at the same time, I need to exercise ownership over them in order to make sure they stay firmly outside the boundary of my self-system. To mention Barbara Johnson's (1980) eminently deconstructionist formula once again, a difference *between* opposites is a difference *within* them. The others are thus an intrinsic part of my identity (by negative definition), but that fact must be denied with a vigor proportionate to the unease that the internal otherness causes me. Hence the latent homosexuality we impute to the rabid homophobe, the anxiety about contamination we impute to the militant racist. And hence, on a level that implicates all of us in the dominant culture, the wish not to know the extent to which a "third world" —dark-skinned (hence dirty), effete (hence effeminate) or sexually insatiable, ignorant or over-cunning, primitive, perverse, shiftless, unruly, irrational, bestial: everything that we dissociate, everything of which we want to emphasize that it "is not and never will be" us—is in fact part of who we are.

Only a small effort at translation is needed to make it clear that, on another level, this mode of theorizing has always been an intrinsic part of psychoanalysis, beginning with Freud all the way to the variety of current discussions (many cited in "Analyzing Multiplicity") of the optimal configuration of the subject in its relations with internal and external otherness. Why, then, are some analysts apparently resistant to "conflating the otherness of world politics with the 'other' in oneself"? We can approach this question by asking a second one: What is the space in which psychoanalytic treatment is conducted?

Particularly where matters of gender and sexuality are concerned, there has been a growing awareness that clinical work reflects larger societal biases from which many of us wish to free ourselves once we become mindful of the harm they do if we unthinkingly reiterate them in working with patients. But alongside the acknowledgment that gender, sexuality, and (much more dimly on the psychoanalytic horizon) race, ethnicity, and class affect the analytic process in a host of ways, there still seems to be a powerful assumption that the treatment takes place in the sacred precinct of "the room."

Now, like everyone who has had an intense analytic experience on and/or behind the couch, I know that "the room" is the zone of a unique form of human relatedness, one that can often feel removed from everyday time and space. This experiential sense of dyadic enclosure is supported by theories that posit the relevance of infant research to psychoanalytic work. I'm referring specifically to those studies that focus on the microinteractions of mother and child as though these were culturally unmarked, as though the child's caretakers were not instructing it, from the outset, about when someone of that child's particular gender, class, ethnicity, and family milieu may or may not cry, laugh, smile, make eye contact, approach, touch, and so on. In contrast to this assumption, I believe that, like the seemingly pristine dyadic space of parent–child interactions, "the room" is in fact saturated with object relations and hence with cultural information from beyond its walls.

I hope I am not being presumptuous in trusting that Mitchell would agree with me here. I don't know whether he would agree with me in deciding how far beyond those walls one should go in locating the cultural influences that can shape the analytic process.

As we see in clinical work every day when dealing with the components of a patient's precarious subjectivity, one way people shore up a sense of self is by rigidly differentiating between "me" and "not-me." Clinical psychoanalysis addresses this strategy by bringing repressed or dissociated components of subjectivity into the patient's awareness in order to make otherness feel tolerable or even positive. On the societal level, as I have noted, the tactic of repudiation appears in exclusionary distinctions between "us" and "them," while proponents of integrated housing, affirmative action, multiculturalism, diversity, and the like share the analyst's aim of bringing together what was disjoined. Another way to safeguard a vulnerable subjectivity is not to place otherness outside a firm boundary but to engulf it, assert what Bromberg calls "omnipotent control" over it, absorb it into the me-system. And the sociopolitical counterpart of this strategy of engulfment? In "Analyzing Multiplicity" I spoke of the imperialist tendency of Europe and the United States to efface the distinctiveness of what used to be called third-world cultures. But nowadays the U.S. does not have to resort to warfare in order to carry out colonization of the other, including the European other.

In a book review entitled "All the World's a Mall," Sanger (2000) discusses the emergence of multinational capitalism: "Wander anywhere abroad, from Malaysia to Japan to France, and it does not take long to find raw resentment that the world economy is now run by 'international standards' that look and feel suspiciously American." The challenge of creating a global economy, he continues, lies in "trying to negotiate an accord among 160 nations about a set of minimum rights for workers that makes sense in both Brussels and Shanghai. . . . It is in this territory where the interests of individual nations come into direct conflict with America's sense of how the post-cold-war world should be molded that a whole new world of foreign policy is being created" (p. 13). The drawing accompanying the piece shows the United States in the form of an octopus whose tentacles extend over the globe. (This was in the *New York Times*, hardly a Gallic anti-American organ.)

It isn't a coincidence, I would suggest, that at the same time as this trend is emerging on the global scale, relational-analytic treatments are becoming increasingly centered around negotiating differences and bringing strongly disparate elements of subjectivity into a larger conversation, both within the patient and between the patient and the analyst. Moreover, as I noted in "Analyzing Multiplicity," the theory underlying such a treatment usually presents itself as the "international standard," as it were: not a particular, local set of interests, but a bias-free generalization about the nature and optimal functioning of a heterogeneous psychic economy. In the debates between monists and modern pluralists, each of these interests is striving to become dominant enough to claim universality for itself. To me, this looks very similar to what many people see as the strategy of the master culture in the U.S. as a whole, now positioning itself as the powerful arbiter of what (to borrow Mitchell's phrase) constitutes "the good life" for one and all in the world.

Mitchell and other readers may or may not agree that the spread of global capitalism under the leadership of the U.S. is to be viewed with some concern; that is a matter of personal opinion and is not at all my focus here. I want simply to point out that there seems to be a parallel between a shift taking place on the geopolitical level and a shift taking place in an increasing number of consulting rooms. You may perhaps disagree that this parallel exists, or, if you grant its existence, that it significantly affects your clinical work. But what I'm suggesting is that, beyond the issues of gender and sexuality of which psychoanalysis is slowly and belatedly becoming aware, we might do well to promote discussion about the ways in which our work as analysts may reflect and thereby tacitly endorse other, perhaps less easily discernible, assumptions in the culture at large.

Mitchell asserts that "the third world is not and never will be European or American." Yet the trend of globalization, based as it is on the spread of electronic communication at an exponential rate, is to ensure that non-Western societies will in fact become economically and culturally "European or [what that increasingly amounts to] American" as soon as possible. I think I may assume that at least some psychoanalyst readers who are aware of this trend have reservations about it. Aren't these akin to the reservations that, on the microcosmic relational scale, make us mindful of the separate subjectivity of the other who is our patient? Not every relational analyst wishes to become politically active, and that is their right. My point is that a postmodern perspective is relational all the way through, not just in the consulting room. We confront the same problems and challenges of otherness as analysts and as citizens.

As I noted, I'm disturbed by some of the implications of Mitchell's use of *American*. In explaining why this is so, my intention is not to single out his comments but to call attention to cultural influences that all of us—and I am no exception—have absorbed and reiterated. What *American* means to you depends on the subject positions you enjoy, or are forced into, in the dominant culture of the U.S. Thus, for the lesbian political theorist Shane Phelan (1995), in the "(hetero)sexist social ontology" of this country, "there are two distinct groups: 'Americans' and 'gays and lesbians.' This ontology is shared among Americans of all political stripes. As an example, remember Ross Perot's statement in the 1992 presidential campaign that he would not have 'homosexuals and adulterers' in his cabinet because they would be 'controversial' with 'the American people'" (pp. 334–335). And consider the words of a Maryland congressman reporting "that of recently awarded scholarly prizes, half went to those with Oriental names, a sixth [to those] with Indian names, and the rest to what we would consider normal Americans" (Delgado and Stefancic 1994, p. 99). These definitions of what it is to be "American" are internalized in ways that ominously trouble Mitchell's distinction between "Americans" and "the others." For example, I know a woman of Asian origin who has been in this country since the age of two, spoke English at home, is thoroughly acculturated, is in a longstanding relationship with a white man, and is a U.S. citizen. I have often heard her say "an American" to refer to a white person. For her, then, a salient social distinction, absorbed from the larger culture, is "Americans" and "nonwhite persons." (People are described all the time as Italian Americans, Jewish Americans, Japanese Americans, African Americans, and so on. But how often do you hear someone described as a Protestant American or a British American?)

Mitchell refers to "the shift from a monadic to a more pluralistic view of self" that he calls "one of the most important changes in psychoanalytic thought over the past several decades".[2] It might be argued that Klein (whom Mitchell notes), Fairbairn, Lacan, and classical Freudians outside the U.S. have always retained some version of a pluralist view of the subject, and that psychoanalysis in this country is an anomaly, one that—thanks to a group of analysts among whom Mitchell figures so prominently—is now being redressed. Though there are several reasons why ego psychology, with its emphasis on control of otherness by a sovereign ego, developed here in the way it did and never caught on elsewhere in the world, I believe it's no coincidence that this school flourished in the years when the U.S. was establishing itself as the world's great superpower.

And is it a coincidence that ego psychology began to lose strength (or, as I suggest in "Analyzing Multiplicity," to shift to a subtler model of hegemony) in the years following the societal upheavals of the '60s and '70s? These were the years when postwar complacency and the normative monoculture were shattered by activism on behalf of rights for blacks, women, and gays, and by a dramatic increase in the self-identification and demand for recognition of a host of hitherto silenced and invisible minorities: Native Americans, the elderly, others. Suddenly, curb cuts and handicap-access ramps were being constructed everywhere for those among us who, we discovered to our shame, had been effectively banished from most of the streets and buildings in the country. More problematically in terms of social resistance, the warehousing of the mentally ill gave way to treatment within the community, busing brought minority children to schools that had been entirely white, and affirmative action plans brought their older siblings and their parents into colleges and the workplace. Women and, increasingly, homosexuals were insistently refusing to remain in the shadows. Formerly invisible populations were now not only present among the majority but, in another important shift, were often unwilling to assimilate to it, to lose their distinctive identities culturally and in terms of empowerment. As the catchphrase has it, the country that had been celebrated as a "melting pot" was now valued for being a "salad bowl."

Is it a coincidence that, in these same years, a "broad shift from a monistic to a more pluralistic view of self" was taking place in psychoanalysis? Was the conceptualizing of a salad-bowl self, as it were, due to the progress of knowledge and the discovery of the true nature of subjectivity, or did it reflect the change taking place in the culture as a whole?

Europeans are starting to struggle with similar problems as they construct their new Union. No longer able to exclude others who "will never be" them, all the nations of the industrialized North, in fact, are confronting tough decisions about trade and immigration policy, bilingual education, and other issues of cultural difference. Why, then, did the branch of relational psychoanalysis that posits a multiple subjectivity in the modern pluralist mode emerge in the U.S. and not in Europe? I would suggest that one reason (among several) is this country's constitutional infrastructure: our federalist system and our system of checks and balances among the executive, legislative, and judiciary branches of government. Every day we read of tensions, often productive, sometimes frustrating, between the claims of states' rights and those of the federal government, and among the branches of the central government itself. Processes of negotiating the competing claims of unity and heterogeneity are taking place on all levels of our society, from the Supreme Court to city council chambers. They make available a model of subjectivity and of the analytic process that many relational analysts and their patients will bring into "the room."

But, as I tried to show, pluralism is not tantamount to postmodernism, and here I want to move on to another part of Mitchell's discussion.

Mitchell argues that I dismiss authenticity and agency as "hopelessly modernist" concepts. On the contrary, I find them among the most hopeful of modernist concepts, and that's why I say that clinical psychoanalysis, at least as we know it now, can't do without them. The point of "Analyzing Multiplicity" is to suggest that there is a tension between postmodern theories and the pragmatic task of relieving the suffering of patients whose subjectivity, like ours, was formed by modernism. For analysands who are weeping amid the rubble of familiar psychic constructions that had seemed so solid and safe, and who are asking us the anguished question, "How can I possibly go on from here?," postmodernism as yet has few ready answers.

Mitchell's expansion of the concept of authenticity so as to take postmodern views into account thus performs a valuable service. It offers a way in which we can gradually modify our thinking without pulling the ground out from under our own feet at this transitional point in the evolution of psychoanalysis, a point in which it can be hard to stand comfortably in either the old paradigm or the new one. Like other analysts who are interested in postmodernism, in my actual clinical work I still often find myself reaching for some version of "authenticity" or "agency," and in that sense Mitchell's preference for taking the time to decide which traditional terms might still be usable is one I respect. On the whole, however, I prefer not to strain to reshape concepts that are so laden with established meanings that their every use has to be supplemented with parenthetical disclaimers and caveats: "(Of course, we need to presume an ambiguous, postmodern notion of truth rather than Truth. . . . [O]f course, we need to presume an ambiguous and complex notion of *I*)." Though the analogy isn't exact, I'm reminded of the measure to which defenders of the Ptolemaic cosmology resorted when Copernicus presented evidence that the Earth, and with it the human being, was not at the center of the planetary system. The Ptolemaists devised an intricate system of epicycles—multiple circles upon orbital circles—in an attempt to bring Copernican theory into accord with an anthropocentric view invested with deep religious import. But, eventually, the epicyclic approach became so elaborate that it collapsed under its own unparsimonious weight. Human beings came to realize that, despite the fact that they had been radically decentered in the universe, life could not only go on but thrive.

I certainly agree that Mitchell's redefinitions of authenticity and agency bring these concepts closer to postmodern thinking. I also grant that, in processes of reconceptualization, words have been known to change their meanings over the years. But I wonder whether it isn't possible to approach the crucially important issue of what "honesty," "self-expression," "responsibility," and "truth" might mean in a postmodern world without bringing quite so much baggage along with us. A deconstructive technique that might be useful in this connection is called *putting under erasure*. In putting a term under erasure, you draw a line through the word denoting it; for example: ~~authenticity~~. This indicates that, given the conceptual system we're steeped in, it's quite impossible to do without the term in discussing a topic (say, subjectivity in clinical psychoanalysis), but that at the same time you would like to call the term into question in ways you proceed to specify. Since this is similar to what Mitchell is doing when he speaks of reworking the notions of authenticity and agency, I hope he will welcome deconstruction as an ally in this venture.

As I noted at the outset, deconstructive practice operates simultaneously inside and outside a paradigm, complicating the binary inside/outside in productive ways. In this reply to Mitchell's thought-provoking discussion, I hope to have done something similar, deconstructing a few of the sociocultural implications of the inside/outside binary formation: psychoanalysis/not-psychoanalysis. This project, I suggest, may be part of what it will mean to be a relational analyst in the United States at the beginning of the twenty-first century. Considering the implications of shifts in psychoanalytic theory, Mitchell says that these involve "a question of ideals of mental health or, more broadly, the good life." But psychoanalysis, I would add, has implications not just for the good life but for the ethical life. My co-editors and I note in our Introduction that there is no question of "politicizing" psychoanalysis: as a set of theories and practices of human relatedness, it is, to use the postmodern tag, always already political. The only question is whether we, as analysts, want to become conscious enough of our political values and assumptions to understand the ways in which these affect our thinking and our work with patients.

## NOTES

1. Like the present paper, "Analyzing Multiplicity" attempts to unsettle either/or formations. For example, Mitchell objects to what he takes to be my characterization of Pizer and Bromberg, preferring to see them "as pluralists, not monists." My aim, however, was to deconstruct the binary structure *modern monist/postmodern pluralist*, with its derogation of one or the other term. I complicate the binary by adding an intermediate category, modern pluralism, and by arguing that all analysts on both sides of the controversy have some version of a mixed model.

2. Mitchell is quite right to point out that Barnaby Barratt needs to be mentioned in any discussion of postmodernism and psychoanalysis. I should have made it clear that I was omitting a reference to him for the reason noted in the Introduction to this volume. Though Barratt is a learned and eloquent exponent of what he considers to be a Derridean approach, like my co-editors I do not see him as adapting it to the constructivist-relational paradigm that, in our view, is the only clinical approach consistent with a postmodern perspective. Co-construction is a process occurring in the intersubjective space between patient and analyst. In contrast, Barratt speaks of the way in which the patient's free association loosens her familiar system of identitarian notions; while this is occurring, the analyst, listening for opportunities to acquaint her with her internal otherness, silently carries on his own private free association. This seems to me to be more a relation of parallel play than the ongoing and intricate mutuality characteristic of a two-person clinical encounter.

# REFERENCES

Benjamin, J. (1995). *Like Subjects, Love Objects. Essays on Recognition and Sexual Difference*. New Haven, CT: Yale University Press.

Cornell, D. (1992). *Deconstruction and the Possibility of Justice*, ed. D. Cornell, M. Rosenfeld, and D. G. Carlson. New York: Routledge.

Critchley, S. (1992). *The Ethics of Deconstruction. Derrida and Levinas*. Oxford, UK and Cambridge, MA: Blackwell.

Delgado, R., and Stefancic, J. (1994). "Imposition." In *Critical White Studies: Looking behind the Mirror*, ed. R. Delgado and J. Stefancic, pp. 98–105. Philadelphia: Temple University Press, 1997.

Derrida, J. (1966). Structure, sign, and play in the discourse of the human sciences. In *Writing and Difference*, trans. A. Bass, pp. 278–293. Chicago: University of Chicago Press, 1978.

Handelman, S. S. (1991). *Fragments of Redemption*. Bloomington, IN: Indiana University Press.

Johnson, B. (1980). *The Critical Difference*. Baltimore, MD and London: Johns Hopkins University Press.

Kearney, R. (1993). Derrida's ethical re-turn. In *Working through Derrida*, ed. G. B. Madison, pp. 28–50. Evanston, IL: Northwestern University Press.

Phelan, S. (1995). The space of justice: lesbians and democratic politics. In *Social Postmodernism*, ed. L. Nicholson and S. Seidman, pp. 332–356. Cambridge, UK: Cambridge University Press.

Sanger, D. E. (2000). All the world's a mall. *The New York Times Book Review*, April 30, p. 13.

# 3

# (Ir)reconcilable Differences: A Postmodern Relational Approach to a Clinical Case of Alleged Satanic Ritual Abuse

*Carolyn Stack*

## INTRODUCTION

In the first frame of my favorite *New Yorker* cartoon a drowning little Timmy calls out to his faithful collie on shore, "Lassie! Get help!!" The second frame depicts our gallant pooch, gesticulating wildly, on the analyst's couch as she tells her story—what story we are left to conjecture. This joke works not only because of the cuteness of the pun but also because the *New Yorker* crowd is privy to the debates about whether psychoanalysis qualifies as science and to the controversies, which have suffused this discipline since its inception, over differing registers of interpretation. In the first frame of the cartoon, "Get help" demands an interpretive response to a literal traumatic event. The second frame espouses an imaginative rendering of the same exclamation. From Freud's shifting views on the seduction images of his hysterical patients to the contemporary positivist-versus-constructivist debates, psychoanalysis has always concerned itself with the ambiguous relation between factual events and phantasmatic productions. This uncertain relation is, of course, not peculiar to psychoanalysis but rather reflects and contributes to an ongoing cultural discourse that problematizes the concept of reality.

The question of what constitutes "reality" is particularly salient at this historical moment. In this postmodern era we can no longer take for granted the kinds of beliefs that previously structured individual identity, interpersonal relations, and our deepest senses of meaning. The deconstructionist critique of hierarchical norms of gender, sex, sexual identity, race, and family relations exposes the primitive thinking of such ideological formations—they are always built on the aggrandizement of one identity or way of being over another. For many of us, particularly those of minority social status, this insight and the possibility of change are welcome news indeed. For others, the erosion of these foundations is a powerful threat, not only to self-esteem, but to identity as well. Likewise, cultural changes in our understanding of memory and the growing comprehension of "reality" as co-constructed according to context and as always open to multiple interpretations undermine our usual modes of organizing subjective experience.

Relational psychoanalysts are grappling actively with the impact of these cultural shifts on concepts of health, disease, and what is curative. The immutable core self of mid-century psychoanalysis cannot survive well in an era in which external forms are no longer stable enough to bind anxiety and organize meaning. Contemporary theorists have supplanted this idea of a core or true self with the imaginative concept of a subjective capacity to bear uncertainty, contradiction, rapid change, and intense affects. We understand our patients' memories less as accurate retrievals and more as narrative retellings that say something about their construction of patterns of experience in relation to others. Furthermore, this concept of narrative retellings argues for inclusion of the construction of experiential memory at the time of specific historical events, across time, and in relation to specific listeners, including the analyst. We now place greater emphasis on the imagination and the creation of what Winnicott (1971) termed *potential space* and what others, following Winnicott, call *play space* or *transitional space*. The work of analysis is now understood more in terms of helping patients to develop relativistic modes of experience (Schafer 1992) and to move fluidly within the discontinuous flux of unconscious and conscious thought and affect—in short, to develop the capacity for reverie.

In my mind this is the ground on which the best of postmodern theory and classical psychoanalysis find a common language (cf. Elliott and Spezzano [1996], who draw upon the work of Castoriadis, Kristeva, Anzieu, Ogden, and Bollas to delineate a theory of the radical imaginary that is common to both postmodernism and psychoanalysis).

I noted earlier that while the precepts of postmodernity are welcomed by many, they pose a threat to others. Nowhere in contemporary culture do we see the manifestations of anxieties about "reality" more than in the eruptions of hysterical epidemics such as the alien abduction, satanic cult, and day-care abuse movements that have multiplied exponentially in the past decade. Numerous historians and social commentators have addressed the cultural anxieties that fuel these movements, arguing that they reflect the perception of a decline in traditional moral values (Victor 1993), the widespread suppression of women's voices (Haaken 1998, Showalter 1997), gender anxiety (Showalter 1997), the North American fear of difference (Nathan 1991), the dangers of institutional controls (Haaken 1998), and a resistance to critical thinking (Kaminer 1999).

While all of these writers touch upon the psychological dimension of such phenomena to varying degrees, few speak to the complex relation between these cultural narratives and individual intrapsychic processes. It makes sense that these contemporary legends serve a function of simultaneously binding and expressing social anxieties. But it also makes sense that specific individuals will be drawn to these movements for particular psychological reasons. It is no surprise that these narratives show up as sites of emotional distress in some of our patients. To explore this juncture of cultural hysteria, the individual psyche, and the transference–countertransference demands in treatment of such a belief, this paper uses a case study of a patient who believed she had participated in a satanic ritual abuse cult. Before I turn to this case I want to outline the psychological commonalities and functions of these belief systems.

## HYSTERICAL MOVEMENTS

These movements, described in the literature as moral panics, contemporary legends, hysterical epidemics, and urban myths, all depend on a kind of primitive thinking that confers badness upon the other, leaving the self as innocent and essentially good. As such, these beliefs provide a haven for people struggling with affects and impulses that are unacceptable to the self. Like prejudice, which also relies on splitting and projection as ways to rid the self of unwanted affects, believers take comfort in the shared placement of violent, sexualized images elsewhere: far away into outer space in the alien fantasies, and into secret, almost otherworldly covens in the satanic fantasies. However, unlike the mythologies of bigotry, these legends produce a supernatural other (Hacking 1995, Kaminer 1999), such as aliens or perpetrators so omnipotent that no whit of evidence is ever found.

Belief in the supernatural is part of the fabric of all cultures, providing community and comfort in the face of existential pain and fear. While traditional religions and New Age spiritualities produce good supernatural entities to watch over us, the satanic ritual and alien abduction movements generate evil beings whose goal is destruction rather than protection. (Organized religions, particularly the cult-like fundamentalist movements, also feature the devil and earth-bound demonic characters, such as homosexuals and sexually active young women, to play out the good-and-evil drama. But for the most part religious and spiritual beliefs rest more on an image of benevolent supernatural beings.) Despite their focus on abuse, hysterical epidemics, like religious and spiritual beliefs, offer comfort through the provision of coherent narratives that make sense of otherwise unbearable, inchoate feelings. Speaking of *The Celestine Prophecy*, Kaminer (1999) writes, "Its message is there is no such thing as a coincidence; there are no chance encounters, no arbitrary events, no reasons for existential angst" (p. 108). In similar ways, the satanic abuse and alien abduction narratives spare the believer from having to grapple with ambiguity, paradoxical experiences, and the complexity of simultaneous, opposing feelings. The hysterical epidemics, then, fall somewhere between religion and psychosis, borrowing from both. They are an attempt to narrate meaning as religions do, and they reflect the psychotic's struggle with what we commonly refer to as reality testing.

Thus, at the individual psychological level, these epidemics provide coherent stories that structure horrific, otherwise indescribable feelings and experiences, as they simultaneously displace these affects outside the self of the believer. Finally, because these mythologies frequently center on an individual who is helplessly victimized and dependent on the intervention of others, they suggest a regression to a site of trauma. I am not arguing that these narratives necessarily speak either to a condition of infancy or to a physical trauma. Rather, the primitive quality of these stories just as readily suggests the imaginative elaboration of a psychological climate that cannot be borne or fully articulated.

## CLINICAL ILLUSTRATION

A woman in her thirties, Hannah was extremely bright, creative, and psychologically sophisticated, yet she held only part-time menial jobs. Even these were a strain on her, as she lived in a constant state of terror, fearing that she might be killed or might be forced to kill someone else at any moment. Similarly, she feared that she would be abandoned by everyone she knew, or that she would have to leave everything and everyone familiar to her. She had no internal predictors of these dangers, no signposts, no specific rules about what would get her into trouble or what would keep her safe. She lived in fear, afraid to speak much of the time, afraid to make herself visible lest she or someone else be annihilated. Some months prior to entering treatment Hannah was mugged and held at gunpoint on the street. The striking element of this experience was her response of profound relief when the gun was at her temple. "For the first time," she said, "the outside matched the inside. In that moment I knew exactly who I was, who the other person was, what was happening, and precisely what I needed to do." In this way, Hannah let me know that a violent mugging was an apt representation of her inner life, and that she hungered for the safety of a narrative that made sense of her psychological distress.

Hannah believed that as a child she had participated in a satanic cult. She had images and somatic experiences that suggested to her that she had been involved in extreme forms of ritual abuse phenomena, such as nationwide conspiracies and government-involved cover-ups, cannibalism, and baby-breeding for the purpose of sacrifice. She had, for example, a specific image of herself with her hand on a knife, a larger hand over hers, as it pressed into the belly of a neonate. She believed that she had been forced to choose between killing a baby or watching her younger brother be killed. Initially in the treatment she believed that, because she told her story to me, she remained in danger from the alleged cult members. She told me that now that I knew her story I was also in danger of being killed. The perpetrators, she suggested, might run me off the road in my car.[1]

The appearance of satanic ritual abuse as a defining narrative in this patient's life raises a number of questions for the relational postmodern analyst. Why is this mythology particularly compelling as an organizing construct for this patient? What intrapsychic and interpersonal functions does it fulfill? What is the psychological meaning of the patient's choice of a highly contested cultural narrative? How does the treatment replicate the structure of this narrative, both as a site of contested meaning and as a story of abuse and helplessness? What do these replications tell us about the patient's experience of self, others, and relationships?

Hannah's belief that she had participated in a satanic cult entered our work on numerous occasions in different ways and with different functions. Initially, her discussion of cult memories did not arouse conflict between us. My empathic stance in response to her terror in the face of her grotesque images, and her rage at media reports that denied the existence of such cults, allowed Hannah and me to move smoothly into related arenas that did not lead to conflict between us. I believed at the time that the satanic cult story served a function similar to the way she psychically organized her experience of being mugged. That is, this narrative structured her confusing psychological experiences into coherent and meaningful form. It provided a story of life-and-death drama descriptive of an unspeakable kind of horror. Because this kind of story was already to be found in popular culture, it appeared to validate the concrete origins of her distress. Simultaneously, because it is a highly contested narrative, it functioned psychically as terrain on which the troubling question of reality could be mapped. Why such a concrete narrative, rather than an imaginative, descriptive one? I conjecture that Hannah's childhood experiences were profoundly confusing and traumatic, to the extent that she could not render them into language. In the following discussion of how the cult narrative played a large role in the inevitable impasses that arose throughout the treatment, we catch a glimpse of Hannah's difficulties finding language and claiming a voice of her own, and of her problematic relational patterns.

The ritual abuse mythology functioned relationally in the treat-ment in a number of ways. First, it provided the context for Hannah's repetitive traumatic conflicts that arose when her reality clashed with a loved other's. Second, it exposed her preoccupation with the psycho-logical functioning of the other and her fear of the other's or her own craziness. And third, it exposed her belief that relationships are inevi-tably sadomasochistically structured.

Some time into the first year of treatment Hannah observed that I did not take quite the same affective stance when she spoke of satanic abuse as when she spoke of other forms of perceived abuse or injustice. Her accurate assumption that I did not believe in the literality of her memories aroused the kind of terror that brought her into treatment in the first place. Her entire sense of self, of reality, and of life-sustain-ing relationship was on the line. She believed that she had to make a choice between maintaining our relationship or maintaining her iden-tity. Each choice demanded an equally powerful and unbearable loss. My wish at the time was to sustain a dialogue with Hannah as deeply as possible inside this conflict, to help her find a language to speak her confusion, her pain, and her intense rage. Yet the fact remained that, when she demanded to know where I stood, I was in a different place than she was. This difficulty between us encompassed Hannah's most troublesome, repetitive psychic conflicts: the turmoil and sense of dan-ger she experienced when her perceptions differed markedly from those of an important other. At this moment, the imaginative terrain had collapsed and Hannah was utterly distraught. I felt frightened for her, afraid that I would lose her, fearful that I was making her unnecessar-ily crazy, and, at times, doubting of my own beliefs.

It seemed to me at these times that the only way Hannah knew to find psychological safety in relation to others was through a kind of twinship. At crucial moments she needed me to be exactly like her and to believe precisely as she did. She experienced my difference as a traumatic intrusion that threatened to engulf her. It became clearer to me how Hannah invited the repetition of intrusive difference, including both her choice of an organizing narrative that would arouse contest and her choice of a therapist who did not believe as she did.[2]

This simultaneous yearning for safety and the less conscious need for intrusive difference exemplifies the workings of the repetition compulsion in treatment. Hannah believed that she wanted us to be exactly alike, and yet she invited the traumatic experience of difference.

Let me give a brief example of how this repetition worked in the treatment. Hannah spoke one day of her belief that reality was utterly defined by others. She attributed this belief to the mind control of cult members. In her imaginative world specific rules were established by others about what she could say and do. She had learned to follow these rules, to mimic having an existence, knowing that if she broke away from the rules tragedy would follow. If, for example, she spoke spontaneously or out of turn, if she named something before I did, either she or I would be killed. Hannah's speech during this exposition was barely audible, hesitant, obtuse, and anxiety laden. We were on delicate ground. I strained to hear her, trying to understand the intricately regulated psychic life that she was attempting to explain. In the following session she was enraged at me for not having challenged her belief that reality was subjectively defined. "Of course there's a reality," she shouted, adopting the stance she had longed for me to take in the previous session.

While I use this vignette as an illustration of how Hannah invited the trauma of intrusive difference, I am mindful of the relational context. The idea of always keeping the field open to interpretation is psychologically and politically important to me, which is why I gravitate toward the postmodern. A different therapist, for whom the dividing lines of reality and fantasy are more sharply drawn, might very well have responded precisely as Hannah wished. I can see in retrospect that my postmodern position—that I privilege uncertainty and paradox—frequently figured as my contribution to the impasses in Hannah's treatment.

This question of how reality gets defined is linked to the second kind of relational work that the satanic abuse narrative performed in treatment. When Hannah's and my realities didn't line up, she demanded that I relinquish my beliefs in the service of hers. At these times I could experience her lifelong conflict firsthand. My choice was between my beliefs and the relationship. At times I felt as though my reality was also on the line. A session occurred about midway through the treatment when Hannah was speaking of her shame and sense of worthlessness. "It's like there's something horrible inside of me that I can't get out," she said. Because her speech was labored and halting, I

played back what she had said and added the word "poison" in my response. ("You feel as though you have been poisoned.") As was often
the case, when I spoke to the metaphorical when she was attempting
to speak of the literal, she was enraged. She spoke angrily of the problems with psychoanalysis, saying that Freud did much damage in his
refusal to believe his hysterics. How many people are constantly hurt,
how many others am I hurting by this persistent move to metaphor
when, according to Hannah, the literal interpretation is obvious? She
was talking about something real inside of her. My next utterance com-
pounded the betrayal. I didn't understand that when she spoke of others being hurt, she was referring to satanic abuse. The dialogue continued as follows:

> *Patient* (in frustration):  But I laid it all out for you.
> *Therapist* (attempting to clarify):  Other people aside from you
>     were literally in danger?
> *Patient*:  More like worse than that—not in danger. It was too
>     late.
> *Therapist* (still in the clarification mode):  People had already been
>     killed?
> *Patient*:  I don't know. I don't know these things.

Suddenly, I realize, *I'm* telling the story of satanic abuse and murder. Hannah, innocently, knows nothing of these kinds of things. We
have switched roles. I have a fleeting fantasy that Hannah will somehow demonically kill me. This fantasy, I later imagine, represents my
fear for my own sanity, a reflection of Hannah's fear for hers, her wish
to kill me for my disruptive intrusions on her reality, and my wish to
kill her for her psychological entrapment. I also imagine that this fantasy of mine and Hannah's preoccupation with murder reflect some
historical antecedents about the danger of relationships. Related to this
terror of madness and death is Hannah's persistent need to have me
understand my part in our impasses. She doesn't need to know the details, she says, but she does need to know that I understand my psychological contribution to our conflicts. I come to understand through these
efforts to control me that relationships for Hannah often involve a
perceived craziness on the other's part and, even worse, the other's absence of self-reflection and psychological responsibility.

Finally, as the above interchange reflects, the satanic abuse narrative provided a space in treatment for Hannah and me to reenact her (and, of course, aspects of my own) sadomasochistic relational patterns. Speaking, for Hannah, was fraught with the terror of retribution. Our sessions usually began with long silences, or she suggested in a child-like voice that I begin. She frequently expressed her wish that I be utterly in control of the speech between us, and that I be ahead of her in defining reality. She insisted that it was my job to name the traumatic events that must have happened to her in the past. As she related fragments of memory and somatic symptoms, she wanted me to tell her that I knew she had been ritually abused, that she had murdered and eaten infants. (I sometimes wonder if her unwitting choice of a postmodernist for an analyst was a wise choice or a traumatic re-enactment!) Conversely, at other times she had to be in total control of me and what happened between us. Her constant demands about my kind of speech, my role in the treatment, and my level of self-reflexivity bespoke her terror of spontaneous communion lest she or another be destroyed.

Unsurprisingly, Hannah's adult relationships re-enacted these patterns. She frequently found others (including prior therapists) who also required the kind of relational merger that Hannah sought. In these relationships one or both of the parties often sacrificed beliefs and needs for the sake of the twinship. These relationships usually ended disastrously when one member attempted to break out of the mold.

It was tempting to believe that Hannah had been traumatized physically and/or sexually. She reported feelings and thoughts, similar to the satanic abuse fragments, that led her to believe she had been sexually abused by her father. She reported that her father was physically abusive and that his rages were explosive and unpredictable. She experienced her mother as extremely self-effacing and easily wounded by her child's intelligence and emotional outbursts.

I have provided my readers with little of Hannah's biographical information. Those who are used to charting pathology through reference to childhood circumstances will be frustrated. My reasons for this omission are several. First, confidentiality is difficult to maintain in such a detailed rendition. Second, Hannah's memory is dissociative and not particularly reliable. With some patients and certain memories we can feel pretty clear that some form of the event being told occurred. That is not so with the kind of traumatic memory that Hannah relies upon.

Third, I am attempting in this paper to delineate a mode of treatment that relies less on linking current symptoms to past events and more on mining the imaginative space created between patient and analyst. We cannot know what really happened in our patients' histories. I mean this in the social constructionist sense that memories are always reconstructions. This is not to say that we cannot sometimes be reasonably sure that particular events happened, but we believe that they are experienced, remembered, told, and retold within specific defining contexts. I also mean this in the psychoanalytic sense: much of our experience, including that which drives us, is unconscious. We often do not know and often can never know literal events in any reliable manner.

These questions of knowing and reality are never more urgent than in cases such as Hannah's, where the patient's thinking has a psychotic quality. With these patients, particularly when their distress is heightened and their demand for solutions is vivid, it is compelling to reach for a genetic narrative to soothe the patient and ourselves. While an important hallmark of psychoanalysis, the concept of familial predeterminants of symptomatology can also be used defensively by both analyst and patient. Psychologically sophisticated patients frequently call upon specific family stories in treatment whenever they come too close to affect-laden material. I am also aware of the times in treatment when a patient's symptom, severe distress, or particularly uncomfortable transference dilemma leads me to prematurely construct an early infancy narrative or to contextualize the patient's distress in a childhood story. Whether I speak this construction or not, its very existence threatens to foreclose what might happen next between the patient and me if the imaginative field were left open.

This easy reach for the literal interpretation is particularly salient in trauma theory. Both psychoanalytic and non-analytic trauma theorists all too frequently make the mistake of assuming that one can always know whether a patient has been sexually abused or not (cf. Davies [1996], Davies and Frawley [1994], Herman [1992] for examples of this ready assumption of abuse from fragmented images, somatic affects, and other symptomatology). Throughout her published work on trauma, Davies (1996) assumes that she knows that her patients have been sexually abused even as she argues eloquently that psychoanalysts must not "hunt for traumatic memories but attempt to reengage traumatic object relationships" (p. 215). For these trauma theorists Hannah's symptoms would have readily elicited the belief that the patient had been sexually abused. For the most part, these theorists leave little room for the possibility that patients might have to find a way to live without knowing whether they were sexually molested or not.[3] This is a juncture where postmodern theory and psychoanalysis meet. Not only patients who have been physically abused but all patients, and all of us, must find ways to live with "not knowing" our histories. Furthermore I believe that the psychological and familial dangers of the analyst's making premature interpretations of abuse far outweigh the dangers of temporarily weathering the psychic turmoil of not constructing a coherent narrative of victimization. Treatments such as Hannah's, in which the patient presents with a fantastical story, make it very clear to us that we cannot—in fact, must not—deduce certainty from fragmented images and a specific list of symptoms. I did not know if Hannah and I could ever know "what happened" in some objectifiable way. What I did know was that this question of knowing and not knowing was precisely the ground of the analytic impasse. I do not believe that satanic cults of the kind that Hannah describes exist. Haaken (1998) writes that the satanic ritual abuse discourse

> both engages and evades the ramifications of human destructiveness. It engages the real harm done to children . . . in the erosion of public education and social welfare institutions. Much like religious revivalism, the SRA movement transports this social crisis into the metaphysical realm, enlisting believers in a displaced struggle against fantastically elaborated and reified enemies. [p. 228]

As individual stories, these hysterical epidemics also narrate patients' psychic horror in the manner they best know how to describe. To paraphrase Haaken, these mythologies also engage and evade the ramifications of human destructiveness both intrapsychically and interpersonally. We cannot know exactly what is best for our patients (Hoffman 1998). But I believe it is imperative that we allow them the chance to stretch their capacities for flexibility, for imaginative play, for moving through a world where so much is rapidly paced, so much is uncertain and multifaceted. It is important that we allow patients the best possible chance of finding their own ground, their own dialectics of certainty and uncertainty. This stance reflects the best that psychoanalysis has to offer and that the postmodern relational theorists have emphasized—the chance to examine life as it is lived, to feel as deeply as possible, to think critically and self-reflexively, to make meaning in relation to others, and to find ways out of rigidly defined repetitious narratives and into more imaginative relations to self and others. Some analysts grappling with postmodern ideas argue that these concepts are useful for the obsessive patient, whereas fragmented patients need help finding ways of experiencing more coherent senses of self (Flax 1990). For these theorists the postmodern ideals of multiple subjectivities and perspectivist ways of understanding look like the fragmented self, dissociative defenses, and paucity of agency that characterize traumatized patients' symptomatology. In contrast, I believe that the traumatized patient,[4] like the obsessive patient, is also trapped in a limited and limiting psychological position. Like the obsessive, the hysterical or fragmented patient suffers from a failure of imagination. She or he is caught in a kind of literalization that belies the possibility of creative psychological engagement with self and others. Thus we might reframe Hannah's problem of fragmenting terror as an obsessional need to bind her anxiety in a singular literal narrative, and as a need that manifests in her demand that her analyst narrate this same constricted story.

From this perspective it appears that psychological safety (which this patient sorely needed) comes through the freedom to play, as opposed to the process of mirroring or other active analytic methods of containment that trauma theory, self psychology, and object relations theories advocate. In these latter two-phase models the analyst offers a holding environment in which her or his empathic listening and mirroring of affects and experience provide the patient with enough safety to consolidate a strong enough sense of self and of self–other boundaries. Because of this initial phase of safety the patient can afford to begin to regress to more disturbed states.

I am arguing instead that experiences of both safety and danger are aroused through the dialectic of negative and positive poles of transference–countertransference phenomena throughout the course of analysis. The more disturbed patient may initially use the appearance of a childlike trust in the analyst as a defense against delivering her or his psychopathology and troubled relational patterns into the treatment. It is within this frame that I place those initial months of treatment with Hannah when her cult stories did not pose a conflict between us. Through the presentation of a childlike aspect of self, Hannah avoided the premature exposure of her psychological damage. Given that numerous prior therapists had let her down either through serious boundary violations or an inability to cope with the extent of her distress, Hannah rightly took some time to check me out. In fact, I do not think that a lengthy mirroring phase could have been created in this particular dyad. Hannah and I held opposing views on her central self-defining narrative, and, as I stated earlier, her choice of a therapist who was bound to arouse conflict in such psychically vulnerable arenas probably carried unconscious intentionality. Furthermore, her profound absence of internal safety, coupled with her psychological acuity, determined the occurrence of early and persistent treatment crises.

The curative work in Hannah's treatment began and continued from the moment she perceived that our realities were profoundly different. Because she had at this point already cast her lot with me, and because she was savvy enough to understand that this conflict was at the center of either her healing or her undoing, she stayed through crisis after crisis. Early in the work she poetically stated that during her prior treatments she had been on a sinking ship throwing overboard all that carried weight. In this treatment, she said, there was nothing left to abandon—she would either sink or sail. I suspect that both possible outcomes held allure for her.

As Hannah worked through the terrifying repercussions of our differences around satanic abuse, the focus of the conflict shifted away from this particular discourse. The heart of her psychotic-like patterns of relating now played out between us, unfettered by the distancing, fantastical narratives of cult abuse. There were times, I must admit, when I found myself longing for the return of the ritual abuse story. At least it was "out there." These were the times when I too felt in danger of going crazy, when Hannah drew on my own primitive unconscious modes of being. At such moments I deeply understood the power of these cultural stories to ward off the chaos of unformulated and terrifying psychological depths. While I did not change my mind about the existence of cult abuse, I did come to know the necessity and function of this particular narrative. I suspect that Hannah knew this, and that this was a kind of shared reality that sufficed for the other kind that she had earlier demanded—that I believe precisely as she did.

I believe the stories that Hannah and I created, and added to and deleted from, enabled her to develop a more flexible sense of self that could better weather the exigencies of life; that could bear strong affects of rage, pleasure, grief, confusion, shame, and joy; that could bear paradox and enigma; and that could also feel utterly certain at times. My hope for Hannah continues to be that she broaden her repertoire of stories in such a way that the ones that hold the deepest meaning, that are the richest affectively and the most interesting, are not only the stories where she is the literal victim of circumstance, where the gun is always at her temple, and where her hand is forever on the knife.

## NOTES

1. Lest my readers think this a simple case of a psychotic delusion, I want to be clear that Hannah's belief in the existence of these kinds of cults is shared by many others, including respected therapists and psychoanalysts. This became particularly clear to me on a number of occasions when I used this case illustration at psychoanalytic conferences and was frequently accused of retraumatizing the patient by not believing her story.

2. My thanks to Richard Nasser for pointing out that, in her initial interview with me, Hannah did not inquire about my thoughts on satanic ritual abuse.

3. Janice Haaken's (1998) work is a notable exception in that she offers a comprehensive theory of sexual abuse in an analytic treatment in her emphasis upon the need for the analyst to stay open to multiple readings. She writes, "The problematic reasoning that has so limited the field of trauma therapy [is] its emphasis on singular causes of disturbing states" (p. 224).

4. I use the term *traumatized* to refer to the cluster of symptoms and relational patterns that frequently, but not necessarily, follow physical trauma.

## REFERENCES

Davies, J. M. (1996). Dissociation, repression and reality testing in the countertransference: the controversy over memory and false memory in the psychoanalytic treatment of adult survivors of childhood sexual abuse. *Psychoanalytic Dialogues* 6:189–218.

Davies, J. M., and Frawley, M. G. (1994). *Treating the Adult Survivor of Childhood Sexual Abuse: A Psychoanalytic Perspective*. New York: Basic Books.

Elliott, A., and Spezzano, C. (1996). Psychoanalysis at its limits: navigating the postmodern turn. *Psychoanalytic Quarterly* 65:52–83.

Flax, J. (1990). *Thinking Fragments: Psychoanalysis, Feminism, and Postmodernism in the Contemporary West*. Berkeley: University of California Press.

Haaken, J. (1998). *Pillar of Salt: Gender, Memory, and the Perils of Looking Back*. New Brunswick, NJ: Rutgers University Press.

Hacking, I. (1995). *Rewriting the Soul: Multiple Personality and the Sciences of Memory*. Princeton, NJ: Princeton University Press.

Herman, J. L. (1992). *Trauma and Recovery*. New York: Basic Books.

Hoffman, I. Z. (1998). *Ritual and Spontaneity in the Psychoanalytic Process: A Dialectical-Constructivist View*. Hillsdale, NJ: Analytic Press.

Kaminer, W. (1999). *Sleeping with Extra-Terrestrials: The Rise of Irrationalism and Perils of Impiety*. New York: Pantheon.

Nathan, D. (1991). *Women and Other Aliens: Essays From the U.S.-Mexico Border*. El Paso, TX: Cinco Puntos Press.

Schafer, R. (1992). *Retelling a Life: Narration and Dialogue in Psychoanalysis*. New York: Basic Books.

Showalter, E. (1997). *Hystories: Hysterical Epidemics and Modern Media*. New York: Columbia University Press.

Victor, J. S. (1993). *Satanic Panic: The Creation of a Contemporary Legend*. Chicago, IL: Open Court.

Winnicott, D. W. (1971). *Playing and Reality*. London: Tavistock.

# Negotiating the Baby and the Bathwater in Psychoanalytic Process: A Discussion of Carolyn Stack's "(Ir)reconcilable Differences"

*Steven H. Cooper*

Where to begin when so much has already been written about postmodern relational approaches to satanic ritual abuse? Just kidding.

Stack has written a fascinating paper describing the incredibly gratifying experience of being able to engender an analytic process and help a patient when both patient and analyst had much reason to doubt that it could ever get off the ground. Her paper is a contribution that I think goes beyond the narrow confines of "postmodern relational," though indeed her work is a fine example of this interpretive stance. She is describing how to spark a capacity for play when the imagination has been drastically truncated through traumatic experience and, worse, when near-psychotic thinking threatens to carry the day.

Since I thought this was such a fine example of analytic work, I will briefly take up a few points that were particularly interesting to me regarding the nature of therapeutic action and interaction in this therapy.

Stack distinguishes between prejudice and believers in movements described as hysterical epidemics, urban myths, and moral panics.

Mythologies of bigotry rely on splitting and devaluation essentially to debase and dehumanize one group so that it can be exterminated or assigned as inferior. She suggests with Hacking (1995) and Kaminer (1999) that hysterical panics, like mythologies of bigotry, rely on the mechanisms of splitting and projection, but that hysterical panics or legends produce a supernatural other such as aliens or perpetrators "so omnipotent that no whit of evidence is ever found." I am more skeptical about a sharp distinction to be made between these two phenomena. The work of Adorno (1950) and Antelme (1957) beautifully illustrates how devaluation, splitting, and projection function in prejudice. Antelme (1957) writes:

> It's because we're men like them that the SS will finally prove powerless before us. It's because they shall have sought to call the unity of this human race into question that they'll finally be crushed. Yet their behavior, and our situation, are only a magnification, an extreme carica-ture—in which nobody wants or is perhaps able to recognize himself— of forms of behavior and of situations that exist in the world, that even make up the existence of that older "real world" we dream about. For in fact everything that happens in that world happens as though there were a number of human species, or rather as though belonging to a single human species wasn't certain, as though you could join the species or leave it, could be halfway in it or belong to it fully, or never belong to it, try though you might for generations, division into races or classes being the canon of the species and sustaining the axiom we're always prepared to use, the ultimate line of defense: "They aren't people like us." [p. 219]

While I don't want to suggest that there aren't differences between sa-tanic mythologies and prejudice, I think there are some important com-mon elements as well. In elevating a supernatural power, I think that humans are debased, made into the subspecies that characterizes the mythologies of bigotry. Splitting, projection, and devaluation function to expel toxic affects and debase the self or other. In Hannah's case, she is in the debased position, hiding for her life, always ready to be killed. Hannah's terror of being killed or abandoned may have at its core profound feelings of being unworthy of care, love, and safety, particu-larly if her fantasies of having killed relate to her own experience of feeling that she could be psychically murdered.

One of the most important things about this treatment was the considerable flexibility and openness that this patient had to Stack's difference with her. I say this only in a relative sense—relative to those countless people who would never bring their convictions about satanic ritual abuse to the office of a psychoanalyst to be explored at all, much less questioned. Some therapists describe clinical decisions they make in which they "lie" to a patient about believing something they really don't believe. In agreement with Stack, I can't imagine trying to lie or distort her position by telling the patient that she believed something she didn't believe. Hannah's considerable emotional strength allowed her to invite Stack to call a spade a spade, which was the foundation on which this work developed. I can imagine saying to a patient that I believe that they believe what they believe and I'll work on trying to understand as much as possible about what and how it is that they believe what they believe. This, of course, was something that Stack compassionately conveyed to Hannah throughout their work. In doing so, Stack appeared to me to be psychically holding the terror and disavowal that Hannah experienced, while maintaining a reality sense outside this realm of psychic terror and psychic reality. Hannah gradually reinternalized this detoxified reality that Stack held so well.

Stack was able to hold her own uncertainty about whether Hannah would be able to tolerate the different organizing mythologies held between the two. In retrospect, we can say that in this treatment it was extremely important that the patient neither asked Stack about her willingness to believe her in the initial session nor fled when finding out more pointedly that Stack did not believe her story in a literal sense. Many patients would never see a therapist who did not believe the veracity of their satanic abuse stories. This patient was eventually able to welcome (albeit with great terror and quite slowly and reluctantly) a form of play regarding reality and past experience that is a part of analytic work and rare within this population.

In the first year of treatment, when Hannah begins to observe Stack's lack of belief in the literality of events she is demonstrating a positive therapeutic development. She is inviting an exploration of difference, a bumping up of two realities in conflict with one another. I don't mean to minimize how profoundly uncertain Stack must have been about whether Hannah would be able to work with multiplicity of meaning, ambiguity, compromise, and paradox. My sense of how different Hannah is, in comparison to people for whom these organizing mythologies are bedrock and immutable narratives, can only be gathered in retrospect from the two of them going through this process and living to tell the tale.

I thought Stack worked with the dialectics of difference between herself and her patient quite masterfully. What happened between the two was expansive for the patient in understanding her sense of past and present. I shy away from the term *curative* as it is used in this paper because I don't think it is a concept that has much relevance to psychoanalysis. Instead I think that psychoanalysis helps expand meaning systems, sometimes including those associated with symptomatic relief (see Caper 1992 for an interesting discussion that questions the concept of cure in psychoanalysis). In holding Hannah's terror, in holding her own uncertainty about whether Hannah could tolerate their differences, and in maintaining her independent sense of a reality outside Hannah's psychic reality, Stack detoxified and suggested a psychic future for Hannah that was not predicated on a killing but on a kind of new experience or beginning, one based less on murder and more on something generative involving the dialectics of difference. Stack succeeded in broadening Hannah's metaphorical realm.

Stack's discussion of how "reality" was explored in the analytic work is complex, and we can only imagine how complex it must have been for both patient and therapist. Hannah alternates between wanting Stack to see things exactly as she sees them and wanting her to articulate more clearly the obvious differences in how she sees things. Stack states that Hannah was upset when Stack did not challenge her belief that reality was not subjectively defined. Stack demonstrates a significant awareness of how her openness to uncertainty and paradox was quite helpful in this process as well as how, in retrospect, it posed problems for Hannah in developing an augmented sense of play. Even though Stack does not believe that Hannah killed babies, she does want to explore Hannah's construction as much as possible. This stance is confusing to Hannah, who is partly trying to consolidate a different sense of reality, more in line with or at least a closer version of Stack's sense of reality.

While I'm extremely appreciative of Stack's criticisms of applying the developmental metaphor too concretely and with too much linearity (e.g., Cooper 2000a), I still like to be able to have some information about development in making my own constructions. I also like to use it metaphorically, if not with my patient, then in my own mind. The language of developmental metaphor, particularly if not taken literally, can help both patient and therapist discuss the meaning (not necessarily the origins) of a belief system. I agree with Bromberg (1998) that we do well not to take the baby metaphor literally, but that we don't have to throw the metaphorical baby out with the bathwater. In fact, Stack and Hannah may have relied on developmental mythologies in the treatment more than we are told in this description of the clinical process.

It is easy for all of us to conflate a few rather different things when we discuss postmodern preference for "always keeping the field open to interpretation" versus what Stack refers to as "other therapists for whom the dividing lines of reality and fantasy are more sharply drawn." I think analysts can be quite oriented to keeping the field open to interpretation but also up front about the fact that certain things are real to them and certain things are not. I have had patients who rather enjoy when I'm up front about when I think something they say is wrong or "crazy," because they know very well from their experience with me that I want to understand and keep things open to interpretation as much as possible. On the one hand, Stack thinks the satanic ritual abuse didn't happen. Maybe that's the reality that Hannah is referring to when she says, "Of course there's a reality," meaning: I know that you don't agree with me about my view, so why not just say it. I find a certain kind of disjunction between Stack's statement that in her "postmodern position I privilege uncertainty and paradox" and her honest reporting to us about how much she didn't believe the ritual abuse to be true. I see these two positions as occurring along different axes, and I wonder if it would have been clearer for Hannah if Stack had presented a more direct picture of how much she didn't believe in the literalness of Hannah's story, while clarifying to her how much she wanted to understand the psychic reality that Hannah experienced. Hannah knows the reality of Stack's difference with her, and I find Stack's statement of always privileging uncertainty and paradox a bit confusing. Stack is interested in exploring uncertainty and paradox within psychic reality. She is applying this stance (with which I entirely agree) to the issue of something factual that must have been confusing to Hannah.

Hoffman (personal communication, 1999) states that there is nothing contradictory about social constructivism and believing that certain things are or aren't true. For example, he views as a fact that there is no God. This, to him, is different from discrediting a belief in God. Stack does not believe that there was an event in which her patient participated in killing babies. This doesn't mean that she isn't interested in trying as hard as possible to understand Hannah's sense that she did kill babies as a part of a satanic ritual. As I read this paper, at times I was confused about how much Stack valued making this distinction more clear to Hannah. I tempered this thought with the sense that maybe what Stack was trying to tell us was that this level of clarification was too toxic a form of intrusive difference for Hannah at most stages of the treatment. Stack decided, perhaps wisely, to suffer the confusion that this conveyed to Hannah rather than scare her away with conveying too bold and stark or too untimely a picture of how much her reality was in conflict with Hannah's.

But there is, in the insistence on privileging uncertainty and paradox, what I call "the return of the repressed positivistic" (Cooper 2000a). What I mean by this is that any epistemological stance involves the therapist's belief that something will be understood if we do such and such. There's no getting around the fact of psychoanalytic life that Stack, like all of us, is insisting on a view of how to get at the truth of the matter and that the patient will be both benefiting and toiling under this insistence on the part of the therapist. Postmodernists, like classicists, are all subject to this phenomenon of a working stance. The return of the repressed positivistic cannot be avoided by any particular stance but is instead a current of analytic work to try to understand. Stack illustrates her ability to consider this current when she tells us how confusing her stance was for Hannah.

Stack did not provide developmental details because of her wish to protect the patient's identity, which understandably holds priority over other wishes to provide detail to her colleagues. This does leave us with many questions, however, in trying to understand the meaning of Hannah's psychic reality. "Why is this mythology particularly compelling as an organizing construct for this patient?" she asks. "What intrapsychic and interpersonal functions does it fulfill?" Without knowing the history of Hannah's interpersonal and representational world it is difficult for me to understand more deeply what went on between

Stack and Hannah. Instead, we are left with a poignant account of how reality was negotiated between the two around an organizing mythology that stretches our more conventional boundaries of reconcilable psychic reality.

Many American relationally oriented analysts who have questioned the linearity of the developmental metaphor (e.g., Benjamin 1988, Cooper 2000a,b, Davies 1994, Hoffman 1994, Mitchell 1988) also believe in the value of using developmental metaphors to create meaning systems. These are not used to create objective reconstructions of what happened. They involve entering into the patient's idiom, partly forged through a conversation with a therapist about what meaning systems "mean" and say about the stories of our lives. At a very speculative level, I wondered about whether Stack analyzed with Hannah her needs for a parental figure who might consolidate her sense of a less toxic reality. Did she want a parent who would help her organize a reality that was not predicated on either killing or being killed? I think Hannah was seeking something that might be understood in a developmental context. I just don't know whether this was a phase of work that occurred in her treatment. Naturally, I am speculating that she's looking for someone who isn't crazy to validate her sense of reality or disconfirm it.

I think that Hannah was drawn to Stack's certainty about what she believes and doesn't believe and that Stack's postmodern position regarding epistemology (uncertainty and openness to new meaning) may have been less relevant to some aspects of the therapeutic action, even though I'm quite sympathetic to Stack's epistemological stance.

The developmental metaphors that we utilize with patients are in the best of circumstances only a part of the evolving meaning systems that drive analytic process. When taken too literally, they encourage regression and distancing, as well as more permanent and stultifying meaning systems. Stack is correct to criticize both the use of these meaning systems in "charting pathology through reference to childhood circumstances" and in developing an objectified or actual story of what happens in an individual's life. The ritualized asymmetry of the therapeutic situation does, however, borrow from developmental experience in ways that can help construct meaning that is complementary to immediate interpersonal engagement. My guess is that Stack and Hannah either used or enacted aspects of developmental phenomena in the considerable progress of this therapeutic work, whether this was articulated or not. A postmodern epistemological stance is not in contradiction with this assertion. Rather, it works in conjunction with developmental and other meaning systems that involve patient and therapist building and tearing down constructed mythologies so that new meanings, jointly developed, can be alloyed and organized.

## REFERENCES

Adorno, T. (1950). *The Authoritarian Personality*. New York: Norton.

Antelme, R. (1957). *The Human Race*. Evanston, IL: Marlboro/Northwestern.

Benjamin, J. (1988). *The Bonds of Love*. New York: Pantheon.

Bromberg, P. (1998). *Standing in the Spaces*. Hillsdale, NJ: Analytic Press.

Caper, R. (1992). Does psychoanalysis heal? *International Journal of Psycho-Analysis* 73:283–292.

Cooper, S. (2000a). *Objects of Hope: Exploring Possibility and Limit in Psychoanalysis*. Hillsdale, NJ: Analytic Press.

——— (2000b). Elements of mutual containment in the analytic process. *Psychoanalytic Dialogues* 10:169–194.

Davies, J. (1994). Love in the afternoon: a relational consideration of desire and dread in the countertransference. *Psychoanalytic Dialogues* 4:153–170.

Hacking, I. (1995). *Rewriting the Soul: Multiple Personality and the Sciences of Memory*. Princeton, NJ: Princeton University Press.

Hoffman, I. (1994). Dialectical thinking and therapeutic action in the psychoanalytic process. *Psychoanalytic Quarterly* 63:187–218.

Kaminer, W. (1999). *Sleeping with Extra-Terrestials: The Rise of Irrationalism and Perils of Impiety*. New York: Pantheon.

Mitchell, S. (1988). *Relational Concepts in Psychoanalysis*. Cambridge, MA: Harvard University Press.

# Response to Steven Cooper's "Negotiating the Baby and the Bathwater in Psychoanalytic Process"

*Carolyn Stack*

Dr. Cooper is right to wonder about the role of developmental narratives in my treatment of Hannah. In agreement with his notion of the "return of the repressed positivistic," I believe that we can never move fully outside a modernist perspective. Because of sociocultural familial arrangements, coupled with the widespread belief that psychological distress links back to early relationships with primary caregivers, it is impossible to conduct an analysis from either side of the couch completely outside the frame of the developmental storyline. Cooper argues that "the language of developmental metaphor, particularly if not taken literally, can help both patient and therapist discuss the meaning (not necessarily the origins) of a belief system." However, I would add that metaphor is not immune to deconstruction. As Cooper suggests, the overreliance in psychoanalysis on family history has raised its own set of problems. It is this overreliance on both literal and metaphorical constructions of family dynamics that I attempted to redress in my essay and about which, in response to Cooper's discussion, I have further thoughts.

Cooper writes, "Without knowing the history of Hannah's inter-personal and representational world it is difficult for me to understand more deeply what went on between Stack and Hannah." This statement speaks to a central vexing dilemma in the treatment because I, too, would say that after many years I knew little about Hannah's history, and yet it was incumbent upon me to deeply understand *something* that was happening between us. The concrete facts that I had about her childhood, her family structure, and her parents' personalities contrib-uted little to a fuller picture of the depth of Hannah's psychological distress. From my perspective, the narrative of what happened between Hannah and me, which I outline in my essay, *is* as detailed a version of Hannah's intrapsychic life and her most important relationships as I could present in condensed form. And I believe that by living through this dynamic narrative with Hannah I did grasp that "something" well enough.

Cooper's response inspired me to think more clearly about my anti-developmental stance. While I have understood my attraction to this position on political grounds (the moment we posit linear development we are inscribing a hierarchy of social norms) and on aesthetic grounds (I believe that any calcified narrative restricts our and our patients' capacities to live full lives), Cooper's discussion led me to another fac-tor. I find that many of my patients are uninterested in developmental narratives and, further, are not inspired by curiosity about their lack of interest. I find myself, as was the case with Hannah, having to work with the narratives that *are* of interest. As Cooper suggests, this position doesn't preclude a construction of a developmental narrative in the analyst's mind. But I found in this particular treatment, as I have found in others, that these explicit or merely fantasized speculations inhib-ited rather than furthered the imaginative unfolding of the therapy.

What do I make of this? Here I do have a developmental fantasy. It seemed to me that a coherent, linear narrative linking her history with her present symptomatology was far from Hannah's psychologi-cal reach, that attempts at constructing this kind of picture were, in Kohutian terms, so experience-distant as to be of little use to her, and that her only hope for some kind of healing was to be able to traverse the maddest terrains of her psyche, holding me as close to the fire as she and I could bear. In the heat of the work, developmental narratives, even speculative ones about Hannah's longings for specific kinds of caretaking, seemed ineffectual at best and wildly tangential at worst. I suspect that for a variety of reasons psychological difficulties for patients like Hannah are not always traceable to simple traumas or identifiable traumatic relational patterns. In many treatments we can link transference and countertransference phenomena to specific memories of childhood or to screen memories that can often be backed up by observations of parental functioning in the present. When we cannot do this, we psychoanalysts often resort to fantasies about the quality of maternal care in infancy and, for some patients, these narratives are useful. As I argued in my essay, we cannot always know what happened in childhood, and the analytic work may consist of the patient learning to live with *not knowing*. This is my developmental narrative: healthy development requires learning to live with the enigmatic.

I am arguing that a kind of "not knowing" haunted Hannah her whole life and that her most important psychological work was to find some footing in the chaos of profound confusion, terror, and psychotic-like thinking. Hannah's own attempts to create a linear narrative (the ritual abuse), which was supported by prior therapists, was retraumatizing to her. I can make up stories that are more plausible: Hannah's memories (both diffuse and specific), family lore, a few indisputable facts, the transference–countertransference dynamics, and the kinds of intimate relationships that she entered into led me to wonder about early sexual abuse, a profound absence of maternal care throughout childhood, and the crazy-making concealment of family secrets. And while Hannah and I came to articulate all of these narratives, it seemed to me that this story-making was not what led to firmer ground. Rather, her growing capacity to bear in my presence her grief about the limitations in her life so far and her rage about the betrayals by, and absence of help from, others provided more of a semblance of agency than she had previously experienced. I am aware that this is precisely the kind of material that developmentalists would mark as the child's helpless longing for adequate parenting and rage at her parents' limitations.

I think that we analytic therapists are too quick to posit this story line, and that this lazy kind of work can limit us. First, the easy reach for the familial metaphor evokes and reinforces the politics of traditional family values. Second, the mother–infant metaphor holds the patient in the narrative of helplessness and victimhood. In the first instance we fail to appreciate the cultural implications of the compulsively repeated story of children who feel unloved and unseen. (For example, is this a story that tells us something about the failure of nuclear family arrangements? Or is it a metaphorical construction in psychoanalysis and the culture at large—evidenced in all those inner-child books—that serves specific sociopolitical purposes?) The blind reiteration of this story robs our patients of the chance to broaden their frameworks to include the sociopolitical. In the second instance, the easy reach for the developmental may foreclose a construction of a more mutual kind of relation—about the parents in fantasy in the past or with the parents in the present, or between therapist and patient.

There were times when my construction of a familial story line was of use to Hannah. Once I suggested that her dissociated periods of panic and silence in treatment reflected a memory. This idea was appealing to her less because it signified a precise memory but more because she saw that I understood that these terrifying psychological experiences had been with her her whole life. There were also times when, out of my own desperation at the chaos of sitting with Hannah, I would reach for a familial story and the work would grind to a halt. Early in the treatment this interpretive move further distanced Hannah. Later in the analysis she had developed enough of an observing ego to comment on the process and enough trust to aggressively confront me. At another time Hannah spoke of her longing to have had me as a mom. In her playful way she suggested that she move into my waiting room. She wouldn't get in the way as long as she could always have me near. We played this out in fantasy. Whether we call this pantomime a redoing of childhood, a trying on of what she didn't get and should have had, or whether we call it the unfolding of her creative imagination in the presence of another—the bearing of not knowing what comes next—perhaps doesn't matter a whole lot. While developmental narratives are often useful in a treatment, I do believe that they must also be open to close scrutiny and that we should be wary of needing them when perhaps our patients do not. I want to thank Steven Cooper for offering me the chance to further my thinking on this matter.

# 4

# Relational Theory and the Postmodern Turn

*Virginia Goldner*

At the 1997 Annual Conference of the Division of Psychoanalysis of the American Psychological Association, I participated in a symposium on "Psychoanalysis and Postmodernism." Two of the presenters were Irwin Hoffman and Donnel Stern, both significant contributors to American relational theory and to the growing clinical literature on postmodernism. The third presenter, Carolyn Grey, addressed issues of class and gender from a postmodernist perspective. As the discussant of these papers, I saw my task as building some intellectual bridges between the postmodern clinical perspective exemplified by Hoffman and Stern and the postmodern critique of identity categories articulated by Grey. I argued that these two traditions of scholarship and practice were mutually essential to one another and to the task of understanding individual subjectivity and the politics of the analytic situation.

Much more has been said along these lines since that conference (see especially Layton 1998), and much of what I said then has a familiar ring nowadays, but I am going to reproduce those remarks, with some modest enhancements, so that Donnel Stern can craft for this book the reply he was not able to make at the time. Stern's further thinking on the matters I raised four years ago will, of course, spark new thoughts of mine, which is precisely the way ideas lurch forward within a community of readers and writers.

In line with the spirit of interdisciplinary conversation that shapes so much of the intellectual culture of postmodernism, I thought I'd begin with a pertinent quote from an unlikely source: Aleksii Antediluvianovich, the "World's Oldest Living Bolshevik," brought to us courtesy of the playwright Tony Kushner (1993). From *Angels in America, Part II*, Act One, Scene One:

> The Great Question before us is Will the Past release us? The Great Question before us is: Can we Change? . . . And Theory? How are we to proceed without *Theory*? What System of Thought have these Reformers to present to . . . the Inevident Welter of fact, event, phenomenon, calamity? Do they have, as we did, a beautiful Theory, as bold, as Grand, as comprehensive a construct? . . . And what have you to offer now, children of this Theory? What have you to offer in its place? . . . If the snake sheds his skin before a new skin is ready, naked he will be in the world, prey to the forces of chaos. Without his skin he will be dismantled, lose coherence and die. Have you, my little serpents, a new skin? [p. 3]

Clearly, Kushner must have been keeping up with the fiery debates that have been raging in our professional journals and conference circuit about who is authorized to speak in the name of the psychoanalytic movement. In our North American context, the Old Bolshevik's Great Question would probably translate into asking whether (if not when) the waning power and authority of classical psychoanalysis will have become completely appropriated by its high visibility challenger, the relational perspective, so aptly named by Charles Spezzano the "American Middle School."

Indeed, it often does seem that the relational-constructivist point of view has already been installed, if not as Aleksii's new Master Narrative—a "paradigm *über alles*" that is no longer possible in this swirling information age—then surely as the paradigm everyone is talking about. And as truth has yielded to taste and science to story line, "talk" becomes a truth method and measure unto itself. In Spezzano's pithy axiom, "truth" is simply "the . . . solution we invent at a particular moment that seems to explain things so well that no one has any interest in pursuing the conversation any further" (Spezzano 1993, p. 179).

But while there may no longer be a hegemonic Old Guard to defeat, relational psychoanalysis still conceives of itself as an anti-establishment movement even as it becomes something of an establishment itself. Purveyors of postmodernism exhibit a similar habit of mind and rhetoric, representing themselves as outsiders even as they operate on an inside track. Although compelled by Foucault's critique of knowledge as disciplinary power, they have been slow to acknowledge or reflect upon how, in the last decade, postmodernism itself has produced a powerful regulatory regime both in the academy and in the wider world of arts and letters.

Yet as Kuhn and Foucault have demonstrated so influentially, such paradoxes are hard-wired into the social processes through which competing paradigms of knowledge develop and come to unseat one another, each temporarily occupying the citadel of truth. The implications of these contradictions for a practice-based knowledge system like psychoanalysis remain to be articulated, but Irwin Hoffman captures the essence of the dilemma for relational analysts when he asks how we can spontaneously and creatively defy tradition once a new tradition emerges that seems to require defiance as a matter of principle (Hoffman 1998).

It is not just that the idealization of spontaneity and authenticity can become its own sort of pressure. The larger problem, addressed by Foucault, is that as any discipline evolves, its melange of aspects begins to congeal into "principles" that transmute into "requirements," which eventually become instrumental "techniques" that must be mastered by anyone claiming to be an "expert" in this newly minted Method and Profession, a process Hoffman, who does not come at this via Foucault, nonetheless also dubs the work of "technical rationality." Quite a perversion of the original radical impulse—being "real" as opposed to being "right."

Are such processes inevitabilities? (How) can we assess whether and when, even in privileging what is absolutely unique, such as the analyst's personal voice, the result can still become another conformist regime of "correct" ideas and technique? Think about how it has now become right to know that you can't know if you're right.

Yet canonizing uncertainty does make it easier to give up the voyeuristic pleasures of the penetrating gaze and the authorizing power of the one-way interpretation. In its place, the postmodern turn gives us reflexivity, the act of making one's own processes the object of one's own observation. This is not reducible to analyzing one's countertransference, since our point of departure is what Hoffman has called the analyst's "superordinate subjectivity," which is, in Donnel Stern's terms, always "embedded in the grip of the field" both relationally and socioculturally (Stern 1997). The technical and moral challenge thus becomes the quest to *decenter* one's subjectivity, not to transcend it.

This way of thinking about postmodern questions of authority and uncertainty can provide a dynamically grounded epistemological justification for Hoffman's notion that relational analysts both "throw away the book" and yet "keep it in the background." Instead of the judgmental, never-satisfied Mother or Father Confessor to whom we have traditionally been beholden, theories of intersubjectivity, social constructionism, and the postmodern turn are permission-giving and responsibility-enhancing. They generate a collective voice of authority that encourages us to question authority and yet to recognize how embedded in its matrix we will always be, to make our *own* decisions about what to pack and what to unpack, while acknowledging how many of those choices have been predetermined by culture and context.

Postmodern theorizing can be seen as a sequence of displacements. The first was the move from the object of theory to the subject who theorizes, and thus from objectivism to epistemology: from the first-order question, "What does the patient lack/need/desire?" to the second-order, "What does the analyst know, and how does s/he know it?" The next move was from the subject who theorizes to the relational context through which any form of knowing is created and meaning performed. This is the shift from the solitary perspective of radical constructivism to the intersubjective relational framework of social constructionism, or from a one- to a two-person psychology of knowing. The third displacement is the move from the dialogical to the discursive, from the intersubjective co-creation of meaning to the discourses and cultural narratives that set the terms for what the dialogical partners can think and know. This is the Foucauldian piece.

Relational psychoanalysis has been essentially preoccupied with the second of these iterations: the social-constructionist project of grounding the work of knowing and of meaning-making in the to and fro of intersubjectivity. Relational thinking has yielded up richly theorized, thickly described renderings of the ordinary epistemological rigors of psychoanalytic collaboration—of the philosophical, linguistic, and intersubjective conditions of ambiguity and indeterminacy through which we construct what we come to know, wringing out every possible implication for the way we work, think, and talk in the analytic situation, and thus making the case on philosophical grounds that the ideal analytic stance can no longer be abstinence and neutrality but must become collaboration and a commitment to uncertainty.

But theorizing the epistemological status of psychoanalytic dialogue without taking the next (Foucauldian) step—from dialogue to discourse—obscures the extent to which the conversational partners, no less their conversation, are embedded in a sociocultural matrix that sets the terms for what can be known, thought, and spoken. Analyst and analysand may co-construct meaning dialogically, but not as equals, since their dialogue is owned by the discourse of psychoanalysis as embodied in the person of the analyst. It is only by threading the social-constructionist process of analytic meaning-making through the deconstructive, critical categories of Foucauldian space that we can observe, *in statu nascendi*, how psychoanalysis holds but also disciplines practitioners and clients alike—how, in the most intimate sense, every analytic encounter is conducted in the shadow of the analytic profession, a powerful Third, as we now like to say. (See Lewis Aron 1999 for an extended exploration of this idea.)

Aron also reminds us that when Europeans were studying other cultures, they suddenly recognized that those "other" people were also studying them, that the object of their gaze was also another subject gazing (Aron 1996). When we ask who is looking and who is being seen, who is doing the naming or the telling of another's life, when we query the relative social power of conversational partners to create meaning, we are asking about the power relations of intersubjectivity as they are revealed in the core question of whether a person is constituted as a subject or is consigned to be an object. This conceptually elegant, morally evocative distillation of cultural politics has been the central project and accomplishment of the political wing of the postmodern enterprise, the work of feminist, Foucauldian, and queer theory.

Foucault argued that modern societies are characterized by the rule of experts, and that knowledge produced within a discursive system legitimates the power of experts who attain their status because of the discourse-specific knowledge they have acquired (Flax 1993). Foucault's analysis of how the creation, systematization, and dissemination of knowledge produce power inequities between those who are in charge of knowledge and those who are the objects of its gaze is particularly relevant to the psychotherapies. A Foucauldian view would insist that we view therapy as a social practice shaped by, and embedded in, an elaborate professional culture that inevitably constrains what can be seen and named and, like all discursive formations, elevates and fore-grounds some ideas and people while marginalizing or devaluing others. By asking, for example, how certain constructs come to appear univer-sal and natural (like "mankind") while others appear narrow and stig-matizing (like "lesbian"), a Foucauldian perspective can illuminate the ways in which psychoanalytic theories create, enforce, and rank the identity categories that become us and through which we are socially defined.

The lack of engagement with this rich critical tradition has been costly for relational psychoanalysis. Issues of power have been under-theorized, while questions of identity and its relation to subjectivity have been completely neglected. Moreover, the exclusion of identity categories, especially gender and sexuality, from the central tenets of psychoanalytic theorizing turns them into topics, when they are, in fact, foundational conditions of personal subjectivity and of relatedness. Their omission as ground-zero concepts from authoritative discussions of ground-zero concepts in relational psychoanalysis creates the danger that gender and sexuality will return to their default settings, where they are codes for "female" and "gay," leaving the Heterosexual Male as our singular standard of universal humanity and of wellness and excellence.

Psychoanalysis cannot escape itself as the founding confessional discourse of our therapeutic society, constructing the very categories of identity through which we experience and evaluate ourselves both in the analytic hour and outside it. Every sentence spoken by the analyst, already saturated with assumptions and categories, inevitably underlined and put in "caps" by the magical powers of transference and the ideali-zation of expertise, is a performative utterance, materializing what is said as it is spoken. Thus we cannot allow foundational identity cat-egories like gender and sexuality to function at face value, because their truth, though false, makes everyone else an exception to be specified, that is, a specimen.

Having argued the case that it is crucial for psychoanalysis to address the ways in which cultural discourses construct and penetrate subjectivity, I want also to repeat that it is equally crucial to search for the subject who creates a world of personal meaning nonetheless. Gender and sexual subjectivity, as Chodorow (1996) has persuasively demonstrated, are not merely "effects" of discourse, as Foucault would have it; they are also personally idiomatic, creative acts. Without incorporating the psychological aspects of identity formation, discourse theory also leaves us with an empty space in our understanding of how minds get made.

Intriguingly, at the conference for which these remarks were originally written, I was struck by how each of the three panelists ignored one or the other of these dimensions almost entirely. Their thinking split right along the gender divide, with the woman focused solely on discourse theory and the critique of identity categories, while the men restricted themselves to psychoanalytic constructivism, broadly defined.

Where Stern's and Hoffman's work suffered from the neglect of Foucauldian categories, Grey's notion of discourse struck me as too one-sided, neglecting a consideration of how the subject comes out to meet it, indeed, even talks back. Discursively speaking, the process of finding ("positioning") oneself in discourse, what Althusser (1971) called "interpellation," requires the creative agency of the subject who says, "Yes, there I am, that's me!"

We need this side of the experience brought forward and theorized as well, because it is here, in the meeting of minds and in the space where mind meets narrative, that each of us crafts a uniquely personal version of the subject positions that make a claim on us. The mechanisms of internalization and the enactment of normative behavior cannot be reduced to a simple linear process through which the external somehow travels from the outside in. Rather, as Judith Butler has argued, these processes are creative, sui generis acts of resignification. To quote Clifford Geertz (1986), "it is the copying that originates" (p. 380).

In the joining of constructivist and deconstructive perspectives we can make a bridge between the intersubjectively emergent self of psychoanalytic dialogue and the self that is discursively produced (by cultural imagery of whatever form, including by psychoanalytic theory itself). Clinical interpretation, for example, can be construed as a text like any other in which the words create a space and a category through which the subject can locate herself and identify. In this clearing, personal subjectivity winds itself around a particular evocation of individuality, a "subject position" in the language of discourse theory. Such moments magnetize unformulated or disavowed aspects of self, creating for the reader or listener or conversational partner the sense of having been "found."

The mass production of identities and the subjectivities to match may be our most reliable growth industry. Indeed, in our moth-eaten families, with their conga-line of caregivers, with parents continually reinventing themselves personally and sexually while children invent cyber-identities that may be unrealizable by the facts of bodies as we know them, psychotherapeutic conversation may have become one of the few remaining cultural bridges linking up these multiple centers of mind and multiple sites of identity. Revisioned and decentered by constructivism and the Foucauldian turn, psychoanalytic work and theory can still take us to the human heart of that force field, where many voices are waiting to speak and be heard.

## REFERENCES

Althusser, L. (1971). *Lenin and Philosophy and Other Essays*. London: New Left Books.

Aron, L. (1996). *A Meeting of Minds: Mutuality in Psychoanalysis*. Hillsdale, NJ: Analytic Press.

——— (1999). Clinical choices and the relational matrix. *Psychoanalytic Dialogues* 9:1–31.

Chodorow, N. (1996). Theoretical gender and clinical gender. *Journal of the American Psychoanalytic Association* 44:215–238.

Dimen, M. (1999). From breakdown to breakthrough. In *Female Sexualities: Contemporary Engagements*, ed. D. Bassin, pp. 407–421. Northvale, NJ: Jason Aronson.

Flax, J. (1993). *Disputed Subjects*. New York: Routledge.

Geertz, C. (1986). Making experiences, authoring selves. In *The Anthropology of Experience*, ed. V. Turner and E. Bruner, pp. 373–381. Chicago: University of Illinois Press.

Hoffman, I. (1998). *Ritual and Spontaneity in the Psychoanalytic Process*. Hillsdale, NJ: Analytic Press.

Kushner, T. (1993). *Angels in America: Perestroika*. New York: Theatre Communications Group.

Layton, L. (1998). *Who's That Girl, Who's That Boy?: Clinical Practice Meets Postmodern Gender Theory*. Northvale, NJ: Jason Aronson.

Spezzano, C. (1993). Psychoanalysis and human conversation. *Psychoanalytic Dialogues* 3:177–208.

Stern, D. (1997). *Unformulated Experience: From Dissociation to Imagination in Psychoanalysis*. Hillsdale, NJ: Analytic Press.

# 5

# What You Know First: Construction and Deconstruction in Relational Psychoanalysis

*Donnel B. Stern*

*What you know first stays with you, my Papa says.*
—Patricia MacLachlan, *What You Know First*

In 1996, I contributed to a panel symposium focused on the intersection of psychoanalysis and postmodernism. (The other presenters were Carolyn Grey and Irwin Hoffman.) By *postmodernism*, I mean to refer to that wide range of ideas and writers who begin from the assertion that knowledge should no longer be thought of as a matter of matching the words we use to a reality that exists separately from us. We should instead think of knowledge as a social product, influenced by the time and place in which it comes to be. Specifically, it was my aim to discuss some of the effects on psychoanalysis of replacing a scientific view with a hermeneutic one. I will say more later about what I mean by *hermeneutic*, but for the time being let me just say that the word refers to the idea that we understand not by uncovering a previously existing, hidden truth, as in older ways of conceiving the matter, but instead by constructing a new truth in dialogue with another person. Contemporary hermeneutics is one of the contributors to postmodernism.

In her discussion, a version of which immediately precedes this chapter in the present volume, Dr. Virginia Goldner expresses her appreciation of the basic orientation that inspired the three papers, especially the way certain aspects of postmodernism are used to describe anew the details of the clinical interaction. But Dr. Goldner also takes issue with all three of us for not rooting our work in the significance of subject positions in discourse. Her position is that psychoanalysis should be grounded in questions about the identity categories that lie at the root of subjectivity, such as gender, sexuality, race, class, and ethnicity. She admonishes us that any social theory, including psychoanalysis, that is not grounded in the explicit study of identity categories risks embedding in its ideas the invisible assumptions and limitations that are such a significant part of what defines identity categories. She also makes the point that it might be precisely because Hoffman and I are male that we do not begin our theorizing in a consideration of subject positions. Perhaps, she goes on to suggest, the fact that we are male means that we have had a less conflicted and more advantageous acquaintance with power (I mean "power" here in the Foucauldian sense of an invisible but productive and shaping social influence, not only in the simpler sense of brute oppression or political repression) than we would have had if we were women, leaving us with that much less reason to develop a sustained interest in, and critique of, identity categories. I will help Dr. Goldner's case a bit by adding that both Hoffman and I are also white and straight, and I will broaden it by noting that her argument really applies not only to Hoffman and me but to most of psychoanalysis. It applies with special emphasis, though, to relational psychoanalysis, precisely because the relational group has been more hospitable to the study of identity categories than any other psychoanalytic orientation, and so Dr. Goldner, and anyone else who believes psychoanalysis should originate in the study of subject positions, has good reason to believe that relational analysts will and should take her argument with particular seriousness. Insofar as Dr. Goldner's criticism is directed to relational analysts, in other words, our interchange is something of a family matter.

I find Dr. Goldner's observations intriguing and helpful, and I have revisited the issues she raised that day over and over again. I was therefore pleased to accept the editors' invitation to commit some of these thoughts to paper in *Bringing the Plague*. Dr. Goldner's part of our interchange is a presentation of the argument I hope I have just summarized fairly, and mine will be a response to her argument.

It is true that my position derives from a less politically charged hermeneutics than Dr. Goldner's. But it seemed to me at the time of the panel, and still does now, that her criticism of the three of us really ought to be accompanied by a description of the ways in which our thinking contains undesirable biases, or at least unconsidered ones, that could be understood to be the result of not basing our views in a consideration of subject positions. The question should not be whether psychoanalysts *ought* to think in one way or another; we should be focusing instead on specifying the unintended assumptions and effects of the ways in which we actually *do* think. It seems to me that, unless Dr. Goldner lays out the very particular problems she believes are inherent in approaching psychoanalysis as Hoffman does or as I do, her argument comes perilously close to being a claim about the right way to think.

I will do no more than mention this point, though, because I know perfectly well that Dr. Goldner does not intend to make it. I do think her case would be strengthened by a more specific analysis of the views she is criticizing, but I also think it is important for those of us who, like me, are sympathetic to Dr. Goldner's position but do not construct our psychoanalytic thinking as she recommends, to ask ourselves how we have arrived at our positions and to imagine how we can preserve what is most important about them while accepting that we must do more to acknowledge and investigate the crucial constitutive properties of subject positions and their accompanying unconscious identity categories.

## PERSONAL SOURCES

In looking for a way to think about the sources of ideas in a life, one turns to history—and in the case of one's own ideas, one turns to one's own history. It seems to me that the enduring significance of "what you know first" has something important to do with why Dr. Goldner and I approach the relation of postmodernism and psychoanalysis in different ways. In the 1970s I did a clinical internship at a Veterans Administration Hospital in the Midwest as part of my doctoral training in clinical psychology. My very first piece of work, assigned to me by a senior psychiatrist, was the diagnostic assessment of a young man. It was my first piece of clinical writing, and so, after carrying out the requisite projectives and intelligence testing and conducting a couple of interviews, I constructed the report with the greatest care, following the ideal—which I naively assumed everyone who wrote and read such things shared—that clinical descriptions should be precise and detailed, but couched in everyday language. I felt proud that I had the opportunity, finally, to do serious written work in psychology, to participate in the tradition that had been handed down across the generations by such icons of clinical acuity as Dostoevsky, Graham Greene, and Freud.

I was actually quite pleased with the outcome of my work, and so when the psychiatrist who had requested it summoned me to her office, I was unprepared for the upbraiding I received. She told me that what I had given her was quite unacceptable, no more than an untrained person could do, and certainly of no use at all to her. I was to do the whole report over again, adhering to principles more in keeping with the profession I was attempting to join.

This set of instructions may sound obscure, but I thought I understood them, because I added to what she said her barely suppressed rage, her stiff posture, and the even more rigid attitude that told me not to risk asking her even a single question about what she meant. On the basis of the conclusions to which these observations led me, I stayed up late that night translating what I had written into the language of libido theory—a language that is no doubt bad enough in German, but in English becomes a tool so clumsy that any clinical description fashioned in its terms is hopelessly ponderous and uninspired. I knew I was robbing what I had already written of whatever vitality and particularity I had managed to capture and convey.

The following day I typed my revised report and left it in the psychiatrist's mailbox. A day later she called me into her office once again, but this time she proceeded to marvel at how well I suddenly seemed to understand what was required of a psychologist. The report, she averred, was now first-rate. Why? Because now it was *scientific*! It was clear to her that I could not have learned so much so fast, and so she could not escape the conclusion that I had been capable of doing this kind of work before. Why in the world hadn't I given her this report in the first place?

My success was costly. Over the following months, and to my dismay, the psychiatrist lobbied the Psychology Service to assign to me, and to me only, all evaluations she ordered. I managed to evade many of these requests, but by no means all of them. My skill at wielding the language of drive, which had been fine for a beginner, became distressingly good as the months passed, but the words never ceased feeling like sledges, and what I was doing with them continued to make me feel more like an offensive tackle than the writer I had wanted to be. I was relieved to run across several volumes of Norman Mailer that had been secreted for some reason on the highest shelves of the tiny psychiatry library. Largely as a result of trying to escape what I was supposed to be writing, I think I spent more time at the hospital that year reading Mailer than doing anything else.

Along the way, though, I did discover Ernest Schachtel's (1966) scoring method for the Rorschach, which is a phenomenological approach more related to philosophy, poetry, and the practice of psychoanalysis than it is to psychometrics. It is a work of profundity and conviction. I also came across Schachtel's other book, *Metamorphosis* (1959), a series of deeply erudite and aesthetically aware psychoanalytic essays written in poetic and completely untechnical language, that became, for me, one of the half-dozen most influential psychoanalytic texts. Eventually I was also drawn to Harry Stack Sullivan's way of understanding human living, because he (and those who developed his work into a more fully psychoanalytic perspective—see Levenson 1972, 1983, 1991, Lionells et al. 1995, Stern et al. 1995) wrote not about a second-order theory of human existence but about the meanings that accrued from internalized patterns of interpersonal interaction. And whereas theories based in drive tended to portray external reality as the projection of the inner world, interpersonal writers emphasized instead that the internal world is the result of what has happened in one's outer world and how one has understood and participated in those events. It seemed to me in the mid-1970s, when I began psychoanalytic training at the William Alanson White Institute in New York City, the center of interpersonal writing and teaching, that interpersonal psychoanalysts wrote about experience itself, not about a theory once removed from it; you could find in these writings what was actually familiar in day-to-day life. This was a psychoanalysis about meaning, not one that tried to position itself as science as the ego psychology of Hartmann, Kris, Loewenstein, and Rapaport had done. The elegance of ego psychology still drew me, but I was also aware that many analysts had begun to feel that metapsychology—which was, after all, ego psychology's raison d'être—was uncomfortably distant from actual clinical practice. Interpersonal pychoanalysis was the kind of approach the VA psychiatrist would have found godawful, and judging from the work of the inter-personal writers whose work I grew to admire during my psychoanalytic training, it was just the way I wanted to learn to work, think, and write.[1]

## KNOWING HERMENEUTICS FIRST

It was from within this orientation that, as a psychoanalytic candidate and early graduate analyst, I observed the revolution in Freud-ian theory—the death of metapsychology—that I have already mentioned. This reinvigoration of mainstream psychoanalysis fired my imagination. Led by George Klein (1969, 1976), Roy Schafer (1976, 1983), and Merton Gill (1976), and continuing in the work of Donald Spence (1982) and many others, Freudian psychoanalysis was recast as a hermeneutic or narrative discipline, not a scientific one: as psychology or clinical theory, not as metapsychology. I had long thought of psychoanalysis in this way, but I had not had the word "hermeneutic" to describe it. As I began to look into the philosophy that lay behind the work of Schafer and Spence, I discovered a new way of grasping the nature of understanding, a way that was based not in science but in the nature of meaning and the telling of good and useful stories, and that seemed to me to have everything to do with clinical understanding. Eventually I came to feel that hermeneutics, especially the ontological hermeneutics of the philosopher Hans-Georg Gadamer, offered a model not only for the means by which we construct interpretations, but also for what actually transpires in the clinical situation, that is, for clinical process itself (Stern 1990, 1991, 1997).

Gadamer's theory of understanding is a way of approaching the question of how we grasp whatever truth is conveyed by the texts, plays, paintings, or persons we are faced with. The process is inevitably dialogic, a point that was attractive to one who, like me, was immersed in interpersonal psychoanalysis. (These were the years just before the advent of what was to become relational psychoanalysis.)

The concept of the horizon is central. Here is Gadamer's (1960) definition:

> Every finite present has its limitations. We define the concept of "situation" by saying that it represents a standpoint that limits the possibility of vision. Hence an essential part of the concept of situation is the concept of "horizon." The horizon is the range of vision that includes everything that can be seen from a particular vantage point. [p. 269]

Gadamer teaches that one must allow whatever one is trying to understand to pose questions to oneself; one is then open to the questions this phenomenon provokes; one allows whatever is to be grasped to "have its truth" inside one's own experience. In psychoanalysis, this "thing" is whatever the patient is saying and doing, as well as the analyst's own experience. "The working out of the hermeneutical situation means the achievement of the right horizon of enquiry for the questions evoked by the encounter" (p. 269).

That is, in successful episodes of understanding, one manages to grasp the other person's perspective so fully that there is what Gadamer calls a "fusion of horizons." This fusion includes all the relevant experience, which means that, especially in psychoanalysis, it is liable to be deeply laden with affect. The affect may not be labeled as such, but since it cannot actually be separated from the meanings to be understood, it is part and parcel of any act of understanding. We separate thought, language, and affect only at the peril of intellectualization. Experience is the only really relevant category in the hermeneutic examination of understanding. When we break experience into different kinds of pieces, we are liable to lose the experience-near intentions of clinical psychoanalysis and unwittingly substitute abstraction. And so, in this discussion of understanding, I presume the presence of affect, sometimes a great deal of affect, at every single turn.

In the fusion of horizons, then, whether one agrees with the other or not, one understands the other's meaning within the other's frame of reference—the other's affect-laden frame of reference—which one understands fully enough to meld it with one's own: one sees how and why the other means what he or she says. It is the other's frame of reference that Gadamer means when he refers to "the achievement of the right horizon of enquiry."

As a matter of fact, since all experience requires interpretive understanding, each moment, while it may not deserve to be called a fusion of horizons, is at least an imperfect version (sometimes *very* imperfect) of such a thing, a tiny interpretive event, an episode of understanding. The ongoing mutual construction or co-construction of meaning in this way is the process of living itself.

Gadamer intends to discourage unthinking reliance on any method of understanding, including science. Each method—including science, of course—has its value, but that value disappears as soon as we take the method for truth itself, as if there were only one valid way of understanding. Truth is multiple in Gadamer's view, so multiple that several contradictory views are sometimes all simultaneously true. Each method of achieving understanding must itself be subjected to hermeneutic analysis, so that its particular way of dividing the world into observable and invisible—its distribution of light and darkness, its systematic biases—can be known and thereby taken into account. It is not our methods of arriving at understanding that are basic, then; what is basic is the ongoing and dialogic process of hermeneutic analysis, which cannot be described as a technique but as the intention to grasp what the other means, an intention that is actualized in whatever way seems best at any particular moment. No one can really say, Gadamer claims, how it is that we accomplish understanding, how it is that we find a way to allow each view to "have its truth." If this description already seems to you to mirror the nature of interpersonal and relational psychoanalytic inquiry, including our current dissatisfaction with the idea of specifying a standard psychoanalytic technique, then you have gotten ahead of my argument and you see what it was about this non-psychoanalytic literature that drew a psychoanalyst to it.

It is only in language that we can accomplish a fusion of horizons, because it is language that makes our construction of a horizon possible in the first place—and that is so whether the horizon in question is the very particular and shifting horizon that characterizes each person's world or the more generic horizons that define what can be meaningful in any culture. Since horizons do change, understanding is historically specific. Understanding is inevitably historical and contextual, and that is so whether we are considering the tiny context of an individual life or the ideas circulating in a culture. This was one of the insights that excited me so much about Roy Schafer's (1983) work: what is said and done in psychoanalysis takes its meaning as much from the treatment context itself as it does from the events under discussion. An account of a psychoanalytic treatment is the same as its history, and it is continuously being remade. Although Schafer did not take the next step, this line of thought falls quite naturally into the emphasis on co-construction and the transference–countertransference matrix of relational psychoanalysis (e.g., Aron 1996, Mitchell 1988).

On what do we stand, though, when we attempt to grasp the conditions of existence in someone else's world? It is here that Gadamer's ideas are in conflict with certain other strands of postmodern thought, and it is here that what may appear to be a disagreement between Dr. Goldner and me is focused. It is Gadamer's position that, ever since the Enlightenment, truth has been treated as if it is simply there to see, if we can but let the veils fall from our eyes. Truth has been treated for centuries as if it were self-evident, and is only obscured by error, most particularly by the distortions introduced by bias or prejudice. We have constructed a way of life in which prejudice is always suspect, always to be decried and expunged. For Gadamer, because he rejects the possibility of any kind of "objective" or nonconstructed truth, that place on which we stand in the effort to grasp the other's experience is inevitably—prejudice itself.

Think of it this way. Our only means of knowing are the means of our cultures. As a matter of fact, culture is probably best described, according to Gadamer, as an immense set of linguistic criteria for what counts as meaning and experience, and an equally extensive set of linguistic tools to use in invoking these criteria. Culture, in other words, is a defining and enveloping way of knowing, and it is language in which all of this is shaped, or in Foucault's term, sedimented.

So far, so good: this much is familiar in any postmodern view. But Gadamer must go further, because he is not a relativist; he is convinced that there is such a thing as reality. He proposes a perspectival realism, in which reality can never be apprehended directly but only by means of the perspectives offered by language (i.e., by culture). Reality, whatever it actually is, sets constraints beyond which assertions are untrue. But reality does not set truth criteria; many things can be true. Whatever it is, reality is so complex and manifold that it allows many interpretations of the same phenomenon—assuming, of course, that different cultures start by dividing up the world into the same set of phenomena, which Gadamer is quick to recognize they do not.

Here we reach the point I want most to emphasize: in belonging to our cultures, each of us belongs to and participates in traditions of interpretation. If we begin from Gadamer's perspectival realism, these ways of constructing reality must each "have their truth"; each must, in one way or another, capture something valid or true about the world. Now, what is tradition except the sum total of our prejudices? Therefore, we have no choice, says Gadamer, but to ground our new understandings on our prejudices. Our prejudices are the very condition of our being. That is not a problem to be solved, but a reality to be accepted; and so if there is anything wrong here, it is not that we depend on prejudice to understand, but that we incorrectly and unrealistically characterize prejudice as distortion that must be removed.

The nature of understanding, then—the hermeneutic circle—can be described as follows (Stern 1994):

> When we read a text, we try to allow the meanings in the text to reach us. But we can do that only by supplying a context within which to receive them. We must supply "forestructures" of understanding, or "preconceptions," or "prejudices." We must select these contexts; they are not given.
>
> The process of understanding, then, goes something like this: To begin with, a new meaning "hits" us. It is contextless. But because we know something about what this meaning might be on the basis of the preceding moments, or on the basis of past experience with this category of meanings, we have in mind a relatively small collection of contexts that might be appropriate for whatever is going to arise. When the new meaning hits us, we understand it only partially, but we are able to sense enough about it to select the context that we feel fits it best. The meaning is then completed by the context we have selected, the process of understanding has come full circle, and then we are ready for the next attempt to understand. . . .
>
> On first consideration, the hermeneutic circle may make understanding seem impossible. How is it that we vacate our prior understandings enough to allow the perception of new meaning? How can we select the right context within which to hear a new meaning without already know-

ing what the new meaning is? I hope it at least makes sense that the different theories of hermeneutics all revolve around the ways in which solipsism can be avoided. Palmer [1969] puts it this way: "How can a text be understood when the condition for its understanding is already to have understood what it is about?" [p. 25]. The hermeneutic circle is a paradox. [pp. 447–448]

Gadamer's work has received its share of criticism for his willingness to rely on tradition. What do we do with the racist or sexist ideologies, for instance? Do we look for their "truth"? In the view of Georgia Warnke (1987), who offers a fine exposition of, and apologia for, Gadamer's work, Gadamer's answer to such questions was to reiterate

the equation of understanding and dialogue. Opportunism in interpretation is ruled out by the conditions of genuine understanding in which interpreters are concerned with the truth of the subject-matter at issue and are open to the alteration of their perspective that the object may require of them. [p. 118]

Ideology, that is, can be identified by its rigidity; it is not interested in genuine conversation, and it is certainly not interested in change. And so the answer is that yes, we probably should look for the "truth" of racist or sexist ideologies—at least the truth as seen by its authors. We cannot set in motion genuine conversation in these cases, of course, but we may still be able to understand the context in which the views make their own objectionable kind of sense. We do not comprehend even the most odious views until we grasp the world from which they arise. Until we accomplish such understanding, the only tool we have to combat what we disagree with is force.

The problem with this perspective, of course, is that it seems to apply only to views that are actually expressed, opinions that reach explicit existence in language. To think this way seems not to take account of the insidiousness of ideology, the way ideology undercuts freedom while remaining completely invisible. Warnke tells us that the problem is as follows: "Even if hermeneutic understanding can go beyond a focus on the truth of expressed claims to an analysis of the presuppositions behind them, . . . it remains tied to a society's explicit or implicit self-understanding" (p. 116). Gadamer says that hermeneutics can articulate what has not yet been articulated; it can help us formulate the unformulated. But that may not be enough, for, as Warnke also succinctly writes, "Ideological claims do not simply leave the assumptions behind them implicit; they rather articulate them in such a way that it becomes difficult to disentangle the warranted part of the claims from the unwarranted" (p. 115).

Gadamer did not merely accept this objection, of course; he did offer a response. In his eyes, the core of his critics' argument was the following: if we are to observe explicitly the effects of ideology, we must avoid having to submit all truth claims to hermeneutic inspection, because dialogue or conversation—the medium of hermeneutic study—is itself inevitably contaminated by ideology. And so the only way to make such contaminated conversation unnecessary is to assume that right-thinking human society has some essential core, some objective standard of freedom against which we can judge unfreedom. This was, in fact, the view taken by Habermas in his debate with Gadamer (see Warnke [1987] for an account of this interchange); and before Habermas, it was, of course, the view taken by Marx. It is Gadamer's point, though, that as soon as we posit an essence that precedes hermeneutic reflection—that is, as soon as we accept that there is an objective standard for human emancipation—what we are actually subverting is not ideology at all, but our freedom to examine the presuppositions that underlie any and every thought. Any objective definition of freedom excludes from critical inspection some aspect of political life.

Gadamer produced the main body of his work just prior to the wide dissemination of the ideas of Derrida, Foucault, and Lacan. We know now, from these latter writers, that we do not need objectively verifiable standards to judge the presence and influence of ideology. We can instead question the functions of cultural practices by trying to see them as the effects of power, and we do that, at least in part, by investigating the ways in which subject positions, or identity categories, are invisibly defined and supported more by what they are not than by what they are. (Familiar examples are the way heterosexuality has been argued to be defined by its opposition to, and difference from, homosexuality, or the way being white is defined by not being a person of color, or being a man by not being a woman, and so on.)

Gadamer's thought continues to be crucial to me. His conceptions of prejudice and tradition are thoroughly interwoven in my understanding of transference and countertransference. I am still smack in the midst of exploring them (Stern 1997). Nevertheless, over the last few years, as a result of exchanges such as the one Dr. Goldner and I had on the podium that day,[2] I have not been able to rid myself of the nagging and disquieting worry that no matter how thoughtfully Gadamer presents his reliance on tradition, and no matter how clear he is that new understandings require us to formulate our prejudices, disembed ourselves from them, and sacrifice them whenever we have the opportunity, to place tradition at the root of understanding may be unintentionally to court conservatism. And so the upshot is this: the freedoms offered by rejecting a psychoanalysis based in science, by the deconstruction of metapsychology, and by the embrace of a thoroughly clinical theory, may not be freedom enough.

## KNOWING FEMINISM FIRST

In the terms that are relevant to this discussion, then, my first psychoanalytic commitment was to understanding clinical work in interpersonal and hermeneutic terms. It was a commitment I understood to be clinical, aesthetic, and intellectual in nature; in those days its political and moral implications did not seem primary to me. At that time, I did not yet understand that the intellectual and the moral-political are inextricable from one another.

I imagine Dr. Goldner's entry into psychoanalysis somewhat differently. I do not know the details of her history, but I do know that she has been interested in social theory for many years. Her psychoanalytic work on sex and gender is well known. It is my impression that during the years in the 1970s when I was becoming fascinated with hermeneutics, she was deeply involved in the morals, politics, and intellectual life of feminism.

In its beginning, feminism was more or less exclusively occupied with what it meant to be a woman and how women's experience was shaped. Eventually, though, while this initial commitment was of course maintained, the interests of many feminists widened. One of the reasons was that the study of sex and gender had brought more and more attention to the view that these two phenomena were relatively independent of one another, meaning that the study of women and the study of men each required more categories than one. A second and related broadening influence was that more and more feminists began to be impressed with the idea that the identity of women could not be considered separate from the consideration of other identity categories, including men. Today, it is my impression that many feminist writers base their studies not only on the identities of women, but also on the recognition that everyone organizes meaning around unconscious aspects of all kinds of gender identity, and since all identity categories are interwined, each playing its part in defining the others, this point means that the study of women requires the study of identity categories that are not-woman as well. Thinking this way may make it more natural for feminist psychoanalysts than most other analysts to consider the significance of subject positions in discourse, including many subject positions that are not expressly concerned with either sex or gender. Through the feminist psychoanalysts I know and have read, who are among those interested in a wide variety of unconscious identity politics, I have become much more aware of the way identity categories constitute subjectivity.

Here we reach what may be a point of contradiction with Gadamer's hermeneutics, for in the psychology of subject positions and identity categories, it is what is *absent*—the operations of power, which are exactly what is most difficult to describe—that must be known. What is *present*—tradition, or the sum of the prejudices of a culture, the history of a culture's interpretive understanding—is precisely what is suspect, because, as we have learned from Foucault, cultures are both parents and offspring to unconscious power relations.

And yet if we do not stand on the ground of the traditions of our cultures in analyzing the operations of power, on what ground do we stand? There is no other. Gadamer's hermeneutics seems to offer too little consideration of power, but the psychology of identity categories, while it does remedy that problem, seems to have no choice but to rely on tradition. If we are to describe the workings of power, we must find ways to reinvigorate and redirect the only experiential tools at our disposal. The interpretive traditions of our cultures are the only ores there are to mine. In clinical psychoanalysis and psychotherapy, analysts deconstruct the narratives their patients have always told about their lives, along with some of their own, and analysts also deconstruct the narratives that, only in retrospect, they find they and their patients have been telling about the analytic relationship itself. But analysts also tell new stories along the way; they cannot help it. Narrative abhors a void, so that as soon as one story is deconstructed, another flows in to fill the space, like water to a level. One of the consequences is that, as Muriel Dimen (1997) writes in a different context (she is referring here to narratives of gender identity and development in a wider discussion of women's desire), we and our patients "cannot help but (re)present the normative structures [we] mean to deconstruct" (p. 543). We cannot escape power, in other words, only struggle in it and with it. But that much we can do. Treating theories of gender as aspects of tradition, as Dimen also goes on to say:

> At the same time, however, theories of gender as social construction index its historical multiplicity, revealing women's desire as the contradictory thing it is—present here and absent there, flaring here, doused there, flickering still elsewhere, its ambiguity, difficulty, and elusiveness the alternate truth of all, of anyone's desire. [p. 543]

The sum of our interpretive traditions, that is, no matter how determined they may be by the relations of power, are the only "indices" we have.

## TWO ORIENTATIONS TO UNCONSCIOUS MEANING AND INTERPRETATION

And so, in relational psychoanalysis, we have two orientations to the problems of unconscious meaning and its interpretation. Each of them seems to correspond to one of the ways of coming to a postmodern psychoanalysis, to "what you know first": the *hermeneutic/narrative orientation*, often known as *constructivism*, seems to be the approach to postmodern psychoanalysis based in respect for the truth of art and aesthetics, a particular attraction to the details of clinical process, and a dissatisfaction with science as the arbiter of what counts as experience; and what I will call (adapting Foucault to the purpose) the *power/knowledge orientation*, or *deconstruction*, seems to have been adopted by those whose way into psychoanalysis was influenced most by feminism and other critiques of the social order.

## The Hermeneutic/Narrative Orientation, or Constructivism

The first orientation arises from the intention (now more or less fulfilled, at least in some sectors) to unseat science as the sole arbiter of truth. This way of thinking is a hermeneutics of clinical process that de-emphasizes metapsychologies and emphasizes instead the generative value of the traditions that make up cultures. It focuses on the construction of experience and understanding, looking to mutual understanding and agreement on meaning among the community of interpreters as criteria of truth value. Narrative is often the metaphor used for the understandings we make, and the emphasis is on the means of this understanding from one moment to the next. The unconscious is portrayed as that which has not yet been reflected upon in language. The task, in this orientation, is finding or formulating the truth value of that which is already available in some form or other (i.e., what is available may be unconscious, but unformulated). Formulation may entail the construction of meanings that did not exist before, but these meanings grow from pre-reflective experience that actually did exist. One understands from within the position one already occupies; unconscious or pre-reflective meanings are in some way embedded in what is already visible. In this orientation, the most basic analysis of all human phenomena is hermeneutic analysis, and that would include the analysis of power relations. In a dialogue conducted between two people sincerely trying to converse, even power relations should become understandable. The dialogic understanding of hermeneutic analysis is primary, and the process by which it occurs is a constructive process. New meanings are constructions.

## The Power/Knowledge Orientation, or Deconstruction

The second orientation arises from the intention to make psychoanalysis sensitive to political life and the operations of power. The primary activity is the analysis of the individualized, unconscious political effects of each patient's life history, embedded as it is in the social order, and the politically motivated construction of each analytic pair's analytic history. This clinical history is also viewed as embedded in its wider social context. What does it mean, for example, for a man to treat a woman, or vice versa? A gay man or lesbian treated by a straight therapist? By a gay or lesbian therapist? What does it mean for a man to *choose* to be treated by a woman, and vice versa? And so on. In this orientation, like the other, there is a de-emphasis of metapsychology, but in this case it is replaced with an emphasis on power as a productive (Foucauldian) force in the construction of experience. Instead of looking for the truth value embedded in what *is* presented, the task here is finding the truth value that is *not* presented, the meanings that are unavailable—perhaps both consciously *and* unconsciously—precisely because they are prevented by what *is* available. Meanings that are operative but invisible are not embedded in what is already known, but actually missing. In this view, one does not aim to understand from within the position one already occupies, but tries instead to understand how the position one occupies has already been shaped by power; the question is how one is always already in power's grip.

The power/knowledge orientation would probably encourage us to analyze hermeneutics itself as an expression of power. The hermeneutic acceptance of the possibility of mutuality, and the optimism that lies behind the assumption that we can construct new and better narratives merely on the basis of our desire to understand one another, would be portrayed as too easy: at best, well-intentioned but naïve, at worst a denial or obfuscation of the operations of power, a tool of those who already occupy powerful positions and want to keep them. Foucault tells us that the influence of power is often, or even usually, unconscious, but of course the fact that its exercise may be "unintentional" hardly relieves us of moral responsibility, and the unconsciousness of the whole operation only magnifies its effects. Gadamer's hermeneutics, it would have to be argued, so firmly planted in its confidence in honest dialogue, in its position that truth arises through grasping the view of the other, would never have been invented by the powerless. Those with little power know that truth depends on who you are talking to: you can accept that the powerful *believe* they want to understand you, but you're liable to be trampled if you don't maintain your confidence that you know better. Depending on the power disparities between the parties conducting a dialogue, then—disparities that might not even be observable by the parties themselves—the dialogic understanding of hermeneutic analysis is often suspect. It is the analysis of power relations that is primary, not hermeneutic analysis, and the process by which this kind of analysis takes place is not constructive, but *de*constructive. New meanings are less the outcome of a process of attempting to create new meanings than they are the result of the flexibility that arises when old, arbitrary meanings are challenged and taken apart.

## A CLINICAL PSYCHOANALYSIS
## THAT BRIDGES THE DIFFERENCE

Are we confronted, then, with just another version of the issue that led Dr. Goldner to take pen in hand in the first place? I don't think so. Dr. Goldner begins with the observation that some psychoanalytic positions take into account the unconscious relations of power (i.e., identity categories and subject positions) and others do not. It is hard to disagree there, but we can now see that this observation is only half the story. We could just as validly observe that some positions explicitly take into account dialogic understanding more than others.

In psychoanalysis—at least in relational psychoanalysis—mutuality and dialogic understanding were from the beginning keystones in the theoretical arch. The by-now familiar claim that the analyst's personal participation in the treatment is inevitable, continuous, and even continuously unconscious leads to the equally typical relational and interpersonal position that the analyst's experience is never transparent to his or her own scrutiny, that he or she is always involved with the patient in ways that will not become knowable until later—if, indeed, they are ever known at all. Under any circumstances but especially under these, mutuality and dialogue would seem to be essential, because the analyst, just like the patient, needs to listen to the patient's impressions of him or her and wonder about his or her impact. For the process to be mutative, in other words, the two participants must understand one another.

That is a deceptively simple thing to say, and yet one way to read the first seventy years of psychoanalysis is as a history of ignoring it. Interpersonal experience in the Freudian models of those years was understood as the externalization of interior life—but only the patient's life. Apart from the expectable comprehension of what was actually said, there was usually no need for the patient to understand why the analyst took the positions he or she did, because the analyst represented authority. While it is common practice in many fields to believe that

benign authorities, if they are to help those over whom they have control, must understand the poor souls, it is equally *un*common for it to
be considered important for the powerless to understand those in power.
Such a thing is irrelevant at best. Insistence on it is probably disrespect-
ful, perhaps mutinous. And so, for many years in psychoanalysis, the
analyst may have needed to examine his or her experience for evidence
of the patient's projections, but unless the analyst was insufficiently
analyzed and therefore inappropriately involved with the patient, the
analyst's experience was not believed to be directly affected, and the
patient was not believed to have anything of import to contribute to
the analyst's understanding of him- or herself.

There was often a certain subtlety to this one-sided consideration
of the analytic relationship. For instance, there was no denial, even in
those days, that the analyst's experience was *responsive* to the patient's
presence, as "anyone's" (so the story went) would be; good clinicians have
always recognized the significance of unconscious communication. But
this responsiveness was understood to be more passive than participatory;
it was seen as a registration of the patient's impact, not direct and active
involvement. Any active involvement with the patient was condemned
as neurotic contamination of the otherwise pristine analytic field. Registration and responsiveness are very different, indeed, especially when
we add the usual relational insistence that the analyst's expectable involvement is replete with unconscious agendas of the analyst's own.

To have the goal that analyst and patient understand one another,
however, is not necessarily to require that they agree. They do not even
necessarily have to characterize the way they treat one another in just
the same way. As a matter of fact, the case could be (and has been)
made that one of the most important criteria for termination is that the
participants can freely and openly disagree about their perceptions of
one another (e.g., Wolstein 1987).

The only fruitful disagreements in clinical psychoanalysis are those
in which the analyst and the analysand each eventually understand why
the other takes the position he or she does. Without such understanding, both agreement and disagreement are specious, more the expressions
of an interpersonal process that needs to be analyzed than anything else.
We could go as far as to say that for the relational psychoanalyst, so wary
of prescriptive approaches, the detailed clinical exegesis of the very
particular successes and failures of mutuality and dialogic understand-

ing in any single treatment is as close as one can come to describing clinical technique.

And so here we come full circle, to Gadamer, for what I have just said about the conduct of clinical psychoanalysis in a relational model is, as I warned before, entirely congruent with Gadamer's thought. Gadamer's position is that all understanding comes about as a result of the successful negotiation of the hermeneutic circle. I have already suggested that Gadamer may spend too little time discussing the obstacles to this negotiation, obstacles that include the ways identity categories shape clinical interaction, but it turns out that it is precisely in the examination of these obstacles that relational psychoanalysis comes into the picture. In the hands of a thoughtful clinician and a collaborative patient, relational psychoanalysis is a means (a deeply imperfect means) of disembedding the psychoanalyst and the patient from some of their respective unseen expectations of one another, expectations that include the effects of unconscious subject positions.

It seems that we have here something like a dialectic, then, or if not a formal dialectic, at least some kind of a relationship between a foreground and background, between terms that each require the other. On the one hand, we must assess the contribution of identity positions to the ongoing structuring of the clinical interaction, but on the other hand, we can do that only by struggling toward mutual understanding. We must then simultaneously admit that if this "mutual understanding" has even a prayer of being valid, it must be a continuous struggle with the recognition of its own incompleteness and inadequacy—that is, with the unconscious limitations that are inevitably imposed by the various unconscious aspects of who our social worlds have decreed us to be. If I put this in the terms of the two conceptions of unconscious meaning and interpretation I described above, it looks like this to me: The contribution of the power/knowledge or deconstructivist position to clinical work can only be formulated by applying the constructivist approach, and the constructivist approach must constantly be questioned, because its adequacy is always being undermined by the unconscious power relations it embodies.

My answer to Dr. Goldner, then, is that she and I both have a point. She is right that positions such as mine did not grow from an appreciation of the formative significance of unconscious identity categories, but our positions did grow from the other means by which postmodernism and psychoanalysis can be related—that is, from an appreciation of the hermeneutic process of clinical understanding. Dr. Goldner needs to add my perspective to hers, just as I need to add hers to mine. Psychoanalysis needs both, and they need one another. The power/knowledge position needs the mutuality of the constructivist position if the power/knowledge position is to be a clinical theory, and the constructivist approach needs the doubt and skepticism of the power/knowledge perspective if it is to preserve the precious awareness that important parts of ourselves will always be strange, incomprehensible, and even destructive. Relational psychoanalysis must not be allowed to degenerate into an easy and empty therapeutic optimism in which, if two people are just willing enough, "everything" (whatever that would be) can be understood and melted away. We need to be continuously reminded that our motives can be mysterious and dark, that we are active participants in social projects we would prefer to believe belong only to "other" people. We need to preserve the capacity of psychoanalysis to disturb us, revealing our secret complicity in fantasies we reject and activities we abhor. The hermeneutic pole keeps possibility alive; the power/knowledge perspective keeps us honest.

And yet, as fitting as I believe it is to put the problem this way, significant differences do remain, differences that just will not so tidily fold into a dialectic. All is not conciliation here; there exists an unavoidable and indissoluble tension between the two points of view (see also the interchange between Sass [1995a,b] and Barratt [1995a,b]). The constructivist view, on the one hand, is that we must find ways to be open to the untapped and unformed possibilities of tradition and its prejudices, while from the power/knowledge perspective the word "tradition" is merely a way to refer to the sum total of the power relations in a culture, power relations that must be deconstructed in order to learn anything that really matters. In one case, we must look to the community of knowledgeable interpreters as the arbiter and carrier of tradition; in the other, we must devise critiques of ideology that expose the ways in which the community of interpreters is held hostage by ideology—indeed, perhaps even defined by ideology. One perspective trusts and values genuine conversation above all else; the other instead places its highest value on the revelation of the invisible power relations that, like the language that makes up the interchange, make conversation as much a straitjacket as a means of mutual understanding. I have tried to show that these oppositions can coexist, and that there are ways in which understanding what each has to offer softens their differences. I have even tried to say that their coexistence can be mutually beneficial. But the two perspectives do approach the problems differently: there is no getting around that point. Perhaps the most optimistic way of putting the issue is to say that, for coexistence to be useful, it must be explicitly recognized, and for it to be recognized, we must give the same degree of our attention to how the two ways of thinking diverge as we expend on noticing the ways in which they contribute to the same project.

## WHAT YOU *REALLY* KNOW FIRST

I have suggested that Dr. Goldner and I arrived at our positions because of what we knew first: she arrived through feminism, and I through hermeneutics and its exegesis of clinical process. But is it enough to say that? *Why* did I begin in hermeneutics and not feminism? *Why* did Dr. Goldner start out in feminism and not hermeneutics? *Why*, on the panel that inspired this exchange between Dr. Goldner and me, did the two women (Dr. Grey and Dr. Goldner) take the power/knowledge orientation, while the two men (Dr. Hoffman and I) took the constructivist tack? Part of the answer must be that feminists tend to be women, of course, so that women tend to be disproportionately represented among postmodern psychoanalysts with the power/knowledge orientation, at least those in the United States and Britain (besides Goldner and the editors of this volume, I think right away of Jessica Benjamin, Muriel Dimen, Jane Flax, Adrienne Harris, Juliet Mitchell, and Jacqueline Rose).

But I have begun to think that there may be something reciprocal on the other side of the equation, something rather unexpected: Is there something about hermeneutics in psychoanalysis that attracts *men?* When I thought about it, I realized that virtually every one of the writers who have made explicitly hermeneutic/narrativist/constructivist contributions to psychoanalysis has been a man. The point surprised me enough that I feel it requires explicit scholarly documentation. And so, to begin with, there were Roy Schafer (1976, 1983, 1992), Donald Spence (1982), Merton Gill (1976, 1995), George Klein (1969, 1976), and Robert Steele (1979); and later on came (just to name a few) James Phillips (1991), Carlo Strenger (1991), Philip Cushman (1995), Stephen Mitchell (Greenberg and Mitchell 1983, Mitchell 1988, 1993, 1997),

Irwin Hoffman (1999), Robert Stolorow and his colleagues (see Atwood and Stolorow [1984] for the most explicit statement of their philosophical views), and Louis Sass (1988, 1992, Sass and Woolfolk 1988). The only woman I can think of who has been a significant contributor to this literature is Donna Orange (1995), and this during a period in which women have become as prominent as men in psychoanalysis as a whole.[3] Furthermore, this is a group of men with special relevance to the topic at hand, because some of them are among the most prominent interpreters of postmodernism in contemporary psychoanalysis. Is it possible that, among those interested in the relation of psychoanalysis and postmodernism, the constructivists tend to be men, while the power/knowledge group is more heavily weighted with women?

As all psychologists once had to learn in their courses on experimental method, you can't support a hypothesis with the same data you used to derive it in the first place. And so I tried to imagine a little test of my observation. What might serve the purpose?

I then remembered that a very good book of essays and discussions called *Hermeneutics and Psychological Theory: Interpretive Perspectives on Personality, Psychotherapy, and Psychopathology* (Messer et al. 1988) was sitting on my shelf. Aha! Granted, not all the writers were psychoanalysts, but many of them were. I counted seventeen contributors. Fifteen were men and two were women, a finding that seemed to lend at least moderate support to my hypothesis. However, then I noticed that three of the writers were from the other camp: they had been brought into the project as contributors to the final section of the book, "Critique of Ideology."

Of these three, two were the women.

'Nuf said.

So why *are* such a preponderance of hermeneutic psychoanalysts men? That is a question that would be worth a paper of its own. I don't say this because I am ready to write that paper, however. I actually have no idea why there should be an association of men and hermeneutics. Perhaps Dr. Goldner's speculations about the matter are helpful here. For the time being, though, the best I can do is to recognize that the difference between "knowing hermeneutics first" and "knowing feminism first," however heuristic it is, is by no means the last word on the origins of the constructivist and power/knowledge orientations.

No matter how open-minded the practitioners of any conceptual approach may be, their thinking is marked—limited—by its origins, though often in ways that escape detection; this is the lesson of Foucault. People, too, are marked by their origins, of course; that is the lesson of Freud. Like change in clinical psychoanalysis, change in the life of the mind—change in our cherished ideas—is more basically a matter of loss than a matter of growth. Taking on the new is often not so difficult, really; it tends to happen by itself as soon as we are able to allow it. But giving up the old is another thing. The great difficulty is becoming able to see that the old is there in the first place, and thus that it *can* be given up. In their different ways, that is the aim of both the constructionist and the deconstructionist orientations to meaning.

In the poem I have quoted in my epigraph, the little girl who speaks the words "What you know first stays with you, my Papa says" is preparing to move away from her farm home on the prairie, the only place she has ever known, a place that has been good for her, to a new and unfamiliar land far away, where (she is told by her parents) the sounds of the ocean will replace the soughing of the wind in the one tree she can see and hear out her window. She will lose all her friends and all the farm animals she knows, all the sights and sounds of her everyday world. She thinks long and hard about running away and living hidden by a stream in the countryside, finding one grownup or another to take care of her. But eventually she gathers a little bag of dust and a couple of leaves to remember by, and with which to teach her baby brother, who will be too young to remember, and she moves on with the rest of her family. At the end of the story we are meant to believe she will always love what she knew first. But we are also meant to believe that she will find a new home wherever she arrives, and that she will create it by bringing to it her capacity to love the old one.

In one way or another, we are all constantly in the midst of choosing whether or not to face the fact that we must leave home. Ironically enough it is Heidegger, a man too ready to accept the comforts of belonging to the regime in power (and without whom neither Gadamer's work nor Foucault's would have been possible), who is probably more responsible than anyone else for our conviction today that an authentic life requires the acceptance of not-being-at-home-in-the-world (*Unheimlichkeit*). Dr. Goldner, among others, has forced me to broaden my view and thus to leave yet another home of mine, and I am grateful to her for that. May we all have the courage, wherever we arrive, to make home anew, however precarious, temporary, and partial our postmodern sympathies make us recognize homes to be.

## NOTES

1. Besides Schachtel (1959, 1966) and Sullivan (1940, 1953, 1954, 1956, 1962, 1964), at that time this group included (among others) Erich Fromm (1941, 1947, 1951, 1955, 1960), Frieda Fromm-Reichmann (1955), Clara Thompson (1964), Edward Tauber (Tauber and Green 1959), Leslie Farber (1966), Harold Searles (1979), Edgar Levenson (1972), Erwin Singer (1965), and Benjamin Wolstein (1954, 1959).

2. I thank Muriel Dimen, Adrienne Harris, Emmanuel Kaftal, and Lawrence Jacobson for many other influential conversations in the same vein, especially those concerning Lacan.

3. It is true that Jessica Benjamin studied with Jürgen Habermas, one of the most prominent hermeneutic philosophers of our day. This fact does not contradict my thesis, though, but supports it, since Habermas has expressed sharp disagreement with Gadamer over precisely the issue at hand: how to deny ideology the power to distort human freedom. Habermas says we must define emancipation first, in absolute terms, and only then turn to hermeneutics. The nature of human freedom, in other words, must be established prior to the attempt to understand. Only in this way can we even hope to prevent ideology from overtaking and systematically distorting hermeneutic understanding in the service of power. Despite sharing a great deal with Gadamer, then, Habermas, who is one of the few hermeneutic philosophers to address psychoanalysis (he actually uses psychoanalysis as a model for what hermeneutic understanding should be), is one of the staunchest advocates of the power/knowledge position outlined in the text (see especially Habermas 1971), as is Benjamin herself, of course.

## REFERENCES

Aron, L. (1996). *A Meeting of Minds: Mutuality in Psychoanalysis.* Hillsdale, NJ: Analytic Press.

Atwood, G. E., and Stolorow, R. D. (1984). *Structures of Subjectivity: Explorations in Psychoanalytic Phenomenology.* Hillsdale, NJ: Analytic Press.

Barratt, B. B. (1995a). Review of *Madness and Modernism: Insanity in the Light of Modern Art, Literature, and Thought* by Louis A. Sass. *Psychoanalytic Dialogues* 5:113–121.

——— (1995b). Reply to Louis A. Sass. *Psychoanalytic Dialogues* 5:137–144.

Cushman, P. (1995). *Constructing the Self, Constructing America: A Cultural History of Psychotherapy*. Reading, MA: Addison-Wesley.

Dimen, M. (1997). The engagement between psychoanalysis and feminism: a report from the front. *Contemporary Psychoanalysis* 33: 527–548.

Farber, L. (1966). *The Ways of the Will*. New York: Basic Books.

Fromm, E. (1941). *Escape from Freedom*. New York: Rinehart.

——— (1947). *Man for Himself*. New York: Rinehart.

——— (1950). *Psychoanalysis and Religion*. New Haven, CT: Yale University Press.

——— (1951). *The Forgotten Language*. New York: Holt, Rinehart and Winston.

——— (1955). *The Sane Society*. New York: Holt, Rinehart and Winston.

——— (1960). Psychoanalysis and Zen Buddhism. In *Zen Buddhism and Psychoanalysis*, ed. D. T. Suzuki, E. Fromm, and R. DeMartino, pp. 77–141. New York: Grove.

Fromm-Reichmann, F. (1955). *Principles of Intensive Psychotherapy*. Chicago: University of Chicago Press.

Gadamer, H.-G. (1960). *Truth and Method*, trans. and ed. G. Barden and J. Cumming. New York: Seabury Press, 1975.

Gill, M. M. (1976). Psychology is not metapsychology. In *Psychology vs. Metapsychology: Psychoanalytic Essays in Memory of George S. Klein. Psychological Issues*, Monograph 36, pp. 71–105. New York: International Universities Press.

——— (1995). *Psychoanalysis in Transition*. Hillsdale, NJ: Analytic Press.

Greenberg, J. R., and Mitchell, S. A. (1983). *Object Relations in Psychoanalytic Theory*. Cambridge, MA: Harvard University Press.

Habermas, J. (1971). *Knowledge and Human Interests*, trans. J. Shapiro. Boston: Beacon.

Hoffman, I. Z. (1999). *Ritual and Spontaneity in the Psychoanalytic Process*. Hillsdale, NJ: Analytic Press.

Klein, G. (1969). Freud's two theories of sexuality. In *Clinical-Cognitive Psychology: Models and Integrations*, ed. L. Breger, pp. 136–181. Englewood Cliffs, NJ: Prentice Hall.

——— (1976). *Psychoanalytic Theory: An Exploration of Essentials*. New York: International Universities Press.

Levenson, E. A. (1972). *The Fallacy of Understanding*. New York: Basic Books.

——— (1983). *The Ambiguity of Change*. New York: Basic Books.

—— (1991). *The Purloined Self: Selected Papers*, ed. A. Feiner. New York: Contemporary Psychoanalysis Books.

Lionells, M., Fiscalini, J., Mann, C. M., and Stern, D. B., eds. (1995). *The Handbook of Interpersonal Psychoanalysis*. Hillsdale, NJ: Analytic Press.

MacLachlan, P. (1955). *What You Know First*. New York: HarperCollins.

Messer, S. B., Sass, L. A., and Woolfolk, R. L., eds. (1988). *Hermeneutics and Psychological Theory*. New Brunswick, NJ: Rutgers University Press.

Mitchell, S. A. (1988). *Relational Concepts in Psychoanalysis*. Cambridge, MA: Harvard University Press.

—— (1993). *Hope and Dread in Psychoanalysis*. New York: Basic Books.

—— (1997). *Influence and Autonomy in Psychoanalysis*. Hillsdale, NJ: Analytic Press.

Orange, D. M. (1995). *Emotional Understanding: Studies in Psychoanalytic Epistemology*. New York: Guilford.

Palmer, R. E. (1969). *Hermeneutics: Interpretation Theory in Schleiermacher, Dilthey, Heidegger, and Gadamer*. Evanston, IL: Northwestern University Press.

Phillips, J. (1991). Hermeneutics in psychoanalysis: review and reconsideration. *Psychoanalysis and Contemporary Thought* 14:371–424.

Sass, L. A. (1988). Humanism, hermeneutics, and humanistic psychoanalysis: differing conceptions of subjectivity. *Psychoanalysis and Contemporary Thought* 12:433–504.

—— (1992). The epic of disbelief: the postmodernist turn in contemporary psychoanalysis. In *Psychology and Postmodernism*, ed. S. Kvale, pp. 166–182. London: Sage.

—— (1995a). Review of *Psychoanalysis and the Postmodern Impulse: Knowing and Being since Freud's Psychology* by Barnaby Barratt. *Psychoanalytic Dialogues* 5:123–136.

—— (1995b). Reply to Barnaby B. Barratt. *Psychoanalytic Dialogues* 5:145–149.

Sass, L. A., and Woolfolk, R. (1988). Psychoanalysis and the hermeneutic turn: a critique of *Narrative Truth and Historical Truth*. *Journal of the American Psychoanalytic Association* 36:429–454.

Schachtel, E. (1959). *Metamorphosis*. New York: Basic Books.

—— (1966). *Experiential Foundations of Rorschach's Test*. New York: Basic Books.

Schafer, R. (1976). *A New Language for Psychoanalysis*. New Haven, CT: Yale University Press.

—— (1983). *The Analytic Attitude*. New York: Basic Books.

—— (1992). *Retelling a Life*. New York: Basic Books.

Searles, H. F. (1979). *Countertransference and Related Subjects*. New York: International Universities Press.

Singer, E. (1965). *Key Concepts in Psychotherapy*. New York: Basic Books.

Spence, D. P. (1982). *Narrative Truth and Historical Truth: Meaning and Interpretation in Psychoanalysis*. New York: Norton.

Steele, R. S. (1979). Psychoanalysis and hermeneutics. *International Review of Psycho-Analysis* 6:389–411.

Stern, D. B. (1990). Courting surprise: unbidden perceptions in clinical practice. *Contemporary Psychoanalysis* 26:452–478.

——— (1991). A philosophy for the embedded analyst: Gadamer's hermeneutics and the social paradigm of psychoanalysis. *Contemporary Psychoanalysis* 27:51–80.

——— (1994). Empathy is interpretation (and who ever said it wasn't?). *Psychoanalytic Dialogues* 4:441–471.

——— (1997) *Unformulated Experience: From Dissociation to Imagination in Psychoanalysis*. Hillsdale, NJ: Analytic Press.

Stern, D. B., Mann, C. H., Kantor, S., and Schlesinger, G., eds. (1995). *Pioneers of Interpersonal Psychoanalysis*. Hillsdale, NJ: Analytic Press.

Stolorow, R. D., Brandchaft, B., and Atwood, G. E. (1987). *Psychoanalytic Treatment: An Intersubjective Approach*. Hillsdale, NJ: Analytic Press.

Strenger, C. (1991). Between hermeneutics and science: an essay on the epistemology of psychoanalysis. *Psychological Issues*, Monograph 59. New York: International Universities Press.

Sullivan, H. S. (1940). *Conceptions of Modern Psychiatry*. New York: Norton, 1953.

——— (1953). *The Psychiatric Interview*, ed. H. S. Perry and M. L. Gawel. New York: Norton.

——— (1954). *The Interpersonal Theory of Psychiatry*, ed. H. S. Perry and M. L. Gawel. New York: Norton.

——— (1956). *Clinical Studies in Psychiatry*, ed. H. S. Perry, M. L. Gawel, and M. Gibbon. New York: Norton.

——— (1962). *Schizophrenia as a Human Process*. New York: Norton.

——— (1964). *The Fusion of Psychiatry and Social Science*. New York: Norton.

Tauber, E. S., and Green, M. R. (1959). *Prelogical Experience*. New York: Basic Books.

Thompson, C. M. (1964). *Interpersonal Psychoanalysis: The Selected Papers of Clara M. Thompson*, ed. M. R. Green. New York: Basic Books.

Warnke, G. (1987). *Gadamer: Hermeneutics, Tradition and Reason*. Stanford, CA: Stanford University Press.

Wolstein, B. (1954). *Transference*. New York: Grune & Stratton.

——— (1959). *Countertransference*. New York: Grune & Stratton.

——— (1987). Anxiety and the psychic center of the psychoanalytic self. *Contemporary Psychoanalysis* 23:631–658.

# 6

# Cultural Hierarchies, Splitting, and the Heterosexist Unconscious

*Lynne Layton*

In *Who's That Girl? Who's That Boy?: Clinical Practice Meets Postmodern Gender Theory* (Layton 1998), I put forth a theory of gender identity that drew both on work by relational analytic feminists, such as Benjamin (1988), Chodorow (1978), Dimen (1991), Goldner (1991), and Harris (1991), as well as on work by poststructuralist feminists, particularly Butler (1990a,b, 1993, 1995). The impetus for my project was the sense that the relational feminist theories of Chodorow, Benjamin, and others were being relegated to the dustbin of history because of their essentialism, heterosexism, and an array of other charges brought against them by postmodern and poststructuralist gender theorists. As a clinician, I was far from ready to throw their work out because I found that much that Chodorow and Benjamin had theorized as characterizing the psychic conflicts and psychic structure of men and women was helpful in understanding my clients. For instance, it did seem to me that many men exhibited a defensive kind of autonomy built on a suppression of dependency needs. I also found Benjamin's thoughts about gender and heterosexual love compelling: that is, that a healthy desire to hold wishes for both assertion and recognition in tension breaks down in a culture built on gender inequality, one in which mothers are not endowed with the subjectivity necessary to be either a recognizing agent or a recognized subject. Fathers, she and Chodorow both argued, recognize the subjective agency of boys but not of girls. In such a world, Benjamin (1988) wrote, masculinity is grounded in an omnipotent denial of dependency, omnipotence being the version of assertion that emerges when the assertion–recognition dialectic breaks down. Femininity, on the other hand, is grounded in the distorted version of pure recognition: submission. Heterosexual desire emerges in this context of two half-people, each seeking to restore the dialectic in which a subject asserts a self that is recognized by another subject whose assertions are also recognized. Benjamin finds that the breakdown of the assertion–recognition dialectic leads to relations of domination and submission and to a relational logic of doer and done-to that shores up many aspects of a hierarchically organized capitalist–patriarchal system.

Not only did I find the work of these relational feminists useful in understanding my predominantly heterosexual, white, middle-class clients, but I also found it helpful in understanding the conflicts presented in works of fiction and film created by African-American artists such as Toni Morrison, or by working-class lesbian artists such as Dorothy Allison. So postmodern claims that Chodorow's and Benjamin's theories are white, middle-class, and heterosexist were not fully convincing to me and did not warrant my either ignoring their work or restricting its clinical use to the white, middle-class, heterosexual client.

At the same time, I found compelling postmodern claims for the fluidity of gender, the multiplicity of psychic and cultural life, the importance of understanding gender as always already classed, raced, and sexed. It became clear to me that the category "woman" was usually deployed by white, middle-class, heterosexual thinkers whose theories described only women like themselves while suggesting, by use of the category, that *all* women were like themselves. I was particularly engaged by the work of Butler (1990a,b), who, drawing on Foucault (1973, 1979, 1980), alerts clinicians to the way psychoanalytic narratives of development tend to reinforce a sexist and heterosexist status quo. Foucault and Butler suggest that clinicians do not just discover what their patients are about, they create it. For example, Butler is very clear on the fact that, in any given time period, only certain kinds of people count as fully human subjects, while others are considered deviants; in any given time period, only certain modes of agency are conceivable. Political realities dictate what counts and what doesn't, and clinicians, along with other cultural experts, enforce particular views of normalcy.

With regard to gender, poststructuralist feminists maintain that the category *masculinity* is in no way the mutually exclusive opposite of *femininity*; rather, masculinity exists as a category only by defining itself as what is not feminine. The two categories are meaningless except in relation to one another. Further, the relation between the categories is hierarchical, a differential power relation. The defining characteristics of masculinity have cultural value; what masculinity repudiates has less value. In general, the poststructuralist position holds that the first identity element in the pairs male/female, white/nonwhite, heterosexual/homosexual, middle class/working class is the element that holds the power; it is culturally defined as it is by splitting off and projecting onto the other unwanted attributes (attributes both disdained and desired precisely *because* they are prohibited to those who hold the dominant position: for example, emotionality becomes the despised *and* longed for antithesis of rational objectivity. For an analysis of the way this ambivalence works psychically and culturally, see Bhabha [1983]). The power to ensure that such splitting will continue to take place on the psychic level inheres in the institutionalized racism, sexism, class inequality, and homophobia that mark the dominant culture.

As many cultural theorists have argued in the past ten or fifteen years (e.g., Connell 1995, Higginbotham 1992), masculinity and femininity do not exist in isolation from other identity elements: black working-class heterosexual femininity, black middle-class heterosexual femininity, and black working- or middle-class homosexual femininity are four different ways of experiencing gender. Thus, when speaking of dominant social categories, cultural theorists have taught us that it is more accurate to say that it is upper-class white, heterosexual masculinity—rather than just masculinity—that wields the most clout. Indeed, the former is defined by repudiating all the other possible combinations of masculinity and femininity. On the cultural level, it is this repudiation that marks these categories as products of splitting.

In putting the two bodies of work into conversation, I argued that the hallmark of much of both relational analytic feminism and poststructuralist feminism is the premise that dominant categories of gender, race, sexuality, and class are derived from processes of splitting that are mandated by culturally sanctioned sexism, racism, heterosexism, and classism. Relational analytic feminists provide a sense of how the cultural processes described by poststructuralist feminists work on the psychic level, on the level of how these categories are lived. On the psychic level, we find the kind of splitting with which clinicians are most familiar. The following is an example of how dominant white heterosexual masculinity might be constituted psychically. A white, upper-middle-class, male patient of mine, who struggles with not feeling masculine enough, reports one day his sense that the men in his firm who get rewarded are the macho pigs with no conscience. This observation fits firmly within his interpretation of his family history, in which, in several generations, one son has been picked by parents to be a feminized nice guy and one is molded to be an ambitious shark. My patient has disidentified with the sharks, but, since that was his only template for masculinity, he feels feminine and lesser. He frequently complains about the men in his firm who get more attention from management than he, and one day he tells me a story about one such favorite. This man apparently proudly related to his secretary that when his 4-year-old son called him on the phone, sobbing inconsolably, he yelled at him to pull down his pants. Then he asked him what was between his legs. "A penis," the son sobbed. "Right," Dad replied. "So stop crying." This simple lesson in masculinity well demonstrates poststructuralist arguments about how gender categories work. This boy learns that to be a boy means not to be a girl. To be a boy means not to cry when something goes wrong; that's what girls do. To be a boy is to hide your vulnerability, to be stoic. He is taught, then, that culturally sanctioned masculinity is invulnerable, stoic. Masculine vulnerability will be culturally invisible to this boy and others like him; he will always feel feminine in relation to what he takes to be masculinity. He might only be able to recognize as masculine such images of dominant masculinity as the Marlboro Man or the heroes of action films, cultural images that are seamlessly macho (despite deconstructionist revelations that the Marlboro Man was gay).

But how do things operate on the psychic level, where conflicts about masculinity render no image seamless? Will this boy's vulnerabilities disappear? No: they will be defended against, split off, projected. Masculinity as not-femininity, as stoicism, then, might be psychically defined as a continuous vigilance against getting caught being a girl—getting caught and being shamed. The relative conscious versus unconscious status of one's vigilance might depend on the degree of gender wounding that took place in one's history, for example, the degree to which humiliation has played a role in one's gender formation.[1] We might hypothesize that those who are most rigid in their definitions of such identity categories as masculine or feminine are likely to be those who have had a greater degree of psychic wounding in their history. But they inhabit one end of what I take to be a continuum: all of us are forced, to some extent, to constitute these categories in a dichotomized fashion; doing so involves some degree of psychic wounding.

What we need to look for when we are trying to understand gender clinically is, as Butler (1995) puts it, not only what is performed or enacted, but what is culturally barred from performance, and how the performed and the unperformed, the latter of which is often unconscious, condition each other. To understand heterosexual desire, we have to look at what men and women split off and then yearn for in the other who seems to have it—how masculinity and femininity operate as split-off complements of one another. As all clinicians know, what is split off from consciousness does not disappear but rather haunts the psyche and, in fact, produces the very form taken by its so-called opposite (thus this poststructuralist way of understanding gender stands in clear opposition to, for example, Stone Center theorists (Miller et al. [1991]), who understand masculinity and femininity as discrete). Let us take another example, this time with femininity. When a girl splits off her assertiveness because assertiveness has been gendered masculine or because she's been made to feel bad for being assertive, it is the very splitting off of assertiveness that produces the kind of passivity that now defines her as an exemplary good girl (Layton 2000). Does her assertiveness disappear? I think not. Autonomous strivings will haunt even the most self-effacing of women, just as entitled grandiosity often haunts a style predominantly marked by self-deprecation; some of these strivings will look like defensive autonomy, some not, depending on what versions of autonomy and attachment have been available.

What else do these examples of the formation of dominant masculinity and femininity reveal? I think one of the most important things they reveal is that gender and other identity categories are inextricably tied to our very ways of loving, attaching, and defining what it is our minds and bodies can and cannot do in the world. Chodorow's *Reproduction of Mothering* (1978) and Benjamin's *The Bonds of Love* (1988) still perhaps give the best descriptions of culturally dominant versions of masculinity and femininity, the agency and attachment patterns that characterize them, and the relational patterns that ensue from them. These are the versions most idealized by white, upper-middle-class patriarchal heterosexual culture. In the masculine version, dependency and attachment needs are split off, and this very split creates the defensive autonomy synonymous with dominant masculinity. In the feminine version, autonomy needs are split off, and this very split creates the self-effacing incapacity to put one's needs before those of others that we celebrate as dominant femininity. As I have argued elsewhere (1998), these dominant versions are best thought of as two subtypes of narcissism, reflecting two different kinds of culturally dominant disturbances of the relationship between attachment and agency.

To respond to the postmodern critique that the relational feminist view of gender is essentialist and based only on white, middle-class heterosexuals, I suggest that these dominant gender positions do not exhaustively define our performance of gender or our own understanding of it, but that they almost inevitably form part of everyone's gender experience (whether as something to emulate, feel inadequate in relation to, or rebel against). The narcissistic positions of dominant masculinity and femininity, however, come into conflict with other, non-dominant versions of gender that circulate in the culture (in art, on TV) and in our families, for example, the non-defensively assertive female or the vulnerable yet competent male. British cultural studies theorist Stuart Hall (1980) has a cultural model of reading that is helpful here. Hall has written about the way members of a culture interpret cultural texts. Rather than assume, as some theorists do, that culture imposes its own preferred, dominant reading on all its heterogeneous members, Hall argues that producers of cultural texts cannot predict how their messages will be interpreted; in fact, one can only know the meaning of a text when one knows what the receivers have made of it. Hall draws on insights from deconstruction and semiotics to argue that the reason a reading cannot be predicted in advance is that, first, audience members have multiple and conflicting aspects to their identities, and, second, linguistic phenomena never have one unique and stable meaning; they mean differently in different contexts and are multivalent even in a given context. Hall proposes, then, that one can read a text in concert with the preferred meaning, that is, with the meaning that likely shores up the values of dominant culture. Or one can come up with what he calls a negotiated reading, a reading that is partially in line with the preferred version and partially inflected to respond to an aspect of the reader's identity that is not consonant with the values of dominant culture. Finally, one can provide an oppositional reading of a text, as, for example, when the Declaration of Independence is read not as a statement of what exists in America—the preferred reading that those in power would like us to endorse—but as an uncompleted project that legitimates the demand for equality for all those not yet truly equal. According to Hall, all readings occur in specific historical circumstances, and all readings are subject to the constraints of unequal power relations (which distinguishes his view from that of liberal pluralism).

The way we connect gender with possibilities for attachment and agency is determined by our own idiosyncratic histories and our cultural positionings in relation to other cultural positionings (see Chodorow 1995), and this involves the very way male and female parent figures talk to, hold, play with, and separate from their male and female babies. My sense is that there is constant struggle and conflict between dominant and non-dominant gender internalizations. Non-dominant gender positions contest dominant ones for pride of place. And there are other challenges to narcissistic dominant gender positions as well. For one, I believe that we take in many versions of attachment and agency as we develop, and not all of these are grounded in narcissistic doer–done-to relations in which only one member of a dyad is a subject. Again, the latter mode is dominant, but not exhaustive. Here, I would distinguish my view from a Kleinian one, in which the narcissistic—or paranoid-schizoid—mode would be a universal and enduring feature of development and also would alternate with a depressive, more relational mode (see, for example, Sweetnam 1996). What I am arguing instead is that the narcissistic positions are traumatically inflicted by cultural inequities such as sexism, racism, and homophobia, and that their dominance would recede were the world to be less hierarchically and hatefully structured. Some modes of relating do indeed keep the assertion–recognition dialectic in tension, and such ways of being may be drawn on to contest subject–object relations. Further, as I have elaborated more fully elsewhere (1998), gender identity is not *only* a product of identifications. For example, we might remember ourselves as little girls doing with our bodies a variety of things that we may later be told are not ladylike or that we may later find are dangerous to do in public, but that, nevertheless, we have done and so know that girls can do. Putting together a sense of being a girl with a sense of what the body can do is also a part of gender identity formation.

Despite all evidence of gender multiplicity and fluidity, however, I do believe that each of us, no matter what our race, class, or sexuality, contends in some way psychically with dominant gender, race, class, and sexual categories, because the dominant categories hold the power to define what a proper race, class, gender, and sexuality is. Non-dominant versions generally carry some shame—shame generated by looking at them through the lens of dominant prescriptions (on race and such double consciousness, see DuBois 1903; on class, see Walkerdine 1997; on gender, see Berger 1977). To a greater or lesser extent, we all contend with the psychic consequences of the continual splitting that living these categories "properly" requires.

The above suggests that when we think about the dynamic unconscious, we must think about it as a gendered, raced, sexed, and classed entity formed in a crucible of power hierarchies. The identity elements are intertwined not only with one another but with what we come to think of as our agency—what we can do—and our possibilities for attachment—how we connect to others, how we love (no one, perhaps, has better described the effects of racism and sexism on how men and women love than has Toni Morrison in her fictional oeuvre). I have begun to use the term *normative unconscious* to account for a range of clinical theories and practices that replicate rather than challenge the splits demanded by dominant identity categories, by the racism, sexism, classism, and homophobia in which these categories are forged.

Identities are constituted in relation to cultural norms, and norms are generally embodied in those whose love and approval we most want and desperately need. To live a race or a gender or a sexed identity "properly," that is, in accord with dominant cultural norms, one has to split off those parts of self that do not have approval. The unconscious pushes for enactment both of what is split off and of the resulting conflict between the split poles. Most cultural-studies perspectives on the unconscious accentuate the fact that what is split off always threatens to undo the apparently stable identity clung to by the subject. Such perspectives seem to equate destabilizing with progressive, and so they figure the unconscious as a progressive force. In fact, however, both sides of the conflict, what is split off and what remains, become marked by the process of having become split in the first place: neither side of the split, in itself, is progressive, or even transgressive of cultural norms. Successful clinical work eventuates in a reworking of the split, and what emerges from that work is something new, something that resembles neither pole, and so is potentially progressive.

Nonetheless, it is true that what is split off and unconscious threatens to undo conscious identities. There is a force that works to defuse that threat, however, and that force is also unconscious. In many (though certainly not all) cases, this force works to keep dominant cultural norms in place. It is this instance of unconscious life that I am calling normative. The normative unconscious is a significant locus of dominant ideology: it works to legitimate cultural inequalities of all kinds and so contributes to the reproduction of the status quo. It is the unconscious support of what we think of as "common sense"; indeed, I want to argue that the prejudices often attributed to ethnocentric blind spots are better understood as products of unconscious conflict. The normative unconscious draws its power from the fact that internal threats not only threaten identity but also threaten relationships—the intimate relationships within which the identity was forged in the first place (for example, the love that one obtains for being a very good girl; see Goldner [1991] for other examples). Any threat to the attachment is rigorously defended against, consciously and unconsciously. In clinical work, normative unconscious processes are manifest primarily in the repetition compulsion and in resistance, each of which represents a great psychic investment in maintaining things as they are and in keeping what is split off out of consciousness.

In this essay, I focus more narrowly on what I call a *heterosexist unconscious*. My choice of term pays tribute to the many gay and lesbian theorists who have pointed to the way homophobia marks clinical theory and practice (Corbett 1993, Domenici and Lesser 1995, Lesser 1997, Magee and Miller 1996, O'Connor and Ryan 1993, Schwartz 1992, 1995, Stack 1999), particularly to the way most psychoanalytic theories have made desire and identification mutually exclusive (that is, the normative demand that we identify with the same sex and love the opposite sex). The drive to make desire and identification mutually exclusive in theory and practice, they claim and I agree, is motivated by a defense against same-sex longings.[2]

I use the term as well to account for the clinical theories and practices that enforce dominant gender categories and their endemic splits. Rather than use the term *sexist unconscious*, I prefer *heterosexist* because I have found convincing many feminist theorists' arguments about the way gender and sexuality are intertwined. Benjamin's theory (1988), as mentioned above, for example, describes the way gender splitting creates men and women who come respectively to incarnate pure assertion and pure submission, and who therefore each need to find what he or she is missing in the other. Butler's theory (1990a,b, 1995) comes at compulsory heterosexuality from the opposite direction, arguing that the cultural taboo on same-sex desire demands that we split off this desire, which issues in a loss that we are not allowed to grieve. When children split off the ungrievable same-sex desire, they turn into oedipal children. In other words, one does not simply move into the oedipal stage via a process of culture-free phylogenetic unfolding of discrete stages; rather, one enters the oedipal stage having already become heterosexualized via this process of splitting off the same-sex desire characteristic of the negative Oedipus. Heterosexuality, then, is haunted by the same-sex desire that the taboo requires we split off—to be heterosexual is to be always vigilantly guarding against awareness of same-sex desire.

But there is more to Butler's theory than a focus on the creation of a sexuality. The taboo against same-sex desire creates men and women whose very gender identity rests on the shaky foundation of this haunted heterosexuality. To be a woman, Butler writes, is defined by the impossibility of loving a woman. If one finds oneself desiring a person of the same sex, one's very gender identity is thrown into question. To be a man, under the dictates of dominant masculinity that I described earlier, requires not only a repudiation of those attributes deemed feminine but a repudiation of same-sex desire. Again, this makes it clear that ways of being agentic and ways of loving are inextricably tied to identity categories. The heterosexist unconscious, then, unconsciously polices the splits on which dominant gender and sexual categories rest. It operates in the building of theory as well as in the consulting room.

In recent work (Layton 2000, Layton and Bertone 1998), I have looked at two different bodies of clinical theory that I believe are among the many marked by this heterosexist unconscious: intersubjective theory and theories of psychic bisexuality. The choice of these two may be fortuitous, but I think I chose the former because it is the theory most inclusive of previously marginalized identities, and I think I chose the latter because it is considered to be on the cutting edge of feminist analytic theory. Thus, as many have assured me, I would likely find even more egregious instances of heterosexism in other areas of analytic theory; my thought is, however, that it makes sense to look at the best of what is out there and examine its assumptions. Here I would like to recapitulate my critique of certain manifestations of intersubjective theory and then present some clinical instances of the way heterosexism operates unconsciously.

## THE HETEROSEXIST UNCONSCIOUS IN CONTEMPORARY PSYCHOANALYTIC THEORY AND PRACTICE

As clinicians concerned with increasing or rendering more flexible our clients' options for autonomy and for opening up the kind of attachment in which both partners exist as subjects, we need to be as aware as possible of the kinds of splitting that make up the way our patients define their gender and their sexuality. To do so, we also must be aware of our own cultural positions and how our gender, race, class, and sexual positionings play out in treatment. It seems to me that relational psychoanalytic models, with their developing theoretical focus on the effects not just of the client's but of the therapist's subjectivity, provide a good beginning for dealing with the way identity and power operate in a treatment. In its social constructivist variant, relational theory suggests that therapist and patient co-construct the treatment; the analyst's unconscious is every bit as much a part of the treatment as the patient's (Aron 1991, 1992, 1996, Hoffman 1983, 1987, 1998, Mitchell 1988, 1993, 1997, Pizer 1998). But most of the "mainstream" work that has been done on the therapist's subjectivity thus far has been about the therapist's psychodynamics. In this work, there is no accounting for how the therapist's psychodynamics are inflected by the therapist's race, gender, and sexuality.[3] If, as I have argued, the way we relate to others and the way we assert ourselves are inextricable from gender, race, sexual, and class identities, then such omissions can be very problematic. My broad critique of this work is that the normative and heterosexist unconscious operates within it to exclude gender, race, class, and sexuality from considerations of either the analyst's or the patient's subjectivity. This is, of course, a charge that one could make about most analytic theories—psychodynamics are rarely thought of as constituted by these identity categories (sometimes the patient's dynamics are thought of as inflected by gender or sexuality, but this is rarely if ever considered in discussions of the analyst's subjectivity; an exception is Davies [1994]). The following discussion of a published case (Gerson 1996), in which a white male analyst disclosed a lie he had told to his female patient, well illustrates how problematic it can be to be unaware of the gender and sex positionings of both patient and therapist. It illustrates as well the way culturally dominant gender and sexual assumptions are marked by splitting.

This vignette begins when the analyst tells the reader that, in early September, he had known he would have to be out of town in November and had told all of his patients in a timely fashion, save one, Ms. A. Just two days before he is to leave, he tells her that an emergency has come up and he will have to be away for a few days. In their one remaining session, the patient free associates to a number of crises that might have come up for her analyst. The analyst feels guilty, not only for having lied but also for having caused further worry. Having read about the potential usefulness of countertransference disclosures while the therapist is away, and having felt that, in an intersubjective analysis, it simply would not do just to accept his own hypotheses about why he had done such a thing, he decides he will tell her that he lied. He does so, and he follows up by asking her why she thinks he lied. Her first response is the very opposite of what he had hypothesized. He had thought he hadn't told her because of her characteristic hostile-dependent response. But she says she thinks he didn't tell her because he liked her and didn't want to leave her. This leads to a reverie on his part, and he recalls that "in early September" she had learned of a possible job promotion in June that would have led to her moving and ending the analysis (note the repeat of "in early September," suggesting an unconscious connection between this information and the time when he first knew he had to be away). Her potential departure had not been taken up much in the analysis. Suddenly he is aware of how fond he is of her and that he will miss her. In this reverie, he acknowledges his dependence on her: "I thought to

myself that I had reversed the role not to avoid her anger at my departure but rather to be consoled by her for the loss I would feel upon her
departure" (pp. 638). But when he speaks next, he says, "Just as you wish
to be dependent on me, I too can have a wish to keep you dependent on
me" (p. 638). This slight shift in laguage exemplifies precisely the subtle
way in which dominant gender dynamics can be normalized in treatment,
the way therapy can subtly keep gender inequalities and the gender splits
that secure inequality in place. For while to himself the therapist can acknowledge being dependent on this less powerful female, to her he can
only express a wish that he presumes each of them shares, to have her
remain dependent on him. At first, the patient is flattered; she finds it
touching. On the next day there are references "to her ambivalent feelings about her possible departure" (p. 638). But over the next several sessions, she gets more depressed and "the predominant theme once again
became her difficulties in imagining and maintaining a positive feeling
about herself as a woman. In various ways we came back to the theme of
how hard it was for her to imagine being the object of someone else's
desire" (p. 638).

What struck me in reading this section of the vignette was the
possibility that patient and therapist were unconsciously colluding in
an enactment both of traditional gender splitting (in which the male
is autonomous and not dependent, the female dependent and not autonomous) and of compulsory heterosexuality. Somehow the issue had
shifted from her autonomous possible departure to whether or not she
was desirable to a man. And my guess is that the shift occurred because
the therapist continued to lie when he told her that what he had wished
for was that she be dependent on him. When he told her that, it seems
she became ambivalent about her departure and then quickly fell into
an old relational pattern of feeling undesirable to a man. What might
have happened if he had told her that his enactment had to do with
his dependency on her and with his conflict about her autonomy, and
if he had made it clear that that conflict was *his* problem, not hers? And
what might have happened had he noticed that the question of sexual
desirability was a defensive reaction on both their parts, a theme she
and he retreated to when something else was at stake, in this case her
autonomy?

As the vignette continues, these questions about how dominant
culture splits autonomy and dependence, autonomy and sexual desir-

ability, get ever more complicated. Ms. A. arrives one day wearing a man's pair of high-top sneakers. Her analyst notes that some time ago they had agreed that the sneakers are "symbolic of her attempts to resolve a variety of conflicts about her femininity via masculine identifications" (p. 639). But whose conflicts about femininity were emerging, hers or his—or might we talk about a heterosexual collusion between the two, a heterosexist unconscious? Ms. A.'s response might have spoken of her despair about ever being able to escape from traditional male–female relations, in which not only are dependency and autonomy split and gendered, but female autonomy is reduced to the capacity to attract a male, to sexual desirability. Ms. A.'s wearing of the sneakers might in fact have expressed refusal to be attractive to a male who had not accepted her as an autonomous subject and who had not acknowledged his dependency.

The vignette continues with a sequence that sheds some light on these questions. On the day she wears the sneakers, she tells her therapist that, the evening before, she had a fantasy of bringing him to orgasm. She was silent, then said she did not want to tell him the details because they might be too provocative. The analyst was surprised because she had often described detailed erotic fantasies during the analysis. He asked her what she thought might happen if she told and he became aroused. She replied that she feared he would become angry with her and disgusted as well. Then she recalled a memory:

> One summer day, she was in her room alone and began to masturbate while lying on her bed. Suddenly her father appeared in the doorway, looked at her, and then turned away and left abruptly. In the instant that she saw him, Ms. A. recalled seeing a look of disgust on his face, a look that until this moment she had associated with his displeasure at her subsequent and significant weight problems during adolescence. This memory served to illuminate her contemporary conviction that all men would react to her sexuality with disgust. [p. 639]

Ms. A. is inviting her analyst to re-enact a traumatic memory here, and the fact that he does not question traditional heterosexual dynamics perhaps causes him to re-enact it and to reinforce the law of heterosexuality. It seems that Ms. A.'s father was reacting not just to her sexual act, an act that requires no other, but to an autonomous act—one in which she was *not* trying to be desirable to a man. And the vignette suggests that the father may have been not, or not only, disgusted by watching her masturbate, but aroused (suggested by Ms. A. telling the therapist she is afraid that if he is aroused he will become angry and disgusted). Perhaps Ms. A. gains weight both to protect her father from acknowledging his arousal and to make his disgust appear to be her fault.

This calls to mind poststructuralist psychoanalyst Luce Irigaray's (1985) assertion that our Freudian forefathers could not tolerate their desire for their daughters and so sublimated this desire in the pleasures of law-making and law-enforcing. The oedipal law says it is the daughter, not the father, who has sexual desire—and not for her mother, but for him. The forefathers created the law of Oedipus, in which girls turn away from their mothers and from pleasure in their own bodies to move toward the father, and they created the law that makes penis envy the bedrock of female development. Traditional gender and heterosexual dynamics tend to reduce a woman's agency to sexual agency and tend to presuppose that there is a man on the other end of a woman's desire. The force of the oedipal law, as Irigaray says, is to prohibit a woman from symbolizing a relation to her own body and to her mother (and so to her origin); the phallus is then free to inhabit the place of origin. Irigaray asserts that women who follow this prescribed trajectory necessarily become hysterics; alienated from the capacity to symbolize and enact their own desire, they can do nothing but try to mime what men say their desire should be.

Raised within the parameters of such dynamics, Ms. A. consciously thinks her father was disgusted by her undesirability, but her father was, it seems, both aroused and disgusted by her masturbation. Like a good girl, Ms. A. consciously interprets the event in the frame of male desire when the event seems to have had more to do with female autonomy, the autonomous sexuality of her masturbation. But perhaps she is aware of this on an unconscious level—perhaps gaining weight, like wearing high-top sneakers, is, among other things, her way of preserving her autonomy, her way of refusing to be feminine and to be desirable to men who can neither affirm her autonomy nor own their need.

Unfortunately, the therapist, too, interprets in the frame of male desire. The rest of the vignette circles around the question: Is Ms. A. (and her sexuality) desirable to men or not? And so the therapist misses another chance to get at the conflict over female autonomy and male dependence. He concludes that Ms. A.'s conflict about her sexual excitement created an intersubjective resistance that manifested in both his and Ms. A.'s difficulty sustaining positive feelings about her: "the other's affectionate idea or feeling about her could not be held in mind, but rather, invoked defensive undoing, denial, and repression" (p. 640). But I think what the therapist had difficulty sustaining was not an idea of Ms. A. as desirable but an image of Ms. A. as simultaneously autonomous and connected. And this difficulty had something to do first with a problem acknowledging his dependence on her, and second, as the enactment unfolded, with a pull to reduce connection *and* autonomy to desirability. Both of these difficulties stem from the performance of unconscious sexist and heterosexist norms.

The enactment that takes place in this vignette followed what Ms. A. seems to have perceived as the therapist's ambivalence about her growing autonomy. Within the enactment, when Ms. A. was autonomous, she resisted being desirable to a man (the mode of connection prescribed by the heterosexual contract), and her way of being desirable to the therapist was to downplay her autonomy and collude with his desire for her to remain dependent on him. Although the therapist had earlier described her as retreating "from experiencing herself as a competent *and* attractive woman" (p. 637, emphasis added), during the enactment he tends to collapse autonomy, sexual excitement, and desirability to men. The therapist's way of splitting, gendering, and sexualizing autonomy and connection seems to have re-evoked the patient's characteristic way of splitting, gendering, and sexualizing autonomy and connection. What gets played out then is a reenactment of dominant masculinity, femininity, and heterosexuality. Maintaining the split between male autonomy and female dependency, as well as collapsing female autonomy into female heterosexual desire, keeps the case in a heterosexual frame—a frame that might fruitfully have been analyzed.

## CLINICAL VICISSITUDES OF
## A HETEROSEXIST UNCONSCIOUS

I would like to conclude by looking at some of my own clinical work, which suggests some further examples of the way the heterosexist unconscious operates in the consulting room. I've spent a lot of conscious time thinking about these issues, and I can truly say that no matter how aware I am of them, I catch my heterosexist unconscious in operation more than I would like to admit. For example, once I was telling a lesbian colleague about my sense that women talk about feeling trapped in relationships much less frequently than men. She noted that her lesbian clients frequently talk about feeling trapped in relationships. That tendency to build theory around white, middle-class, heterosexual women and call it a theory of women is one thing that reveals the operation of a heterosexist unconscious. Again, I see this not simply as a matter of ignorance, of not knowing about other ways of being. Rather, I see it as a manifestation of unconscious conflict, of a motivated suppression of what has been split off in order to take on an identity in conformity with dominant, hierarchical social norms. The clinical examples below illustrate a few of the kinds of splits that enact and reveal heterosexist unconscious processes. They include instances in which identification and desire are split, in which autonomy and connection are gendered and split, and in which heterosexuality and homosexuality are lived as mutually exclusive opposites.

### Heterosexualizing a Homosexual Patient

In the following vignette, I believe that I "perform" Judith Butler's theory of how the classic split between desire and identification described above comes into psychic being. A nominally[4] lesbian female patient falls madly in love with me and details her erotic fantasies over the course of two or three sessions. In the third session, I pick up on a criticism she's made of her partner earlier in the session: "she doesn't ever touch me in the right way." I later note that since we keep her erotic desire for me in fantasy, I'll never touch her the wrong way. This is just the slight she needs to feel humiliated; she had actually been thinking we might become sexual someday. While I think such a rupture was inevitable, I'm also quite certain that I made my comment not to be helpful to her, as I consciously thought, but rather to allay my own anxiety, as I, a nominal heterosexual, was becoming aroused. The patient's sexual fantasies end abruptly, and soon a period begins in which she experiments with what she considers femininity: she paints her nails, she wears make-up, she buys a dress for the first time in years. This is a very playful period, which I enjoy immensely and so undoubtedly encourage. It is only a year later, when she informs me that she wishes she could wear sweatshirts, pants, and hiking boots every day—because, she says, that's who she is—that I begin to think back to the "femininity" period. I wonder if the comment I made that ended the sexual fantasy has led the patient to retreat from desire to identification, a way of connecting with which she thought I might be more comfortable. In retrospect, I believe that in expressing my discomfort with my own same-sex desire, I brought about the performance of the culturally mandated split between identification and desire. To some extent, I heterosexualized the patient.

## Splitting and Gendering Autonomy and Connection

Jane is a 35-year-old nominally heterosexual client who entered treatment when she was abandoned by a man with whom she had fallen in love. Over time, I came to understand that, as for many heterosexual women, love carried the fantasy for her of resolving a lot of her autonomy strivings. But unlike the classic form of heterosexual romance described so well by Benjamin, in which the woman lives vicariously through the idealized man's agency, Jane, whose angry and oppressed mother told her to make sure she has a career and doesn't just go from being some man's daughter to being some man's wife, fantasizes that her boyfriends might provide the means for her better to actualize her career aspirations. I missed this nuance when I assumed that what Jane wanted was to be taken care of (I still have plenty of female patients for whom this is the case. For them, their hard-won career exists side by side, in what we might think of as parallel play, with their desire to have men pay for everything and make most of the decisions. I take this up toward the end of this essay). This is an important nuance, because Jane, like most of my clients, is struggling in her own unique way to integrate autonomy and connection. Unfortunately, the heterosexist imperative, as my earlier examples indicate, makes it nearly impossible to integrate the two, for the kind of autonomy associated with masculinity is defined by its repudiation of dependence (and its notion of dependence unconsciously equates any need for others with infantile helplessness. This illustrates the way that attributes that get split off and repudiated take on a distorted and monstrous form.)

Jane's difficulties in finding a partner have to do with her father's wish to keep his daughters all to himself, with the impossibility of executing her mother's command to be *not* like her, but also with a feeling that she is not feminine. Like most people with whom she comes in contact, she associates most of the activities she likes with masculinity; this association makes her feel less feminine, and, we must now add, less lovable. For Jane, it is impossible to feel competent and attractive at the same time (to hold what she has marked out as masculinity together with what she has marked out as femininity). In one session she lays out the dilemma of the independent female. The session begins as she wonders about her relationship to male authority figures, particularly her boss. She recognizes that she has always put forward her opinions forcefully, but notes that at those times when her view has prevailed, she has done something to sabotage her success. For example, she might express a different opinion from her boss on how a project ought to be done. If he lets her follow through with her plan, she might at some point oversleep and miss an important meeting crucial to the project. She feels guilty because she believes that her autonomous move has in some way destroyed her boss: autonomy destroys relationship. Her self-sabotage re-empowers her boss; she spends a period of time toiling silently and submissively until she feels she has made reparation.

When I ask her to associate to feeling competent and opinionated, she recalls that by the time she was 14 autonomy struggles with her father had led her to associate female independence with badness. She remembers a few more incidents that reveal that at a very young age she had begun to connect her competence with masculine qualities, which include being opinionated, and that this connection made her feel less feminine. Her next association is to rooming with two women on a trip and wondering if she would be better off seeking love from a woman. She had been in love with her college roommate, and this has always made her wonder if she was really straight. If we follow her thoughts, they go from a feeling that independence is bad if you're a female. The only way to be good and independent is to be a male. But if you have male qualities, you can't be feminine. If you're not feminine, you're not lovable to a man. And if you're not lovable to a man, maybe you're a lesbian. It is indeed possible that she will end up with a woman and we do explore her same-sex desire in the treatment. But for my current purposes what is most striking about her thought is the fact that she cannot hold either the gender possibilities or the sexual possibilities together because they have been culturally and then psychically dichotomized. Each time she, and all others like her, enact the split, the cultural dichotomies gain legitimacy.

### "Either You're Straight or You're Gay"

The following vignette reveals a patient's way of dichotomizing hetero- and homosexuality and the way that these carry his difficulty integrating autonomy and connection. John, a 25-year-old nominally heterosexual male patient, is having a hard time thinking about commitment to his new girlfriend. She wants them to agree not to date others. For him, this would mean he's committing to marriage, so he is thinking of breaking up. I wonder aloud whether he is using his all-or-nothing thinking defensively so as not to allow himself to continue to have the good times he's been having with this girlfriend. "Why would I do that?," he asks. I suggest that perhaps he doesn't feel he deserves good things. This observation is based on the fact that every time he buys something new he immediately wonders whether it's the good thing, the right thing, the manly thing. We've understood this in terms of his constant feelings of inadequacy, but here I look at another aspect: he keeps himself from enjoying what he's got. Another source of his conflict is class: he's got a lot more than anyone in his maternal family of origin has had and his hippie mother scoffs at any sign of materialism; her ex-husband, John's father, represents the sell-out businessman that she disdains. Within this discussion a question comes up as to whether or not he thinks of himself as a good person, one deserving of good things. I recall that his mother used to vilify him and his sister with curses and wonder if this treatment contributed to his taking on a sense of himself as bad. As he begins to think about his early life he develops a headache and starts to panic about his sexuality, something that occurs in similar circumstances from time to time.

Why has this homosexual panic come up now? To him, the meaning is that if he's really gay, how could he possibly commit to his girlfriend? Homosexual panic replaces heterosexual panic; both are defenses against connection. In great pain, he tells me about two incidents from his childhood that make him wonder if he's gay. Note that John was abandoned by his father and his cravings for male recognition are as intense as is his avoidance of closeness to men. In eighth grade, there was a boy who was clearly the ideal male in John's eyes and in the eyes of all the girls. He was athletic, handsome, and all the girls wanted him. This is the kind of male to whom John is usually attracted. John recalls one day giving this boy a backrub. He says he doesn't recall it feeling sexual. He wonders: "Did I want to be with him? Or did I just want to be like him? To have all the girls want me, too?" The second memory is from sixth grade. He wanted to shock everyone and he chose to do so by kissing all the boys on the cheek.

My sense is that, in this instance, the sexuality question is both a connection with and a defensive move away from his fear of remembering what it felt like to be disdained by his mother and abandoned by his father. Father's abandonment left him feeling that his love for his father was no good; his desire for his father was, in a way, mocked. It may be that this wound brought into being a split between desiring men and identifying with them. John's identificatory capacities are in fact as fragile as his desire. Any experience of vulnerability can make him feel like an inadequate male. When he feels that way, his associations move quickly from "I am an inadequate male" to "I am not male" to "I am female" to "I am not heterosexual" to "I am gay."

At this clinical moment, I choose to point to his either/or construction: If I'm really gay, he says, how could I commit to my girlfriend? I ask him what if he's attracted to both sexes. He sneers and tells me that, from what he's heard, that's not possible. Either you're straight or you're gay.[5]

In the heterosexist unconscious, homosexuality is split off and causes both sex and gender panic. That is what John is experiencing. Were the therapist to collude with John, what you might see is an unconscious agreement not to question the either/or of straight/gay or the either/or of to be/to have. A therapist might work with John to see that what he wanted was to be the adequate male, not to have him (as in the Greenson example that so baffled his patient Lance; see note 2, this chapter). The heterosexism here is in denying that being and having are intertwined or in suggesting that they're only discrete with regard to gender choice. In fact, the primary desire that drives many heterosexual relationships is grounded in the female's wish to be like her chosen male partner (for a theoretical attempt to ground the way being and having are developmentally intertwined, see Benjamin 1991, 1995). As it turned out, John later drew on my challenge to the either/or to enable him to stay connected to his girlfriend even when fantasizing about men.

## Two Good Girls

I want to end this discussion of the clinical appearance of the heterosexist unconscious with a particular manifestation of it that I am currently finding most difficult to think my way through. Here, the patient's female and heterosexual identifications are ego-syntonic and culturally approved. She derives esteem from performing her gender properly; yet this proper performance, I am coming to see, is the very site of her distress. I think of those cases I mentioned above, in which a female goes through years of training to be a professional and yet her capacity to be autonomous seems like mere window-dressing and does not seem integrated at all with her desire to have a man take over. One of my clients has suffered for years from her tendency to fall in love with wonderfully kind working-class men who can't provide her with the materially rich lifestyle she seems to want (and her mother definitely wants her to have). I have recently come to see that part of our work is to understand why, if she wants these material things so badly, she keeps herself in a job in which she makes barely enough to subsist (she is a professional and could be making a lot more money than she does). Asking this question revealed her deep feelings of incompetence, feelings she keeps hidden behind her adorable and sexy appearance and her culturally approved-of heterosexual desire to marry a rich man.[6] It took me a long time to ask this question, though, and I think that's because both she and I saw her gender performance as normal and non-problematic.

Another of my clients, who is the youngest female in a family with two older brothers, suffers terribly from a familial sexism in which the brothers make all the decisions and both brothers and mother are highly critical of any decision she might make. This occurs in part because her autonomy, as expressed in any contrary opinion, threatens the shaky masculinity of the eldest brother, a masculinity that mother has sought to protect, particularly since the father's death, by allowing him to be "in charge." The family enactment of traditional gender roles has made it highly conflictual for my client to have opinions and desires of her own and has made her seek out men who make all the decisions. She came to therapy not to deal with sexism but rather because she was chronically depressed. We could understand her depression in terms of a classic autonomy struggle, but I would argue that the very way she conceptualizes being a female and loving a man, the very shape of her agency and attachment styles, are conditioned by the gender assumptions that operate in her family and in large parts of the culture. The classic autonomy struggle is simultaneously a struggle over the way she lives her gender and sexuality.

An interesting clinical moment occurred with this client when she told me she had seen a new movie and had loved it. I had seen the movie and found the plot compelling, but I was appalled by the film as well, for it was one of the most misogynist movies I had seen in quite a while. For a few weeks I wondered whether or not it was appropriate to inquire whether she had noticed the sexism in the film—after all, we're not here to do film criticism, nor are we here to critique our clients' aesthetic choices. But an opening soon emerged when she brought up the fact that in the time since she had broken off a relationship with a boyfriend of three years, several of her friends had begun to tell her that they did not think he had been very nice to her. I then brought up my concerns about her reaction to the movie, and we began to explore the effects of her blindness to sexism. As it happens, in the three years in which she was dating her boyfriend, her heterosexist unconscious had operated so effectively that I had never heard a thing to suggest that he didn't treat her well. When she was beginning to express the dissatisfaction that led to the break-up, I had no idea why she was so suddenly dissatisfied with him, in part because she expressed the problem in terms of wanting a wealthier man who would take more control. My vision of the boyfriend was of a loving man who wanted her to be more assertive. Because she didn't notice the sexism, we didn't get an opportunity to look at it until the relationship was over and the friends started speaking up.[7]

My client is becoming increasingly aware of the fact that she has a blind spot for sexist dynamics, a result of the fact that to be loved in her family is to comply with a system in which only the male has agency (and the female is the agent reassuring the male that he's the only agent around). The therapeutic challenge in this case is how to make conscious the way dominant versions of gender and sexuality have made my patient sick, even though her proper performance of them is her main vehicle for getting love and approval. Challenging as well is the fact that, if you are anything like me, you may be delighted to have such very good girls in your practice and might miss the fact that the transference–countertransference dynamic is precisely constituted by your desire for a good patient and the patient's desire to be good. You may, in fact, not notice that it is not only the "good" but the "girl" that is symptomatic and in need of interpretation.

Indeed, it was late in the treatment that I recognized she was not nearly as good a girl as I'd thought. In fact, she fairly frequently controlled how deeply the treatment could go by suggesting that she was too fragile that day or week to talk about difficult things. In going along with this, I fear that I all too frequently colluded with her sense/fear that she was not an agent and missed the fact that, in some way, she was running the show and not being the compliant patient I had thought she was. In fact, *I* had often been the non-agentic good girl; *I* was the compliant one.

## CONCLUSION

To conclude, I would urge that we think more about what this notion of a heterosexist or normative unconscious might add to our understanding of the dynamic unconscious. For Sigmund Freud, the unconscious contained unacceptable id impulses; for Anna Freud, the unconscious also contained the defenses against the emergence of these impulses; for Winnicott, the unconscious contained the spontaneous strivings of the true self; for Mitchell and others in the relational school, the unconscious contains the products of relational conflict. My discussion of the heterosexist unconscious suggests at least two corrections to the way the unconscious is conceptualized by many theoreticians in the relational school, particularly those who are not explicitly feminist. First, psychic conflicts involving dependence and independence, the way we love and the way we assert ourselves, are inextricable from the gender, race, sex, and class positions we inhabit, so any discussion of the unconscious must look at the way these categories are imbricated with conflict. Second, the unconscious is as permeated by cultural norms as is the conscious mind. The unconscious is not a space that is free of norms, nor is it a space that can be conceptualized solely as resistant to norms. Indeed, it seems to me that the dynamic unconscious oper-ates in at least two modes: it strives to overcome the traumatic experi-ences that create it and it repeats the traumatic experiences that create it. Because of the nature of conflict, it is likely that the two modes most frequently operate simultaneously. Usually we are seeking to avoid pain by repeating what has caused pain in the first place or by using defenses that continue to make impossible the performance of the very ways of being that might be necessary to heal the pain. I have tried to argue that an important piece of the repetition compulsion has to do with the fact that cultural approval and familial love are often contingent upon performing dominant versions of gender, race, sex, and class identities. As Butler and others have argued, the repetition keeps the cultural norms in place, legitimates their dominance, and shuts out other ways of being that might contest those norms. Theoretical stances and clini-cal practices that are not mindful of these operations are, unfortunately, more than likely to sustain them. And so I urge that we be aware not only of how the heterosexist/normative unconscious operates in our patients but how it operates in the intersubjective space that we estab-lish between our patients and ourselves.

## NOTES

1. My patient, humiliated by his father in a way that made him feel feminine, might be at one end of a continuum, the end at which trauma-induced splitting creates unconscious conflict about gender. The world be-comes divided up according to gender stereotypes, and all sorts of capaci-ties begin to carry gender connotations (see Layton 1998, chapter 7). At another point of the continuum, I offer the following example: my 6-year-old nephew spends the entire weekend of my visit periodically kissing and hugging me. When it's time for me to go, we all travel to the airport. On our arrival, a car pulls up carrying one of his friends. The two boys run around the airport and when it's time for me to leave, I call him over and ask for/ offer a kiss good-bye. I kiss him, and he wipes his mouth in disdain. I then tell him I'm onto him, that I know he's just wiping it off because he doesn't want his friend to see. He smiles mischievously and walks away. For him, gender proscriptions are conscious: he knows in what contexts it's safe to kiss, and in what contexts you must fear humiliation for such behavior. I hope

this will continue to operate on the conscious level as he ages—but, let's face it, it still isn't a very desirable outcome.

2. One can perhaps find no better example than in Greenson's classic 1968 paper on the necessity for boys to disidentify from their mothers. When his 5-year-old patient, Lance, who was "lively, intelligent, well-oriented" and yet "consumed by the wish to be a female," gave Greenson permission to be the princess Barbie with which they were playing, Greenson replied, "I don't want to *be* the princess, I want to dance with her" (p. 371). Greenson teaches Lance to distinguish between being and having. "Lance," he reports, "was baffled. I repeated this several times until the boy permitted me to dance with the princess. He watched this, puzzled and upset. . . . Shortly after this episode, Lance no longer referred to the Barbie doll as 'I' or 'we' but only as 'she'" (p. 371).

3. Exceptions include feminist theorists discussed earlier (e.g., Benjamin 1988, Dimen 1991, Goldner 1991, Harris 1991, Layton 1998); those who deconstruct the heteronormativity of what one might call "mainstream" relational theory, also discussed earlier (e.g., Lesser 1997, Magee and Miller 1996, Schwartz 1992, Stack 1999); and those who focus on race and intersubjectivity (e.g., Altman 2000, Leary 1997a,b, Thompson 1995, Yi 1998).

4. I use the word "nominal" throughout this discussion when referring to sexual preference. I do so because I believe the deconstructionist argument is correct: that these categories are psychically constituted only in relation to one another. The term also captures the fact that people designate or name themselves by means of the cultural categories available to them. I do not mean to suggest that the categories ought necessarily to be abolished. People live their lives in accord with the designations they take on, and so they create communities around their definitions of these categories.

5. It is precisely this cultural position, apparent in both heterosexual and homosexual discourses, that bisexual writers deplore (e.g., du Plessis 1996, Eadie 1996, Michel 1996), as it renders bisexuality invisible. Bisexual authors make it clear that it is possible not only for heterosexuals but also for gays and lesbians to evidence what I have defined as a heterosexist unconscious. For my discussion of the way psychoanalytic discourse similarly renders bisexuality invisible, see Layton 2000.

6. Most of my clinical examples here clearly reveal the way that class and race are also bound up with the proper performance of gender and sexuality. For this reason, it may be misleading that I have distinguished the term "heterosexist" unconscious from the more overarching "normative" unconscious. I leave it to the reader to determine which term might be more accurate.

7. For me, this example points to what may be a significant limitation of individual treatment.

# REFERENCES

Altman, N. (2000). Black and white thinking: a psychoanalyst reconsiders race. *Psychoanalytic Dialogues* 10:589–605.

Aron, L. (1991). The patient's experience of the analyst's subjectivity. *Psychoanalytic Dialogues* 1:29–51.

———— (1992). Interpretation as expression of the analyst's subjectivity. *Psychoanalytic Dialogues* 2:475–507.

———— (1996). *A Meeting of Minds: Mutuality in Psychoanalysis.* Hillsdale, NJ: Analytic Press.

Benjamin, J. (1988). *The Bonds of Love.* New York: Pantheon.

———— (1991). Father and daughter: identification with difference—a contribution to gender heterodoxy. *Psychoanalytic Dialogues* 1:277–299.

———— (1995). *Like Subjects, Love Objects. Essays on Recognition and Sexual Difference.* New Haven, CT: Yale University Press.

Berger, J. (1977). *Ways of Seeing.* New York: Penguin.

Bhabha, H. (1983). The other question—the stereotype and colonial discourse. *Screen* 24:18–36.

Butler, J. (1990a). *Gender Trouble: Feminism and the Subversion of Identity.* New York and London: Routledge.

———— (1990b). Gender trouble, feminist theory, and psychoanalytic discourse. In *Feminism/Postmodernism*, ed. L. J. Nicholson, pp. 324–340. New York and London: Routledge.

———— (1993). *Bodies That Matter.* New York and London: Routledge.

———— (1995). Melancholy gender—refused identification. *Psychoanalytic Dialogues* 5:165–180.

Chodorow, N. J. (1978). *The Reproduction of Mothering.* Berkeley: University of California Press.

———— (1995). Gender as a personal and cultural construction. *Signs* 20:516–544.

Connell, R. W. (1995). *Masculinities.* Berkeley: University of California Press.

Corbett, K. (1993). The mystery of homosexuality. *Psychoanalytic Psychology* 10:345–357.

Davies, J. M. (1994). Love in the afternoon: a relational reconsideration of desire and dread in the countertransference. *Psychoanalytic Dialogues* 4:153–170.

Dimen, M. (1991). Deconstructing difference: gender, splitting, and transitional space. *Psychoanalytic Dialogues* 1:335–352.

Domenici, T., and Lesser, R. C., eds. (1995). *Disorienting Sexuality: Psychoanalytic Reappraisals of Sexual Identities.* New York: Routledge.

Du Bois, W. E. B. (1903). *The Souls of Black Folk.* New York: Penguin, 1989.

du Plessis, M. (1996). Blatantly bisexual; or, unthinking queer theory. In *RePresenting Bisexualities,* ed. D. E. Hall and M. Pramaggiore, pp. 19–54. New York and London: New York University Press.

Eadie, J. (1996). Being who we are (and anyone else we want to be). In *Bisexual Horizons,* ed. S. Rose, C. Stevens, et al., pp. 16–20. London: Lawrence & Wishart.

Foucault, M. (1973). *Madness and Civilization: A History of Insanity in the Age of Reason,* trans. R. Howard. New York: Vintage.

——— (1979). *Discipline and Punish: The Birth of the Prison,* trans. A. Sheridan. New York: Vintage.

——— (1980). *The History of Sexuality. Volume 1: An Introduction,* trans. R. Hurley. New York: Vintage.

Gerson, S. (1996). Neutrality, resistance, and self-disclosure in an intersubjective psychoanalysis. *Psychoanalytic Dialogues* 6:623–645.

Goldner, V. (1991). Toward a critical relational theory of gender. *Psychoanalytic Dialogues* 1:249–272.

Greenson, R. (1968). Dis-identifying from mother: its special importance for the boy. *International Journal of Psycho-Analysis* 49:370–374.

Hall, S. (1980). Encoding/decoding. In *Culture, Media, Language: Working Papers in Cultural Studies, 1972–79,* ed. S. Hall, D. Hobson, A. Lowe, and P. Willis, pp. 128–138. London: Hutchinson.

Harris, A. (1991). Gender as contradiction. *Psychoanalytic Dialogues* 1/2:197–224.

Higginbotham, E. B. (1992). African-American women's history and the metalanguage of race. *Signs* 17:251–274.

Hoffman, I. Z. (1983). The patient as interpreter of the analyst's experience. *Contemporary Psychoanalysis* 19:389–422.

——— (1987). The value of uncertainty in psychoanalytic practice. *Contemporary Psychoanalysis* 23:205–215.

——— (1998). *Ritual and Spontaneity in the Psychoanalytic Process. A Dialectical-Constructivist View.* Hillsdale, NJ: Analytic Press.

Irigaray, L. (1985). The blind spot of an old dream of symmetry. In *Speculum of the Other Woman,* trans. G. Gill, pp. 13–129. Ithaca, NY: Cornell University Press.

Layton, L. (1998). *Who's That Girl? Who's That Boy?: Clinical Practice Meets Postmodern Gender Theory.* Northvale, NJ: Jason Aronson.

——— (2000). The psychopolitics of bisexuality. *Studies in Gender and Sexuality* 1:41–60.

Layton, L., and Bertone, K. L. (1998). What's disclosed in self-disclosures? Gender, sexuality, and the analyst's subjectivity: commentary. *Psychoanalytic Dialogues* 8:731–739.

Leary, K. (1997a). Race in psychoanalytic space. *Gender & Psychoanalysis* 2/2:157–172.

———— (1997b). Race, self-disclosure, and "forbidden talk": race and ethnicity in contemporary clinical practice. *Psychoanalytic Quarterly* 66:163–189.

Lesser, R. C. (1997). A plea for throwing development out with the bathwater: discussion. *Gender & Psychoanalysis* 2:379–388.

Magee, M., and Miller, D. C. (1996). What sex is an amaryllis? What gender is lesbian? Looking for something to hold it all. *Gender & Psychoanalysis* 1:139–170.

Michel, F. (1996). Do bats eat cats? Reading what bisexuality does. In *RePresenting Bisexualities*, ed. D. E. Hall and M. Pramaggiore, pp. 55–69. New York and London: New York University Press.

Miller, J. B., Jordan, J., Kaplan, A., et al. (1991). *Women's Growth in Connection*. New York: Guilford.

Mitchell, S. A. (1988). *Relational Concepts in Psychoanalysis*. Cambridge, MA: Harvard University Press.

———— (1993). *Hope and Dread in Psychoanalysis*. New York: Basic Books.

———— (1997). *Influence and Autonomy in Psychoanalysis*. Hillsdale, NJ: Analytic Press.

O'Connor, N., and Ryan, J. (1993). *Wild Desires and Mistaken Identities. Lesbianism and Psychoanalysis*. London: Virago.

Pizer, S. (1998). *Building Bridges: The Negotiation of Paradox in Psychoanalysis*. Hillsdale, NJ: Analytic Press.

Schwartz, D. (1992). Commentary on Jessica Benjamin's "Father and Daughter: Identification with Difference—a Contribution to Gender Heterodoxy." *Psychoanalytic Dialogues* 2:411–416.

———— (1995). Retaining classical concepts—hidden costs: commentary on Lewis Aron's "The Internalized Primal Scene." *Psychoanalytic Dialogues* 5:239–248.

Stack, C. (1999). Psychoanalysis meets queer theory: an encounter with the terrifying other. *Gender & Psychoanalysis* 4:71–87.

Sweetnam, A. (1996). The changing contexts of gender: between fixed and fluid experience. *Psychoanalytic Dialogues* 6:437–459.

Thompson, C. L. (1995). Self-definition by opposition: a consequence of minority status. *Psychoanalytic Psychology* 12/4:533–545.

Walkerdine, V. (1997). *Daddy's Girl: Young Girls and Popular Culture*. Cambridge, MA: Harvard University Press.

Yi, K. Y. (1998). Transference and race: an intersubjective conceptualization. *Psychoanalytic Psychology* 15/2:245–261.

# 6a

# Response to Layton

*Kimberlyn Leary*

Lynne Layton is adept in the rough-and-tumble world of contemporary gender theorizing. Her chapter "Cultural Hierarchies, Splitting, and the Heterosexist Unconscious" is a savvy but highly accessible account of the impact of postmodern thinking on psychoanalytic gender theory. Much of her discussion centers on an appreciation of the ways in which power relations lie at the heart of gender practices. Layton is attuned to the ways postmodern critiques unmask specific normative forms to show how the cultural machinery behind them preserves power for those in positions of dominance and control. As a result, traditional gender forms are highly contingent. In Layton's hands, we can acknowledge anew the way in which masculinity and femininity are contextual, and, in a certain critical sense, do not exist apart from our subjective experience of gender. Our sense of ourselves as men and women is created in the matrix of mind and body, psyche and society.

This is, of course, by now a familiar view in contemporary psychoanalysis. As Layton notes, it is also a perspective that is often used to refute the work of relational feminist theorists whose attention to relational competence in gendered contexts is decried as being essentialistic, heterosexist, and reinforcing of existing gender boundaries and roles.

For Layton, such charges seem shortsighted. In this chapter, she turns her attention to the very postmodern accounts that are often viewed as the theoretical successors to relational feminism. She does so to examine the ways in which psychoanalytic practices of all kinds can be implicated as subtly enforcing traditional prescriptions of normalcy and restricting the range of identity expressions, even when their intention is otherwise. Along the way, Layton challenges us to consider what it might mean for our work if we were to grapple more strenuously with a notion of our own analytic theories and techniques as already raced, sexed, and classed entities.

By raising these questions in the context of intersubjective and relational analytic models, Layton creatively and usefully pushes the postmodern project still further. She is aware that contemporary analytic models aim to be inclusive of previously marginalized identities. At the same time, she still finds in them an abdication from a full consideration of the way in which gender, race, class, and sexual positioning play out in treatment. She locates some of the continuing gender tension within contemporary clinical practices. In doing so, Layton convincingly demonstrates the power that inheres in deconstructive critiques.

During the last twenty-five years, relational and intersubjective psychoanalytic models have yielded an array of concepts and techniques that many believe have enabled us to apprehend better the suffering of our patients and to extend ourselves as analysts to ameliorate their pain more effectively (cf. Hoffman 1996). "One-person" formulations, with their near-exclusive focus on the analyst's authoritative rendering of the analysand's subjectivity, have given way to an understanding of psychoanalytic treatment as a co-constructed collaboration between patient and analyst. All forms of psychoanalytic treatment now recognize that the curative potential of an analysis depends on a series of interactive events mutually experienced by both patient and analyst (Mitchell 1995). Our understanding of what it means to be an analyst vis-à-vis our patients has shifted dramatically. The range of experiences we now consider to be analytic has undergone a similar transformation.

Much of this change has been understood as a corrective to the orthodoxy of psychoanalysis as it has been practiced in the United States, particularly in the context of what was once the exclusionary "closed shop" of the American Psychoanalytic Association (Aron 1996). A number of analytic thinkers (e.g., Mitchell, Ehrenberg, Renik, Hoffman, and many others) have carefully argued for an appreciation of classical analytic constructs as contingent, rather than universal and based on institutional forms dedicated to preserving power for those in positions of dominance and control. The thrust of much of contemporary theory has, in my view, skillfully used postmodern thinking to advance agendas of restoration and revitalization.

At the same time, psychoanalytic authors have not always been mindful of the ways that postmodern solutions can also bring new problems that equally require our attention (Leary 1994). In this respect, it is useful to remember that postmodern discourses are not theories in and of themselves. Rather, they involve critiques that are meant to destabilize existing constructs. In finding the tensions and inconsistencies in an idea previously assumed to represent an essential truth, a new conceptual space opens—one that reveals the ambiguity of lived human experience. In this respect, postmodern commentaries address virtual spaces rather than real places (Leary 1996). Like the technology of virtual reality, the conceptual space opened up by postmodernism is fictive and retains its shape only temporarily. When true to form, postmodern commentaries always involve repeating cycles of constitution, collapse, and recomposition.

At times, theorists inside and outside of psychoanalysis can unwittingly adopt postmodern critiques to lay authoritative claim to this conceptual space and use it to legitimate new events of importance (Leary 1996). This can be seen when a critique of traditional theory is employed to reveal, for instance, the clinical reality of intersubjectivity or the universality of clinical enactments. In this way, postmodern commentaries can be deployed in such a way that they gravitate to the "real" and to elucidating the facts of the matter. These are, of course, the very conclusions these inquiries were meant to deconstruct. As a result, the conceptual space opened up by the critique shrinks a bit. This is not a problem, in and of itself. However, the new facts now demand deconstruction to the extent they have become essentialistic ways of thinking about what an analytic experience *really* involves. We encounter new problems when we fail to investigate our current ways of think-ing—and the purposes they serve—as thoroughly as we engaged with the original critique.

I believe that Layton introduces the term *normative unconscious* to refer to a similar state of affairs. She uses this designation, and the spe-cific form she calls the *heterosexist unconscious* with respect to gender practice, to account for the range of theories and techniques that she believes unwittingly replicate rather than challenge the splitting and projections required by dominant identity categories as a function of racism, homophobia, classism, and sexism. Layton argues that we must become aware of the way in which the normative and heterosexist un-conscious operates to occlude race, class, and sexuality from consider-ations of either the patient's or the analyst's subjectivity.

Surely Layton is correct on that score. She notes that only a few psychoanalytic writers have attempted to account for the manner in which the analyst's psychodynamics are inflected by his or her racial, sexual, and gender positioning. If we look beyond the borders of theory to institutional practice, few analytic institutes teach courses in cross-cultural psychoanalysis or racial and ethnic issues in treatment. Those that do very often relegate such topics to courses investigating "Spe-cial Problems" or to elective sequences tacked on to the end of the academic year. The result is that an effort at inclusion culminates in unconsciously "exoticizing" or further marginalizing racial and ethnic experience. Thus the solution begets a new problem requiring our attention.

Layton uses several clinical vignettes to illustrate the problems that can arise when analysts remain unaware of the gender and sexual posi-tions they occupy and the way in which such culturally dominant pat-terns are marked by splitting. Her reading of Gerson (1996) is potent, and she makes a persuasive case for the possibility that patient and analyst colluded in an enactment of traditional gender splitting. Im-portantly, Layton is concerned with the way subtle shifts in language can move the trajectory of a clinical sequence in the direction of, as she puts it, "normalizing" dominant gender dynamics.

With respect to Gerson's vignette, Layton wonders if a different outcome might have been possible if the analyst had conveyed that the conflict over dependency was his problem, rather than Ms. A.'s. Yet what most impressed me about Gerson's case (both his original report and Layton's summary of it) was that Gerson's intention and his technique were directed at inspiring a very different conversation with his patient. When Gerson owns up to a lie with Ms. A., he is attempting to invite his patient into a different type of dialogue than they have apparently had before this session and one that implicates him as a vulnerable subject, prone to interferences of his own. What is interesting, as Layton details, is just how easily patient and analyst could be moved instead into a connivance that reinstantiates autonomy as the province of men and dependent attachment as the site of female subjectivity.

Layton notices a similar gravitation in her work with her own patients. She notices *after the fact* the way she deflects her nominally lesbian patient's desire ("since we keep her erotic desire for me a fantasy") and unconsciously supports her patient's defensive retreat into an identification with her analyst. Here, as in Gerson's vignette, patient and analyst subtly accommodate themselves to a way of being with each other that preserves the analyst's comfort and reinforces traditional dichotomies (e.g., between desire and identification).

Layton admits that she catches her own heterosexist unconscious in operation more than she would like to admit. Her honesty is compelling and, I think, a model for our efforts to open ourselves up to truly grapple with our susceptibility to the cultural milieu in which we live and work. Such an effort requires a willingness to engage with our own practices in ways that will expose us to ideas that we may not wish to claim easily as our own.

In my own efforts to understand the impact of race and ethnicity in the analytic exchange, I have recently turned to the study of what I term *racial enactments*, for what they might contribute to our understanding of the intersubjectivity of race and racial experience. By *racial enactment*, I am designating interactive sequences that embody the actualization in the clinical situation of cultural attitudes toward race and racial difference. Racial enactments may have much in common with Layton's normative unconscious.

In a recent paper (Leary 2000), I describe a "social enactment" around race (in which a white analyst assumed that I was the African-American analyst he had hoped to meet at a professional meeting) and a clinical enactment (in which an African-American patient and I "negotiated," in effect, who between us was authentically black). I argue that in both instances, albeit in different ways, the principals fell quite unwittingly into racial enactments. Despite the conscious intent to forge new connections and to establish better communication, we instead managed to actualize some of the tensions, stereotypes, and prejudices of the culture in which we live. I suggest that these exchanges indicate the way in which each of us found in ourselves an unintended bit of racism and ethnocentrism that was exposed as being our own.

Renik (1993, 1996), among others, has persuasively argued that enactments constitute irreducible, rather than special, forms of clinical relating. He has advocated that we reconfigure technique to account for the fact that the analyst cannot know fully how he or she is participating in the exchange, making clinical understanding retrospective rather than predictive. More recently (1997), he has suggested that analytic effectiveness can be facilitated by a collaborative method. In order for this to occur, he writes, "the patient has to feel free to perceive and discuss the analyst's activity; and in order for this to happen, the analyst has to be ready to submit his or her activity to scrutiny" (p. 11).

I think collaborative methods may have particular utility in the analysis of racial material and gender experience. In each they would require a conversation approaching a frank exchange of views, along with recognition of the emotional positions from which we articulate those views. With respect to race, this would include, for example, the fear of being labeled racist or the fear of being further marginalized.

Collaborative methods may be viewed as supporting the patient's agency and as providing an opportunity for the patient's voice to be heard. The patient is encouraged—perhaps even required—to offer his or her perspective on the analyst and the analyst's activity. This, in turn, requires the analyst to really listen to things he or she may not wish to hear, including his or her complicity in racial matters and the patient's perception of the analyst's racial experiencing, racial conflicts, or both. Thus emphasizing clinical collaborations with respect to racial experience shifts therapeutic aims. Rather than try to transcend difference, for instance, patient and analyst endeavor to live with their differences and to subject those differences to careful consideration.

Layton engages us in a similar process with respect to the heterosexist unconscious. She argues that practices consistent with the heterosexist unconscious will intrude into intersubjective clinical space as a matter of course. As with all enactments, we are unlikely to catch ourselves before the fact. More often we will find ourselves replicating modes of functioning that we do not consciously endorse, understanding that we have done so only later on. At such times, our patients may be freer to notice our regress into stereotyped thinking, even as we may have a greater purchase on their adoption of cultural practices that limit their full expression of self. Thus Layton invites us to appreciate the innovations in theory and practice that have propelled psychoanalysis into the twenty-first century even as she challenges us to question them rigorously and, in so doing, recognize the work that still lies ahead.

## REFERENCES

Aron, L. (1996). *A Meeting of Minds: Mutuality in Psychoanalysis.* Hillsdale, NJ: Analytic Press.

Gerson, S. (1996). Neutrality, resistance, and self-disclosure in an inter-subjective psychoanalysis. *Psychoanalytic Dialogues* 6(5):623–646.

Hoffman, I. (1996). The intimate and ironic authority of the psychoanalyst's presence. *Psychoanalytic Quarterly* 65(1):102–136.

Leary, K. (1994). Psychoanalytic problems and postmodern solutions. *Psychoanalytic Quarterly* 63:433–465.

———— (1996). Repressed memories and clinical practice. *Women and Therapy* 19(1):61–77.

———— (2000). Racial enactments in dynamic treatment. *Psychoanalytic Dialogues* 10:639–654.

Mitchell, S. A. (1995). Interaction in the Kleinian and the interpersonal traditions. *Contemporary Psychoanalysis* 3:65–91.

Renik, O. (1993). Analytic interaction: conceptualizing technique in the light of the analyst's irreducible subjectivity. *Psychoanalytic Quarterly* 62:553–571.

———— (1996). The perils of neutrality. *Psychoanalytic Quarterly* 65:495–517.

———— (1997). *Collaboration between patient and analyst.* Unpublished manuscript.

# 7

# A Dialogue on Racial Melancholia[1]

## David L. Eng and Shinhee Han

*I wondered if whiteness were contagious. If it were, then surely I had caught it.
I imagined this "condition" affected the way I walked, talked, dressed, danced,
and at its most advanced stage, the way I looked at the world and at other people.*
—*Caucasia*

## THE "CONDITION" OF WHITENESS

Configuring whiteness as contagion, Birdie Lee, the narrator of
Danzy Senna's *Caucasia* (1998), connects assimilation to illness and
disease. Separated from her African-American activist father, Birdie
Lee and her blue-blooded mother flee from the law in a racialized and
radicalized 1970s Boston. Eventually, the two take up residence in New
Hampshire, where Birdie passes as "Jesse" and for white.[2]

This assimilation into the whiteness of New Hampshire plagues
Birdie, who wonders if "I had actually become Jesse, and it was this girl,

this Birdie Lee who haunted these streets, searching for ghosts, who was the lie" (p. 329). This vexing "condition" of whiteness not only alters the narrator's physical world: the manner in which Birdie walks, talks, dresses, and dances; moreover, it also configures the sphere of the affective: the ways in which Birdie ultimately apprehends the world and its occupants around her. Physically and psychically haunted, Birdie/Jesse feels "contaminated" (p. 329).

This is the condition of racial melancholia.

## IN PLACE OF A DIALOGUE

This essay is the result of a series of sustained dialogues on racial melancholia that we recorded in the autumn and winter of 1998. We—a Chinese-American male professor in the humanities and a Korean-American female psychotherapist—transcribed and edited these dialogues, rewriting them into the present form. However, we hope that our rather distinct disciplinary approaches to psychoanalysis, from literary theory as well as clinical practice, not only remain clear but also work to supplement one another. The pressing need to consider carefully methods by which a more speculative approach to psychoanalysis might enhance clinical applications, and vice-versa, is urgent. This essay is, in part, a critical response to the disturbing patterns of depression that we have been witnessing in a significant and growing number of Asian-American students with whom we interact on a regular basis. "A dialogue on racial melancholia" provides, then, an opportunity for us to propose several ways of addressing race in psychoanalysis, a topic largely neglected in this field.

As Freud's privileged theory of unresolved grief, melancholia presents a compelling framework in which to conceptualize registers of loss and depression attendant on both psychic and material processes of assimilation.[3] While Freud typically casts melancholia as pathological, we are more concerned with exploring this psychic condition as a de-pathologized structure of feeling. From this particular vantage, melancholia might be thought of as underpinning our everyday conflicts and struggles with experiences of immigration, assimilation, and racialization.[4] Furthermore, even though melancholia is often conceived of in terms of individual loss and suffering, we are interested in addressing group identifications. As such, some of our observations bring together different minority groups—people of color as well as gays and lesbians—from widely disparate historical, juridical, cultural, social, and economic backgrounds. We are wary of generalizing, but we also hope that in forging theoretical links among these various minority groups we might develop new intellectual, clinical, and political coalitions.

This essay is framed by two larger questions: How might psychoanalytic theory and clinical practice be leveraged to think about not only sexual but also racial identifications? How might we focus on these crossings in psychoanalysis to discuss, in particular, processes of immigration, assimilation, and racialization underpinning the formation of Asian-American subjectivity?

## ASSIMILATION AS/AND MELANCHOLIA

Freud's theory of melancholia provides a provocative model for considering how processes of assimilation work in this country and how the depression that characterizes so much of our contemporary culture at the turn of this century might be thought about in relation to particularly marked social groups. In the United States today, assimilation into mainstream culture for people of color still means adopting a set of dominant norms and ideals—whiteness, heterosexuality, middle-class family values—often foreclosed to them. The loss of these norms, the reiterated loss of whiteness as an ideal, for example, establishes one melancholic framework for delineating assimilation and racialization processes in the United States precisely as a series of failed and unresolved integrations.

Let us return for a moment to Freud's 1917 essay, "Mourning and Melancholia," in which he attempts to draw a clear distinction between these two psychic states through the question of "successful" and "failed" resolutions of loss. Freud reminds us at the start of this essay that mourning is "regularly the reaction to the loss of a loved person, or to the loss of some abstraction which has taken the place of one, such as one's country, liberty, an ideal, and so on. In some people the same influences produce melancholia instead of mourning and we consequently suspect them of a pathological disposition" (p. 243). Mourning, unlike melancholia, is a psychic process in which the loss of an object or ideal occasions the withdrawal of libido from that object or ideal. This withdrawal cannot be enacted at once; instead it is a gradual letting go. Libido is detached bit by bit so that, eventually, the mourner is able to declare the object dead and to invest in new objects. In Freud's initial definition of the concept, melancholia is pathological precisely because it is a mourning without end. Interminable grief is the result of the melancholic's inability to resolve the various conflicts and ambivalences that the loss of the loved object or ideal effects. In other words, the melancholic cannot "get over" this loss, cannot work it out in order to invest in new objects.

To the extent that ideals of whiteness for Asian Americans (and other groups of color) remain unattainable, processes of assimilation are suspended, conflicted, and unresolved. The irresolution of this process places the concept of assimilation within a melancholic framework. Put otherwise, mourning describes a finite process that might be reasonably aligned with the popular American myth of immigration, assimilation, and the melting pot for dominant white ethnic groups. In contrast, melancholia describes an unresolved process that might usefully describe the unstable immigration and suspended assimilation of Asian Americans into the national fabric. This suspended assimilation—this inability to blend into the "melting pot" of America—suggests that, for Asian Americans, ideals of whiteness are continually estranged. They remain at an unattainable distance, at once a compelling fantasy and a lost ideal.

In configuring assimilation and melancholia in this particular manner, it is important to challenge Freud's contention that melancholia ensues from a "pathological disposition," that it emerges from the disturbance of a one-person psychology rather than the disruption of an intersubjective relationship. In our model, we must emphasize that the inability to "get over" the lost ideal of whiteness is less individual than social. For instance, Asian Americans are typically seen by the mainstream as perpetual foreigners based on skin color and facial features. Despite the fact that they may be United States-born or despite however long they may have resided here, Asian Americans are continually perceived as eccentric to the nation. At other times, Asian Americans are recognized as hyper-model minorities—inhumanly productive—and hence pathological to the nation. In both scenarios, mainstream refusal to see Asian Americans as part and parcel of the American "melting pot" landscape is less an individual failure to blend in with the whole than a socially determined interdiction. Indeed, Freud suggests in "Mourning and Melancholia" that melancholia may proceed from "environmental influences" (p. 243) rather than internal conditions that threaten the existence of the object or ideal.

Freud goes on to delineate the debilitating psychic consequences of melancholia. When faced with unresolved grief, the melancholic preserves the lost object or ideal by incorporating it into the ego and establishing an ambivalent identification with it—ambivalent precisely because of the unresolved and conflicted nature of this forfeiture. From a slightly different perspective, we might say that the melancholic makes every conceivable effort to retain the lost object, to keep it alive within the domain of the psyche. However, the tremendous costs of maintaining this ongoing relationship to the lost object or ideal are psychically damaging. Freud notes that the "distinguishing mental features of melancholia are a profoundly painful dejection, cessation of interest in the outside world, loss of the capacity to love, inhibition of all activity, and a lowering of the self-regarding feelings to a degree that finds utterance in self-reproaches and self-revilings, and culminates in a delusional expectation of punishment" (p. 244).

In identifying with the lost object, the melancholic is able to preserve it but only as a type of haunted, ghostly identification. That is, the melancholic assumes the emptiness of the lost object or ideal, identifies with this emptiness, and thus participates in his or her own self-denigration and ruination of self-esteem. Freud summarizes the distinction between mourning and melancholia in this oft-quoted citation: "In mourning it is the world which has become poor and empty; in melancholia it is the ego itself" (p. 246). He contends that melancholia is one of the most difficult of psychic conditions both to confront and to cure as it is largely an unconscious process. "In yet other cases," Freud observes,

one feels justified in maintaining the belief that a loss of the kind occurred, but one cannot see clearly what it is that has been lost, and it is all the more reasonable to suppose that the patient cannot consciously perceive what he has lost either. This, indeed, might be so even if the patient is aware of the loss which has given rise to his melancholia, but only in the sense that he knows *whom* he has lost but not *what* he has lost in him. [p. 245, Freud's emphasis]

Freud tells us that the depression often accompanying melancholia is extremely dangerous, characterized by the tendency to suicide. Here, we must add, suicide may not merely be physical; it may also be a psychical erasure of one's identity—racial, sexual, or gender identity, for example.

## NATIONAL MELANCHOLIA

For Asian Americans and other groups of color, suspended assimilation into mainstream culture may not only involve severe personal consequences; ultimately, it also constitutes the foundation for a type of national melancholia—a national haunting—with negative social effects. In Senna's *Caucasia*, the ambivalence characterizing whiteness leaves the narrator with the constant and eerie feeling of "contamination."[5]

Writing about the nature of collective identifications, Freud (1921) notes, "In a group every sentiment and act is contagious, and contagious to such a degree that an individual readily sacrifices his personal interest to the collective interest. This is an aptitude very contrary to his nature, and of which a man is scarcely capable, except when he makes part of a group" (p. 75). Our dialogue on racial melancholia insists on thinking about what happens when the demand to sacrifice personal to collective interest is accompanied not by inclusion within, but rather exclusion by, the larger group.

As we know, the formation of the United States quite literally entailed—and continues to entail—a history of institutionalized exclusions, from Japanese-American internment to immigration exclusion acts legislated by Congress, brokered by the Executive, and upheld by the Judiciary against every Asian immigrant group.[6] For example, Chinese Americans experienced one of the longest juridical histories of immigration exclusion as well as bars to naturalization and citizenship from 1882 to 1943. Yet few people realize that the first exclusion laws against a particular ethnic group were passed against the Chinese. These laws were followed by a series of further exclusion acts culminating in the 1924 National Origins Act and the Tyding–McDuffie Act of 1934 that effectively halted all Asian immigration and naturalization. At the same time, other laws were instituted against miscegenation and ownership of private property.

Discourses of American exceptionalism and democratic myths of liberty, individualism, and inclusion force a misremembering of these exclusions, an enforced psychic amnesia that can only return as a type of repetitive national haunting, a type of negative or absent presence.[7] The popular "model minority" stereotype that clings to Asian Americans is both a product and productive of this negative or absent presence.[8] In its compulsive restaging, the model minority stereotype homogenizes widely disparate Asian-American racial and ethnic groups by generalizing them all as economically or academically successful, with no personal or familial problems to speak of. In this manner, the stereotype not only works to deny the heterogeneity, hybridity, and multiplicity of various Asian-American groups that do not fit its ideals of model citizenry;[9] it also functions as a national tool that erases and manages the history of these institutionalized exclusions. The pervasiveness of the model minority stereotype in our contemporary vocabulary works, then, as a melancholic mechanism facilitating the erasure and loss of repressed Asian-American histories and identities. These histories and identities can only return as a type of ghostly presence. In this sense, the Asian-American model minority *subject* also endures in the United States as a melancholic national *object*—a haunting specter to democratic ideals of inclusion that cannot quite "get over" the histories of these legislated proscriptions of loss.

Before moving on, we would like to extend our observations on the psychic consequences that this model of national melancholia exacts upon the individual Asian-American psyche. One compelling example comes from Maxine Hong Kingston's *China Men* (1980). In Kingston's historical novel, the narrator speculates wildly about the disappearance of "The Grandfather of the Sierra Nevada Mountains" after he helps to complete the transcontinental railroad, the greatest technological feat of the nineteenth century: "Maybe he hadn't died in San Francisco, it was just his papers that burned; it was just that his existence was outlawed by Chinese Exclusion Acts. The family called him Fleaman. They did not understand his accomplishments as an American ancestor, a holding, homing ancestor of this place" (p. 151). Kingston understands that the law's refusal to recognize Chinese Americans as citizens "outlaws" their existence, placing them under erasure. At the same time she also underscores how this national refusal gains its efficacy through a simultaneous psychic internalization of its interdicting imperatives on the part of excluded Asian-American subjects. That is, the Grandfather's own family refuses to recognize him. They cannot perceive his accomplishments building the railroad as legitimizing his membership in the American nation. How, in turn, can it be possible to see themselves as legitimate members of this society?

In this regard, racial melancholia might be described as splitting the Asian-American psyche. This cleaving might be productively thought about in terms of an altered, racialized model of classic Freudian fetishism.[10] That is, assimilation into the national fabric demands a psychic splitting on the part of the Asian-American subject who knows and does not know, at once, that she or he is part of the larger group. In the early 1970s, two Asian-American psychologists, Derald and Stanley Sue (1971), coined the term "Marginal Man." Described by the Sues as an Asian-American male subject who desires to assimilate into mainstream American society at any cost, the Marginal Man faithfully subscribes to the ideals of assimilation only through an elaborate self-denial of the daily acts of institutionalized racism directed against him. In "Chinese American Personality and Mental Health," the two write about the complex psychological defenses that the Marginal Man must necessarily employ in order to "function" within American society. The Marginal Man finds it "difficult to admit widespread racism since to do so would be to say that he aspires to join a racist society" (p. 42). Caught in this untenable contradiction, he must necessarily become a split subject—one who exhibits a faithful allegiance to the universal norms of abstract equality and collective national membership at the same time that he displays an uncomfortable understanding of his utter disenfranchisement from these democratic ideals.

Birdie's unresolved assimilation into the whiteness of New Hampshire gives us a final reflection on the psychic effects of splitting in racial melancholia on the level of the signifier. Through the twinning of her name, the impossible mulatto child is marked by doubleness: Birdie (mulatto) → Jesse (white). Here, Birdie/Jesse is the object of melancholia for a nation organized by an ecology of whiteness. At the same time, she is the subject of melancholia, a girl haunted by ghosts. It is difficult not to notice that much of contemporary ethnic literature in the United States is characterized by ghosts and by hauntings from both these perspectives—the objects and subjects of national melancholia. For instance, the subtitle of Maxine Hong Kingston's well-known *The Woman*

*Warrior* (1976) is "Memoirs of a Girlhood Among Ghosts." In "Unspeakable Things Unspoken: The Afro-American Presence in American Literature," the Nobel laureate Toni Morrison (1989) writes that the African-American presence is "the ghost in the machine" (p. 11).

## MIMICRY, OR THE MELANCHOLIC MACHINE

Racial melancholia as psychic splitting and national dis-ease opens upon the interconnected terrain of mimicry, ambivalence, and the stereotype. Homi Bhabha's seminal essay, "Of Mimicry and Man: The Ambivalence of Colonial Discourse" (1984), is crucial here. Bhabha describes the ways in which a colonial regime impels the colonized subject to mimic Western ideals of whiteness. At the same time, this mimicry is also condemned to failure. Bhabha writes, "Colonial mimicry is the desire for a reformed, recognizable Other, as *a subject of a difference that is almost the same, but not quite*. Which is to say, that the discourse of mimicry is constructed around an *ambivalence*; in order to be effective, mimicry must continually reproduce its slippage, its excess, its difference. . . . *Almost the same but not white*" (pp. 126, 130, Bhabha's emphasis). Bhabha has located and labeled the social imperative to assimilate as the colonial structure of mimicry. He marks not only this social imperative but also its inevitable built-in failure. This doubling of difference that is almost the same, but not quite, almost the same but not white, results in ambivalence, which comes to define the failure of mimicry.

Here we would like to connect Bhabha's observations on mimicry in the material space of the colonized with its transposition into the psychic domain through the logic of melancholia. It is important to remember that, like Bhabha's analysis of mimicry, Freud marks ambivalence as one of melancholia's defining characteristics. In describing the genealogy of ambivalence in melancholia, Freud himself (1917) moves from the domain of the material to the register of the psychic. He notes that the "conflict due to ambivalence, which sometimes arises from real experiences, sometimes more from constitutional factors, must not be overlooked among the preconditions of melancholia" (p. 251). Melancholia not only traces an internalized pathological identification with what was once an external and now lost ideal. In this moving from outside to inside (from Bhabha to Freud, as it were) we also get a strong sense of how social injunctions of mimicry configure individual psychic structures as split and dis-eased—another angle from which to consider the cleaving of the Marginal Man. The ambivalence that comes to define Freud's concept of melancholia is one that finds its origins in the social—in colonial and racial structures impelling systems of mimicry and man.

It is crucial to extend Bhabha's theories on colonial mimicry to domestic contexts of racialization in order to consider how we might usefully track this concept to explore further the material and psychic contours of racial melancholia for Asian Americans. One potential site of investigation is the stereotype. In an earlier essay entitled "The Other Question: Stereotype, Discrimination, and the Discourse of Colonialism" (1983/1994), Bhabha also aligns ambivalence and splitting with the stereotype, suggesting that the process of mimicry and the phenomenon of the stereotype might be considered together. The stereotype, Bhabha writes, "is a form of knowledge and identification that vacillates between what is always 'in place,' already known, and something that must be anxiously repeated . . . for it is the force of ambivalence that gives the colonial stereotype its currency" (p. 66).

If we conceptualize the model minority myth as a privileged stereotype through which Asian Americans appear as subjects in the contemporary social domain, then we gain a more refined understanding of how mimicry specifically functions as a material practice in racial melancholia. That is, Asians Americans are forced to mimic the model minority stereotype in order to be recognized by mainstream society—in order *to be* at all. To the extent, however, that this mimicry of the model minority stereotype functions only to estrange Asian Americans from mainstream norms and ideals (as well as from themselves), mimicry can only operate as a melancholic process. As both a social and a psychic malady, mimicry distances Asian Americans from the mimetic ideals of the nation. Through the mobilization and exploitation of the model minority stereotype, mimicry for Asian Americans is always a partial success as well as a partial failure to assimilate into regimes of whiteness.

Let us analyze this dynamic from yet another angle. While Asian Americans are now largely thought of as "model minorities" living out the "American Dream," this stereotyped dream of material success is partial because it is at most configured as economic achievement. The "success" of the model minority myth comes to mask our lack of political and cultural representation. It covers over our inability to gain "full" subjectivities—to be politicians, athletes, and activists, for example—to be recognized as "All American." To occupy the model minority position, Asian-American subjects must follow this prescribed model of economic integration and forfeit political representation as well as cultural voice. In other words, they must not contest the dominant order of things; they must not "rock the boat" or draw attention to themselves. It is difficult for Asian Americans to express any legitimate political, economic, or social needs, as the stereotype demands not only an enclosed but also a passive self-sufficiency.

From an academic point of view, the model minority stereotype also delineates Asian-American students as academically successful but rarely "well-rounded"—well-rounded in tacit comparison to the unmarked (white) student body. Here is another example of Bhabha's concept of mimicry as *nearly* successful imitation. This near-successful assimilation attempts to cover over that gap—the failure of "well-roundedness"—as well as that unavoidable ambivalence resulting from this tacit comparison in which the Asian-American student is seen as lacking. This material failure leads to a psychic ambivalence that works to characterize the colonized subject's identifications with dominant ideals of whiteness as a pathological identification. This is an ambivalence that opens upon the landscape of melancholia and depression for many of the Asian-American students with whom we come into contact on a regular basis. Those Asian Americans who do not fit into the "model minority" stereotype (and this is probably a majority of Asian-American students) are altogether erased from—not seen in—mainstream society. Like Kingston's grandfather in *China Men*, they are often rejected by their own families as well.[11]

The difficulty of negotiating this unwieldy stereotype is that, unlike most pejorative stereotypes of African Americans (but not unlike the myth of the black athlete), the model minority myth is considered to be a "positive" representation, an "exceptional" model for this racial group. In this regard, not only mainstream society but also Asian Americans themselves become attached to, and split by, its seemingly admirable qualities without recognizing its simultaneous liabilities—what Wendy Brown terms a "wounded attachment."[12]

According to Bhabha, in its doubleness the stereotype, like mimicry, creates a gap embedded in an unrecognized structure of material and psychic ambivalence. In Gish Jen's *Typical American* (1991), for instance, we encounter Ralph Chang who chases the American Dream through his attempts to build a fried-chicken kingdom, the "Chicken Palace." Eventually, the franchise fails, the "a" falling off the sign so that "Chicken Palace" becomes "Chicken P__lace." This falling off is the linguistic corollary to the gap in the American Dream that Ralph unsuccessfully attempts to mime. Perhaps it is in this gap, in this emptiness, that Freud's theory of melancholia emerges and dwells. It is in this gap, this loss of whiteness, that the negotiation between mourning and melancholia is staged.

## MOURNING/MELANCHOLIA/IMMIGRATION

This structure of mimicry gestures to the partial success and partial failure to mourn our identifications with whiteness. Moreover, it gestures to our partial success and partial failure to mourn our identifications and affiliations with our "original" Asian cultures. Thus far, we have been focusing on the loss of whiteness as an ideal structuring the assimilation and racialization processes of Asian Americans. However, the lost object can be multifaceted. Since the reformation of the 1965 Immigration and Nationality Act, there are more first-generation Asian-American immigrants living in the United States today than any others. A majority of Asian-American college students are the offspring of this generation. Hence many of our clinical observations lead us to a more concerted focus on the relationship of mourning and melancholia to questions of immigration and intergenerational losses involving Asian identity.

The experience of immigration itself is based on a structure of mourning. When one leaves one's country of origin—voluntarily or involuntarily—there are a host of losses both concrete and abstract that must be mourned. These include homeland, family, language, identity, property, status in the community; the list goes on. In Freud's theory of mourning one works through and finds closure to these losses by investing in new objects, in the American Dream, for example. Our attention to the problematics of mimicry, ambivalence, and the stereotype, as well as our earlier analysis of the history of juridical exclusions of Asian Americans, reveals a social structure that prevents the immigrant from full assimilation. From another perspective, it might be said to deny him or her the capacity to invest in new objects. The inability to invest in new objects, we must remember, is part of Freud's definition of melancholia. Given our current discussion of the ways in which Asian-American immigrants are foreclosed from fully assimilating, are they perpetually consigned to a melancholic status? If so, how do we begin to address Freud's notion of melancholia as pathological? Clearly not all Asian-American immigrants are confined to melancholic or depressive states. If this is the case, how do they negotiate their losses? And how do their offspring inherit and inhabit these losses?

If the losses suffered by the first generation are not resolved and mourned in the process of assimilation—if libido is not replenished by the investment in new objects, new communities, and new ideals—then the melancholia that ensues from this condition can be transferred to the second generation. At the same time, however, can the hope of assimilation and mastery of the American Dream also be transferred? If so, mourning and melancholia are reenacted and lived out by the children in their own attempts to assimilate and to negotiate the American Dream. Here, immigration and assimilation might be said to characterize a process involving not just mourning or melancholia but the intergenerational negotiation between mourning *and* melancholia. Configured as such, this notion begins to depathologize melancholia by situating it as the inherent unfolding and outcome of the mourning process that underwrites the losses of the immigration experience.

Let us turn to a clinical example. Elaine, a U.S.-born Korean-American female college student, grew up in Texas. Her father is a professor and her mother is a homemaker. An academic dean referred Elaine (to Ms. Han) because she was at risk of failing her first year in college. In a tearful presentation, Elaine reported, "My parents have sacrificed everything to raise me here. If my parents had stayed in Korea, my mom would be so much happier and not depressed. She would have friends to speak Korean with, my father would be a famous professor, and we would be better off socially and economically. I wouldn't be so pressured to succeed. They sacrificed everything for me, and now it's up to me to please them, and to do well in school." When asked the reasons for her academic probation, she responded, "I didn't do well because at a certain point I didn't care anymore, and I became depressed."

Elaine's case is an illustration of an intergenerational transference between the immigrant parents and child, which might usefully be described through the logic of melancholia. The loss experienced by the parents' failure to achieve the American Dream—to achieve a standard of living greater than that which they could have putatively achieved in Korea—is a loss transferred onto and incorporated by Elaine for her to "work out" and to repair. In particular, she reenacts these losses through her relationship with her mother. Elaine's depression is a result of internalized guilt and residual anger that she not only feels toward but also identifies with in her mother. Through this incorporation, she also functions as the placeholder of her mother's depression. This mother–daughter predicament has been widely debated in feminist circles.[13] Here, the question is how racial difference comes to intersect what is a strongly gendered formation.

This crossing of sexual and racial difference is a very common narrative in Asian-American literature, especially Asian-American women's writing. Numerous stories portray the first generation (or, alternately, the second generation, depending on the particular historical moment and ethnic group) as being a lost generation—bereft, traumatized, with few material or psychic resources.[14] Is it, however, only at the moment in which the first generation acknowledges its failure to achieve the American Dream that this theme of first-generation sacrifice emerges to be retroactively projected onto the second generation? In other words, are Asian-American parents as completely selfless as the theme of sacrifice suggests, or is this theme a compensatory gesture that attaches itself to the parents' losses and failures? Could the ambition of Elaine's father to become a professor in an American university have motivated their family's immigration? Sacrifice, it is important to remember, is built upon the assumption of non-equivalence and the melancholic notion that what is forfeited and lost can never be recuperated. In turn, do children of immigrants "repay" this sacrifice only by repeating and perpetuating its melancholic logic, by berating and sacrificing themselves?

Yet can sacrifice also be considered the displaced residue of hope—a hope for the reparation of melancholia, of the American Dream? Can hope also be transferred from parent to child, and from child to parent? Elaine's case evokes Rea Tajiri's stunning video, *History and Memory* (1991). *History and Memory* is about a young Japanese-American girl whose parents endure internment during World War II. While her mother has repressed all memories of the interment experience, the daughter has nightmares that she cannot explain: recurring images of a young woman at a watering well. The daughter is depressed, and the parents argue over the etiology of her depression. Eventually, the daughter discovers that these nightmares are reenactments of the mother's histories in camp. Ironically, the mother has history but no memory, while the daughter has memory but no history. For both mother and daughter, history and memory do not come together until the daughter visits the former site of the internment camp, Poston. Here she realizes that it is her mother's history that she remembers.

Tajiri's video is a compelling example of the ways in which historical traumas of loss are unconsciously passed down from one generation to another. It illustrates Freud's maxim that the losses experienced in melancholia are often unconscious ones. Yet, at the same time, it also diverges from Freud's conception of the disease insofar as it posits a theory of melancholia that is not individual but intergenerationally shared among members of a social group—Japanese Americans. It also departs from Freud's definition of melancholia as pathology and permanence. Here, the hope for psychic health is stitched into the fabric of melancholia, but only as an optative gesture that must be redeemed by subsequent generations. In contrast to Freud's contention that melancholia is a classic, one-person psychological state—a permanent psychic condition if not solved within a generation—Tajiri's version of melancholia approaches this condition from a different perspective. It redefines our theory of racial melancholia as an intersubjective psychic state focused on bonds among people, a state that might be addressed and resolved across generations. Indeed, in *History and Memory* the daughter's return to Poston initiates an incipient healing process in her mother.

In melancholia, the subject's turning from outside—intersubjective —to inside—intrapsychic—threatens to render the social invisible. What is striking in both Elaine's case and *History and Memory* is the manner in which the daughters' bodies and voices become substitutes for those of the mothers—not just the mothers' bodies and voices but also something that is unconsciously lost in them. To return to Freud (1917), the melancholic "knows *whom* he has lost but not *what* he has lost in him" (p. 245). Elaine's narrative and the daughters' nightmares are not their own histories. These daughters have absorbed and been saturated by their mothers' losses. The mothers' voices haunt the daughters. These losses and voices are melancholically displaced from the external world into the internal world of the psyche. The anger that these daughters feel toward the loved object is internalized as depression. Freud (1917) reminds us that the reproaches against the self are, in fact, displaced reproaches against the loved object that have been shifted onto the individual's own ego.

In this respect, melancholia might be said to trace a trajectory from love to hate of the lost object. This hate is subsequently transformed into self-hate in the course of moving from the outside world into the internalized domain of the psyche. As such, the internal monologue that the daughters direct toward themselves should rightly be an external dialogue between daughter and mother. Judith Butler (1997) writes,

> The melancholic would have *said something*, if he or she could, but did not, and now believes in the sustaining power of the voice. Vainly, the melancholic now says what he or she would have said, addressed only to himself [*sic*], as one who is already split off from himself, but whose power of self-address depends upon this self-forfeiture. The melancholic thus burrows in a direction opposite to that in which he might find a fresher trace of the lost other, attempting to resolve the loss through psychic substitutions and compounding the loss as he goes. [p. 182, Butler's emphasis]

This turning from outside to inside threatens to erase the *political* bases of melancholia. When Asian-American students seek therapy, for example, their mental health issues—overwhelmingly perceived as intergenerational familial conflicts—are often diagnosed as exclusively symptomatic of *cultural* (not political) conflicts. That is, by configuring Asian cultural difference as the source of all intergenerational disease, Asian culture comes to serve as an alibi or a scapegoat for a panoply of mental health issues. These issues may, in fact, trace their etiology not to questions of Asian cultural difference but rather to forms of institutionalized racism and economic exploitation. The segregation of

Asian-American health issues into the domain of cultural difference thus covers over the need to investigate structural questions of social inequity as they circulate both in and outside of the therapeutic space of the clinic. For instance, not to recognize the history of Japanese internment when analyzing Tajiri's mother–daughter relationship serves not only to repress and to deny this history but also to redouble and to intensify the source of the daughter's melancholia.

Lisa Lowe (1996) writes that

> interpreting Asian American culture exclusively in terms of the master narratives of generational conflict and filial relation essentializes Asian American culture, obscuring the particularities and incommensurabilities of class, gender, and national diversities among Asians. The reduction of the cultural politics of racialized ethnic groups, like Asian Americans, to first-generation/second-generation struggles displaces social differences into a privatized familial opposition. Such reduction contributes to the aestheticizing commodification of Asian American *cultural* differences, while denying the immigrant histories of material exclusion and differentiation. [p. 63, Lowe's emphasis]

A therapeutic process that attributes cultural differences solely to intergenerational conflict may not only result in the failure to cure; it may also serve to further endanger the mental health of the Asian-American patient.

## MOURNING/MELANCHOLIA/LANGUAGE

This discussion of intergenerational immigration issues brings us to the corollary issue of language. Nelson, a first-generation Japanese-American student who emigrated from Osaka to New Jersey when he was 5, sought therapy (with Ms. Han), presenting chronic struggles with depression associated with identity conflicts regarding race. He is the eldest child with two siblings, a brother and a sister, both of whom were born in the United States. Before Nelson entered school, his mother spoke only Japanese to the children. When Nelson started kindergarten, his teacher strongly advised the mother to replace Japanese with English at home if she wanted her children to assimilate and to become successful students. Despite the mother's broken English, she followed the teacher's instruction assiduously, speaking only English to her children. Nelson recounts a story that later took place in grade school. During a reading lesson, he mispronounced "crooked" (two syllables) as "crookd" (one syllable). His teacher shamed him publicly for this failed mimicry, demanding to know where he learned to (mis)pronounce such a simple word. Nelson reluctantly replied that he learned this pronunciation from his mother. He remembers, in particular, the social embarrassment and ridicule of his classmates.

What we learn about Nelson's case is this: while his original connection to the primary object—the mother—was through the Japanese language, this connection was abruptly interrupted by a foreign property, English. The mother's "poor" mimicry of English abandoned and revised the earliest mother–son attachment, one brokered in Japanese. As such, Nelson could no longer mirror himself from his mother, in Japanese or in English. This estrangement from language—native and foreign—is a double loss. While acquiring a new language, English, should be perceived as a positive cognitive development, what is not often acknowledged or emphasized enough is the concomitant psychic trauma triggered by the loss of what had once been safe, nurturing, and familiar to the young child—Japanese.

The loss of Japanese as a safe and nurturing object reveals another concrete way to think about racial melancholia in relation to Asian-American immigration and assimilation. In Nelson's case, melancholia results not only from a thwarted identification with a dominant ideal of unattainable whiteness but from also a vexed relationship to a compromised Japaneseness. Nelson's analytic situation reveals how on two fronts ideals of whiteness and ideals of Asianness are lost and unresolved for the Asian-American subject. In both instances, language is the privileged vehicle by which standards of successful assimilation and failed imitation are measured. In this sense, language itself might be thought of as a kind of stereotype, as demanding a flawless mimicry on the part of the young Nelson whose poor performance leads him to shame and self-abasement.

Nelson's transition from Japanese to English is another good example of the negotiation between mourning *and* melancholia in the immigration and assimilation process. That is, while he suffers a loss and revaluation of his "mother" tongue, his transition into the "adopted" language (or ideal) of English is anything but smooth. We need to emphasize that the shaming ritual to which the grade school teacher subjected Nelson—one all too common in the Darwinian space of the classroom—is one that not merely makes his transition into English difficult but also demonizes the mother (the mother tongue and accent) at the same time. What was once a loved and safe object is retroactively transformed into an object of insecurity and shame. To the extent that the mother originally represents the safe notion of "home," Nelson's estrangement from his mother, and his mother tongue, renders it *unheimlich*—unhomelike, unfamiliar, uncanny.[15]

The relationship between language and assimilation into national citizenry is developed in a short story by Monique T. D. Truong (1991). "Kelly" is about a young Vietnamese refugee girl, Thuy-Mai, who finds herself in the improbable space of a 1975 North Carolina classroom. Truong's narrator writes a distressing epistolary monologue to her one and only (and now absent) friend from that dark period of her life—Kelly. In doing so, she mimes the melancholic logic discussed above. That is, an intersubjective external dialogue meant for two parties is melancholically internalized and transformed into an intrasubjective interminable monologue, remarkable for its anger and depressed solipsism. What is an epistle, after all, but an impassioned (but not necessarily answered) plea to the other?

Truong writes about their grade school teacher:

> Kelly, remember how Mrs. Hammerick talked about Veteran's Day? How about the Day of Infamy when the Japanese bombed Pearl Harbor? Mrs. Hammerick, you know, the mayor's wife, always had a sweet something surrounding her like she had spent too much time pulling taffy. . . . Kelly, you only knew that she liked the Beths and the Susans cause they wore pink and never bulged and buckled out of their shirt plackets. I was scared of her like no dark corners could ever scare me. You have to know that all the while she was teaching us history she was telling, with her language for the deaf, blind, and dumb; she was telling all the boys in our class that I was Pearl and my last name was Harbor. They understood her like she was speaking French and their names were all Claude and Pierre. [p. 42]

Truong's story expands our discussion of language and its effects on the constitution of good and bad national subjects. Here, Mrs. Hammerick's common language for the "deaf, blind, and dumb"—a language from which Thuy-Mai is emphatically excluded—is used to create good and bad students within the institutionalized space of the classroom. The Susans and the Beths, the Claudes and the Pierres are all, as Louis Althusser (1971) would put it, "interpellated" by the mayor's wife as good citizen-subjects of the classroom and consequently the nation. Truong emphasizes how education is a primary site through which narratives of national group identity are established, reinforced, and normalized. At the same time, the Vietnamese refugee, Thuy-Mai, is pathologized as the Asian enemy, dismissively labeled "Pearl Harbor," erroneously conflated with the Japanese, and implicitly rendered a menace to the coherence of the U.S. nation-state. Mrs. Hammerick is, of course, not literally speaking French. However, Truong's attention to language underscores the ways in which an unconscious discourse of racism is circulated in the space of the classroom as a nationalizing tract. Furthermore, as Lisa Lowe (1996) points out, Mrs. Hammerick's nationalizing tract is also a gendered discourse: "The narrator's observations that the teacher's history lesson addresses 'all the boys' further instantiates how the American nationalist narrative recognizes, recruits, and incorporates male subjects, while 'feminizing' and silencing the students who do not conform to that notion of patriotic subjectivity" (p. 55). Racialized subjects, such as Nelson and Thuy-Mai, become "good" citizens when they identify with the paternal state and accept, as Lowe summarizes, "the terms of this identification by subordinating [their] racial difference and denying [their] ties with the feminized and racialized 'motherland'" (p. 56).

## ON GOOD AND BAD RACIALIZED OBJECTS

In the case of Nelson, the teacher's shaming of the mother brings her image into crisis, reconfiguring her return in the guise of a "bad" mother. Like Elaine, Nelson, as the Asian-American child of immigrant parents, becomes the arbiter not only of his mother's ambitions and losses but also of his own. His attempts to "reinstate" his first love object and caretaker—the Japanese mother—as well as his first language— Japanese—are tortuous and compromised.

Nelson's case history brings us to the work of Melanie Klein on good and bad objects, which might be usefully factored into our discussion of racial melancholia for Asian Americans. In "Mourning and Its

Relation to Manic-Depressive States" (1940), Klein extends Freud's theory on mourning. She writes that "while it is true that the characteristic feature of normal mourning is the individual's setting up the lost loved object inside himself, he is not doing so for the first time but, through the work of mourning, is reinstating that object as well as all his loved *internal* objects which he feels he has lost. He is, therefore, *recovering* what he had already attained in childhood" (pp. 165–166, Klein's emphasis). States of mourning in adult life are dealt with and resolved through the alignment of the lost object with all the "loved internal objects" of infancy. This clustering of the lost object with the good objects of the past is, as Klein points out, an attempt to recover and hence to reinstate the securities of infancy before the mother was split into good and bad (a necessary but impossible project). In this manner, the loved object is "preserved in safety inside oneself" and depression can be negotiated (p. 119).

Unlike Freud's, then, Klein's formulation of mourning, as well as her prescription for psychic health, depend on the introjection of the lost object, retaining it through a melancholic logic of internalization, but an internalization that attempts to reinstate the lost object by aligning it with a cluster of good internal objects.[16]

Klein warns us, however, of the difficulties often accompanying this rebuilding of the inner world, this recovery and reinstatement of the lost object as "good." Depression will surely ensue, Klein warns us, when the lost object cannot be clustered with the good objects of the past. In particular, she writes about the advent of depression through the forfeiture of the "good" mother. In "A Contribution to the Psychogenesis of Manic-Depressive States," Klein (1935) observes that from

> the very beginning of psychic development there is a constant correlation of real objects with those installed within the ego. It is for this reason that the anxiety I have just described manifests itself in a child's exaggerated fixation to its mother or whoever looks after it. The absence of the mother arouses in the child anxiety lest it should be handed over to bad objects, external and internalized, either *because* of her death or because of her return in the guise of a '*bad*' mother. [p. 121, Klein's emphasis]

Nelson's case shows what happens when the mother returns in the guise of a "bad" mother precisely through the loss—the death— of "Japaneseness." Nelson's "good" mother of infancy returns as a "bad" mother of childhood at the moment of the teacher's sudden linguistic interdiction. After this childhood trauma, Nelson cannot easily repair and realign an image of the mother as "bad" with his earlier perceptions of this nurturing figure. Klein summarizes:

> In some patients who had turned away from their mother in dislike or hate, or used other mechanisms to get away from her, I have found that there existed in their minds nevertheless a beautiful picture of the mother, but one which was felt to be a *picture* of her only, not her real self. The real object was felt to be unattractive—really an injured, incurable and therefore dreaded person. The beautiful picture had been dissociated from the real object but had never been given up and played a great part in the specific ways of their sublimations. [p. 125, Klein's emphasis]

Nelson's case history challenges us to consider what must be shorn away from the shamed Japanese mother in order to reinstate her to a world of loved internal objects, in order to create from her a "beautiful picture." In this instance, it would seem that it is racial difference—Japaneseness—itself that must be dissociated from the figure of the injured and dreaded mother in order for this reinstatement to occur. In turn, however, through the shaming of his mother and mother tongue as well as his attempts to repair them, Nelson's Japanese identity becomes dissociated from him, repressed into the unconscious and transformed into a bad object. Nelson's case history emphatically underscores the way in which good attachments to a primary object can be threatened and transformed into bad attachments *specifically through the axis of race*.

What we are proposing here is the refinement of Klein's theory into an account of "good" and "bad" *racialized* objects. Nelson and his mother are bound together as mourners. The mother becomes overwhelmed with guilt about her broken English. She transfers the burden of this trauma, as well as the burden of hope, onto Nelson's shoulders. As such, Nelson attempts to save himself by reinstating his mother (and thus his own ego) as good object. His fixation with perfecting his English is indicative of an obsessional mechanism that negotiates the depressive position for him. This process of perfecting English might be seen as Nelson's displaced attempt to preserve the image of the beautiful Japanese mother. His efforts to reinstate an image of beauty can never be fulfilled (for him or for anyone). However, these attempts are a "necessary failure," for Klein warns that if this image of beauty is removed completely—if the death wish against the mother is fulfilled—then guilt is not reduced but in fact heightened. Were this to happen, the self-abasement accompanying melancholia's guilt and ambivalence would only redouble.

Indeed, the racial melancholia that underwrites Nelson's unresolved loss of the Japanese mother renders the attempt to reinstate extraordinarily tenuous. This compromising of Nelson's efforts vexes the "proper" work of mourning, leaving him depressed. Klein (1935) states, "the ego endeavors to keep the good apart from the bad, and the real from the phantasmatic objects" (p. 123). However, it may be that the racial melancholia and depression that ensue for Nelson can be avoided only through the most difficult psychic process of dissociation: splitting off Japaneseness from the figure of the mother as well as segregating racial and sexual difference. Klein comments, "The attempts to save the loved object, to repair and restore it, attempts which in the state of depression are coupled with despair, since the ego doubts its capacity to achieve this restoration, are determining factors for all sublimations and the whole of the ego development" (p. 124). Nelson's chronic depression and sustained ambivalence toward the figure of his mother indicate the tortuous process of reinstatement that clearly impedes proper ego development. It is racial difference that must be attended to here.

At this point, we would like to return to Butler. In *The Psychic Life of Power* (1997), Butler observes that melancholia instantiates a psychic topography in which the ego constitutively emerges in relation to a superego that admonishes it and judges it to be lacking. Melancholia, Butler states, "produces the possibility for the representation of psychic life" (p. 177). She makes this claim through a deconstruction of mourning and melancholia. In his first account of the disease, Freud contrasts the pathological condition of melancholia to the normal work of mourning. However, later in "The Ego and the Id" (1923), Freud is moved to revise this earlier distinction between mourning and melancholia. He must do so, Butler notes, when he realizes that the ego itself is composed of abandoned object-cathexes internalized as constitutive identifications: "But let us remember that in "The Ego and the Id" Freud himself acknowledges that melancholy, the unfinished process of grieving, is central to the formation of identifications that form the ego.

Indeed, identifications formed from unfinished grief are the modes in which the lost object is incorporated and phantasmatically preserved in and as the ego" (Butler 1997, p. 132). If the ego is composed of its lost attachments, then there would be no ego—indeed, no distinction between inside and outside—without the internalization of loss along melancholic lines. Melancholia thus instantiates the very logic by which the ego and its psychic landscape are constituted. It is only after this partition of internal and external worlds that the work of mourning—that subjectivity itself—becomes possible.[17]

Butler (1997) aligns this deconstruction of mourning and melancholia with the social emergence of gender and a system of compulsory heterosexuality. She focuses on Freud's contention, in "The Ego and the Id," that the primary lost object of desire for the little boy is the father. As such, Butler argues, heterosexual male subjectivity is created melancholically through the father's forfeiture as an object of desire and his internalization as a primary and constitutive identification. She writes that heterosexual identity is thus

> purchased through a melancholic incorporation of the love that it dis- avows: the man who insists upon the coherence of his heterosexuality will claim that he never loved another man, and hence never lost an- other man. That love, that attachment becomes subject to a double dis- avowal, a never having loved, and a never having lost. This "never-never" thus founds the heterosexual subject, as it were; it is an identity based upon the refusal to avow an attachment and, hence, the refusal to grieve. [pp. 139–140]

Butler concludes that in opposition to a concept of (hetero)sexuality that is said to reflect a natural gendered order, gender in this case is understood to be composed of precisely what remains melancholically disavowed in sexuality.

Klein's theory of good and bad objects is a useful theoretical supple- ment here because she addresses something unaddressed in Butler. If a system of gender melancholy instantiates compulsory male heterosexu- ality, we nevertheless do not typically describe the normative male sub- ject as melancholic or depressed. In other words, as Adam Phillips (1997) suggests, if the normative heterosexual male claims to be rela- tively untroubled by this disavowal, is it the task of the psychoanalyst to engineer its undoing? Here the clinical implications of this undoing diverge from the speculative payoff of rethinking a system of compulsory heterosexuality.

In both cases, however, Klein's notion of the good and the bad object—of "recovery" and "reinstatement"—allows us to understand how certain losses are grieved because they are not, perhaps, even seen as losses but as social gains. These gains include access to political, economic, and cultural privilege; alignment with whiteness (disavowal of Asianness) and the nation; and "full" subjectivity and a sense of belonging. In other words, the loss of the father as object of desire for the little boy can be more acceptably mourned than other losses, for this "forfeiture" has widespread social support and approbation. Indeed, it provides the very foundation of oedipalization. As such, it is seen not as an abandonment but as a culturally rewarded transaction. To return to Phillips, we must continue to ask why it is that the normative heterosexual male can claim to be untroubled by his melancholic disavowals.

Let us contrast this normative story of oedipalization and the "loss" of the father to Nelson's compromised loss of the mother and the mother tongue. Our present deconstruction of mourning and melancholia tells us it is crucial to recognize that all identities are built on loss. Loss is symptomatic of ego formation, for both dominant as well as marginalized subjects. The crucial point to investigate, then, is the social and psychic status of that lost object—idealized or devalued—and the ways in which that lost object can or cannot be reinstated into the psychic life of the individual in order to rebuild an internal world. It is Klein who lends us a theoretical account that enables us to make these distinctions.

## DEPATHOLOGIZING MELANCHOLIA

The process of assimilation is a negotiation between mourning *and* melancholia. The ethnic subject does not inhabit one or the other, but mourning and melancholia coexist at once in the process of assimilation. This continuum between mourning and melancholia allows us to understand the negotiation of racial melancholia as *conflict* rather than *damage*. Indeed, might we consider damage the intrasubjective displacement of a necessarily intersubjective dynamic of conflict? This attention to racial melancholia as conflict rather than damage not only renders it a productive category but also removes Asian Americans from the position of solipsistic "victims." We are dissatisfied with the assumption that minority subjectivities are permanently damaged—forever injured and incapable of ever being whole. Our theory of intersubjective conflict, intergenerationally shared, evokes Klein's notion of rebuilding on a communal level. This notion of communal rebuilding provides the foundation for the reparation of individual psyches as well as group identities.

The discussion of immigration, assimilation, and racialization pursued here develops them as issues involving the fluid negotiation between mourning and melancholia. In this manner, melancholia is neither pathological nor permanent but, as José Esteban Muñoz (1999) eloquently suggests, "a structure of feeling"—a structure of everyday life. Muñoz states that, for queers as well as for people of color, melancholia is not a pathology but an integral part of daily existence and survival. He provides a corrective to Freud's vision of melancholia as a destructive force, stating that it is instead part of the "process of dealing with all the catastrophes that occur in the lives of people of color, lesbians, and gay men. I have proposed a different understanding of melancholia that does not see it as a pathology or as a self-absorbed mood that inhibits activism. Rather, it is a mechanism that helps us (re)construct identity and take our dead with us to the various battles we must wage in their names—and in our names" (p. 74).

Within the continuum of mourning and melancholia, there is a productive gap that the various issues under discussion here—immigration, assimilation, and racialization; mimicry, ambivalence, and the stereotype; sacrifice, loss, and reinstatement—inhabit. The material and psychic negotiations of these various issues are the conflicts with which Asian Americans struggle on an everyday basis. This struggle does not necessarily result in damage but is ultimately a productive and a necessary process. It is the work of rebuilding. "Suffering," Klein writes, "can become productive" (1940, p. 163). She adds:

> It seems that every advance in the process of mourning results in a deepening in the individual's relation to his inner objects, in the happiness of regaining them after they were felt to be lost ('Paradise Lost and Regained'), in an increased trust in them and love for them because they proved to be good and helpful after all. This is similar to the way in which the young child step by step builds up his experiences but also from the ways in which he overcomes frustrations and unpleasant experiences, nevertheless retaining his good objects (externally and internally). [p. 164]

We would like to think about the numerous difficulties of Asian-American immigration, assimilation, and racialization processes in terms of "Paradise Lost and Regained."

In the work of racial melancholia, too, there lies a nascent ethical and political project. Freud (1917) originally describes the melancholic's inability to get over loss in rather negative terms. We would like instead to focus on the melancholic's absolute refusal to relinquish the other—to forfeit alterity—at any cost. In this essay, Freud lays out the provocative idea that in melancholia "the shadow of the object fell upon the ego" (p. 249). In most of the Freudian oeuvre it is indubitably the ego that rules; his majesty the ego's narcissism reigns supreme. Throughout his writings, Jacques Lacan (1991) emphasizes the narcissism of the ego even more, reversing this particular formulation by insisting that it is always the shadow of the ego that falls upon the object. In our present formulation, however, we have the loved object, not the ego, holding sway. Racial melancholia thus delineates one psychic process in which the loved object is so overwhelmingly important to and beloved by the ego that the ego is willing to preserve it even at the cost of its own self. In the transferential aspects of melancholic identifications, Freud suggests, "is the expression of there being something in common which may signify love" (1917, p. 250).

This community of love, as W. R. D. Fairbairn (1954), Jessica Benjamin (1998), Christopher Bollas (1987), and others have noted, is possible only through the aggressive and militant preservation of the loved and lost object. Hence, the melancholic process is one way in which socially disparaged objects—racially and sexually depriviledged others—live on in the psychic realm. This behavior, Freud remarks, proceeds from an attitude of "revolt" (1917, p. 248) on the part of the ego. It displays the ego's melancholic yet militant refusal to allow certain objects to disappear into oblivion. In this way, Freud tells us, "love escapes extinction" (p. 257). This preservation of the threatened object might be seen, then, as a type of ethical hold on the part of the melancholic ego. The mourner, in contrast, has no such ethics. The mourner is perfectly content to kill off the lost object, declaring it to be dead yet again within the domain of the psyche.

While the ambivalence, anger, and rage that characterize this preservation of the lost object threaten the ego's stability, we do not imagine that this threat is the result of some ontological tendency on the part of the melancholic; it is a social threat. Ambivalence, rage, and anger are the internalized refractions of an ecology of whiteness bent on the obliteration of cherished minority subjectivities. If the loved object is not going to live out there, the melancholic emphatically avers, then it is going to live here inside of me. Along with Freud, "we only wonder why a man has to be ill before he can be accessible to a truth of this kind" (1917, p. 246). It is the melancholic who helps us come face to face with this social truth. It is the melancholic who teaches us that "in the last resort we must begin to love in order not to fall ill" (Freud 1914, p. 85).

Both Judith Butler and Douglas Crimp (1989) isolate the call of melancholia in the age of AIDS as one in which the loss of a public language to mourn a seemingly endless series of young male deaths triggers the absolute need to think about melancholia and activism. Muñoz (1999) highlights the communal nature of this activist project—the community-oriented aspect of group as opposed to individual losses, identifications, and activism: "Communal mourning, by its very nature, is an immensely complicated text to read, for we do not mourn just one lost object or other, but we also mourn as a 'whole'—or, put another way, as a contingent and temporary collection of fragments that is experiencing a loss of its parts" (p. 73). A series of unresolved fragments, we come together as a contingent whole. We gain social recognition in the face of this communal loss.

There is a militant refusal on the part of the ego—better yet, a series of egos—to let go, and this militant refusal is at the heart of melancholia's productive political potentials. Paradoxically, in this instance, the ego's death drive may be the very precondition for survival, the beginning of a strategy for living and for living on. Butler (1997) asks of melancholia: "Is the psychic violence of conscience not a refracted indictment of the social forms that have made certain kinds of losses ungrievable?" (p. 185). And Crimp (1989) ends his essay with this simple and moving call: "Militancy, of course, then, but mourning too: mourning *and* militancy" (p. 18, his emphasis). We would like to pause here to insert yet another permutation of this political project in relation to the Asian-American immigration, assimilation, and racialization processes we have been discussing throughout this essay: "mourning *and* melancholia."

## EPILOGUE: LIVING MELANCHOLIA

This essay is an engagement with psychoanalysis and racial difference that belongs neither in the speculative nor in the clinical arena proper. Rather, like our theory of racial melancholia, it exists in a gap between two spheres, seeking to establish a productive relationship between them. We wrote this essay with the hope of proffering a number of new critical interventions significant to both realms. We wrote it with the desire to understand better our students, our communities, and ourselves.

It also occurs to us that our dialogue—crossing into the often disparate realms of the literary and the clinical—is an exercise in new models of communal interaction that we advocate in our various discussions of the everyday living out of racial melancholia by Asian Americans. Much of our focus reexamines the ways in which the genealogy of racial melancholia as individual pathology functions in terms of larger social group identities. Indeed, it is our belief that the refusal to view identities under social erasure as individual pathology and permanent damage lies in the communal appropriation of melancholia, its reformulation as a structure of everyday life that annuls the multitude of losses an unforgiving social world continually demands.

To that end, we conclude with a few words on one strategy of community building within the space of the university. A recent, albeit contested, trend in the academy is the establishing of Asian-American Studies programs. In the face of this trend, the model-minority stereotype is consistently marshaled by university administrations as proof that Asian Americans neither are in want of any special recognition nor have any particular needs as a distinct and socially marked group. The popular vision of Asian Americans as model minorities, as having the best of both worlds (two cultures, two languages), is a multicultural fantasy in the age of diversity management. Our investigation here of immigration, assimilation, and racialization as conflicted and unresolved processes of mourning and melancholia reveals the link between East and West as less than fluid. For Asian Americans, the reparation of these unresolved processes requires a public language, a public space where these conflicts can be acknowledged and negotiated.

In their ideal form, Asian-American Studies programs provide this publicity, a physical and psychic space to bring together various fragmented parts—intellectual, social, political, cultural—to compose, borrowing from Winnicott (1965), a "holding environment," a "whole" environment. This type of public space ultimately facilitates the creation of new representations of Asian Americans emerging from that gap of ambivalence between mourning and melancholia. These new representations not only contest conventional ways in which Asian Americans have been traditionally apprehended but also reformulate the very meanings of *Asian American* within the public sphere.

In the final analysis, this essay has been an exercise for us to mourn the various passings of Asian-American students who no longer felt tied to our present world, such that it is. However, this dialogue—this production of new ideas about the conditions and constraints of racial melancholia—should not be taken as a summary moment. Instead, it might be understood as an initial engagement in the continued work of mourning and melancholia, and in the rebuilding of new communities.

## NOTES

1. We would like to thank Neil Altman, Muriel Dimen, David Kazanjian, Tazuko Shibusawa, Carolyn Stack, Serena Volpp, and Sophie Volpp for their generous advice and expert help in the revision of this essay.

2. "Jesse" presents herself as Jewish (and thus not black), significantly complicating the racial complexities of "whiteness" in Senna's novel. While "Jesse" is marked differently from the WASPs populating her New Hampshire environment, her part-Jewish background is mobilized so that she can "pass." It is ostensibly used as an explanation for her dark skin tone and hair.

3. It is important to remember that melancholia and depression are not synonymous psychic conditions, although they often coexist and can trigger one another.

4. The relationship between melancholia and processes of immigration, assimilation, and racialization is underdeveloped in both Asian-American Studies and clinical practice. We suggest that those interested in this intersection read Asian-American literature by authors such as Frank Chin (1988), Maxine Hong Kingston (1976), Wendy Law-Yone (1983), Chang-rae Lee (1995), Fae Myenne Ng (1993), Hualing Nieh (1981), and Chay Yew (1997). For a discussion of Asian-American immigration, see Sucheng Chan (1991), Bill Ong Hing (1993), and Lisa Lowe (1996). For a discussion of Asian-American immigration and mental health issues, see Salman Akhtar (1995) and Yu-Wen Ying (1997).

5. Here Senna is reconfiguring a long history of "contamination" that racializes individuals with "one-drop" of black blood as colored. There is also a long history that configures immigrants as diseased and contaminated, carriers of illness who infect the national body politic. The theme of "contamination" is thus one location to think about the intersections of African-American and Asian-American racialization processes.

6. For a history of these immigration exclusion acts see Chan (1991), Hing (1993), and Lowe (1996).

7. See Anne Anlin Cheng (1997), pp. 51–52.

8. For a history of the model minority stereotype, see Bob H. Suzuki (1977). For a critique of the model minority thesis in terms of Asian, white, and black relations, see Mari Matsuda (1996).

9. For an elaboration of the concepts of "heterogeneity, hybridity, and multiplicity," see Lowe (1996), pp. 60–83.

10. See Freud's essays "Fetishism" (1927) and "Splitting of the Ego in the Process of Defence" (1938). This argument on racial fetishization and the following discussion on the "Marginal Man" come from David L. Eng (2001), chapters 1 and 4.

11. Tazuko Shibusawa (personal correspondence, 1999) points out that we must also consider how the model minority stereotype dovetails with a Confucian tradition within East Asian societies. This tradition mandates a strict hierarchical relationship between individual family members and between individual family units and the political representatives of the state.

12. For an elaboration of this concept, see Wendy Brown (1995). In particular, see chapter 3, "Wounded Attachments," pp. 52–76, in which Brown writes:

> But in its attempts to displace its suffering, identity structured by *ressentiment* at the same time becomes invested in its own subjection. This investment lies not only in its discovery of a site of blame for its hurt will, not only in its acquisition of recognition through its history of subjection (a recognition predicated on injury now righteously revalued), but also in the satisfactions of revenge, which ceaselessly reenact even as they redistribute the injuries of marginalization and subordination in a liberal discursive order that alternately denies the very possibility of these things and blames those who experience them for their own condition. Identity politics structured by *ressentiment* reverse without subverting this blaming structure; they do not subject to critique the sovereign subject of accountability that liberal individualism presupposes, nor the economy of inclusion and exclusion that liberal universalism establishes. [p. 70]

13. See, for example, Kristeva (1980).

14. The question of generational sacrifice is historically as well as ethnically specific. For example, during the exclusion era, many first-generation Asian immigrants were barred from naturalization and citizenship. Designated as "sojourners" in the U.S., they exhibited a strong identification with their home country. Consequently, it was the second generation during this historical period (especially those born on U.S. soil) who exhibited the stronger characteristics of a lost generation, for instance, the Nisei interned during World War II.

After the 1965 reformation of the Immigration and Nationality Act, Asian immigrants—and in much larger numbers—were legally guaranteed access to the space of the nation-state as citizens. The narrative of sacrifice thus attaches itself more strongly to these first-generation immigrants, whose hopes for assimilation and integration into the national fabric are quite evident.

15. See Freud's essay on "The Uncanny" (1919). For a discussion of the uncanny and nation building, see Sau-ling Wong (1993), chapter 2 and Priscilla Wald (1995), chapter 1.

16. It might be useful here to consider Freud's notion of mourning and melancholia against Abraham and Torok's (1994) concept of "introjection" versus "incorporation."

17. Butler writes that, in melancholia, the

> inability to declare such a loss signifies the "retraction" or "absorption" of the loss by the ego. Clearly, the ego does not literally take an object inside itself, as if the ego were a kind of shelter prior to its melancholy. The psychological discourses and its various "parts" miss the crucial point that melancholy is precisely what interiorizes the psyche, that is, makes it possible to refer to the psyche through such topographical tropes. The turn from object to ego is the movement that makes the distinction between them possible, that marks the division, the separation or loss, that forms the ego to begin with. In this sense, the turn from the object to the ego fails successfully to substitute the latter for the former, but does succeed in marking and perpetuating the partition between the two. The turn thus produces the divide between ego and object, the internal and external worlds that it appears to presume. [p. 170]

## REFERENCES

Abraham, N., and Torok, M. (1994). Mourning or melancholia: introjection versus incorporation. In *The Shell and the Kernel, Volume 1*, ed. N. T. Rand, pp. 125–138. Chicago: University of Chicago Press.

Akhtar, S. (1995). A third individuation: immigration, identity, and the psychoanalytic process. *Journal of the American Psychoanalytic Association* 43(4):1051–1084.

Althusser, L. (1971). Ideology and ideological state apparatuses (notes towards an investigation). In *Lenin and Philosophy and Other Essays*, ed. B. Brewster, pp. 127–186. New York: Monthly Review Press.

Benjamin, J. (1998) *The Shadow of the Other: Intersubjectivity and Gender in Psychoanalysis*. New York: Routledge.

Bhabha, H. K. (1983). The other question: stereotype, discrimination, and the discourse of colonialism. In *The Location of Culture*, pp. 66–84. London: Routledge, 1994.

———— (1984). Of mimicry and man: the ambivalence of colonial discourse. *October* 28 (Spring):125–133.

Bollas, C. (1987). *The Shadow of the Object: Psychoanalysis of the Unthought Known*. New York: Columbia University Press.

Brown, W. (1995). *States of Injury: Power and Freedom in Late Modernity*. Princeton, NJ: Princeton University Press.

Butler, J. (1997). *The Psychic Life of Power: Theories in Subjection*. Stanford, CA: Stanford University Press.

Chan, S., ed. (1991). *Entry Denied: Exclusion and the Chinese Community in America, 1882–1943*. Philadelphia: Temple University Press.

Cheng, A. A. (1997). The melancholy of race. *Kenyon Review* 19(1):49–61.

Chin, F. (1988). *The Chinaman Pacific and Frisco R.R. Co*. Minneapolis, MN: Coffee House Press.

Crimp, D. L. (1989). Mourning and militancy. *October* (Winter):3–18.

Eng, D. L. (2001). *Racial Castration: Managing Masculinity in Asian America*. Durham, NC: Duke University Press.

Fairbairn, W. R. D. (1954). *An Object-Relations Theory of the Personality*. New York: Basic Books.

Freud, S. (1914). On narcissism: an introduction. *Standard Edition* 14:67–103.

———— (1917). Mourning and melancholia. *Standard Edition* 14:243–258.

———— (1919). The uncanny. *Standard Edition* 17:217–248.

———— (1921). Group psychology and the analysis of the ego. *Standard Edition* 18:69–143.

———— (1923). The ego and the id. *Standard Edition* 19:1–59.

———— (1927). Fetishism. *Standard Edition* 21:152–157.

———— (1938). Splitting of the ego in the process of defence. *Standard Edition* 23:275–278.

Hing, B. O. (1993). *Making and Remaking Asian America Through Immigration Policy, 1850–1990*. Stanford, CA: Stanford University Press.

Jen, G. (1991). *Typical American*. Boston: Houghton Mifflin.

Kingston, M. H. (1976). *The Woman Warrior*. New York: Vintage, 1989.

———— (1980). *China Men*. New York: Vintage, 1989.

Klein, M. (1935). A contribution to the psychogenesis of manic-depressive states. In *The Selected Melanie Klein*, ed. J. Mitchell, pp. 116–145. New York: Free Press, 1987.

———— (1940). Mourning and its relation to manic-depressive states. In *The Selected Melanie Klein*, ed. J. Mitchell, pp. 146–174. New York: Free Press, 1987.

Kristeva, J. (1980). *Desire in Language: A Semiotic Approach to Literature and Art*. New York: Columbia University Press.

Lacan, J. (1991). *The Seminar of Jacques Lacan, Book II: The Ego in Freud's Theory and in the Technique of Psychoanalysis, 1954–1955*. New York: Norton.

Law-Yone, W. (1983). *The Coffin Tree*. Boston: Beacon, 1987.

Lee, C. (1995). *Native Speaker*. New York: Riverhead Books.

Lowe, L. (1996). *Immigrant Acts: On Asian-American Cultural Politics*. Durham, NC: Duke University Press.

Matsuda, M. (1996). We will not be used: are Asian Americans the racial bourgeoisie? In *Where Is Your Body? and Other Essays on Race, Gender, and the Law*, pp. 149–159. Boston: Beacon.

Morrison, T. (1989). Unspeakable things unspoken: the Afro-American presence in American literature. *Michigan Quarterly Review* 28 (Winter):1–34.

Muñoz, J. E. (1999). *Disidentifications: Queers of Color and the Performance of Politics*. Minneapolis: University of Minnesota Press.

Ng, F. M. (1993). *Bone*. New York: Hyperion.

Nieh, H. (1981). *Mulberry and Peach*. Boston: Beacon, 1988.

Phillips, A. (1997). Keeping it moving: commentary on Judith Butler's "Melancholy Gender/Refused Identification." In J. Butler, *The Psychic Life of Power*, pp. 151–159. Stanford, CA: Stanford University Press.

Senna, D. (1998). *Caucasia*. New York: Riverhead Books.

Sue, S., and Sue, D. W. (1971). Chinese-American personality and mental health. *Amerasia Journal* 1(2):36–49.

Suzuki, B. H. (1977). Education and the socialization of Asian Americans: a revisionist analysis of the model minority thesis. *Amerasia Journal* 4(2):23–51.

Tajiri, R., dir. (1991). *History and Memory*. New York: Women Make Movies.

Truong, M. T. D. (1991). Kelly. *Amerasia Journal* 17(2): 41–48.

Wald, P. (1995). *Constituting Americans: Cultural Anxiety and Narrative Form*. Durham, NC: Duke University Press.

Winnicott, D. W. (1965). *The Maturational Processes and the Facilitating Environment.* New York: International Universities Press.

Wong, S. (1993). *Reading Asian-American Literature: From Necessity to Extravagance.* Princeton, NJ: Princeton University Press.

Yew, C. (1997). *Porcelain.* New York: Grove.

Ying, Y. (1997). Psychotherapy for East Asian Americans with major depression. In *Working with Asian Americans: A Guide for Clinicians*, ed. E. Lee, pp. 252–264. New York: Guilford.

# Discussion of "A Dialogue on Racial Melancholia"

*Ronnie C. Lesser*

It is with pleasure that I enter this eloquent dialogue between Eng and Han. By joining their discussion I heed their directive to read their paper as a particular moment in an ongoing engagement with "Mourning and Melancholia" (Freud 1917), rather than as a final word. It is in this spirit that I will articulate both my enthusiasm for and my disappointment with different aspects of their paper. I join this discourse from various subject positions, some of which differ from Eng and Han's in significant ways: Eastern-European Jewish, middle class, baby boomer, lesbian, psychoanalyst. Like Birdie, the protagonist in *Caucasia* (Senna 1998), I am someone on the border, both an insider and an outsider, experienced with some kinds of culturally induced melancholia and, because of privilege, exempt from others.

I was enthusiastic about Eng and Han's discussion for many different reasons. Most important, it makes conscious a subject that haunts psychoanalysis (and, for that matter, "Mourning and Melancholia"): race. Consider the paradox that race is so rarely discussed in psychoanalysis, even though Freud, and most of the Jewish psychoanalysts around him in the early years, were victims of racial trauma. Racialized hatred of Jews cast its shadow on Freud's life and work. Anti-Semitism was present not only within Austrian culture, but in science as well. According to Gilman (1993), the idea of Jews as a different, diseased, incurable race was central to scientific paradigms. It was of strategic importance for any Jew who became a physician (a profession that was closed to Jews prior to the nineteenth century) to find a way to deal with racism in science.

Freud used the rhetoric of psychoanalysis both to deny his own racial melancholia and to work it through (Gilman 1993). By highlighting the sexual difference as if it alone were what counted, racialized identifications and desires became marginalized. Issues concerning how subjects become racialized, as well as the extent to which gendered subjectivity might rely on or be tangled up with racial assumptions, were, and continue to be, rarely considered (Walton 1997).

Eng and Han's discussion of race is also important because it illuminates the intersection between the cultural and the psychological. The traditional psychoanalytic view assumes a psyche independent of culture. By focusing on the psychological and cultural aspects of race as interlocking constructions, Eng and Han contextualize psychoanalytic theory. From this perspective, the melancholia experienced by some racialized subjects is culturally induced. An individual pathology model will simply not do.

The image of the indissociability of the social and the psychological is a thread that runs through much of the paper. In their description of the model-minority myth, for example, Eng and Han discuss the way that Asian-American subjectivity is configured by this cultural stereotype. In this context, Asian Americans are impelled to mimic the stereotype in order to gain visibility and acceptance in mainstream culture. Sadly and ironically, this mimicry estranges them from both mainstream culture and themselves.

I would like to add to Eng and Han's description of the psychological ramifications of the model-minority myth, its political purposes. According to Takaki (1999), the model-minority myth has a long history. In 1870, prior to the exclusionary policies cited by Eng and Han, it was already in full swing when it was used to keep other racialized groups in line. Consider two events that occurred in that year: when

Southern planters were confronted with wage-earning blacks and be-gan to have labor conflicts with them, a coalition of planters transported 500 Chinese immigrant workers to Louisiana and Mississippi in order to pit them against black wage earners. Newspaper reports from that time show that the Chinese immigrant laborers were touted as examples of obedient, conscientious workers. They were meant to serve as cau-tionary models for the newly freed blacks. This strategy was also used in the North in the same year, when Chinese laborers were transported to break a strike by Irish workers. Again they were touted by the news-papers as inexpensive, obedient, highly efficient laborers.

The model-minority myth in its present incarnation has yet an-other purpose: when Asian Americans are praised as examples of im-migrants who made it through their own private efforts, this is meant to convey that they didn't need the help of affirmative action or wel-fare. Thus this cultural stereotype has been consistently used to advance a conservative, racist agenda (Takaki 1999).

Eng and Han deploy the concept of racial melancholia in several provocative ways. They are particularly interested in the melancholia that they contend Asian Americans experience, while making it clear that they also believe that other racialized groups, as well as sexual mi-norities, experience similar melancholia. In this instantiation, racial melancholia represents the feelings of loss and contamination experi-enced by those who are forced to mimic an idealized whiteness that they can never achieve (in Bhabha's words, cited by Eng and Han, "almost the same but not white"). Here Eng and Han meld Bhabha's discourse on mimicry in colonial regimes with Freud's observations of melancho-lia in psychic registers. Racial melancholia is viewed as originating in colonialism and racism, which impel both mimicry and failure. It is fur-ther exacerbated by the fact that for the purposes of assimilation Asian Americans must relinquish their original ethnic identity, at the same time as cultural bias contaminates their good feeling about this iden-tity. They are then in the unenviable position of having given up an old identity without the possibility of a positive replacement.

The theme of the indissociability of the social and the psychologi-cal is repeated in the discussion of intergenerational transference. If the losses experienced by the first generation are not resolved, melancholia may be transmitted to the second generation. The concept of inter-generational transference is quite fascinating. From this perspective, daughters absorb their mothers' losses unconsciously, so that, as Eng and Han point out, their bodies and voices become "substitutes for those of the mothers—not just the mothers' bodies and voices, but also something that is unconsciously lost in them." Thus daughters' internal self-reproaches must be viewed as dialogues in which they are addressing their mothers.

This concept illuminates an aspect of my work with a patient I'll call Ms. B.

> Ms. B's mother grew up in China where, when she was 2, her family gave her away to another woman and she never saw her biological parents again. The expectation was that in exchange for the care she received from her adoptive mother, she would always take care of her. Yet when she grew up, political events in China threatened her freedom, and she moved to America, leaving her adoptive mother behind. Although she became a lawyer and made enough money to send some to her adoptive mother, she never saw her again. She was depressed much of her life, unable to succeed professionally, and was often critical and rejecting of Ms. B., repeating the theme of maternal rejection. She became psychotically depressed in her 50s, and, after several hospitalizations, killed herself.
>
> Ms. B. suffers from intense feelings of guilt about the fact that when her mother first became ill Ms. B. had just graduated from college and had made the decision to live with her American boyfriend, far away from her mother. Like her mother before her, she put her needs first instead of staying home to take care of her parent. Since her mother's death, having anything positive in her own life—be it money, relationships, a job—causes her to become paralyzed with depression, anxiety, and suicidal impulses. Her self-reproaches are often conscious "dialogues" with her mother, in which she begs her forgiveness for not being more successful at the same time as she is reproached by her for not being a higher functioning adult. Complicating the dialogue is her mother's other voice rebuking her for striving for success and abandoning her. The themes that her mother never resolved—her own feelings about the trauma of being rejected by her biological mother, her guilt about leaving her adoptive mother, and her ambivalence about

meeting her own needs—haunt Ms. B., making any positive step she takes in her life fraught with anxiety and conflict.

I found Eng and Han's description of whiteness as contagion of particular interest. It is of the utmost importance to stress that whiteness contaminates not only non-white people but also so-called white people. I find this a radical way to think about racial melancholia: as a description of the subjectivity of white people. What is whiteness but a precarious, panicked, and heinously violent construction that naturalizes itself at the expense of others? Eng and Han write of our nation being haunted by its dissociated violence toward those that it excludes, at the same time as it touts itself as democratic. This subject is grist for the mill in the analyses of all white Americans, but I imagine that it rarely occurs. If relational psychoanalysis is going to make a real difference it must analyze this omission, as well as develop clinical strategies to ensure that race (along with other cultural issues) enters consulting rooms.

In this context I was disappointed that Eng and Han dismissed the idea that race should be brought up by analysts with their white patients who are "untroubled" by their whiteness. Like Phillips (1997) whom they cite, and who similarly begs the question of whether analysts should problematize heterosexuality in heterosexual men who are untroubled by it, they seem to believe that analysts would be imposing their values if they were to intervene in cases where white people don't bring up race as a problem. Here Eng and Han drop the theme of the indissociability of the social and the psychological (a subject they have developed throughout their paper) and bifurcate them. How could it be possible that any white person growing up in our racist culture can be truly "untroubled" by race? Since our work as analysts consists largely of bringing up issues with which patients believe they are untroubled, why do we make exceptions when it comes to "untroubled" whiteness and "untroubled" male heterosexuality? By not troubling these issues, analysts are imposing their values about what's important to analyze and what doesn't count.

It is shocking to consider that most analyses of white patients proceed without examining whiteness and racism, even though these treatments occur in an American society haunted by racism and violence toward racialized others. The fact that race is most often brought up by white analysts when patients are non-white is itself a form of racism, since it perpetuates the heinous myth that white is unmarked and non-white marked. (This always reminds me of how, when I was a child, packs of Crayola crayons always had a crayon that was labeled "flesh." The fact that the color matched the skin tone of only very light-skinned white people seemed to convey the message that this was the color "normal" flesh should be.)

I was also disappointed that Eng and Han insufficiently problematized the American Dream. While it is indisputable that all people should have equal access to success in America, aren't movies like *American Beauty* and other dire cultural markers telling us that the much-touted American Dream is a nightmare, not only for those who are excluded from it but also for those who have achieved it? Consider that the contemporary American Dream (as opposed to a more progressive dream of the past) seems limited to equal access to instant gratification and acquisition of material goods, a way of life we are spreading across the world (along with genetically altered food) through global capitalism, the latest version of imperialism. Though so many of our patients suffer from American-Dream sickness, it has been unfashionable in psychoanalysis to discuss this malady since the days of Erich Fromm (1941), with the important exception of the work of Philip Cushman (1990, 1995). Perhaps psychoanalysts, along with much of the American public, are bamboozled by the media into thinking that both American capitalism and global capitalism are overwhelmingly positive. Thus, in the late '90s, we heard a lot about how well the economy was doing (as many of us made money on the stock market) and not very much about how the gap between the rich and the poor was growing larger all the time. Unlike the last years of the nineteenth century, when grossly exploitative capitalism gave rise to labor unions and socialism, capitalism today appears virtually unopposed (Bellah 1999), although a small but increasing number of protests by labor and environmental activists offer a ray of hope. This lack of opposition is recapitulated in psychoanalysis, where an examination of the ways that capitalism affects American psyches is missing from most of contemporary theory and clinical practice.

Exactly how to bring issues of race and capitalism into consulting rooms is a question that I find particularly vexing. In clinical situations where the patient is driven by greed and deeply troubled by feelings of emptiness, the issue is accessible. Here I am thinking of Mr. J., a patient whom I've seen for many years.

> Mr. J. entered analysis with chronic feelings of emptiness, depression, and lack of connection to himself and other people. Although his work as a stock analyst for a European bank netted him a huge amount of money each year, he always felt that he didn't have enough. The more money he made, the more he acquired and the more he had to make, a vicious cycle that Cushman (1990) sees as critical to the empty selves that capitalism requires. Much of Mr. J.'s money was spent on buying attention and respect from other people, a tactic that left him feeling powerful but exploited. Making a lot of money was a desperate but culturally lauded maneuver of a man who had never felt connected to his parents and knew no other way of connecting with people. While at the beginning of his analysis he felt that he was being sucked dry by other people's needs and demands, and was unaware that he himself had any needs other than making a lot of money, in later years he came to feel identified with a dream image of a starving, homeless man. Accepting this image as part of himself, and realizing that he was starving for emotional connection, changed his relationship to money.

In other clinical situations, where issues of race and American-Dream sickness are more subtle, it is harder to know how to intervene. Consider Ms. D., a patient who was on the verge of losing her license as an accountant when I first began working with her.

> A woman with progressive leanings in the '60s, she had spent the intervening years bucking authority by getting herself into all sorts of professional trouble, in addition to having two psychotic breaks. During long periods of not working (after being fired from job after job), she would feel like her old radical self, free and unfettered, as she stayed home and watched soap operas. For the past few years, Ms. D. has held down a job as an accountant for a firm that represents the most conservative elements in society. She loves her job and is doing very well, and her old pattern of self-sabotage is absent. Ironically, her position is antithetical to her values (as well

as my own), a subject that I've not broached out of fear that her newly developed capacity to take care of herself will become undone. Knowing how to intervene in clinical situations like this is an area that relational psychoanalysis needs to address.

I was also disappointed with the last section of Eng and Han's paper because of their idealization of melancholics (at the expense of mourners, of all people!). While I understand that Eng and Han are trying to find a theoretical strategy for preserving the original good object, they seem to forget that grief is historically and culturally specific. Thus they take issue with the Freud of "Mourning and Melancholia" for his view that mourning should have a clear beginning and end, without recognizing that Freud's vision was a reflection of a modern Western view of grief. From the modern perspective, grief was seen as something the mourner should recover from relatively quickly so she could get back to normal functioning (Stroebe et al. 1992). The stress was on rationality and efficiency, as opposed to the older, romantic view of grief.

The romantic perspective granted centrality to everlasting love. Those who would give up functional and pragmatic goals for love were praised. Marriage was characterized as a communion of souls and friendships as lifelong commitments. Grief signaled the significance of the other and the strength of one's bond to her. Dissolving bonds with the dead meant that the relationship was superficial, and this reflected poorly on the mourner. Valor consisted of sustaining bonds to the deceased despite a broken heart. A study of fifty-six diary accounts of grief from the nineteenth century found little evidence that bonds to the deceased were ever broken. Praying for the dead was seen as keeping a caring relationship alive. The loved one's wishes were often used to guide action.

According to Stroebe and colleagues (1992), different cultures construct mourning in vastly different ways. In Japan, maintaining a tie to the deceased is accepted and sustained by religious rituals. Native American Hopi, on the other hand, forget the deceased as soon as possible and carry on as usual. This has to do with their belief that the spirit of a dead person becomes depersonalized and no longer Hopi, and thus is feared. Contact with death brings pollution. Many rites having to do with spirits end with a ritual designed to cut off contact.

In addition to not contextualizing mourning, Eng and Han idealize melancholics, losing sight of the clinical fact that depressed people are emotionally and physically depleted, as well as consumed by self-reproaches. I don't envision an army of melancholics overthrowing the tyranny of whiteness anytime soon. Therapy would have to help them redirect the sadistic attacks on themselves outward, in order to empower selves exhausted by culturally induced self-hatred.

I also thought that Eng and Han could have further developed the idea that racial melancholia always preserves an ambivalent relationship to the object (Freud 1917). From this perspective, racialized people should be viewed as hating as well as loving the whiteness that eludes them. Cultural forces collude to ensure that this hatred is turned against themselves. Liberating this anger would enable racial melancholics to develop a more critical view of the fragility, violence, and fictive nature of whiteness, to see through a culture of whiteness that idealizes itself at their expense, and to refuse a society that took a detour away from a progressive American Dream toward a dream of the acquisition of material goods.

## REFERENCES

Bellah, R. (1999). The ethics of polarization in the United States and the world. In *The Good Citizen*, ed. D. Batstone and E. Mendieta, pp. 14–29. New York: Routledge.

Cushman, P. (1990). Why the self is empty: toward a historically situated psychology. *American Psychologist* 45:599–611.

——— (1995). *Constructing the Self, Constructing America*. Menlo Park, CA: Addison Wesley.

Freud, S. (1917). Mourning and melancholia. *Standard Edition* 14:237–259.

Fromm, E. (1941). *Escape from Freedom*. New York: Avon, 1969.

Gilman, S. (1993). *Freud, Race and Gender*. Princeton, NJ: Princeton University Press.

Phillips, A. (1997). Keeping it moving: commentary on Judith Butler's "Melancholy Gender/Refused Identification." In J. Butler, *The Psychic Life of Power*, pp. 151–159. Stanford, CA: Stanford University Press.

Senna, D. (1998). *Caucasia*. New York: Riverhead Books.

Stroebe, M., Gergen, M., Gergen, K., and Stroebe, W. (1992). Broken hearts or broken bonds: love and death in historical perspective. *American Psychologist* 47(10):1205–1213.

Takaki, R. (1999). Race at the end of history. In *The Good Citizen*, ed. D. Batstone and E. Mendieta, pp. 81–93. New York: Routledge.

Walton, J. (1997). Re-placing race in (white) psychoanalytic discourse: founding narratives of feminism. In *Female Subjects in Black and White: Race, Psychoanalysis, Feminism*, ed. E. Abel, B. Christian, and H. Moglen, pp. 223–252. Berkeley: University of California Press.

# 8

# Doctor Fell

## Michael Bronski

### PART ONE. JOURNAL

September 24, 1995

Just signed the contract for *Flesh and the Word*. I guess I have to think about doing an essay now. We had talked about my writing about blood and cutting. It seemed like a good idea at the time. Am I ready for this? Usually I have no trouble writing about anything in my sexual history—s/m, public sex, intimate moments with a lover, piercing, sex as a salve for death, jerking off on death beds, piss, violence. Why should this be any different? This is what writers do; we write. About ourselves, about what happens, about life. And it's a great subject—and the essay is sure to be mentioned in the reviews as, well, cutting edge.

October 5, 1995

Made notes on *Flesh and the Word* essay. Nothing feels right. I have no idea of what tone to strike—lurid, medical, religious, psychological, confessional? The whole thing makes me uneasy. It should be simple: for six years, in several relationships, part of our sex play was that we cut each other with razors, scalpels, Exacto blades. Sometimes we did temporary piercings with needles, usually to draw blood. No big deal. Assume an honest, open tone and simply describe the experiences. Don't forget to mention that it was the most potent sexual stimulation I have ever encountered. Leave out the fact that we were on drugs (you wouldn't want to give cutting and blood sports a bad name).

October 17, 1995

Essay going nowhere. Realize the problem is that it is supposed to be sexy. The actual experiences were sexy, but how do you convince readers who may well be appalled by the very idea? On the other hand, everyone likes gory movies, slasher films where sex and anxiety are bound together and released in the oozing and spattering of red fluid. The problem is that, as often as not, what's sexy in real life is boring on the page. Bad sex is always more interesting to write about than good sex; it's where the conflict is, where the tensions lie. The problem with writing about cutting is that nothing happens: cut and bleed. No thrashing legs, pulsating cocks, heavy moaning, and guttural sobs. It's not the stuff of pornography but of dreams and unreason; the fairy tale, fearful myth; the unspoken, elliptical spaces left unarticulated.

> *I do not like thee, Doctor Fell.*
> *The reason why, I cannot tell.*
> *But this I know and know full well,*
> *I do not like thee, Doctor Fell.*

I've always loved this nursery rhyme, even when I was a child. It resonates with longing and dread. Odd that the man—Jim—who introduced me to cutting, with whom I did it for five years, whose scars I still carry and who died more than a decade ago (with the scars he carried from me), was a doctor and a Vietnam vet. Sometimes, on acid, he would remember the horrors of battlefield surgery, and cry, and praise me for having protested the war. And then we would cut each other. I would try not to cry because this was *his* time: his memories, my blood, and his way of finally gaining control. Not just moving the torn, bruised flesh of young men from the muddied trenches of war into his living room. That was only one part. But shedding the shame and humiliation so connected with his desire in this setting—he was a Marine, the stuff that porn is made of—and making it real, palpable. The intensity was suffocating, heart binding. "Do you trust me?" he would ask. "Do you trust me?"

The question felt superfluous, heart binding. Trust wasn't an issue; it was beyond being a given. It was a state of mind, a reality of us together: of sharpness and recoil, of grace under pressure as slice and skin become one. Trust, like love, is diminished when articulated. Trust, like fear, can vanish when examined. The cutting and the gradual flow of blood—first a trickle, then a tributary, never more than that—was a demanded physical and emotional release. But it was so sexy, so *driven*. The fifteen years between then and now slip away; I can feel my heart beat, place my hand on the breastbone—a tattoo, a pulse: blood, blood, blood. I still love thee, Doctor Fell, the reason why I cannot tell, or even remember clearly, but I remember those long nights with hot black tea laced with bourbon, lemon, and MDA, and the almost unimaginable intimacy of scalpel to skin, of steady hand to willing flesh.

## ESSAY. PART ONE

The living room in Jim's South End apartment is dark, candle-lit. A hard music beat on low volume comes from the radio. It is three A.M. We came home from the Ramrod twenty minutes ago, high on energy, cruising, MDA, a little acid, and each other. We've been going out for four months. Walta, my lover of six years, is at home. Jim is my other life, my non-domestic dark side, where the wild things are. At home I feel loved and secure, bookish, smart, even respected. Here I feel beautiful, desired, wanted, needed. I am no longer the geeky, friendless high-school kid jerking off thinking about juvenile delinquents and hoods, James Dean and the wild ones with their antisocial attitudes and slicked-back hair. In Jim's eyes I become someone who lives in the world, lives in my body. With Jim I move through the bar as though I should be there, as though *we* should be there. Ripped dirty jeans, T-shirts, leather jackets: these were the uniforms of the rebels of my youth. I have become my childhood dreams. I have become the men I feared.

We are alone. We dragged no tricks back with us; our own bodies are still enough to excite and enthrall. The room is hot, the heat turned up against the winter outside. On the far wall, above a low, long chest, is a mahogany-framed mirror—seven feet by seven feet—that dominates and enlarges the room. We move the candles in front of it, and the cave-like room becomes magical. We make tea and carefully (or not so carefully) doctor it with sweet bourbon and sugar to mask the bitterness of more MDA.

We talk and laugh about someone at the bar, my arm around Jim, his hand under my shirt. We kiss and allow ourselves the pleasures of small movements, affectionate gestures. I feel myself both leaving my body and entering it. Like a transformed beast in a fairy tale, I feel my flesh changing around me: it is a body I like, that I want to touch, that feels right. Jim's hand is on my nipples, and I have a hand in his pants, kneading his cock through the jock strap, feeling the foreskin shift and move with my fingers.

We kiss again and Jim gets up to piss. I begin to rearrange the room, moving candles away from the mirror, adjusting the music to increase the volume and lower the bass, and, from the drawers of the antique captain's desk, taking the scalpels. They are instruments meant for healing. In my heightened consciousness I think about the "art of healing"—a derisive term that Jim uses to blaspheme and dismiss his experience "in country." This moment before we begin cutting is a prelude, an *introit*: "O most precious blood" floats through my mind, a refrain from a litany to the Sacred Heart. Jim comes from the bathroom as I turn on the crane's-neck lamp and focus its 150–watt bulb on the mirror. The effect is mesmerizing. Jim has taken off his shirt and jeans. He wears only boots, socks, and his jock strap; his six-foot-five-inch body—long sinewy arms, flattish ass, slight potbelly, shaved head—moves in and out of the mirrored light.

I remove my shirt, pants, boots and cast them into the corner. Jim opens a sterile package. The plastic crinkles, my body responds. I stretch my arms. I've done this before. You have to get the blood moving through the skin, bring it to the surface: tension, tightness keeps it in. I run my hands over my pectorals, down my thighs, play with my nipples, watch my body in the mirror. I am beautiful, I think. Who is this person? Not me, surely not me. Not as I know myself in the real world, the world of books and politics, or the reality outside this room, this Bluebeard's castle (soon to become the dreaded eighth chamber), this amalgamation of Cocteau and Klimt, decadent and barbarous with dark corners and silver glints.

I stand in front of the mirror and inhabit the warmth from within and without. I run my fingers through my long hair and throw my head back—half Garbo in *Camille*, half Brando in *Streetcar*—and feel Jim's hand roam my chest as he chooses where to cut. I reposition my head and, staring at the body in the mirror— my body—watch as Jim makes feathery cuts around my nipples. I flex my pectorals. Pink lines form on my upper chest, Tina Turner chants "What's Love Got To Do With It" in my mind or on the radio, the pink turns rose, then vermillion, then crimson as it gathers and trickles, eddies and flows. I flex and breathe deep, stretch my arms above my head, savoring the pull of muscle and the tightness of skin. But most of all I watch. Watch as the blood—my blood—begins to run down my chest, glistening and gesticulating with a life of its own. This is who I am, I think. This is my body. Altarboy Latin hums in my head: *Et introibo ad altare Dei: ad Deum qui laetificat juventutem meam.* Then will I go to the altar of God, the God of my gladness and joy. Jim whispers in my ear, "Look at it look at it I love you look at it." I am in my body and beyond it, I have made it do what I want it to. I am transfigured and scarred, transfixed and left wanting more. More cuts, more pleasure, more warmth, more refuge from the hard life of the real world, from my past, from the person I was as a child, an adolescent, yesterday. I am the man in the mirror, the man standing next to me, holding me and cutting me, the man in my body and outside of it watching it live and bleed, move and breathe. I am . . . .

## PART TWO. JOURNAL

November 3, 1995

Decided essay is too difficult to write. I'll be misunderstood, misinterpreted, and have a hard time getting dates. I should think I'm beyond worrying about most of that, after cultivating a reputation as a sexual renegade. What here is making me uncomfortable? My depictions of my cutting experiences are detailed and verifiable (I just looked at the fading scars on my chest and legs, running my fingers over them in memory and dispassionate awe), but the essay feels false to me. Is it over-romanticized? All those candles and references to fairy tales? Is it too consciously spiritual with its insistence on high-Catholic kitsch? Or is it simply too, well, literary? And why not? It's for a volume of literary essays.

November 7, 1995

Journal entry of four days ago is complete shit. I know perfectly well what is missing from the essay: honesty and truth. Not that the cutting didn't happen and (at its best) was romantic, fairy-tale-like, affirming, and tremendously potent. So what am I leaving out? That as much as I loved Jim, I thought he was fucked up about sex and his own sexual desires? That his s/m practices, including cutting, were mostly vain attempts to break through the crushing repression of his Southern boyhood and his horrible feelings about himself? That for the first year we were together (out of five) he would have to leave the room after coming, so he could be alone? That some of those times he cried? Or that Jim died of AIDS in 1986? Who knows how he got it? After 1981 we only had safe sex and our bloodletting was always carefully executed. But I know that the only way he could have sex with other people was to get totally fucked up, and half the time he didn't know what he was doing.

The romanticism of our blood games—and my presentation of it—is countered by the fact that there was often blood dripped all over the floor and furniture from other men he brought home. Jim's sexual abandon was an attempt to break through his own repression, but it was an attempt that was fraught with denial, hurt, fear, and potential harm to himself and others. Acting out doesn't always bring you through to the other side. And what does this mean in an essay that is promoting all kinds of sexual experimentation in the name of sexual freedom and health? Should I mention that my first attractions to blood and sex were watching Christopher Lee's sexy Dracula movies as a child in the late '50s—*The Horror of Dracula, The Brides of Dracula*—with the elegantly handsome Count repeatedly shown with blood dripping from his open mouth? These movies, which always ended in the deaths of mere mortals but held out the idea of resurrection and life for the outcast vampires, excited and titillated me: I always wanted to be overcome, drained, depleted by the beautiful Count, who in my life became a sexually fucked-up Vietnam vet who held me in his arms and made me feel beautiful.

What else am I leaving out? That while I was seeing Jim (from 1979 to 1984) I was involved in a deeply committed relationship with Walta Borawski, a relationship that was to last twenty years until Walta's death in 1994. Walta and Jim and I spent a lot of time figuring out how to be non-monogamous. Sometimes it worked; sometimes it didn't. It felt, and still feels, like a noble experiment, an attempt to remake life to fit our own needs and desires. And what does it mean that, while I rhapsodize now about my cutting and piercing experiences with Jim, I *never* talked about them with Walta? That I would wear sweatpants and T-shirts to bed for weeks at a time to hide the fresh scars, as if Walta couldn't figure it out anyway. What does it mean that I trusted Jim—my boyfriend, my exotic, exciting porn fantasy—enough to cut my flesh with scalpels, and yet I couldn't trust Walta—the love of my life, the man who has meant more to me than anyone else and whose loss I mourn every day—enough even to speak to him about this part of my life? Was I lying to Walta by hiding (or attempting to hide) these sexual activities with Jim? Am I lying now by not disclosing more circumstantial details—some important, some not—in this essay?

The idea of what is truthful and what is not is arbitrary. We can only approximate truth. Did I feel great about my cutting experiences all the time? Of course not. Would I write about that? I don't know. We write to give at least the appearance of truth, and we hope that our readers believe us. But even careless readers must realize that these "journal" entries are fake, cribbed from Nabokov and John Fowles and others: a literary device used to contextualize and move my story, my agenda, along. All, of course, in the pursuit of "truth" and "honesty."

Moments after Walta died—at 9:05 P.M. on February 9, 1994 at home, in our apartment, in the bed I inherited from Jim in which he had died eight years earlier—I sat next to him and talked to him for the last time. My first thought was to apologize for all the times I may have hurt him by my relationship with Jim. Why is this harder to confess than any of the details of cutting and bleeding, of sexual extravagance and erotic dalliance? What does this say about trust and truth—fragile concepts at best—and about the decisions we make? Why, when I write this, can I feel my heartbeat, feel the pulse in my wrists (I just felt it, fingers on veins, blood beneath fragile bones) and an inexplicable stirring in my cock?

Should I also mention (for full disclosure) that while taking care of Walta during his illness I accidentally gave myself several sticks with needles that might well have been contaminated? (It's so easy, no matter how careful—and I was careful, very careful, all the time.) That if I am HIV positive—I've never been tested—it was because transmission occurred (accidentally, incidentally) while I was taking care of, nursing to his death, the man I loved? That the blood running down my chest, down my legs, that Jim's blood and the blood of tricks and other friends, conflates in my mind with the blood of my dying lover. Death and grief, lust and love: inseparable. That the romance of the scalpel slicing through my skin is nothing compared to the sharp, frightening reality of the jab of the needle in the thumb, the fear that pierces the heart and disorders the mind: the realization that blood is never innocent, that truth is always elusive, and that trust, real trust—in love, in science, in the sureness of hand and the caress of the smile—is always beyond the grasp, beyond certainty, beyond control.

## ESSAY. PART TWO

The living room is glowing now. Not only with the candles and the reflected lamplight but with the heat of our bodies. I stand in front of the mirror and watch myself. A simple flex will increase the trickle of blood down my chest; arching my torso to one side will change the course of the fluid, now carmine in color as it oxidizes and finds its way into the world, outside of the body. Jim lies on the couch watching me, enjoying my self-involved pantomime. I pull on my cock. It is soft, but full of feeling. I can feel the sexual excitement in my belly and down my thighs: I feel polymorphously perverse, dazed by my own lack of inhibitions and overwhelmed by desire.

My self-entertainment ends and I begin to make us more tea. In the kitchen, waiting for the kettle to boil, I look at my chest and marvel at the patterns, now drying and crusting. Jim is in the bedroom looking for the restraints (tossed beneath the bed after he took them off last night's trick) and appears in the kitchen, wanting my help in fastening the buckles. We adjust the black leather cuffs, finish making the tea—sugar, lemon, bourbon—and, returning to the living room, sit on the floor, our backs resting on the couch. The tea is hot and sustaining; its heady fragrance intoxicates. Jim says it smells like hibiscus, a memory of his youth. We kiss, and I run my hands over his chest, pulling the skin taut and relaxing it like a moiré silk or the most subtle of velvets.

Tea finished, we stand in front of the mirror. I flex and watch the now dry blood crinkle and flake. Jim holds up his arms, and I stand on a chair to slip a long rawhide cord through the D-bolts of the restraints and around the not-so-subtly-placed hook in the ceiling. I pull the rawhide taut; he raises his arms, relaxes. The cord holds tight and I deftly knot. Climbing off the chair I readjust the light (Jim is taller than I am) to highlight his form in the glass. He plays with the tension—up on his toes, down again, shrugging shoulders and then forcing them down—until he is comfortable. I stand to his side and run my hands over his skin, play with his nipples. Jim's eyes are closed. What is he thinking? About me? About last night, a trick whom he has wanted for months and who finally got the courage to go home with him? About being a teenager, and the smell of hibiscus, and the terror of sex with other boys? About Vietnam and the flesh and blood and mud of operations in the trenches, the removal of shrapnel from legs and arms before muscles swelled and became gangrenous, trapped in too-tight membrane casings? He sways, and I hold him still with my hand and then carefully open the hermetically sealed package and remove the blade.

"Open your eyes," I whisper. He does. "Where?" I whisper. "Here?" I touch the skin above his nipple. "Here?" I run my hand along his breastbone. "Here?" I touch the flesh on the uppermost part of his abdomen. "Yes." "Where?" "There." I press on the soft center, pinch the skin, knead it, redden it, make it ready for the cut. "Watch," I say. "I love you." I steady my hand and slide the blade, ever so gently, across the expanse of white epidermis. A three-inch arc appears. We both look in the mirror amazed, confounded by the beauty of it. From pink, to rose, to vermillion, to crimson (who knew there were so many shades of red?), it rises to the surface magically and begins to weep. Slowly at first. Jim tenses his body, holds it, relaxes. Tenses and relaxes. The blood rises and then begins to run: rivulets almost afraid to give in to the gravity that pulls them down. "Do you like it?" I ask. "Do you want more?" The question is needless. "Here." "Here?" "Here." I create a feather pattern over his nipples, alternating light with deeper strokes. Jim likes to see a lot of blood. It is not a matter of cutting deep, just of time and tension, patience and gravity.

I cut lower on his belly and we watch. Wait and watch. "Shave me," he asks quietly. There is a hospital safety razor on the chest. I reach for it and remove the stubble of his pubic hair—we did this two weeks ago—with short, quick strokes. Around the soft cock, the inner thighs, the top of the scrotum. Carefully, carefully. He is clean, more naked than ever. And suddenly he tenses his whole body: once, twice, again and again and again. This is what he wanted. What he has waited for. The blood runs more freely, past his nipples, his rib cage, each rib showing as his body stretches, over his belly and down onto his cock and balls. It runs down the foreskin, slowly. He watches in silence, rapt with the extraordinary grace of it. Lost in some private reverie. This is what he wanted. This is what he always wants. Suspended, displayed, unable to help himself, and watching as rivulets of blood dam at the tip of his gathered foreskin and then fall, drop by drop, to the floor. Like some martyr in a Renaissance painting, he glows in the mirror. Is this some image of himself from Catholic childhood? Some reparation for not being good, or holy, or man enough? Is this transcendence? In the silence Tina Turner, again, chants "What's Love Got To Do With It"—she has a hit; it's on every twenty minutes; it is the theme of the evening—but you can almost hear the precious droplets, tiny amounts of jewel-like fluid, fall and shatter as they hit the floor. I look in the mirror. It is like a dream. But whose? And then I see that Jim is crying.

## PART THREE. JOURNAL

December 2, 1995

Have just reread what I've written after putting it away for a few weeks. Does it work? Is it sexy? Or sexy enough? Is it "truthful"? Can it be more truthful? Is it too much about relationships and not enough about cutting? Have I cheated the reader of an essay by admitting that I've already made up part of the form, even if the content is real—is this an egregious infringement against the "truth" of the essay?

Jim and I had an intense sexual relationship for almost five years. A great deal of the dynamic between us was that I took care of Jim: sexually, psychologically. It was still intense when we were breaking up in 1984. One of the last times we had sex—we were already in the process of separating—I had him tied to a chair, beat his chest and arms with a switch, and then cut him with a scalpel. There was much blood because it had risen to the surface. We were angry at each other, yet he still trusted me to enact our old rituals. After we broke up, my fury at him was nearly out of control. How could a man who trusted me to cut him when he was tied up not trust me enough to love me, to believe in the depth of my love for him? We broke up and continued speaking, if only to argue. Walta was both upset and relieved. Jim left me for another man, Patrick, who loved him without any demands, who lived only to be loved by Jim. Maybe in the mirror Jim's dream was to find the perfect lover, the man he did not have to be tied up to love, the man who would not remind him of his guilt about Vietnam, who did not protest the war, whose appeal was that "trust" and "truth" were completely defined by Jim. What happened? Where did "trust" and "truth" discontinue and career apart? Can you trust with your body and not trust with your heart? I think Walta felt more betrayed by my grief at losing Jim than he did by my sexual relationship with him. It was easy to hide scars in bed with T-shirts and sweatpants; it was nearly impossible to hide my desolation when Jim told me he "just wanted to be friends."

December 12, 1995

Can I write about "honesty" and "truth" without talking about Vince? I started seeing Vince after Jim and I broke up. I never men-

290 / Bringing the Plague

tioned it to Walta. Or rather, Walta and I never talked about it. Vince
was a distraction from my loss of Jim. Our sex was energized and extravagant. He let me beat him, tie him up, cut him. His capacity for
this abuse and pain was endless. He fell in love with me—a fact he never
felt permission to state—and I used him to get over Jim. My grief and
anger fueled the affair. Was I hitting Jim when I hit Vince? Was he my
whipping boy, or simply a substitute? Once, in the middle of a long,
somewhat drunken night, I said that I loved him. The words hung in
the air. He had never said these words to me, but they were true for him.
I did say them, but they weren't true for me. The next week he asked
tactfully if I had uttered those words. He remembered that I had, but
he thought he might have made it up. I said I didn't know.

We continued the intense sex for another year and a half. Neither
of us could seem to get enough. Did I love him? I don't know. Was I
using him? Probably. Was he using me? For what? Attention, sex, love?
I gave him some of that. When I cut him, it wasn't like cutting Jim: it
was exciting but perfunctory, surgical, and almost not sexual. It was
about Jim. It was about me. It was about me wanting control again.
"Trust," "love," "honesty." Is it enough to say that those words have no
real meaning detached from actions and intentions? Is it enough to say
"I'm sorry" now? Is it enough to say anything?

My last date with Vince was June 13, 1986. The day Jim was diagnosed with PCP. I was at the hospital and stayed there for the night.
Sitting by Jim's bedside, I watched as they set up a transfusion; his body
was so depleted that he needed red blood cells immediately. He had
ignored the fact that he was sick for at least six months—was this the
doctor-in-denial or the saint-in-the-making? I watched the blood, thick
and heavy with concentrated plasma, drip from the plastic bag into the
clear tubing, through the large-gauged needle into Jim's vein. I never
slept with Vince again, or tied him up, or beat him, or cut him. Jim
needed me. I won. I was back in his life.

December 23, 1995

I've lost track of what this essay is about: me, cutting, Jim, Walta,
Vince. The impossibility of knowing, really knowing, what is "true," what
is "honest." Every story takes on its own life in the telling. But is "truth"
(like God) in the details? Everything I've written is "true"—except for

lots of the details. Did we have two cups of tea or just one before I cut Jim? How long did I wear sweatpants to bed to hide my scars? Was Jim really suspended from a hook in the ceiling, or did he just stretch his arms above his head? What do these details matter if my emotional material is honest? Am I a trustworthy narrator? Writers are manipulators. We spin tales, we use facts and ideas in an attempt to convince ourselves and readers that what we are writing is true, but we do this to bring attention to ourselves. To place ourselves front and center. This essay is about me, not about Jim, or Walta, or Vince, or cutting. It is about my life, my feelings, my grief, and my sorrow. This is what writers do.

December 28, 1995

I sit here running my fingers over the scars on my chest and my legs. They are fading now, most of them gone. Here or there is a line, a bump, a bit of raised skin, perhaps whiter than the surrounding flesh. I touch my flesh and pull at it. Does it change with age? Does it mean to me now what it meant then? How could it? What could? Fifteen years— never mind AIDS, politics, culture, aging, loss, fear—is a long time. I look at the bed next to me, its brass in need of polishing, and think of Jim and then Walta dying in it. I look at my life and think, "It's not too bad. I'm here. I am writing this. This is what writers do. They remember, they try to tell the truth, and they write—about themselves." My fingers roam my chest, pinch my nipples. I think about Jim's white, fish-belly flesh; Walta's hairy, darker skin; Vince's pliant, scarred arms. I think of Walta and Jim and love and trust, and where we fail and where we succeed, but sometimes fail in the long or the short run. Flesh is what joins us and what keeps us apart.

I always thought Hamlet's line was, "Oh, that this too, too solid flesh would melt." But someone just told me it is "sullied," not "solid," and that made sense. Flesh isn't solid; it isn't marble, or noble, or pure, but tender and ready to bruise, and tear, and hurt. Like "truth" and "honesty" and even "love," it can be inexplicably ruptured, ripped, and torn apart. It is ripe for decay on its inevitable journey to becoming lifeless, inert, what we—as a last resort—have to call dead. Like "honesty," "truth," and "love," it is also negotiable; we can make it do what we want (sometimes); we can do to it what we want (often); we can misuse and abuse it, but we cannot deny that it is there, that it is us.

I think about cutting Jim, about being cut. About what that meant to me then and means to me now. I feel my scars and think about cutting again. But with whom? Who would do this? Jim is dead. I never even talked about cutting with Walta. Vince is very sick, and we haven't spoken for almost a decade. Feeling my skin, I decide—one last time—to cut myself. Will it be sexual? My cock feels nothing. Will it be an experiment in remembrance? I can remember. I have remembered. Is it an easy way to end this piece? A cheap, exploitative shot? What do I feel writing this? What does my skin feel, my flesh, aging as it is on its journey to death? Do I have your attention? This is what writers do.

## ESSAY. PART THREE

I've turned up the heat in the house. It is cold outside. I've made a strong cup of tea with bourbon and sugar and lemon and have warmed myself within and without. I find the needles I saved from when Walta was sick and look at them in their sterile paper and plastic wrappers. I forget which is thinner, 20G1 or 25G5/8? These are things I used to know. How odd to hold these slim packages in my hand. Three years ago I would deftly open them, remove the needle, and irrigate Walta's Hickman catheter or flush his feeding tube with saline and heparin. Fifteen years ago I would open these packages and carefully push the needle through Jim's and Vince's flesh. Which has more meaning for me now in memory? I nursed Walta and at times even made him better; he needed me and I was there. I gave Jim and Vince pleasure, at times even ecstatic joy. Did they need me? Could anyone else have done this for them? And me? I learned, I received pleasure, I grappled with the mysteries of flesh, my own and others'. I entered worlds I never dreamed existed—of sex, of fantasy, of fear, of AIDS, of death—and I became who I am today. Oh, that this too, too sullied flesh would melt.

I am lying on the brass bed next to my desk. I rub my chest, my nipples, warm them with my palms. I unwrap the needle and breathe deep. I've done this before. I can do this now. I hold the tip of the needle—the thinner of the two—to the almost pink-beige areola of my nipple. I breathe, I look at my chest and remember the whiteness of skin, the tension of muscle, the love of other men, their bodies and their trust. I trusted them, and why not now? Why not myself? I hesitate, and then I push without thinking, without feeling, without memory. The needle slides, cleanly, and then sticks. I see the skin on the other side of the nipple poking pointed; the needle has not broken through. I breathe and push again. There is a little pain, a poke, and that is it. The tip of the needle is exposed, and its shaft emerges clean and bright. My breath comes back, and I stare at the shiny needle. What does it mean? Have I recreated a moment from my past? Did I think this would bring back Jim or Walta? Bring back some sense of their presence, of their being, of their desire? Or is it to bring back my own desire for them? The needle feels hot, the skin surrounding it feels warm. I rotate the tiny steel rod and feel nothing: a slight pull, a tiny tug deep inside my flesh.

I reach next to me and open the single-edged razor from its package—not sterile, but clean, new—and hold it up. Can I do this? Without pausing or hesitating I reach down with my left hand and stroke the skin around the pierced nipple. I can feel the tension from the needle below. I stroke and warm the flesh, and again without pausing I look down and with the blade in my right hand sketch—delicately, almost imperceptibly—an arc across the skin. There is no pain; there is no feeling at all. I breathe and wait. Nothing. I breathe more. My hand trembles: tension, anxiety, fear? I remember Jim in the mirror, Vince on the floor, Walta in bed sick and frail, hardly able to talk or help himself. Do I cut again? I'm too tense. There is no blood because I can't relax. Tense, relax, tense, relax. There is no gravity; I am lying down. Tense, relax, tense, relax. I am holding my breath as I remember Jim in his hospital bed, his face gaunt, Walta at home holding my hand so hard it hurt. Tense, relax, love, trust, truth, pressure, trust, tense, relax. All of the men I have loved, really loved, in my life are dead. I am here. I think about Vietnam and Jim and dead boys covered in blood. I think about the needle in my thumb, my panic. There is no blood. Tense, relax. Tense, relax. I stand up. Breathe. Tense, relax. I look in the mirror on the wall across from the bed. The room is dark. I see Jim's picture on the wall above my desk. Walta watches from across the room. I feel hot and look again in the mirror. The arc is pink, almost rose. I breathe, tense, relax. Suddenly the rose turns deeper—a lovely color—and almost imperceptibly the new color emerges from the top of the arc and slowly travels to its end: as if by will alone a single drop of crimson, scarlet, carmine blood forms and runs down my chest. It stops, and I stare at it in the mirror. I don't feel like a saint, I don't feel beautiful, I don't feel sexy. I just feel alive and begin to cry.

This isn't about Jim or Vince, or Walta whom I miss every day in so many ways. This is about me. This is what writers do. We write and try to tell the truth and sometimes bleed and try to convince you that this is about life, about what happens, about ourselves.

# The Disturbance of Sex: A Letter to Michael Bronski

## Muriel Dimen

Dear Michael Bronski,

You know, this is going to be very hard. I mean, *cutting*? I've read "Dr. Fell" many times, gasping all the way. No doubt you intended exactly this reaction, in all its intensity. Do you too react like that sometimes? Disbelieving. Horrified. Fascinated. Repelled. Did the drugs help you through the Scylla of disgust and the Charybdis of anxiety? "Don't forget to mention that it was the most potent sexual stimulation I have ever encountered," you say. "Leave out the fact that we were on drugs (you wouldn't want to give cutting and blood sports a bad name)." Oh, what would we do without our fabulous irony?

You are one good writer, Michael. I don't know you, although friends of mine have read your work. The struggle "Doctor Fell" recounts impresses (itself on) me: reader gets writer because writer makes reader struggle to(o) understand. The effort you make to articulate the ambivalence of (your writing about) your sexual practices gives the lie to psychoanalysts like Janine Chasseguet-Smirgel (1985) who think perverts are liars.

Whoops. I'm on the brink of political incorrectness, aren't I? You know, of course, that, in the traditional psychoanalytic lexicon, you are a pervert. The new, more liberal lingo softens the swipe: it's just your practices, not your character, that are perverse.

Somehow, though, I have the feeling you don't mind my using this cutting terminology. Your passion makes me think you understand the effort to work irony and liberation into the same sentence. Perhaps you too have wondered whether perversion, like queer, can be reappropriated as part of what Ken Corbett (2001), interpreting the tropes of invert and queer in culture and psychoanalysis, calls "the efforts of theorists and activists to assume and empower [and privilege] a marginal position" (p. 2). Cutting-edge strategy, to be sure, but perhaps you might also share Corbett's suspicion that to render the marginal a privileged site of knowledge, critique, and revolution is as idealizing as the marginalizing and pathologizing term, *invert*, is demonizing; "neither the invert nor the queer sufficiently problematizes homosexual subjectivity" (p. 4).

Do I digress? My target here is precisely the binary, specifically, psychoanalytic marginalization, its divide-and-conquer approach: there's "us" and there's "them," the " normal" and, well, take your pick: the invert, the queer, the pervert, perhaps the woman (de Beauvoir 1952), even devotees of oral sex (Dimen 2000). Chasseguet-Smirgel (1985) wields that binary like a rapier. Unlike "us," she insists, perverts hate the truth. "The perverse solution" tempts us to replace the love for truth with "a taste for sham" (p. 26). Well, I disagree. It's far better to abrogate the binary rather than maintain it. Privileging ambiguity salutes the complication of life and love and sex, letting them be as mixed-up and nutty on the page as they are in the light of day and dark of night. I would have Chasseguet-Smirgel and those who agree with her consider your agonized *fort/da*: "Journal entry of four days ago is complete shit. I know perfectly well what is missing from the essay: honesty and truth."

But who doesn't lie about their sexual pleasure? Bill Clinton's not alone here, you know. Okay, so maybe "lie" is too strong. What Chasseguet-Smirgel doesn't consider is the hot wire coupling sex and secrecy for everyone in our part of the world and of history. Sexual passion situates shame, and under the cover of privacy we can indulge pleasures that in the air of public life might grow embarrassing. As Zen Buddhist Sallie Tisdale (1995) puts it in *Talk Dirty to Me*, "Tongues loosen during orgasm, things get said that would never be said otherwise" (p. 280). Remember Gordon Lightfoot's verse about the room where you do what you don't confess? He was talking about prostitutes, I think, but of course one reason gents go to whorehouses is to do what they can't at home. Did you see *Analyze This?* Robert De Niro, playing a Mafia don, has commandeered Billy Crystal as his shrink. Crystal asks De Niro why he has a girl friend, since he's already got a wife. Duh. "Are you nuts?" sputters De Niro. "You think I . . . with my wife . . . the mouth that she kisses my children goodnight with?" Talk about madonna/whore. Shame, excitement, pleasure, disgust—which, as Freud said, "the sexual instinct in its strength enjoys overriding" (1905, p. 152). Isn't that what you write about too, Michael?

Recognizing the way sex invites mendacity, you tell us of your own temptation to dissemble: "[W]hat am I leaving out? That as much as I loved Jim, I thought he was fucked up about sex and his own sexual desires? That his s/m practices, including cutting, were mostly vain attempts to break through the crushing repression of his Southern boyhood and his horrible feelings about himself? That for the first year we were together (out of five) he would have to leave the room after coming, so he could be alone? That some of these times he cried?" Pretty powerful stuff, damage and healing, not to mention love and hate, and it's interesting that you found yourself on the brink of omitting these particular complications. Perhaps what you were inclined to leave out is the ambiguity, the both/and inhabiting the space between binaries, the paradoxes of desire for which speech fails us. Sex may be reckoned in the Symbolic, but it takes place in the Real (Dean 1994).

For whom is sexuality not a cure? The scalpels, you say, "are instruments meant for healing." You know, Michael, you touch here on the crux of contemporary psychoanalytic thought, in which sex is rarely about sex. Mostly, these days, it's about selfhood and its matrix, the ligatures of life, not the erotics of tension and discharge but the repair of the self and the mutilated capacity to love. Now we take our clinical cue not from disorders of desire but from disturbances of self and relatedness—splits in the psyche, maladies of object-love, infirmities of intimacy. You too respond to this tension between sex and attachment when, worrying about how the essay is going, you ask yourself, "Is it too much about relationship and not enough about cutting?" Indeed, you say on the next page, "I think Walta felt more betrayed by my grief at losing Jim than he did by my sexual relationship with him." And certainly we can see in your story of Jim what Stephen Mitchell (1988) writes about: sex as a search for security, for open and honest connection (Jim keeps asking whether you trust him) and sex as an escape (Jim's tricking) from the constraints of intimacy—the lover's demands, intrusive or otherwise, or the paralysis induced by the hate that always accompanies love. Absolutely we could find in his rage and hatred what Robert Stoller (1979) saw: sexuality as infiltrated with hostility and conducted for revenge. Do you think that what Virginia Goldner (1989) discerns in couples showed up in your intimacies with Jim: an intense, addictive, and acrid mix of sex, gender, love/hate, and reparation? I'm not sure about this last, but I do know that you yourself understood Jim to use s/m and cutting as a means to break out of a repressed childhood in a sexually hypocritical culture (I think that's what you suggest by identifying it as "Southern") and to cure his feelings of, one must suppose, shame and inadequacy about his own need for others.

But what about you? One wants to know. When my study group read "Doctor Fell," they noticed that, while you pinpointed the suffering implicated in Jim's sexual practices, you did not bring yourself under the same clinical eye. I mean, I know you're not a clinician, and clinical acumen would not be a criterion by which I would judge this piece of writing, but you do diagnose Jim and you do suggest that his sexuality was a way to cure his own illness. What about you? Yes, he's "the beautiful Count" in whose arms you are overcome, drained, and depleted. But how did you get there? A word or two, to parallel those you offer about Jim, would have been welcome, would have answered the craving "Doctor Fell" incites in the unsettled, sympathetic, or even combative reader. Otherwise, one is left asking what wounds of yours were healed by those scalpels. I haven't forgotten what you've told us about high school. But who among us bookish types wasn't a miserable nerd way back then? One does feel that the extremity of the treatment, sex-as-therapy, must have something to do with the extremity of the injury. Did you just forget to tell us? Or did you decide not to? Were you lying? Why?

"Doctor Fell" challenges clinical minds, and it's not only the blood sports that do it. There's something else that may be even more difficult: the relation between truth and irony. Like most postmoderns, your premise is the impossibility of truth, a small problem whose solution, you propose, is irony. "The idea of what is truthful and what is not is arbitrary," you say. Nowadays most psychoanalysts, I among them, would agree that we can only approximate truth. A conservative fringe (e.g., Grünbaum 1984) still holds that psychoanalysis can and should ape (a caricature of) the scientific method, a wishful thought, found in most of the soft, social sciences, which Richard Rorty (1993) cleverly dubs "physics envy" (p. 28).

More likely, however, your average clinician understands that we deal in approximations to causes and cures of illness. We don't always know exactly why someone gets ill or why we fall sick in the way we do or even precisely what a symptom might be. Frieda Fromm-Reichmann (1950) reports on a patient, one of whose chief symptoms had been "the delusion of the appearance of 'The Line.'" Neither the therapist nor, perhaps, the patient, was absolutely certain what "The Line" was. What mattered was that the patient could respond to the therapist's inquiry, "telling him each time what event preceded the appearance of 'The Line,' until they finally discovered what type of events in the patient's life created its appearance." We no longer pursue the Holy Grail of historical truth; we construct narratives instead (Schafer 1994), and they emerge from or in the intersubjectively created meanings of the analytic dyad. The ultimate disappearance of "The Line" "seem[ed] to . . . contribute greatly to the general improvement in the patient's condition" (p. 19). Psychoanalysis isn't science, it's hermeneutics.

Irony is deep in the heart of psychoanalysis. Freud's (1908) real message, for example, was the irony of sublimation, as announced by the scare quotes in the title of one of his grandest essays, "'Civilized' Sexual Morality and Modern Nervousness." What civilization gives with one hand, it takes away with the other. It gives us culture but takes away peace of mind. A society founded on sexual repression creates the habitat required for human survival but so fills its citizens with hate, despair, fear, and rage that they draw into themselves, their sickness undermining the very society they call home. American psychoanalysis might be better off, I think, if it occasionally cut that relentless, smiley-face, anything-is-possible, traditional pursuit-of-happiness brashness with a *soupçon* of irony.

But there is a truth people come to therapy to find: feeling better. People hurt, they want help, they look to therapy, and therapists want to help them. Hence another interesting tension. Psychoanalysis, in

Freud's eyes, was a trinity: a body of knowledge, a technique of research, and a method of cure. Famously, the first and second parts interested him much more than the third. As objects of knowledge, consequently, theory and research came to have more cachet than treatment. Probably one reason that object relations theory has become so popular is its righting of that balance. Psychoanalysis, argued Harry Guntrip (1969), is a psycho*therapy*, a healing process, a treatment for disorders of psychic reality and (as the Sullivanians put it) problems in living. The work of Winnicott (1975), Fairbairn (1952), and Sullivan (1953), coalescing in and later transforming the second half of the psychoanalytic century, brought suffering and healing out of the shadows and into the psychoanalytic limelight. As we have seen, the "triumph of the therapeutic" has influenced you, too.

So the clinical relationship between truth and irony really is interesting. There is a truth people want, and it's called healing. It may be, however, that the route to healing passes through irony (a possibility of which Lacanian thought makes great use). Clinical practice necessarily takes place in a briar patch of uncertainties—the obscurity of cause, the trial-and-error of therapy, the incompleteness of result, the post-hoc quality of knowledge. As things begin to fall apart, you, the patient, come into treatment with two conflicting goals: to change your mind and practice so you can feel better, and to keep things the same by restoring your neurotic structure to working order. In the context of the therapeutic relationship, with all its inevitably personal over- and undertones, you, the therapist, try to intensify insight as a means to help your patient, while your patient is torn between the effort to feel better and the wish/need to remain committed to suffering. At therapy's end, cynicism and bitterness are not uncommon: you understand more, you have even changed in very definite and deep ways, but still, what happened happened, you are who you are, you are who you were. Analyst as well as patient must swallow the disappointment. Welcome to "ordinary unhappiness." Irony is the only stance possible on the inevitable failure of psychoanalytic "cure."

So it makes me feel uncomfortable when you say, "Did I feel great about my cutting experiences all the time? Of course not. Would I write about that? I don't know." I'm not sure I trust you. Why are you being so coy? Don't you want to probe your ambivalence about cutting? It would be a complicated task, but a very engrossing one. It would intensify the irony. Do you fear such doubt would compromise your political agenda? Using a psychoanalytic locution (oddly, one diagnostic of illness or at least of resistance to the analytic process) you write, not without irony, "Acting out doesn't always bring you through to the other side. And what does this mean in an essay that is promoting all kinds of sexual experimentation in the name of sexual freedom and health?" Perhaps, were the dark side of the dark side, your unease with the erotics of scalpels, cuts, pain, and blood, to be explored, the liberation project would be advanced rather than impeded.

Why wouldn't it be an advance for your readers to think about the dark and light sides of everything, from therapy to sex, from life to death? Somehow I feel it's not fair of you to stop right there. Is the reader to be the one left holding the bag of conformity and timidity? I wish you would say what you mean by "Of course not." That grain of sand contains a world, and I wonder if it is a world you want to shock, a world you, shocked, inhabit too. You appeal here to some common sense that you don't spell out, an earnest common sense that is implicitly spurned, mocked, the butt of a joke. Implied is the italicized thought with which I began this letter: *cutting?* "*Cutting?* You must be joking! Who would want to do that?" Are we to align that "Of course not" with the bookish domesticity of love and relationship? You describe your ambivalence about loving/hating Jim and loving Walta, about the contrast between your domestic state of feeling "loved and secure, bookish, smart, even respected" and your "non-domestic dark side, where the wild things are," where you are no longer the geek: "Ripped dirty jeans, T-shirts, leather jackets. . . . I have become my childhood dreams. I have become the men I feared." Should we believe you? I think you are also the geek you were who is not so sure about that bloody world of leather and scars. Why can't you let the contradiction stand as paradox? It worries me when you say, "We write to give the appearance of truth, and we hope that our readers believe us. But even careless readers must realize that these 'journal' entries are fake, cribbed from Nabokov and John Fowles and others: a literary device used to contextualize and move my story, my agenda, along. All, of course, in the pursuit of 'truth' and 'honesty.'" This letter to you isn't fake. It's a form. It's a literary device that helps me respond to the engaging and disturbing form you chose. But there are both truth and irony in it.

So now let me approach the end of this formal communication. As I was reading what I'd written, preparatory to coming to this point,

I saw the double meaning in Sallie Tisdale's (1995) observation about orgasm. Let me repeat it here: "Tongues loosen during orgasm, things get said that would never be said otherwise" (p. 280). When I quoted it, I was talking about lies. Now I see the other side, the truth Tisdale was talking about. By "otherwise" she means that, in the light of day, you cannot articulate that which, as you tip over from the pinnacle of passion down the other side of the mountain, is perfectly clear and accessible and safe. It's as though we inhabit parallel universes, each with its own rules, its own canon. Indeed, if we can't leave the waking universe dominated by the reality and performance principles, we can never have a really good time in the sexual universe, that extraordinary place lying somewhere between dream and daily life.

There's a clinical way of thinking about this duality of truth in sex, one that I hesitate to invoke because it is ordinarily diagnostic and thus redolent of pathology. But since it also hints at irony, let me try it out, Michael, and then you can tell me if it furthers emancipation, a project to which, as you know, Freud in his duality was also committed. If we all lie about sex—to others if not to ourselves—doesn't sexuality also always take place in a dissociated state? I am suggesting, in the matter of sex, an erotic continuum between lying and disavowing (I am willing to believe that Bill dissociated his adventures with Monica, as did O.J. his with Nicole). While dissociation, the splitting of consciousness described by Pierre Janet as hysteria's central pathology, has been most recently discussed in relation to psychic trauma and the recovery of memories of various kinds of abuse, this "severing of the normal connections between memory, knowledge, and emotion" (Herman 1992, pp. 34–35) may find itself in civilian life as well. Jody Davies (n.d.) suggests as much when she argues that "a significant piece of infantile sexuality [may be] inherently unformulated and significantly unmentalized psychic content, . . . not repressed . . . but indeed dissociated in a manner that involves being overwhelmed, invaded and symbolically unmediated" (p. 10). Initially, Davies thinks, "the intrapsychic structure or, more aptly put, 'structurelessness' of childhood sexuality might be compared to and have much in common with the internal qualities of traumatic experience" (p. 8). In the parent–child relationship, she points out, sexual feeling, unlike, say, anger or love or jealousy, is rarely dealt with: "children's erotic experiences are in large measure the one area of intense emotional and physiological arousal that . . . parents do not help them to process and contain" (p. 6). Sexuality comes to seem Other, which in fact it might be. Davies, following Laplanche (1976), proposes that sexuality may be implanted in the child, transplanted, more or less whole, more or less directly, from the parental unconscious as an "alien internal entity" (p. 24) that feels disturbingly familiar and incomprehensible at once.

Sex—its passion and pleasure as much as its anxiety and disgust— takes place in an exceptional, even, one might say, an extraordinary state of mind because it evolves, as Davies puts it, outside "an internalized relational context" (p. 7). Freud's (1905) definition of instinct as lying "on the frontier between the mental and the physical" (p. 168) chimes in here. Today, as we work through our Cartesian heritage of dualism, that definition, so potent and prescient, requires a little emendation: that frontier expands into a region that we might call "bodymind" (Dimen 2000, Wrye 1998), a liminal territory inhabited by sex, by us as we do sex. To put it differently, sexuality, located in bodymind and therefore apart from the familiar binaries of rational adulthood, sits on the margin of linguistically encoded experience, making itself known at least as much in kinesthetics, in sensorimotor mnemonics, in semiosis (Kristeva 1983), as in symbolic representation.

In my course "Sexuality in Relational Perspective," I once asked my students, all psychoanalytic candidates, whether, in order to have good sex, you have to dissociate. "But then you wouldn't know what happened," exclaimed one student. "You wouldn't know whether you had a good time or not." I was stumped for the moment, but now I see that we were both right. Daily life militates against remembering erotic life; to put it differently, the erotic fantasy that visits you on the job is the counterpart to the laundry list that floats into your mind as you struggle against the descent into or ascent toward desire. Virginia Goldner (1999) writes: "The erotic, which Stoller and many others have likened to the dramaturgical, requires, like any piece of theatre, the willing and complete suspension of disbelief. Turning up the house-lights, even for a passing thought, breaks the spell" (p. 20). Carolyn Stack (personal communication), in her edit of the first draft of this epistolary essay, put it this way: "We all conceal and fabricate in our stories about our own sexual pleasures because of the differences between the states of consciousness of doing and not doing sex." Occurring outside the intersubjective realm, sexual experience becomes en-coded as that which did and did not happen.

Are you familiar with that mundane reluctance, when you're in a relationship that's been going on for some time, to get into the sack? The challenges of ordinary dissociation visit us daily. As gays and queers and even some straight people know, this ennui is not merely the mat-rimonial vicissitude it is conventionally held to be. Tom Domenici (personal communication) said that, among his mostly gay (male) cli-entele, one member of a couple will not infrequently respond to the other's sexual invitation with a (not always ironic) demurral, "But didn't we just do that last week?" Even "lesbian bed death" (Lindenbaum 1985) might fall under this rubric. Sexuality has its discontents not only because of civilization but also because it runs by different rules, dif-ferent truths, if you will, than waking and even sleeping life.

To put it differently, in sex you inhabit primary process and sec-ondary process at once. You step from one universe into another, sort of like the journey from the late twentieth to the late nineteenth cen-tury made by the protagonist in Jack Finney's *Time and Again* (1995), in which an inventor, inspired by the Einsteinian idea that time bends, finds a way to step from the now to the then as though crossing the banks of a stream doubling back on itself. In 1892 (the time period, strangely enough, into which Finney's hero steps), Freud (Breuer and Freud 1895) asks his patient, Miss Lucy R., a governess, "But if you knew you loved your employer why didn't you tell me?" She replies "I didn't know—or rather I didn't want to know. I wanted to drive it out of my head and not think of it again; and I believe latterly I have succeeded" (p. 117). In a footnote he says, "I have never managed to give a better description than this of the strange state of mind in which one knows and does not know a thing at the same time" (p. 117, n. 1). Ordinary dissociation, I would call it: you're in bed or on a chair or hung from the ceiling, you're doing something that in some other ordinary con-text you would not want to be doing or maybe not be seen doing, and you know that you would not want to do that even as you are totally immersed in the passion of the moment.

So, Michael, the structure of your essay, as well as some of the details of your sexual practice, tell us about this dissociation, this man-agement of incompatible truths. Alternating between "journal" entry and "essay," you raise and lower the house lights. By showing and shocking and dismaying, you tell how this suspension of disbelief works: the ordinary dissociativeness of sexuality, in the light of day, under the pitiless glare of writing and symbolic representation, fails to conceal the pathetic ordinariness of sex, "the expense of spirit in a waste of shame," the wet mess, the limp organ, the blood on the floor: "The romanticism of our blood games—and my presentation of it—is countered by the fact that there was often blood dripped all over the floor and furniture from other men he brought home."

You have to know and not know in order to have really good sex, because sex is so weird altogether: the genitals, primitive and grotesque; the extraordinary space between dream and reality holding erotic states of mind; the abundance of paradoxes, for example, generated by "the moment before" (Dimen 1999). Once a student of mine said, "I don't know why Freud emphasized discharge as the be-all and end-all of sex, why he thought the moment of orgasm is the greatest pleasure. As far as I'm concerned it's the moment before, when you're just hanging on and you want it to go on and on and you don't want to stop." He was describing a liminal state that I've called *Lust*, one to which Freud (1905) paid but marginal attention in the *Three Essays*. "The only appropriate word in the German language, *Lust*, is unfortunately ambiguous and is used to denote the experience of a need and of its gratification" (p. 135, n. 2, added 1910). In the interests of scientific clarity, Freud dismissed this term, but in so doing he lost a lot. Way down deep, *Lust* means not the conclusion of discharge, but the penultimate moment of peak excitement when being excited is both enough and not enough, when each rise in excitement is, paradoxically, satisfying. Orgiastic. I would not want to do without orgasm—catharsis—myself. But isn't the pleasure of *Lust* equally central? A need calling for satisfaction, a satisfaction becoming a thrilling need. An excitement whose gratification is simultaneously exciting. Both "lost to the world" and in the world at once (Bach 1998). A doubling of feeling, a doubled and potently contradictory state whose end one craves and fears. If the closure of climax is devoutly to be wished, do we, or at least some of us, not savor it all the more because, in achieving it, we must let go of the extraordinary poignancy of sustained excitement in the moment before?

In a means–ends culture, it is counterintuitive, even if totally compelling, to enjoy that penultimate moment of peak excitement, when being excited is both enough and not enough, when each rise in excitement is, paradoxically, satisfying. Foreplay may be for girls, but one reason so many guys keep returning over and over again to hookers or peep shows is that they love the build-up, the fantasy and anticipation, the moment before. So do you. Otherwise, why all that paraphernalia, the tea doctored "with sweet bourbon and sugar to mask the bitterness of more MDA," the mirrors, the rearranging of candles and adjusting of music, all that romance you write of? "This moment before [you say the very words] we begin cutting is a prelude, an *introit*." Remember Jack Nicholson in *Carnal Knowledge*? Rita Moreno, playing his high-class whore, forgets the lines to the drama they routinely enact, and so he loses his hard-on. Furious, he insists they take it from the top. He re-enters her apartment and repeats his opening lines so that, this time, she can get hers just right and he can float into his fantasy of a white-skinned, red-lipped, blonde-haired figure-skater, her snowy costume barely distinguishable from the ice she silently skims.

Is the "moment before" the sacred moment? Is coming profane? Ruth Stein (1998), following Georges Bataille, reframes the common idea that "sexuality profanes the sacred" by asking whether or not "*the sacred* [including sexuality] *violates* ('*profanes*') *secular life*, such as work, thrift, reason, everyday conduct and feelings" (p. 256). How smart and yet, in the end, how contrary to your approach and, I would say, to sex itself. Stein's reversal splits, idealizing sex and demonizing the everyday. How much more suitable the paradoxical, the juxtaposed rather than the opposed. For my money, sex is a place not of either/or but of both/and, which is why it's so disturbing, "monstrous" says Stein after Bataille (p. 257). In sex, the dissociation one needs to maintain ordinary, related consciousness breaks down. Of course one thinks here of Leo Bersani (1989), who, also influenced by Bataille, theorizes the shattered self of sex, which, if it showed up on the street, would wind up in the gutter or the loony bin. Like a night-blooming flower, the dread of sexual shattering, often masked by love's first blood and the idealization of romance, echoes the dread one feels at any threshold where boundaries are transgressed, whether facing the blank page/canvas/screen, or sitting down on your *zafu* to meditate, or plunging into the water for a swim, or starting an analytic session. This dread is what your juxtaposition of (are they really?) fake journal entries and (real?) essay fragments creates in the reader, Michael, a very successful mimesis of the disturbance of sex.

With all very best wishes,
Muriel Dimen

## REFERENCES

Bach, S. (1998). Colloquium on Sexuality in Psychoanalysis, Postdoctoral Program in Psychotherapy and Psychoanalysis, New York University, New York, March.

Bersani, L. (1989). "Is the rectum a grave?" In *AIDS: Cultural Analysis/Cultural Action*, ed. D. Crimp, pp. 197–222. Cambridge, MA: MIT Press.

Breuer, J., and Freud, S. (1895). "Miss Lucy R." Studies on hysteria. *Standard Edition* 2:106–124.

Chasseguet-Smirgel, J. (1985). *Creativity and Perversion*. New York: Norton.

Corbett, K. (2001). More life. *Psychoanalytic Dialogues* 11:313–335.

Davies, J. (n.d.). *Too hot to handle: containing and symbolizing erotic overstimulation in the realms of the traumatic and the transgressive*. Unpublished manuscript.

Dean, T. (1994). Bodies that mutter. *Pre/Text* 15:81–117.

de Beauvoir, S. (1952). *The Second Sex*, trans. H. M. Parshley. New York: Vintage.

Dimen, M. (1999). Between lust and libido: sex, psychoanalysis, and the moment before. *Psychoanalytic Dialogues* 9:415–440.

––––––– (2000). The body as Rorschach. *Studies in Gender and Sexuality* 1:9–39.

Fairbairn, W. R. D. (1952). *Psychoanalytic Studies of the Personality*. London: Routledge & Kegan Paul.

Finney, J. (1995). *Time and Again*. New York: Scribner.

Freud, S. (1905). Three essays on the theory of sexuality. *Standard Edition* 7:135–248.

––––––– (1908). "Civilized" sexual morality and modern nervousness. *Standard Edition* 9:181–204.

Fromm-Reichmann, F. (1950). *Principles of Intensive Psychotherapy*. Chicago: University of Chicago Press.

Goldner, V. (1989). Sex, power, and gender: the politics of passion. In *Intimate Environments: Sex, Intimacy, and Gender*, ed. D. Kantor and B. F. Okun, pp. 28–53. New York: Guilford.

———— (1999). *Theorizing gender and sexual subjectivity*. Paper presented to the Westchester Center for the Study of Psychoanalysis and Psychotherapy 25th Anniversary Conference, Tarrytown, NY, March.

Grünbaum, A. (1984). *The Foundations of Psychoanalysis*. Berkeley: University of California Press.

Guntrip, H. (1969). *Schizoid Phenomena, Object-Relations, and the Self*. New York: International Universities Press.

Herman, J. L. (1992). *Trauma and Recovery*. New York: Basic Books.

Kristeva, J. (1983). *Tales of Love*, trans. L. S. Roudiez. New York: Columbia University Press.

Laplanche, J. (1976). *Life and Death in Psychoanalysis*, trans. J. Mehlman. Baltimore, MD: Johns Hopkins University Press.

Lindenbaum, J. (1985). The shattering of an illusion: the problem of competition in lesbian relationships. *Feminist Studies* 11(1):85–103.

Mitchell, S. A. (1988). *Relational Concepts in Psychoanalysis: An Integration*. Cambridge, MA: Harvard University Press.

Rorty, R. (1993). Centers of moral gravity. *Psychoanalytic Dialogues* 3:21–28.

Schafer, R. (1994). *Retelling a Life*. New York: Basic Books.

Stein, R. (1998). The poignant, the excessive and the enigmatic in sexuality. *International Journal of Psycho-Analysis* 79:253–268.

Stoller, R. J. (1979). *Sexual Excitement*. New York: Pantheon.

Sullivan, H. S. (1953). *The Interpersonal Theory of Psychiatry*. New York: Norton.

Tisdale, S. (1995). *Talk Dirty to Me*. New York: Doubleday.

Winnicott, D. W. (1975). *Through Paediatrics to Psycho-Analysis*. New York: Basic Books.

Wrye, H. K. (1998). The embodiment of desire: relinking the bodymind with the analytic dyad. In *Relational Perspectives on the Body*, ed. L. Aron and F. S. Anderson, pp. 97–116. Hillsdale, NJ: Analytic Press.

# 8b

# Sex, Death, and the Limits of Irony: A Reply to Muriel Dimen

*Michael Bronski*

Dear Muriel,

Thank you for your thoughtful, provocative, and challenging reply to "Dr. Fell." As someone who writes for publication you surely know the (often unarticulated) trepidation of committing words to paper, images and ideas to print.

You have said so much about "Dr. Fell" that I am not sure where to begin in response. Which is ironic, really, because as a freelance journalist who turns out copy on order and on deadline I am usually not at a loss for words. But then questions of irony are, in your piece, the order of the day. I am intrigued by the idea—you cite Chasseguet-Smirgel, but it is a ubiquitous idea in much of mainstream culture—that perverts hate the truth. This phrase to me is delicious, for, ironically, as a pervert, I believe it to be completely true. And, ironically, I love this phrase. But doesn't Chasseguet-Smirgel's idea only work—as she would presume, being deeply wedded to a binary view of the world—if the perverted are always on the outside, are always the other? The "truth," as it is so carefully and lovingly called, is almost always what is held as a cherished belief by those in the dominant culture: those with power, those who have the power to name, and, as it follows, to name-call.

I want to write a little about being a pervert but first want to admit some serious qualms about entering into this dialogue/response with you. I have always been eager to enter into the political fray, but here, in the context of this book, I feel not so much vulnerable as at a disadvantage. I suspect that many (perhaps even the majority) of readers of this book are going to be negatively judgmental, even antagonistic to "Dr. Fell." The editors of this volume have told me of two instances in which members of psychoanalytic groups expressed violent responses to it. I have enormous respect for psychoanalysis, which I have read widely and used in my own work, but I have no illusions that a majority of our readers here will judge me as a pervert. The conjuring of the phantom of Chasseguet-Smirgel as a stand-in for the sex-negative judgmentalism of some aspects of the psychoanalytic community avoids, I think, the harsher reality that innumerably more psychoanalytic professionals share her views, or at least some aspect of them. Am I being defensive, or paranoid, in imagining many readers shaking their heads as they read the details of cutting and bleeding? Or even, as they do their best not to judge too quickly, silently enumerate the technical language of pathologies that might be used to describe my actions and feelings? Let us not forget that it was only in 1973 that the APA removed homosexuality from its list of mental illnesses in the *DSM-III*. Nor let us forget that there are currently APA members—often fueled and fueling right wing media pundits such as "Dr." Laura Schlessinger—who constantly lobby for it to be reinstated. And, let's face it, plain old vanilla homosexuality is moderately acceptable compared to sadomasochism or cutting.

Even as you and I are in dialogue here, will my words not be read, by some, as elaborate self-justifications for perverted behaviors? So I must say at the beginning, since this dialogue is appearing in a book intended for (perhaps non-traditional) psychoanalysts, that we are not on equal ground. And I must add, as well, that part of what I want to talk about here are ways in which I feel that your response contributes to that unequal ground.

But now some background on my perversion. In many ways I have, over the course of the past thirty years, become a professional pervert.

That is to say that a great deal of my energy has gone into working in the Gay Liberation Movement and writing (both for pay and for free) about issues connected to homosexuality. And as a perverted writer and activist I have also become, in the eyes of Chasseguet-Smirgel and others, a liar: "gay is good"; queer-baiting hurts; children and teens have queer desires; children and teens should be able to act on their queer desires; institutional heterosexuality is stifling and dangerous; the nuclear family is a dangerous place for gay people; the nuclear family is, by and large, a dangerous place for women and children. These are the lies that I have spent more than half my life thinking about and promoting. They are the lies that I think will bring about a greater degree of safety, honesty, and happiness in the world. To reverse-paraphrase that well-known, first-century Jewish heretic: the lies will set you free. Or as the Lesbian Avengers say: SUBVERSION THROUGH PERVERSION.

As you see, I take my perversion seriously. And to make living in this world a little easier I have learned to take my irony as, if not more, seriously. One of the ways that homosexuals (as well as other marginalized groups) have learned to survive in a world that hates them is to rely upon the comfort and the possibilities of "truth" (or at least understanding) that might be found in irony. Indeed, there is a strong historical thread—camp—running through gay male culture that is predicated on viewing the world through the lens of irony. Susan Sontag (1966), in her essay "Notes on Camp," states that "the essence of Camp is its love of the unnatural" (p. 275), that it subverts "reality" by seeing "everything in quotation marks. It's not a lamp, but a 'lamp'; not a woman but a 'woman'" (p. 280). Indeed, homosexuals have been so good at this that Sontag claims that "[T]he two pioneering forces of modern sensibility are Jewish moral seriousness and homosexual aestheticism and irony" (p. 290). And perhaps even more importantly she notes that "[C]amp is the solvent of morality. It neutralizes moral indignation, sponsors playfulness" (p. 290).

My attachment to the irony that you write about is fully committed and sustained. I learned in grammar and high school to protect myself from being queerbashed by honing an ironic wit. If that didn't work I tried to be ironic about being queerbashed. The irony here is that I think I learned to deal with queerbashing by being ironic before I learned the often better technique—turning and running. Looking over my 40-something career as a pervert I often feel that not only have I used irony to get through and make sense of my life, but that on some level—as an openly homosexual man—I (and other queers) have literally embodied irony. What else could it mean to simultaneously be a "man" and not a man or to make love but have it called a perversion? Even in the sociology of the Christian Right, homosexuals embody an ironic position: we are less than 2 percent of the population and yet constitute the greatest threat to the nation ever imagined.

It was this ironic body that I tried to convey in "Dr. Fell"—that the "wounded" body was the "healed" body; that the perversions of homosexuality and cutting were good and healthy; that love and hate, fear and hope, devotion and revenge could exist at the same time. Ironically (which does seem to be the word of the day), I did not *choose* the rhetoric of "irony" to express these ideas, it is simply how they existed in my own life and body. The distance, for me here, between and/or and both/and is reflexive, not chosen.

You speak of how "the binary, specifically, psychoanalytic marginalization" is used to "divide and conquer . . . there's 'us' and there's 'them,' the 'normal' and, well, take your pick: the invert, the queer, the pervert, perhaps the woman": a position with which, as a professional pervert, I wholeheartedly agree. And I also agree with Ken Corbett's suggestion that "to render the marginal a privileged site of knowledge, critique, and revolution is as idealizing as the marginalizing and pathologizing term, *invert*, is demonizing." And yet when I step back and think about this I find unexpected qualms, hesitations.

Much of my adult life has been spent doing political organizing around issues of gay, lesbian, and other deviant sexualities. While this has been less about grassroots lobbying to repeal sodomy laws than writing articles and promoting an ideology of various forms of "sexual liberation," it has been impossible for me to not be concerned with the hard, and often cruel, reality of the world (laws, police, arrests) and the difficulties faced by lesbians and gay men in attempting to live everyday and ordinary lives. I imagine that as a well-read, politically aware New Yorker you are all too cognizant of these issues; they are not new and are going to be with us for a long time. But what I have learned over the years is that the best—well, at least the most organized and effective—way of concretely addressing them is from a position of political power predicated in large part on cultivating and embracing that "marginal" site of knowledge, critique, and revolution as "privileged."

Over the years I have come to the realization that, much as I esteem and need my irony, it is not useful or productive in all situations. I want to write that I have always relished the irony and the ambiguity of my body, imagination, and life, but that is not quite correct. Far more then relishing it, I have to admit that it was essential in helping me survive in what at times has been an incredibly hostile and dangerous world, to become the person that I am today. And for this I value it as much as my life. It has also helped me to understand my self, my desires, my sexualities, and my past. It has even allowed me to imagine possible futures. All of this I understand as political: the politics of the self, as R.D. Laing (now so unnecessarily out of fashion) might say. But what I have also come to see is that with regard to actually changing the world—abolishing terrible, dangerous laws, creating support systems for gay and lesbian teens, shaping and supporting a broader sense and reality of a community that will give people the permission and the ability to make the world a safe place in which they can live—irony and ambiguity are not all that helpful.

I understand that this is one of the most prevalent and articulated liberal attacks on postmodernism, and I say it with caution and even some trepidation. It is, of course, the same critique that Martha Nussbaum (1999) has of Judith Butler's work in her celebrated/notorious attack in *The New Republic*. It is true that irony and ambiguity have, in many ways, helped me deal with the process of doing political work—god knows, it can go a long way in making a meeting clogged with bad tempers and process go more easily—but I always come back to the question: Does irony always work toward a larger project of (especially social) liberation? Is simply finding the *both/and* going to rid us of the destructive world of *either/or*? And if not, then how do we do that?

But in my desire to remake the world I have drifted away from the discussion of "Dr. Fell." There is much you have said about the piece that I have found illuminating. But I must admit that there are portions in your response that I find curious, that feel alien to me or do not register on an emotional or psychological level. But before I talk about them let me give a little background on the piece.

I was asked to write an essay for an anthology that my friend Michael Lowenthal was editing. It was the fourth volume in a series entitled *Flesh and the Word: An Anthology of Gay Erotic Writing* (Lowenthal 1997). The first three volumes of the series concentrated on fiction, and Michael thought it would be interesting, and commercially smart, to shift the focus. Memoirs were beginning to be all the rage in publishing—Mary Karr's *The Liar's Club*, Lucy Greely's *The Face*—so volume four was subtitled "Gay Erotic Confessionals." Michael had always urged me to write about my experiences with cutting, so I began working on a piece that became "Dr. Fell."

I give all this background for two reasons. The first is that many people have read the piece and, panic-stricken or overwhelmed by its content, presume that it is simply an outpouring of memory, grief, and unchecked emotion similar to sitting next to someone on a plane and having them tell you a story that is shocking and troubling, but (like the watchers of the proverbial car wreck) you are compelled to listen. As a writer I am pleased by this reaction, because it means that I have touched them in some visceral way. But while this is satisfying, I sometimes feel that such a reaction misses the literary craft and exacting artifice that went into writing the piece.

The writing of "Dr. Fell" deviated from my standard process. I usually know what I want to say and how I want to say it. I am blessed with the ability to write quickly and (usually) concisely. When I sat down, under deadline, to write what was to become "Dr. Fell," I had little idea of where it was going or even what I wanted to say. I fumbled through some false beginnings, but eventually things began to take shape; images came into my mind, the dichotomized journal/essay structure evolved, themes came into focus, and the piece slowly began to unfold. I must admit that "Dr. Fell," as opposed to much of my other writing, felt like a process. I sometimes surprised myself by remembering details and incidents I had not thought about in fifteen years. Sometimes I even shocked myself—as when I confessed that I needed Jim to be sick to feel I had "won" our power plays—by acknowledging something on paper that I had only half-thought before. Writing "Dr. Fell" often provided insights that made it feel like good psychotherapy, but it was never cathartic or even emotionally draining. It never profoundly challenged me, or brought me to new places, a process I imagine would be closer to a successful psychoanalysis.

The other important, even fundamental, condition under which "Dr. Fell" was written was that it was scheduled to appear in a collection marketed as erotica. I do not want to underestimate my enormous emotional investment in the piece, but it was also a work for hire that had to conform to the concerns and pressures of the market. (As a working writer, I am always aware of the "market" in my thoughts or process: I take pride in the fact that I am, in the strict Victorian sense, a "hack writer.") I liked the idea of writing for the genre called erotica, or, as I would prefer, pornography, for it reaffirms my identity as a professional pervert shocking and provoking mainstream culture with aberrant sexuality: subversion through perversion. One of the central challenges that faced me in "Dr. Fell" was balancing the erotic detail and narrative of the piece with its other aspects. How do I explore my experience of cutting, while touching on and describing the myriad other experiences I wanted to examine? This, I believe, is how the "irony" of which you write so suggestively entered and installed itself into "Dr. Fell."

For a number of reasons I needed to structurally create areas of distance in the piece. The first was to allow readers some breathing room––to let them get past that first (for most people) powerful and intensely upsetting idea of cutting the flesh. The second was to find a way to integrate serious emotional and psychological meditations with erotic narratives without harming or displacing the integrity of either. This was tricky, because the pornographic imagination is best indulged through unbroken, masturbatory reverie. Like all fantasies it thrives on single-minded and very focused solitude. For me to bring up other topics, many of which were, indeed, anti-romantic and anti-erotic (isn't irony the enemy of pornography?), would be profoundly contradictory to the pornographic project to which I was, at least partly, committed.

After several failed attempts I intuitively discovered the rhetoric of irony to solve the problem of emotional distance and (in the words of Dr. Johnson in his definition of "oxymoron") "yoke together" such divergent, even contesting, narratives. In retrospect, I see the use of irony in "Dr. Fell" as fitting because the very nature of ironic rhetoric or discourse "queers" a narrative: it interrupts and distances in much the way that Bertolt Brecht's much-praised "alienation technique" allows audiences to partake in a theatrical experience while being able, at the same time, to think about and critique it. This, I believe, is substantively different from what Virginia Goldner refers to as "turning up the houselights" in the theater, thus disrupting the "suspension of disbelief." Brecht's "alienation technique"—which I have tried quite consciously to adapt in "Dr. Fell"—does not simply interrupt the "magical" hold that theater has on an audience but forces that audience to consciously critique what it has accepted as "real" just seconds earlier. Good sex (and good sexual fantasy), like good theater, transports us and supplies us with that unbroken reverie of fantasy (pornographic or not). In Brecht, and I modestly hope in "Dr. Fell," the emotionally and intellectually startling experience is in the dislocations, the dissociations, the in-between spaces. The discovery of those spaces, and the living within them, is to a large degree, I think, a paradox—a conundrum? contradiction? puzzle? mystery?—of conscious human existence.

I say all of this because there are times in your response where I have the uneasy feeling that your reading of "Dr. Fell" takes it too much at face value. I don't *think* I am being defensive, nor do I want, to any degree, to avoid the questions you raise in your response to the piece, but frequently I was puzzled by your comments.

Maybe this has to do with my expectations as a (hack) writer, and your expectations as an (analyst) reader. There are times in your response when you want more from the narrator of the piece. I was at first going to write "when you wanted more from me," and maybe this is part of the/my confusion. I don't see myself as the narrator of "Dr. Fell." Of course I wrote it, and of course all of the details of it are from my life, but the narrator is really someone very different from it. He is carefully constructed as the well-planned split between "essays" and "journals," as consciously plotted as the movements from the "erotic" to the "meditative" and as sharpened as the rhetorical ironic that holds "Dr. Fell" together. It is this irony, perhaps, that best defines him. And, of course, that is my irony as well. But just as we learned in high school that Swift is not Gulliver, it is "Michael Bronski" who is the narrator of "Dr. Fell," not me.

I was confused, then, when you queried my raising the question of what I "considered" leaving out. But my stated hesitation was a literary device, used to engineer the introduction of new ideas and material. And later I wonder what to think when you ask why it wouldn't be an advance for my readers to think about the dark and the light sides of everything. You say, "Somehow I feel it's not fair of you to stop right there. Is the reader to be the one left holding the bag of conformity and timidity?" I tried to do many things in "Dr. Fell," and one of them was to leave the reader, in your phrase, "holding the bag." But I saw that as my gift to the reader. As a writer I don't want to give everything over to the reader, I don't want to explain everything, to make it clear: in fact, it seems to me that my job as a writer is quite often to leave readers "holding the bag" to see where they want to go with it, to see what it is like to have in their hands and minds some approximation of what I have experienced. It is, I think, one of the many spaces that open up in the process of writing/reading, creating/experiencing.

But this is a complicated and always fascinating process/dance. I loved it when you wrote, "So it makes me feel uncomfortable when you say, 'Did I feel great about my cutting experiences all the time? Of course not. Would I write about that? I don't know.' I'm not sure I trust you. Why are you being so coy? Directly probing your ambivalence would be a complicated task, but a very engrossing one. It would intensify the irony. Do you feel that such doubt would compromise your political agenda?" For while part of me, as writer, took this as a criticism—should I have written more about that? was I avoiding something?—another part of me, as writer, was extraordinarily pleased, for I did exactly what I had set out to do: I tricked the reader into not trusting me, into resisting my words, and into finding a new space from which to read and think about "Dr. Fell." Being a writer, for me, entails many things, one of which is discovering that voice, that phrase, that grammatical or broader structure that can resist the simple truth, the easy answer.

I agree with you that truth—in psychoanalysis, and in almost all of existence—is an approximation. Which is why I carefully situated my statements about "truth" ("This is what most writers do. We try to tell the truth.") as being as drenched in irony as the rest of the piece. "Dr. Fell" is a provocative entertainment, all charade and smoke and mirrors, its "truth" residing only in the feelings, desires, and discomfort that it can engender in each reader.

For me the process of writing "Dr. Fell"—well, anything really (you, as a writer, must know what this is like)—was painfully conscious. "Dr. Fell" was not the product of the tongue loosened during sex. A good, or decent, or conscientious writer does not have the luxury of dissociating during the act of writing. This is not to deny that an unconscious process was behind my consciously crafting the piece, but this is not (I think) a form of literary criticism we are talking about. Maybe we are at cross purposes here: on the one hand the writer who crafts and attempts to create a powerful, hard-hitting effect (a "truth") by hiding, hinting at, and even obscuring his meanings to provoke emotions in the reader, and on the other hand the analyst who attempts to discover her own "truth" by questioning and uncovering what she senses is missing.

I have written about this at length because I think it gets to some fundamental points about how we write, and read, and think about ourselves and the world, points that I think will lead to a more complex discussion about the topics in which we are both interested: healing, irony, and liberation.

I must admit that I was quite startled by two sections of your response. The first comes early, when you write, "Do you react like that sometimes? Disbelieving. Horrified. Fascinated. Repelled." I felt pleased at first that my writing had hooked you. But then I was troubled. For while it is you (the reader) who are disbelieving, horrified, fascinated, and repelled, I (as the writer) was not. You construct what seems to be a too easy conflation of our experiences when you add: "Did the drugs help you through the Scylla of disgust and the Charybdis of anxiety?" But my experience with cutting was neither disgusting nor anxiety producing. And, as I read carefully through "Dr. Fell," I saw that these are never words that I use (or would use.) Were *you* disgusted? Filled with anxiety? Is this countertransference? A lack of "ironic" distance? I must admit, trying not be feel defensive, to feeling a little misunderstood, even judged.

This happens for me again when you ask what wounds of mine "were healed by those scalpels. . . . [W]ho among us bookish types wasn't a miserable nerd way back [in high school]? . . . One does feel that the extremity of the treatment, sex-as-therapy, must have something to do with the extremity of the injury. Did you just forget to tell us? Or did you decide not to? Were you lying? Why?" It's hard to know where my reply should begin. It's important to remember that I wrote "Dr. Fell" with an almost entirely gay male audience in mind. When I wrote about how the cutting and blood sports, as well as my attraction to the dangerous image Jim projected, related to my being a gay boy in high school I had concrete specifics in mind: the constant verbal torments, being pushed against lockers, taunts from some teachers, the unending stream of petty and minor humiliations experienced every day. Almost every gay man I have spoken to about "Dr. Fell" understood that this is what I meant; this is a shared experience of so many gay men of my age. I didn't spell it out because I thought that this degree of societal homophobia would be understood by the (gay male) readers. So it shocked me that you read this passage—granted, with its lack of detail—as being about "bookish types" who were "miserable nerds." I didn't feel so much a nerd in high school as the victim of violent homophobic abuse. The "extremity" of my healing treatment, replete with scalpels and blood, feels completely congruent with my experience of being hurt and abused by "normal" people, the perversion and lies of my present life a fitting and just response to the "truth" I was taught as a queer youth.

And I guess (to reverse your earlier queries) I would like to know about you. What was your life like in high school? Were you bookish and nerdy, physically and sexually harassed? What was it like being a "smart" woman? How much of yourself and your history are you willing to bring openly to your response? I understand that all readers bring their idiosyncratic, personal experience to a written piece, and that, in your quest to know more about why "I," the narrator, did what he did and felt what he felt, you wanted more information. This made me think about how interpretative practices can differ so widely from person to person. And also about how writing practices, as well as contexts, can affect reading. That is why I wanted to discuss the disadvantage I felt about discussing "Dr. Fell" in this book. For most readers of *Flesh and the Word*, "Dr. Fell" looked and felt normal. In *Bringing the Plague* I believe this is not true. Context and the market affect reading practices. What I am interested in is finding a way, if possible, to bridge those reading practices—not only in "Dr. Fell," but in speaking to one another and dealing with one another in the myriad intimacies and negotiations of everyday life: for me as a writer, for you as an analyst.

This brings me to what I found most surprising about your response. For me as the writer—although not "the narrator"—and a reader, "Dr. Fell" is hardly about sex at all. It is, rather overwhelmingly, about AIDS, loss, and death; words that I don't think appear once in your response. Just as you are curious about what I have left out of my story intentionally or unconsciously, I, as a reader, am interested in why you do not address AIDS and death. I am certain that for you, as both a clinician and a person living in a cosmopolitan city, AIDS is part of the fabric of your everyday life. Have you had close friends who have died of AIDS? Clients? Has your life been touched in small or large ways by the epidemic? Yet you never mention it. Ironic, isn't it? Obviously, as recounted in "Dr. Fell," it has been the central event of the last two decades of my own life. How central? I realized the depth to which this is true when I (half) joked to a friend a while ago about a difficult breakup I was going through: "Well, sure it's hard. I'm just not used to breaking up without someone dying." She responded with: "Do you know what you just said?" And I did, and it was true. What *would* we do without irony? But in the end they are still dead.

Earlier I spoke of the writing of "Dr. Fell" as being like good psychotherapy. And, in reality, I tried quite consciously to structure it as a series of self-investigative confessions that lead to a "breakthrough," the final attempt at healing in which I bring myself to reenact "the bloody act" (to quote *Macbeth*, a work that is as obsessed with blood and loss). It is true that a great deal of the material in "Dr. Fell's" Essays explores the possibility of healing past injuries through sex. Yet I am much more compelled, as author and reader, by the narration of the healing of the loss caused by AIDS and death. You have written frequently, maybe even mostly, about the relationship of the body to the material and psychic worlds. What I would like to know more about— and what I missed in your response—was your thoughts about the injured, sullied, diseased body that we have all experienced in our lives. I have friends who have worked with you in the reproductive rights movement in New York. Did this experience of working hard to ensure that women's bodies were cared for and safe affect how you think about AIDS? About the incessant fragility of bodies and of lives?

Over the past two decades I, as well as many, many other gay men, have been faced with nearly incalculable losses inflicted by the AIDS epidemic—the losses not only of death, but of community structures, of family networks, of political organization, of sexual experiences, and of art. I personally have lost at least fifty friends, at least three of whom I loved deeply and passionately. We have also, in a unique way for the young and middle-yeared, been repeatedly faced with our own mortality. And all of this has taken place within the larger framework of queer, perverse sexuality. This has caused enormous changes in our lives. I believe one of the most important (and, I think, rarely addressed), of these changes is how to once again turn to sex as a method of healing when it has been consistently demonized by the dominant culture as the primary cause of the injury. What do we do with the gay male sexual body in the age of AIDS? How can the body be used to heal the seemingly ceaseless physical, psychological, and emotional injuries inflicted by the epidemic?

This was always on my mind when I wrote "Dr. Fell": the inevitability of the decay of this "too, too solid—sullied—flesh" on its way to death. All humans deal with the reality of death, but for many gay men this reality is all too immediate and specific. I wrote earlier about how, for me, postmodern irony had particular and definite limitations in political praxis. It also has limitations in dealing with AIDS and death. Irony has helped me survive as a gay man in this world (including the AIDS epidemic), but I have found it useless in the face of death. The binaries of life and death, living and dying feel stark to me, with no in-between space for negotiating irony or even comfort.

What I tried to do in "Dr. Fell" was to find some metaphorical narrative that would take the place—and maybe do the work—of that irony upon which I have usually relied. It is surprising to me that one aspect of this metaphor involved religious imagery and iconography. I was brought up Catholic, and while I have forthrightly rejected that heritage, I have remained very connected to much of the religious symbolism of the Roman Church. Despite all the criticisms leveled at the Church, you have to admit that it is lovingly obsessed with the body, and with the death and decay of that body. As British playwright Joe Orton (1977) has a character remark in a play: "It's Life that defeats the Christian Church. She's always been well-equipped to deal with Death" (pp. 317–318). Part of what I was interested in exploring in "Dr. Fell" was the idea of transfiguration of the body in response to AIDS and loss as a form of healing. In fact, the main source of inspiration for "Dr. Fell" came from a poem, which I have always loved, by the British metaphysical/religious poet Thomas Crashaw, written in 1646. I would like to reprint it, both because it is so moving and because it is so little known.

On the Wounds of Our Crucified Lord

O these wakeful wounds of thine!
    Are they mouths? Or are they eyes?
Be they mouths, or be they eyne,
    Each bleeding part some one supplies.

> Lo! A mouth, whose full bloomed lips
>     At too dear a rate are roses
> Lo! A bloodshot eye! That weeps
>     And many a cruel tear discloses.
>
> O thou who on this foot hast laid
>     Many a kiss and many a tear,
> Now thou shalt have all repaid,
>     Whatsoe'er thy charges were.
>
> This foot hath got a mouth and lips
>     To pay the sweet sum of thy kisses;
> To pay thy tears, an eye that weeps
>     Instead of tears such gems as this is.
>
> The difference only this appears
>     (Nor can the change offend),
> The debt is paid in ruby-tears
>     Which thou in pearls didst lend.

The vividness of Crashaw's images—wounds that become eyes that cry, mouths that offer the possibility of kisses—is remarkable and magical. Here Christ's Passion, a religious journey of salvation, becomes a distinctly human, sexualized passion. These wounds are not passive mutilations of the body; they are "wakeful" and take on a life of their own as they cry. But even more important, these tears are "cruel," not because they are brutal or heartless, but because they are part of a larger plan of transfiguration: the death of Christ to redeem humankind.

This, of course, is a theology that I do not believe. But I do find the metaphor of the hurt, damaged body inviting and resonant. The images of Crashaw's body, some of which I have borrowed for "Dr. Fell" let us see and understand the mutilated, sexualized human body in the language of richness and beauty: drops of blood become jewels, the "full bloomed lips" of a "mouth"-wound are more beautiful than roses. Thus Jim's body in the mirror is imagined, transfigured, as that of a Renaissance saint and martyr; the ritual of the cutting itself becomes religious in its repetitive motions and its candlelit solemnity.

Irony is still present. I worry that "Dr. Fell" contains too much high-Catholic kitsch, and, of course, the very juxtaposition of the Passion with my own passions is queer and perverse. But this irony is really in the service of creating "Dr. Fell." It is not, nor, I believe, can it be, really useful in dealing with the deaths and the losses I and others have faced because of AIDS. Perhaps, by literalizing the fragility of the body, I have transformed, transfigured the either/or spaces opened by irony into the tiny spaces between cut, separated flesh: the eyes and mouths where tears and words can flow. I don't believe in an afterlife or the redemptive Passion of Christ, but over the last two decades I have had to find some language, some metaphor, some way to deal with the reality of the sullied, solid flesh of AIDS as it increasingly encroached upon my waking and dreaming hours. "Dr. Fell" was simply one attempt to do that.

Yours,
Michael Bronski

## REFERENCES

Lowenthal, M. (1997). *Flesh and the Word: Gay Erotic Confessions*. New York: Plume.

Nussbaum, M. (1999). The professor of parody. *The New Republic*, February 22, pp. 37–45.

Orton, J. (1977). The Erpingham camp. In *The Complete Plays*, pp. 277–329. New York: Grove.

Sontag, S. (1966). Notes on camp. In *Against Interpretation and Other Essays*, pp. 275–292. New York: Farrar, Straus & Giroux.

# 9

# The Analyst's Participation: A New Look

*Jay Greenberg*

Over the years, psychoanalysis has grown as a discipline under the impact of one inspired theoretical excess after another. At one moment, a new vision of what moves the world arises out of the idea that neurosis is invariably and inevitably caused by a persistent if conflicted attachment to the perverse incestuous fantasies of infancy. Not long afterward, adherents of an alternative insight triumphantly proclaim that the root of all psychopathology can be found in the tormented and tormenting experience of the infant at the breast. Still later, another revolutionary idea emerges, locating the source of emotional difficulties in the failure of the sufferer's parents to provide the psychic supplies that are needed for healthy development.

Each new theory as it emerges is both wonderful and surprising, the more so for being narrowly focused on a partial truth. Each probes a dimension of our experience that had not been investigated, or investigated in quite the same way, before, and each shows us something new about what it means to be human. It is as if a thin beam of light has been directed toward an area that had been dark forever; we see what had never been seen. But a bright light in the darkness can also be blinding, and areas outside the sweep of the beam grow even darker by comparison.

It takes a while to identify psychoanalytic excess, because each new development generates a powerful sense of excitement. It must have begun right at the beginning. I sometimes imagine Freud and his earliest followers mulling over clinical material, finding new meanings in mundane narratives. There is nothing more thrilling than the sense of being on to something, something that opens up surprising ways of understanding the familiar. Maybe today we envy those early analysts for the wonder they must have felt at their insights, a wonder that no psychoanalyst of our generation can experience in exactly the way that they did. And perhaps the insights worked clinically, for a while at least, *because* they were surprising and wonderful—because they turned peoples' attention in a direction that it had not been turned before.

But what about the one-sidedness of our insights? What makes it so difficult, even after the rush of discovery has passed, to wonder whether something has gotten lost in all the excitement? Why couldn't Freud, caught up as he was in what he was learning about the vicissitudes of Dora's conflicted sexuality, also see that his patient was a pawn in an intricate interpersonal drama that included Freud himself? Why couldn't Kohut, dazzled though *he* was by his insights into ways that parents create their childrens' oedipal miseries, keep in mind that inner conflict inevitably accompanies growth and even life itself? We psychoanalysts constantly praise ourselves, in print and in informal gatherings, for our ability to tolerate the ambiguity that confronts us in our daily work. But at the same time, we meet that ambiguity with an ironclad commitment to an overarching way of understanding what went wrong for our patients and what it will take to help them change. The commitment, although it sustains us through the ups and downs of clinical work and is necessary if we are to fully develop our theories, can easily become so passionate and so exclusive that it forecloses alternatives.

We might hope that, as new ideas emerge, there would come a point at which their adherents could step back and undertake a cooler assessment of their scope. The new ideas could then be seen as supplementing or productively competing with, but not rendering obsolete, everything that had come before. Whether by integration or through a constructive competitive dialogue, new ideas would, over time, be contextualized and tempered. Unfortunately, this tends not to happen in psychoanalysis. Typically, instead of critical assessment, movements are built that isolate the new idea from other psychoanalytic visions. Adherents of these movements create a culture based on the new theory, complete with organizational structures, historical records, leaders, rituals, moralities, and so on. The goal is to preserve the sense of excitement that informed the new insights. Recall that among the first things Freud did when faced with opinions that differed from his own psychoanalytic vision were to create the Committee, to distribute secret rings, and to write "On the History of the Psychoanalytic Movement" (1914a). This sad legacy has persisted throughout our history; ideas remain isolated from other ideas that could deepen, enrich, and challenge them as groups fragment in the face of conceptual disagreement. There are very few psychoanalysts around these days, only Freudians, or Kleinians, or Lacanians, or self psychologists. The schisms are painful to those committed to making psychoanalysis work as a discipline, and they are laughable to those who observe our battles from without.

Today, I am afraid that relational psychoanalysis is in danger of becoming the latest wonderful idea to coalesce into a movement. This would be especially unfortunate because the relational perspective developed explicitly as a reaction to two earlier, related excesses. Both excesses grew out of the euphoria of discovery. First, there was the excess of conceptualizing relations with other people as principally a transformation of our instinctually driven fantasy life. This arose out of new insights into the power of our internal worlds to influence our experience of what goes on around us. And second, there was the excess of seeing the analyst as a dispassionate technician, capable of impartially assessing the analysand's inner state and intervening in ways that could alter the balance of internal forces without exerting much in the way of personal influence. This grew from the excitement that analysts felt when they realized the therapeutic potential of deepened self-understanding.

In this paper my focus will be on contemporary relational approaches to the nature of the analyst's participation in the psychoanalytic process. My goal is to begin a process of examining what the relational model is teaching, to express some of my own developing misgivings, and to raise some warning flags. First, I will outline what I see as an emerging theoretical vision of the nature of the psychoanalytic situation and of the analyst's participation in it. There are four premises that I think are largely accepted by all relational analysts:

1. Far more than the early theorists could let themselves know, the analyst influences the analysand's experience in myriad ways. Much of what the patient thinks and feels is responsive to what the analyst does and even to who he or she is (Aron 1991, 1996, Hoffman 1983, Mitchell 1988). Everything the analyst says (and a great deal that he or she does not say) will affect the patient deeply. This bears heavily on the relational view of the analyst's authority, which is seen as even more powerful than has previously been imagined (Hoffman 1996, Mitchell 1998). Freud's early idea (1937) that incorrect interpretations will simply be ignored by the analysand is widely rejected. Suggestion and personal influence, once the base metal of the despised and disdained psychotherapies, have become both coin of the realm and a prime area of psychoanalytic investigation.

2. Despite its power to affect everything that happens, the impact of the analyst's behavior can never be understood while it is happening. In contemporary terms, enactment is ubiquitous (Hoffman 1991, Renik 1993). A great deal of the work in every analysis is to understand after the fact what has transpired in an unexamined way. On this last point, different relational analysts hold quite divergent positions. Some claim that enactments can eventually be understood and that the dyadic unconscious can be made conscious. Others believe that one enactment simply folds into the next, with systemic change developing even in the absence of any privileged insight into what was intended or even into what happened.

3. Following on this second point, and contra Freud and his followers, there is no technical posture that the analyst can adopt that will guarantee the creation of a predictable atmosphere in the analysis. Neutrality and abstinence, keystones of classical technique, are mythic and therefore empty concepts. More

contemporary stances, like empathy, are equally mythic. Effective analysis can only be conducted in fits and starts, as a result of negotiations within each individual dyad. The aim of these negotiations is to find a way of working, unique to the dyad, that will suit both participants (Greenberg 1995, Pizer 1992, 1998).

4. While the first three points address the analyst's role as a participant in the process, a fourth addresses his or her role as an observer. Even as an observer, the analyst's subjectivity is a ubiquitous presence in the consulting room (Aron 1996, Mitchell 1997). Opinions differ on the extent to which the patient brings something—an unconscious—that can be discovered and known, or whether all meanings are constructed within the dyad. But regardless of where the theorist stands on that point, there is a broad consensus that detached objectivity is a myth: for some relational analysts because there is nothing to be objective about, for others because the analyst's memory and desire can never be avoided or barred. Our countertransference is the air our patients breathe.

It goes without saying that I believe there is much of value in the critique of classical epistemology and the attendant theory of technique that is contained in these principles. For too many years, psychoanalysis was burdened by a more or less phobic avoidance of any acknowledgment of the analyst's participation in the treatment process. Each of the relational principles lays out a new observational field and presents us with new data to consider. "Look at what you have been ignoring," each principle calls out, "and you will understand what could not have been understood before." In this way, the relational critique does what psychoanalysis at its best has always done, reminding us to attend to the unattended and forcing us to acknowledge that it is always what we don't know that affects us most deeply.

The principles I have outlined underlie and inform my own work. But psychoanalytic perspectives can never be fully expressed in abstractions. Whenever a new model develops, a body of clinical writing accumulates alongside the formal theorizing. These writings embody the insights and elaborate the sensibilities of the model's adherents in a way that theory, by its nature, cannot. In this paper I will address a tension that I don't think has been mentioned before, between the teachings of formal relational theory and those implied in many of its most widely accepted clinical narratives. It is in these narratives that the excess I want to address is expressed.

Consider the four principles as I have outlined them. The personal influence of each analyst, the uniqueness of each analytic dyad, the inevitable uncertainty about what is happening at any moment in the treatment, and the consequent unpredictability of the effects of any intervention all suggest that there is no one way of working that can be privileged across the board over any other. Each analyst and each analysand must find the mode of engagement that best serves the analytic goals the participants have defined. There is no way, the relational critique reminds us, to assert the benefit of any technical intervention a priori.

And yet, the clinical examples through which relational authors illustrate their perspective seem always to point us in a particular direction. This is probably true of the narratives of all psychoanalytic traditions. (Mitchell [1992] has made a similar point with respect to the prototypical case histories written by adherents of the classical Freudian, self-psychological, and interpersonal schools.) These narratives carry considerable weight because they express the clinical sensibilities of leading thinkers within the tradition. Consequently, they take their place as important teaching tools that carry what might be called an ethic or an aesthetic of clinical practice.

With this in mind, consider some important and often-cited clinical vignettes reported in the relational literature: Gerson (1996) admits to a patient that he has lied to her, then enlists her collaboration in understanding his reasons for doing so; Davies (1994) confesses her erotic feelings for her patient; Ghent (1995) recognizes that his patient is cold and brings her a blanket; Frederickson (1990) puts his face in front of his patient and screams "Shut up!" I too have contributed to this trend, writing about self disclosures (Greenberg 1986, 1991) and about bringing some of my own extra-clinical personal preferences into conversations with supervisees about technique (Greenberg 1995).

In each of these clinical examples, the analyst has taken a risk, put himself on the line in a highly personal way. In more or less classical terms, he has broken the analytic frame. But then he has done something that has no counterpart in classical descriptions: he has offered himself, *as a person*, to contain the tensions and anxieties that the patient is experiencing as a consequence of being in treatment. This is the moral of so many relational case reports: they focus on periods in the analysis during which tensions around what is happening are becoming unbearable for both participants. Then the tension is broken when the analyst behaves in some startling, unexpected, and highly personal way, when, in Irwin Hoffman's terms, he or she "throws away the book" (Hoffman 1994). In reaction, the patient is able to relinquish some tie to an archaic internal object and to begin, or to resume, doing the work of analysis.

I hope it is clear, especially since I have included examples of my own work in my list, that I am not—for the moment at least—quarreling with any of the specific interventions I have mentioned. I believe that the experiences that emerge from these sorts of interactions can facilitate the analytic process in many cases, and that they are turning points in some treatments. But I also believe that it is time to wonder why the examples in so many of the important relational texts sound so much the same, even as the very idea of the possibility of a standard or uniform technique has been debunked by the relational critique. It seems that we are offered two parallel messages that work at cross purposes to each other. First, we are shown the futility of any attempt to develop a fixed psychoanalytic methodology applicable to all analysts, all analysands, all dyads. But then, alongside of or perhaps overarching this, there is what I have come to think of as a morality play, a series of stories that are highly prescriptive of a way that we should all be working and that put pressure on the reader/analyst to be open enough, flexible enough, and caring enough to respond appropriately.

Clinical examples such as those I have mentioned typically are drawn from moments in which an analysis has become stalled and fraught with tension. Some of this reflects a rhetorical strategy: authors use the examples to illustrate that analytic work can still get done even in the face of the apparent failure of traditional technique. But more than rhetoric is involved; the examples imply a model of treatment and a new way of thinking about an old and fundamental clinical problem. The problem, which has been around from the beginning, is this: there is apparently very little reason why a person would want to be in analysis. Freud struggled with this early on, but it took him quite a while before he answered it in a way that satisfied him. I will take a brief look at the solution Freud came up with, to provide a backdrop for my further discussion of contemporary views.

It was only a few years after he started practicing psychoanalysis that Freud noticed that his patients were looking for something he was not prepared to offer. Obviously daunted by his experience, but speaking, characteristically, with the bravado of a conquistador, he warned aspiring clinicians of a danger that threatened to undermine at least their treatments and perhaps their professional reputations as well. Hysterics, he wrote, invariably prefer a cure by love to a cure by analysis (1914b).

Consider the dilemma that Freud came upon so quickly: the commodity he was selling—self-awareness—was something his customers were not particularly interested in buying. In fact, they had constructed complex and crippling symptoms to avoid the collapse of self-esteem that awareness threatened to bring with it. Freud's patients in the *Studies on Hysteria* (Breuer and Freud 1893–1895) suffered paralyses, hallucinations, debilitating pain, and weakness, all to avoid knowing what analysis revealed to them: that they were in love, or felt angry, or were frightened. The anguish that came with consciousness of these thoughts and feelings, evidently, hurt even more than the pain caused by the symptoms. If ever a cure was worse than a disease, this was it. That is why the patient had become symptomatic in the first place.

And the problem did not stop there. Not only did patients want to avoid self-awareness, but it was also easy for them to assume that their analysts, despite their claims to be mere purveyors of insight, were in fact offering the desired love. Freud quickly realized that in the process of requiring that patients disclose their deepest secrets and creating conditions that made such disclosures possible, the analyst must appear both to demand and to offer a unique form of intimacy. The "special solicitude inherent in the treatment," Freud wrote as early as 1895, could encourage patients to "[become] sexually dependent" on their analysts (Breuer and Freud 1893–1895, p. 302). Thus the stage was set for every treatment to degenerate into a colossal misunderstanding about what was being offered. It did so in the first analysis on record, Breuer's treatment of Anna O., and caused its disastrous end.

The need for a way out of this predicament was apparent from the beginning. And, setting a pattern that he would follow throughout his career, Freud solved the clinical problem with a brilliant and groundbreaking theoretical stretch. He invented the concept of transference, and using it both to guide his own thinking and to influence the way that patients might understand their experience, Freud could say that the patient only thought she wanted the analyst's love. He believed he could demonstrate to the patient that, despite its poignancy and urgency, her belief was ultimately mistaken. It was based on a "false connection" between experience in the present and memories of the past. So far so good. Armed with the conviction that his patient didn't really want him—and, of course, that he had no interest in and had done nothing to encourage her desire—the analyst was able to dissuade the patient from her ardent pursuit.

But whatever the concept of transference revealed and whatever problems it solved, it could not address the question of what motivates the patient to undertake and continue an analysis. Consider: the end result of a successful piece of transference analysis, one that relocated the patient's desire safely in her prehistory, would be a patient who could relinquish her claim on the analyst but not necessarily one who had much interest in pursuing analysis. We might very well be left with little to sustain the patient through the rigors of treatment.

Today, looking back on Freud's struggles with almost a century's worth of hindsight, we are able to give shape to the problem as Freud himself, living through them, could not. So it is easy for us to see why it took Freud quite a while to come up with an explanation for why anyone should want to be in psychoanalysis. In fact, it took him almost two decades; it was only in 1912 that he suggested that alongside of erotic longings, patients must also experience an "unobjectionable positive transference" that would motivate the work. The ideas contained in the patient's "unobjectionable" transference include his or her belief in the value of treatment. They are based in broadly held views of analysis as a discipline and of the analyst as a professional practitioner. Because he or she is a member of a social group that shares these beliefs, the patient comes to analysis with an expectation of being helped and also expecting that the analyst he or she has chosen is interested in providing and competent to provide that help. The unobjectionable positive transference worked in two distinct ways: first, it carried the patients' conviction that analysis, however difficult, would help them to improve their lives. Second, by empowering the person of the analyst, it would lead to realistically based desires to please, to be so-called "good" patients. The unobjectionable positive transference is unobjectionable both because it facilitates the work and, perhaps even more important, because it is based on socially validated and therefore presumptively "realistic" beliefs about what analysis and the analyst can provide.

But the unobjectionable positive transference has not fared very well recently. The beliefs on which it was originally based—beliefs in the knowledge and authority of the analyst and in the efficacy of analytic treatment—have themselves come under widespread criticism. We talk most about attacks from outside, from non-analytic therapists, from academics disdainful of the principles on which psychoanalytic treatment is based, and, perhaps most distressingly, from the managed care companies. But note that the relational critique as I have spelled it out raises many of these same concerns. In fact, it would be fair to say that the relational critique aims at deconstructing many of the beliefs that lie at the core of the unconditional positive transference.

This deconstruction has been healthy for psychoanalysis as a discipline. It has freed us from some ideas about what we are doing and how we are doing it that are based on an archaic philosophical foundation that has isolated us from the intellectual mainstream. But at the same time, it reminds us of our old dilemma. Today we live in a postmodern culture in which claims to knowledge are easily reduced to overvaluation of personal opinion, in which the distinction between authoritative and authoritarian qualities has narrowed, and in which the offer of expertise is seen as tantamount to the wielding of personal power. And in such a culture the unobjectionable positive transference—traditionally the great motivator of treatment—seems not only objectionable but nearly delusional as well. A patient's a priori confidence in the efficacy of psychoanalytic treatment, or in the competence of any individual analyst, is likely to be seen as virtually symptomatic in its own right.

So we need a new answer to the old question of why anyone would want an analysis. The roots of a relational answer, like those of so many foundational principles of relational psychoanalysis, can be traced to the views of Sandor Ferenczi. The analyst, Ferenczi argued, gives the patient more than insight into the workings of the patient's unconscious. Regardless of whether the analyst is aware of it, he or she invariably and inevitably also provides the patient with a new and crucial kind of relational experience (Ferenczi and Rank 1924). This powerful experience does more than give depth and meaning to the insights that emerge from psychoanalytic exploration. Even more fundamentally, because the analyst gratifies a wide range of needs and desires, it motivates the patient to enter and to remain in treatment.

There is much of Ferenczi's sensibility in the clinical teachings embodied in the relational vignettes to which I have alluded. Stated broadly, the idea is that the patient's ability and willingness to participate in the treatment is one facet of the unique relationship that is forged by every analyst and every analysand. Psychoanalysis may not be held in great esteem in our society at large, and its positivist philosophical origins may make it intellectually suspect, but a far more important reality is created by the participants in each analytic dyad. Within this reality, it is asserted, a range of needs and desires are met. Because of this, it is within the relational matrix created by analyst and analysand that the motivation for treatment evolves. Putting things this way, we can see that in contemporary thinking the analytic relationship has replaced the more broadly based beliefs around which Freud believed the unobjectionable positive transference was built.

But it is more accurate to say that the relational answer accounts for only a part of what Freud had in mind. It is true that both answers invoke reality—the broad reality of social consensus for Freud, the reality of the particular dyad in contemporary thinking. But if Freud had had only reality in mind, he would not have called the unobjectionable positive transference a transference; he could have spoken more simply about a judgment that people make that analysis can be a worthwhile project. He did speak of a transference, however, and in doing so he emphasized that there must be something within the patient that makes it possible for him or her to embrace the social consensus and to muster sufficient hopefulness and courage to undertake an arduous treatment. Perhaps even more important, invoking transference directs our attention to the intricate ways in which the motivation for analysis interlocks with, shapes, and is shaped by all the other transferences that get evoked in every treatment. This stands in sharp contrast to the sensibility embodied in many relational vignettes, which tend to emphasize ways in which the analyst can negotiate a way of being that meets an actual need of the patient's. In the new model, the analyst's ability to find and to satisfy crucial needs at crucial times makes analysis possible. Relatively little is said about the patient's hope, or trust, or courage—the transferential and therefore private and internal side of the "unobjectionable positive transference."

Now let me turn to a clinical example that describes a dramatic moment in which the analyst drew his patient back into analysis in a moment when she seemed to be incapable of going on. He did this by acting in a way that he calculated would meet a specific relational need. The example is drawn from a paper by Irwin Hoffman that has become extremely influential (Hoffman 1994). I have chosen to discuss it both because of its importance in contemporary relational discourse, and because as a result of what Hoffman did he and his patient were able to get beyond an apparent standoff and into an extraordinarily rich conversation about what had gone on between them. But there are also some unexamined assumptions embedded in the description of what happened. My purpose will be to isolate and to raise questions about these assumptions, which I believe are similar to the assumptions that guide the accounts presented in many recent relational clinical narratives.

> The patient is a medical student who throughout the treatment has been ambivalent about following what she considers to be rigid analytic rules. Recently she has become increasingly angry and anxious about a series of events in her life outside the analysis. One day she calls to ask for an appointment earlier in the day than usual. Hoffman is unable to arrange the switch, and when the analysand arrives for her regular hour she begins by saying, "I'm here for one reason and one reason only, and that is to get some Valium. If you can't help me get some, I might as well leave right now!" (p. 206). She does wind up staying, however, and Hoffman tries to engage her in a conversation that would give some meaning to her demand.
>
> But the patient continues to insist that all that matters is that she get the Valium and that her analyst, who is, not coincidentally, a psychologist, get it for her. Feeling helpless and desperate in the face of the patient's unwavering insistence, Hoffman finally asks whether she has an internist who might prescribe the medication, and when the patient says she does he says, "Well, if you give me his number I'll call him right now" (p. 207). He makes the call, the physician agrees to give her the prescription, and Hoffman

reports that "After I hung up, the patient and I started to talk and she was receptive for the first time to exploring the meaning of the whole transaction" (p. 208).

Hoffman's vignette, like many recently, is about a patient who, for the moment at least, appears to be incapable of being an analysand in any traditional sense of the word. She cannot see that there is any value in trying to talk about or to understand rather than to gratify what she experiences as an urgent need. Hoffman's clinical decision was to avoid trying to engage the patient in the kind of conversation she was unwilling to have. Instead he chose to do something that would bolster her belief in the value of the analytic relationship. Drawing on his sense of his patient's history and current need, he created a powerful and—for her—unfamiliar type of interpersonal transaction, one that might provide her with some reason to believe in the value of participating in the analysis. In Freud's terms, he gave the patient the material with which she could re-establish an "unobjectionable positive transference." And, in an important sense, his understanding of what he did improves on Freud's idea. For Freud the unobjectionable positive transference is not subject to analysis, while Hoffman argues convincingly that everything about the transaction he created with his patient can and must be subject to intense examination.

The relational experience Hoffman offered his patient required, he tells us, that he engage her personally, not merely as a technician. He needed to demonstrate to her that he could forsake his allegiances to analytic orthodoxy, and perhaps even to analytic propriety, in the name of meeting her where she needed to be met. It is in this meeting that he provided her with both a reason and the means to go on. In Hoffman's own words, the question for the patient was "What did I care about more, her well-being or my analytic purity?" (p. 206). Because the patient cannot believe that he cares about her more than about himself, she cannot participate in the analysis in any way other than by blindly asserting her presumed need. She can move away from this mode of engagement only when he does something in a way that drives home to her both that he cares about her and that he *intends* to behave in a way that will demonstrate this to her. Hoffman accomplished this, he tells us, by "consciously disidentifying with her father" (p. 202), a man who both the patient and the analyst agree is compulsive and tyrannical.

Reading Hoffman's account in the context of my thoughts about psychoanalytic excess, it occurred to me how frequently contemporary clinical vignettes revolve around a similar sequence: in a moment of crisis the analyst creates a transaction that is new and surprising to the patient. The richness of the subsequent conversation about what went on between analyst and analysand is then offered as evidence of the benefits of the intervention. But in contrast to the elaborate description of what eventually happened, relatively little is offered to convince us that talking about a novel experience with the analyst is the thing that will best serve the patient's treatment. Hoffman, like many others writing today, is notably casual about this. There seems to be no question in his mind that creating a surprising transaction in response to the patient's transference demand (in this case, consciously disidentifying with the father) and then exploring it is the best way to help his patient to learn about herself.

But the assumption raises many questions for me. How can we be sure that exploring a transaction is the best way to do an analysis, with this patient or with any other? Why is exploring a transaction in this moment more important or more useful than exploring a resistance, or a transference, or an affect state? Perhaps most important, why is exploring *anything* more important or more useful than allowing whatever is happening to develop further and to deepen?

Hoffman does not raise these questions in his case report, or even acknowledge that they exist. It is this failure that creates the sense of excess that concerns me. His account gives the impression that he is following a longstanding tradition of zealously declaring that one thing or another is a "royal road" to understanding the unconscious without thinking very much about what else might be involved. Consider some other royal roads that have had their heyday: symptoms, dreams, fantasies, resistance, transference, primitive affect states, the history of interpersonal relations, and so on. My point, of course, is to question any reliance on royal roads, not to deny that it can be interesting and illuminating to explore transactions. Let me repeat here that the idea of a "best route" to anything is not supported by the formal relational theory of technique and is, in fact, contradicted by it. But in the sameness of the clinical examples that many relational analysts use to illustrate their theory, in the morality play of which this vignette is one act, the sense that creating and exploring transactions *is* a royal road comes across loud and clear.

A more balanced approach would require the analyst to acknowledge that having arrived at a new place by following a particular route does not imply that this is the only or the best route to get there. It would also require us to acknowledge that every route has its dangers and its limitations. In the remainder of this paper, I will concentrate on two potential sources of difficulty that can arise when the transactions that are inevitably created in every analysis become too much the focus of our inquiry. Neither of these has been discussed enough publicly, although my sense is that both are causing considerable private concern among working analysts.

First, there is the danger that in focusing too much on analyzing "transactions" we are limiting our observational field to what the analyst and the analysand have created together, dyadically. When the priority of this focus is asserted and accepted without comment, we risk losing touch with other, uniquely private and personal dimensions of the patient's experience. Second, there is the danger that when the analyst's role in shaping the patient's experience is emphasized too exclusively, we encourage the analyst to want to provide the patient with a particular kind of experience. This can inflame the analyst's desire to be a good analyst or even to be a good person. The analyst's desire is always a tricky business, and I will return shortly to ways in which I believe that desire is fanned by contemporary relational vignettes.

Consider how the patient's attention can be directed away from private experience and toward the transaction. In Hoffman's clinical narrative he describes an exchange that occurred long before the crucial Valium incident, and that I believe bears decisively on the course that the analysis followed. Beginning sometime in the second year of the treatment, the patient refused to use the couch. This caused Hoffman some anxiety, especially since he was a candidate in training at the time and worried about how his institute would view his handling of the situation. Hoffman tells us a great deal about how he reacted to his patient's refusal, although he mentions nothing about the patient's experience except that "she was not always enthused about analyzing things" (p. 201).

What Hoffman tells us about himself is that he remained in the chair that he sat in when patients were on the couch rather than the one he used when they were sitting up, "as if to say 'You're the one violating the rules, not me.'" He "conveyed to her the various rationales for the use of the couch" (p. 200, fn). He told her he was against her sitting in the chair. He responded to the patient's "mischievous smile" when they discussed the issue with a "slight smile" of his own. And finally there is this: "When she asked me point blank: 'Are you sure the couch is necessary for the process? I think the eye contact is more important for me.' I bluntly replied, 'Well, I don't know about the process, but it might be necessary for me to graduate'" (p. 200).

Consider the impact that this is likely to have on the patient. In all that he is saying and doing Hoffman is communicating a powerful message to the patient. "This analysis is about both of us," he is in effect telling her. "We each have our own motivations for being here, and in understanding what happens it is necessary to take account of my desires and my needs as much as of yours. In fact, we cannot get to the bottom of your experience unless we understand it as significantly reactive to mine." From my point of view, and I think that this is fully compatible with Hoffman's (1996) formal theorizing about the power of the analyst's authority and influence, this constitutes an instruction to the patient about where to look in her attempt to make sense of what she thinks and feels in the analysis. So when, years later, she is feeling distraught about events in her life, despairing about getting any help from her analyst, and angry at him for not agreeing to change her hour that day, she does not think about her feelings, or about her transference, or about her history, or about herself and her own private experience very much at all. Instead, she focuses her gaze on the analyst's behavior, and on how her own experience is a more or less inevitable reaction to it. But consider the analyst's contribution to this assumption of the patient's. Hoffman believes that patients cannot fully explore their part in creating painful feelings until and unless the analyst is willing to acknowledge his contribution to those feelings. And a great deal of the way he has conducted the analysis communicated the same lesson to his patient. He has taught her that what she feels is manufactured within the dyad.

From this, it is a small step for the patient to make the analyst responsible for her experience. And when the pressure she feels becomes unbearable, it is a small further step to demanding that the analyst change his behavior in a way that will relieve some of her pain. On Hoffman's side, it must be difficult to focus on the patient's inner life, because he agrees with her that he is significantly responsible for her emotional experience. Feeling this way, it would have to be hard for him simply to observe and to explore that experience; his anxiety and guilt about his role in causing the patient's despair must lead him to want to act in ways that will help her to feel better. This inclination will be exacerbated when the patient rejects Hoffman's offer to explore and insists on his meeting her presumed need in a more immediate and concrete way.

So if we go back to the beginnings of the analysis, to the roots of the situation that Hoffman defused by heroically throwing away the book, it seems highly plausible that what happened is to a significant extent an artifact of his particular way of working. At least once before at a tense moment in the analysis he has called attention to himself and insisted that the patient take him into account before she looks inward to herself and especially to her various transferences. Perhaps this invited the kind of interpersonal crisis that eventually developed and that led Hoffman to forego exploration temporarily and to embrace action. And perhaps, too, if the analyst had not interpersonalized the treatment from the beginning, the focus might have been less on the "transaction" that involved Hoffman's rescue and more on the depth of the patient's cynicism about the intentions of others and on her despair about being helped. In turn, being able to confront her despair more directly might have opened a space within which she could explore her demand on the analyst more freely.

But to get to this, both participants would have to be less preoccupied with the quality of their relationship and more willing to dwell in an experience that was becoming grim and even terrifying for patient and analyst alike. Hoffman believes that in his struggle to decide how to respond to his patient's demand lies "the heart of what it means to be a new, good object" (p. 207). I largely agree with this formulation, but I am less sure about the assumption that this was a moment in which the patient was best served by an analyst who was struggling to be either a new or a good object. In fact, I am not sure that the patient was best served by the analyst's struggling with the nature of his participation at all, rather than immersing himself more receptively in an ancient experience of his patient's that was engulfing the two of them.

It is always, of course, tempting to find a way to take on the role of a new, good object rather than feeling drawn, inexorably, into enacting something old and ugly. This gets us to the second point I have mentioned, the way that clinical examples can inflame the analyst's desire. Glen Gabbard (1996) has noted that analysts treating patients with a history of sexual abuse are subject to a particular form of desire, which he characterizes as the "wish to avoid identification with the abuser from the patient's past" (p. 7). The point can be generalized to our work with all patients; note Hoffman's expressed wish to distinguish himself from his patient's father. But the issue of the analyst's desire— what it means to him or her to be an analyst, or to serve the patient in one way or another—is far too rarely discussed. While I agree strongly with the relational premise that the analyst's desire can never be neutralized, it would be a mistake to minimize the dangers that are inherent in all desire. Bion (1967) said that the therapist should be without desire at all, and this would certainly include the desire to provide a particular quality of experience, or even the desire to help. In a very different arena, Mahatma Gandhi, in his autobiography (1927–1929), expressed a similar sensibility, arguing that to be a true leader one must transcend all desire and that the desire he had found most difficult to renounce was the desire to serve. For both Bion and Gandhi, desire corrupts. At its most basic level, I want to look at the difficulties that accompany the analyst's desire to create and to participate in an analysis.

Analysts working in today's environment are at special risk of having our desire inflamed. In general, we are operating under conditions that can fairly be described as a state of siege. No working analyst today can be oblivious to the theoretical, clinical, and economic challenges to what we do. The attacks on the analyst's authority and expertise that I have mentioned leave many analysts feeling that they have little to offer their patients except their desire to help. Freud could, perhaps, afford to be a pessimist about psychoanalysis as a therapy because of his unwavering belief in the scientific truths he was discovering. Today, in contrast, the weakening of our belief in analytic theory has intensified our therapeutic zeal. Desire has been further fanned by the economics of the profession and the scarcity of analytic patients. The effects are not only financial; even analysts with thriving psychotherapy practices want to hold on to their analytic patients, because without them the analyst cannot be an analyst at all.

And the teachings of many relational authors, expressed through their clinical examples, add to these forces. These vignettes invariably portray the analyst as bold and courageous, willing to decenter from his own experience or to renounce preferred ways of doing things in order to serve the best interests of the patient. Hoffman, who is adamant that everything the analyst does has a suggestive impact on the patient, must realize that everything admired authors do has a similar effect on their readers. In setting themselves up as models of flexibility, openness, and so on, relational authors create a desire to do and to be likewise. I think many analysts these days are living with the tension of believing that they could revitalize relationships that have been deadened by toxic transferences if only they were braver, or more available, or simply more decent.

Recently I had an experience while doing supervision that illustrated how the analyst's desire can burden the treatment. In many ways, the example reminds me of Hoffman's, although this one is clearly about a moment gone awry. The vignette shares several crucial characteristics with Hoffman's. The patients in both cases suffer from cynicism and despair of a sort that poisons their faith in human contact. Also, in both cases the analyst chafed under the burden of living with the weight of his patient's toxic transference. As a result, each analyst got caught up in a desire to create with the patient a kind of experience that had been missing in the patients' lives. Both analysts believed, either consciously or unconsciously, that they owed this new kind of experience both to the analysand and to themselves. Both also believed that providing the experience involved a disidentification with a parent whose character was seen as a major cause of the patient's despair. And so each analyst acted out of a desire to change what was going on in the analysis. And in doing so, I suggest, each kept the dyad away from a full confrontation with the depth of the patients' transference.

In this second example, an experienced and talented supervisee has been treating a young architect for several years. One of the patient's central problems is a chronic inability to be excited about or even to enjoy his own accomplishments. Despite quite extraordinary abilities, the patient has always found a way to put off getting as much done as he could and to minimize what he does achieve. In the analysis, this has been discussed frequently, mainly traced back to the patient's experience with his depressed father, who always managed to find just the right word to puncture the balloon of anybody who might think that life is worth living.

One day the patient arrived at his session in an ebullient mood. He had completed the design of a house for which he was entirely responsible and had presented it to his difficult and demanding client, who was uncharacteristically enthusiastic. The house would be built exactly as the patient envisioned it.

The analyst was pleased and happy for the patient; in light of the way the patient had described the project it clearly had come out better than anybody expected it to. He was especially pleased that the patient recognized his own accomplishment and was able to enjoy it so unabashedly. But there were a few flies in the ointment. For one thing, although he knew that the meeting with the client was coming up, the patient had said nothing about its being so imminent, and the analyst felt somewhat taken by surprise. For another, the analyst quickly began to feel "talked at," barraged with a stream of description and commentary that, however enthusiastic, left no way for him to join the patient or to feel included in the session. The patient, he said, seemed to be "celebrating behind glass," and the analyst felt his own presence in the room unnecessary at best. Irritated, the analyst soon began to feel sleepy and, of course, guilty about feeling both irritated and sleepy in the face of the patient's newfound ability to describe his success energetically and excitedly.

As the patient continued to describe the experience, he mentioned that probably the analyst was surprised that the project was finished and that the client meeting had taken place so quickly. At this point the analyst spoke for the first time in the session. "Yes," he said, "I was wondering about your not having told me that the meeting was coming up." The effect of this comment on the patient was immediate and devastating. He was crestfallen and deflated, the enthusiasm and energy gone from his voice. Far from being able to enjoy a triumph, he was faced with having failed his analyst. Now it was his turn to be angry. The analyst had done to him just what his father had always done; he had introduced his own bitter sense of failure at just the wrong time and had spoiled any potential that there was to celebrate an important event.

It was at this point that the analyst brought his experience into supervision, feeling guilty and ashamed about what he had done. I agreed that he had acted in a way that had gotten him and the patient away from the experience that was developing in the room. But I was also impressed, despite the different spirit in which the stories were told, with the similarities between his vignette and Hoffman's. As was the case with Hoffman, I believe, what developed between my supervisee and his patient was born out of the meeting of the patient's negative transference and the analyst's desire. Both Hoffman and my supervisee felt excluded by their patients. Hoffman's patient demanded that he not act like an analyst, which he wanted to do, and that he must act like a physician, which he could not do. My supervisee's patient refused to allow his analyst to be the benign, appreciative figure that my supervisee wanted to be.

The difference in the two vignettes, of course, is that my supervisee fell into the trap of repeating something old with his patient, while Hoffman came up with something novel to do. But I am not sure that finding something new to do is necessarily less of a trap than repeating something old. What seems most poignant as well as most similar to me is that in each case the analyst acted out of a desire to be part of things in a way that could heal a piece of the patient's history. And in each case, doing so enacted a role in a romantic fantasy of the patient's (Schafer 1970). Hoffman took on the role of hero in his patient's fantasy—recall that he consciously decided to be a better, more loving father—while my supervisee became the villain. But these roles define and imply each other, so there is less to the difference than meets the eye. The excess in the two examples is the same: it is the excess of wanting to make something happen. And the excess is perpetuated when, in turn, the thing that happens—the transaction—is understood to be what makes analysis possible and also becomes its subject matter.

It is also important that each vignette captures a moment when the patient's transferential attack on the analyst's desire to make something happen—his desire to create an analysis—has made things unbearable. In the face of these attacks, the analyst's desire is likely to be at its most intense, and he will feel most vulnerable about it. Both of these situations went the way they did, I believe, because the analyst was unable to submit to and contain his feelings, his reaction to the terrible moment when analyst and analysand were each the tyrannical, stifling, poisonous father and each the suffering, terrified, rageful child of the other. Moments like these are well known to all analysts, but they always feel like they are happening for the first time. They are moments when we lose our bearings, when any sense of who was doing what to whom seems impossible to come by, when it seems there is nothing and will never be anything to do. Hoffman's vignette, like many in the relational literature, teaches that there *is* something to do, that destructiveness can be overcome, that once the analysand has been rescued understanding can follow. Like all inspired excess, this is sometimes true. But not always, and it should be taught as one place to look among many, one that has possibilities and pitfalls like all the others. The lesson of Hoffman's vignette and those like it stands as a major contribution of relational theory, but we risk losing something uniquely affecting, and uniquely possible within the process of psychoanalytic treatment, if we turn it into a prescription for meeting all or even most of the difficult moments that arise in every analysis.

Let me conclude by recalling the way medieval morality plays worked. The plays were designed to inflame their audiences' desire to reject evil and to do good. I am struck by the similar tone of contemporary relational vignettes. The characters are different, of course. Instead of gluttony, lechery, sloth, hope, and charity, today we read tales of rigidity, authoritarianism, orthodoxy, openness, decentering, and negotiability. But the ending of the plays and the vignettes is strikingly the same: both end optimistically, with the saving of the protagonists' souls. The message of the vignettes is that saving our psychoanalytic souls depends on finding the right way of being with our patients. But, as in the morality plays, there is a great deal of excess in these reports, and, as in the plays, their message can be oppressive. I hope that by taking this beginning look at some of this excess, I have opened the way to a new dialogue that will allow us to realize the potential of relational thinking while helping us to avoid becoming the sort of movement that forecloses possibilities.

## REFERENCES

Aron, L. (1991). The patient's experience of the analyst's subjectivity. *Psychoanalytic Dialogues* 1:29–51.
———— (1996). *A Meeting of Minds: Mutuality in Psychoanalysis*. Hillsdale, NJ: Analytic Press.

Bion, W. (1967). Notes on memory and desire. In *Melanie Klein Today*, vol. 2, *Mainly Practice*, ed. E. B. Spillius, pp. 17–21. London: Routledge, 1988.

Breuer, J., and Freud, S. (1893–1895). Studies on hysteria. *Standard Edition* 2:3–303.

Davies, J. (1994). Love in the afternoon: a relational reconsideration of desire and dread. *Psychoanalytic Dialogues* 4:153–170.

Ferenczi, S., and Rank, O. (1924). *The Development of Psychoanalysis*. Madison, CT: International Universities Press.

Frederickson, J. (1990). Hate in the countertransference as an empathic position. *Contemporary Psychoanalysis* 26:479–495.

Freud, S. (1912). The dynamics of transference. *Standard Edition* 12:97–108.

——— (1914a). On the history of the psychoanalytic movement. *Standard Edition* 14:1–66.

——— (1914b). On narcissism: an introduction. *Standard Edition* 14:67–102.

——— (1937). Constructions in analysis. *Standard Edition* 23:255–269.

Gabbard, G. (1996). Challenges in the analysis of adult patients with histories of childhood sexual abuse. *Canadian Journal of Psychoanalysis* 5:1–25.

Gandhi, M. (1927–1929). *Autobiography: The Story of My Experiments with Truth*. Boston: Beacon, 1957.

Gerson, S. (1996). Neutrality, resistance, and self-disclosure in an intersubjective psychoanalysis. *Psychoanalytic Dialogues* 6:623–645.

Ghent, E. (1995). Interaction in the psychoanalytic situation. *Psychoanalytic Dialogues* 5:479–491.

Greenberg, J. (1986). Theoretical models and the analyst's neutrality. *Contemporary Psychoanalysis* 22:89–106.

——— (1991). *Oedipus and Beyond: A Clinical Theory*. Cambridge, MA: Harvard University Press.

——— (1995). Psychoanalytic technique and the interactive matrix. *Psychoanalytic Quarterly* 64:1–22.

Hoffman, I. (1983). The patient as interpreter of the analyst's experience. *Contemporary Psychoanalysis* 19:389–422.

——— (1991). Discussion: toward a social-constructivist view of the psychoanalytic situation. *Psychoanalytic Dialogues* 1:74–105.

——— (1994). Dialectical thinking and therapeutic action in the psychoanalytic process. *Psychoanalytic Quarterly* 63:187–218.

——— (1996). The intimate and ironic authority of the psychoanalyst's presence. *Psychoanalytic Quarterly* 65:102–136.

Mitchell, S. (1988). *Relational Concepts in Psychoanalysis*. Cambridge, MA: Harvard University Press.

——— (1992). Commentary on Trop and Stolorow's "Defense Analysis in Self Psychology." *Psychoanalytic Dialogues* 2:443–453.

——— (1997). *Influence and Autonomy in Psychoanalysis.* Hillsdale, NJ: Analytic Press.

——— (1998). The analyst's knowledge and authority. *Psychoanalytic Quarterly* 67:1–31.

Pizer, S. (1992). The negotiation of paradox in the analytic process. *Psychoanalytic Dialogues* 2:215–240.

——— (1998). *Building Bridges: The Negotiation of Paradox in Psychoanalysis.* Hillsdale, NJ: Analytic Press.

Renik, O. (1993). Analytic interaction: conceptualizing technique in light of the analyst's irreducible subjectivity. *Psychoanalytic Quarterly* 62:553–571.

Schafer, R. (1970). The psychoanalytic vision of reality. In *A New Language for Psychoanalysis*, pp. 22–56. New Haven, CT: Yale University Press, 1976.

# On Thinking We Know
# What We're Doing:
# Commentary On Greenberg's
# "The Analyst's Participation"

*David Schwartz*

The persistence of mutual attention between psychoanalysis and postmodernism is a natural upshot of their similarities to one another. Both are at least in part radical critiques of the particular empiricist optimism—modernism—that was predominant at the end of the nineteenth century and that has hung on, with and without modification, in different intellectual quarters into the twentieth and now, twenty-first. Although in different ways, Freud and Foucault challenged our faith in the power of raw observation and in the necessarily progressive and truth-discovering nature of science.[1] They are epistemological cousins: Freud insisted that no array of literally given facts spoken by a human fails to betray a more significant story, an unconscious one. Foucault, in a similar vein, contended that all regimes of knowledge, no matter how tried and true, are first and foremost instruments of power. Each enjoins us from swallowing whole the uninterpreted data of the social world. Each says that behind the claims of narratives and texts are unwritten motives and concealed functions. Each argues that human discourse is a multifarious endeavor that always has within it much more than meets the eye.

Now lest it seem as though I am already imagining far more kinship between Freudians and Foucauldians than is actual, let me quickly add that for psychoanalysis the critique of modernism, particularly the deconstruction of science, has been much more ambivalent than it has been for postmodernism. No doubt for every Freudian text that illuminates the fallibility and interpretability of observational discourse, there is one that avows science as the final word that will seal our understanding of, up to now, mysterious phenomena. (Freud's paper, "The Question of a *Weltanschauung*" (1933) is one of the most extended examples of such wholehearted positivism.)[2] But psychoanalysis's sporadic idealization of science is overshadowed by its most fundamental and innovative contribution, the concept of unconscious process, and this concept (which could scarcely be described as empirical or scientific) is also fundamental to postmodernism. More important, from a conceptual point of view, the Foucauldian analysis of culture, especially the culture of knowledge, with its attention to unarticulated functions and motives, would not be possible without the idea of unconscious process. Freud supplied the intellectual world with the concept that has the potential to challenge any intellectual practices, including science and psychoanalysis itself. Foucault took that concept to a new depth and helped spawn an intellectual movement that proceeded to make just those challenges. Psychoanalysts infused with the postmodern spirit (who tend to be relational theorists, either *ab initio* or newly made) have indeed set about questioning psychoanalytic theory and practice from top to bottom. One might say, further illustrating the kinship between postmodernism and psychoanalysis, that such relational theorists are only taking the concept of unconscious countertransference quite seriously, obeying ruthlessly the psychoanalytic and postmodern injunction to self-reflect.

But as I mentioned above, not all accept postmodernism's reciprocating gift to psychoanalysis as an unambiguous boon and thus do not see a marriage of psychoanalysis and postmodernism as only beneficial. Greenberg's paper is one that eyes the arrival of postmodernism with some suspicion even while it seems to recognize some of its virtue. Now to be accurate with respect to both the intent and the text of Greenberg's paper, it does not address postmodernism explicitly; rather, it takes relational psychoanalytic theory as its named subject. But post-modernism is certainly a central character in the story Greenberg wants to tell. He begins by articulating some fundamentals of relational psy-choanalytic theory in terms that emphasize their linkage to post-modernism's epistemological challenge (that various aspects of the analytic situation occur in a realm of profound uncertainty if not utter unknowability), speaks (approvingly) of the relational critique as a "deconstruction," as at least in part an effort to free us "from some ideas . . . that are based on an archaic philosophical foundation that has iso-lated us [psychoanalysts] from the intellectual mainstream," and, in the manner of postmodern criticism, highlights the rhetorical and dis-cursive properties of the text he chooses to analyze. But Greenberg's paper ends with much less emphasis on postmodern themes, either pro or con, and instead shifts gears to pay much closer attention to what he sees as the riskiness of the implicit technical recommendations of the case reports relational theorists have published. And this is precisely what is most intriguing in his paper: it reveals a seemingly unselfcon-scious movement between postmodern and modern psychoanalytic dis-courses. It offers us the opportunity to examine, at least in the work of one thoughtful and innovative psychoanalyst, some correlates of these two approaches to psychoanalytic theorizing and criticism. My frank intention in examining the details of Greenberg's movement between postmodernism and a more traditional, modernist psychoanalytic cri-tique is to strengthen psychoanalysis's engagement with postmodernism, to encourage psychoanalysts to see postmodernism not only as kindred, but as offering a necessary tool to keep psychoanalysis grounded, alive, and persuasive. It seems to me that the psychoanalytic openness and flexibility that Greenberg strives for in both clinical and political realms are most present when his framework is most postmodern and falter when it re-assumes the supervisory (modernist) rhetoric that is more familiar to us.

Up to now I have avoided a potentially difficult yet crucial task in a discussion of this sort: What is meant by "postmodern"? It should probably go without saying that different writers understand this term differently, so that at this point in the history of this idea it behooves me to specify the relatively narrow sense in which I am using it.[3] By "postmodern" I refer to the acknowledgment that most claims to knowl-edge, but especially those in the social realm, that is, what we claim to know about people either as individuals or as aggregates, are suspect on two counts: (1) assertions about human experience are almost always supported by data of ambiguous significance, and (2) such claims generally reflect the interests of the claim-maker, or of the claim-subscriber, which interests often overshadow any rigor that might have accompanied the establishment of any given assertion. Put a bit more simply, what we say we know about people is on very shaky footing and may say as much about us as about them. As we shall see (and as Greenberg seems to know), the apparent conciseness and limitation of these two points are deceptive. They contain a surprisingly large field of implications for psychoanalytic theory and practice.

Greenberg's critique of relational psychoanalytic writing begins roughly one quarter of the way into his paper, where he observes that despite their frequent emphasis on the idiosyncratic nature of all analyses and on the de-privileging of any specific technical interventions by relational authors, their clinical examples seem always to "point us in a particular direction"; that is, an implicit prescriptiveness in their illustrations belies the radically open system they advocate. Greenberg has noticed that the case reports and clinical examples of relational writers are characterized by a particular trope, or rhetorical device, that goes something like: *I was having a difficult time with a patient; it was so difficult and upsetting that either I decided on, or just unconsciously found myself, veering away from the behavior that has traditionally been considered to be within the margins of psychoanalytic practice. I was directive, emotional, flexible, or revealing. I and the patient then conjointly analyzed my unusual, extra-analytic behavior. As a result a great deal of previously unavailable understanding was acquired, and consequently the treatment moved forward.* Frequently enough, this trope is accompanied by a particular attitude on the part of the analyst who narrates it. At its worst it can be self-congratulatory and superior as the narrator makes him- or herself sound heroic in imagined contrast to those less innovative analysts who are stuck in more conventional ways of working. But more frequently the story simply sounds as though the analyst/teller believes he or she is offering an account of an experience that significantly augments our sense of what works best in psychoanalysis and, by implication, a truer sense of human nature.

To the extent that this rhetorical form has become commonplace in relational psychoanalytic writing, it is no surprise that Greenberg is alarmed by it. In general, too little attention has been given to the problems of psychoanalytic case reporting, and focusing on this particular use of clinical material is overdue and necessary. Indeed, from a postmodern point of view this sort of clinical narration exquisitely exemplifies one aspect of psychoanalysis that continues to expose it to defamation and valid epistemological critique. For as Greenberg aptly labels them,[4] such uses of clinical material are morality plays. The hollow epistemological footing and political import of morality plays are easy to see. They push for generalization when all they really support are themselves. Theoretically psychoanalysis and postmodernism are intrinsically sensitive to the idiosyncratic nature and intellectual flimsiness of morality plays. Greenberg does us a service by pointing not only to their invalidity as arguments, but also to the harm they may do as subtly coercive catechisms in the informal canon of psychoanalysis. Heroic accounts of virtuous and humane flexibility can easily become discursive ideals toward which we mistakenly strive, imagining, as their authors may have suggested we do, that extraordinary and off-the-beaten-track measures in behalf of "the relationship" can save the day in the face of human obstinacy and neurosis. Greenberg touches lightly upon the most obvious implication of the prescriptive inflection of many relational clinical narratives: "My point, of course, is to question *any* (emphasis added) reliance on royal roads." From a postmodern perspective this implication should be elaborated. Any claims by an analyst that he or she has had an experience that shows why a patient did what he or she did, or, even more improbably, shows us what the best way to do psychoanalysis is, is first of all false, and perhaps more important, likely to be part of a larger political project, explicit or not and conscious or not. Any time a clinical account gives off the glow of self-congratulation, or more directly asserts to the reader/analyst some recommendation as to what is best to do with one sort of patient or another, and, by implication, what patients need from us technically, either across the board or differentiated by type of patient, we know that the writer has gone too far. Such assertions cannot be warranted by clinical data, and probably not by any humanly attainable data. That is the crucial caveat that postmodernism in psychoanalysis repeats.

Is Greenberg prepared to follow his critique to such an implied conclusion? Is he willing to apply the deconstructive analysis he offers relational writers, more generally, even to his own writing? Or does

Greenberg replace one morality play with another, but less obvious one? The answer is to be found in the particular use to which he puts his critique. For although his essay begins in a postmodern spirit, its ending points up how difficult a relinquishment it is that the postmodern framework asks of psychoanalysis.

Greenberg further analyzes the narrative trope he has highlighted by characterizing its function. He suggests that the particular psychoanalytic problem this rhetoric seeks to address is the question of why a patient would remain in psychoanalysis.[5] Greenberg is arguing that when relational writers offer examples of dramatically difficult moments in analytic treatment they are really contending with a particular clinical/theoretical problem, namely that the solution psychoanalysis offers to people's problems—self-awareness[6]—is usually quite unappealing in the short run, and so we really do not understand why or how people tolerate psychoanalytic treatment. He says the relational solution to this problem is to assert that "the analyst . . . invariably and inevitably . . . provides the patient with a new and crucial kind of relational experience," giving depth and meaning to the insights that emerge and "even more fundamentally" gratifying a wide range of needs and desires, thereby motivating the patient to "enter and . . . remain in treatment."[7] Greenberg's next step is to contrast the relational solution with Freud's response to the same problem. Freud says (as summarized by Greenberg) that successful psychoanalysis depends on an "unobjectionable positive transference," that there is "something *within* [emphasis added] the patient that makes it possible for him or her to embrace the social consensus [regarding the validity of psychoanalysis] and to muster sufficient . . . courage to undertake an arduous treatment."

Greenberg now uses his articulation of a contrast between the relational provision of an external experience and Freud's abstinent (and modest) reliance on internal forces ("something within the patient") as a framework for critically examining Hoffman's relational clinical example. That is to say, he recounts Hoffman's clinical narrative but emphasizes the analyst's choice to encourage the patient to look within herself instead of encouraging her to look to the analytic dyad, both for sustenance and for an explanation of her experience. Greenberg stresses what he sees as Hoffman's efforts to "bolster [the patient's] belief in the value of the analytic relationship" and his direct provision of "a reason and the means to go on." Using Freud's term explicitly,

Greenberg says that Hoffman "*gave the patient* [emphasis added] the material with which she could re-establish an 'unobjectionable positive transference.'" From Greenberg's point of view Hoffman persuaded the patient to remain in treatment through the gratifying provision of interpersonal novelty (the analyst dis-identifying with her father) and the seductive promise to care more about her well-being than about "analytic purity." While Greenberg does not say so explicitly, he has focused on Hoffman's breach of two cardinal prohibitory principles of classically articulated psychoanalytic technique: no suggestion and no gratification, better known as the principles of neutrality and abstinence, respectively.

Having thus oriented Hoffman's narrative around the polarity of the interpersonal versus the intrapsychic, and having highlighted Hoffman's noncompliance with the classical principles of neutrality and abstinence, Greenberg can question whether Hoffman's emphasis on the interpersonal aspects of the dynamics, including a willingness to gratify the patient, was not excessive. He develops the theme of excessive attention to the analytic dyad (including excessive gratification), finally arguing that the patient's effort to elicit a particular behavior from the analyst—to get Valium for her—was itself a negative consequence of the analyst's historically chronic instruction to her to look outward instead of inward. Greenberg is saying that the story Hoffman has offered as illustrating the value of relational technique is in fact an iatrogenic effect of that technical stance: it appears that "what happened is to a significant extent an artifact of [Hoffman's] particular way of working."[8]

Two things happened for me when I read this last sentence: My postmodern heart sank and my deconstructive brain began to buzz. The essay that began with an innovative openness that seemed congenial to postmodernism now sounded an all-too-familiar note. Like many analysts before him, Greenberg was claiming to be able to determine the etiological sequence of an analysis from having read the analyst's report of it. But given the data available, a determination of the mechanism that produced "what happened" in the analysis Hoffman reports is out of human reach. Greenberg's assertions about that mechanism (and therefore the inferences he might attach to it) are no more nor less creditable than Hoffman's (to the extent that Hoffman made an etiological assertion), because the controlled, independent manipulation of variables that assertion of causality logically requires is necessarily absent from all clinical situations and from their reports. The error of imagining causality among events when all we really have is contiguity (or correlation, at best) is an old one, and I feel certain that if anyone invidiously claimed an unfounded causal sequence in a clinical report offered by Greenberg, he would waste no time pointing out the logical fallacy.[9] That is what made my deconstructive brain begin to buzz. I wondered: What are the underlying assumptions that may have permitted Greenberg to fall into the modernist trap of making inferences and claims in a realm that really only permits speculation? What axioms were so cherished or influential that they turned an essay initially concerned to avoid any "ironclad commitment to an overarching way of understanding what [goes] wrong for our patients" and how we should help them, into one that claims to *know* what went wrong in a case report of an analysis presented by its author as an exemplary success? Greenberg had begun his essay by deploying postmodern tools—an analysis of the rhetorical properties of relational clinical texts—but then diminished the rigor and nonpartisan appeal of his argument by representing in his own text those same epistemological problems (moralism and unfounded conviction) that he usefully deconstructed in Hoffman's. A consideration of what may have been the conceptual basis of Greenberg's switch back toward a familiar psychoanalytic discourse may be instructive. Among other things, it can clarify what it is that we must relinquish in order to sustain the postmodernization of psychoanalysis, and what its costs and benefits may be.

We can discover the conceptual basis of Greenberg's return to modernism by scrutinizing his text. Along the way to his conclusion regarding the events described in Hoffman's report and following it, Greenberg articulates or implies a number of cautions, recommendations, and claims about psychoanalytic technique and theoretical change generally. It is in this cautionary tale in the second half of his paper that the content of his modernism becomes most clear. I have distilled three pertinent, seemingly diverse, but actually interlocking assertions from Greenberg's text. They straddle different discursive realms: the psychological, the moral, and the historical. For each, I want to say something about its relation to postmodernism, and then say something concerning the broader cultural meaning of Greenberg's text, emphasizing the significance of these assertions.

1. *There are two differentiable sources of the patient's experience in psychoanalysis: the patient alone (the "uniquely private and personal") and the analytic dyad (the "transactions" that occur between analyst and patient). Of these two sources the patient alone is the therapeutically and epistemologically best focus of analytic attention.* Although Greenberg gives some credence to the analytic dyad as a source of therapeutically useful knowledge about the patient, his linguistic choices repeatedly show us that he regards the patient alone as a superior source of information and analytic work, the site of depth and authenticity.

From the point of view of ordinary linguistic usage, positivist social science, and a wide range of conscious experience, this postulation seems obviously valid. But postmodern epistemology and psychoanalytic practice both challenge it.[10] In fact, we are almost never able to distinguish the "internal" versus the "external" determinants of subjective experience. This is for two reasons. First, there is no methodology to do so. As long as human experience is observed within a social context (such as psychoanalysis), it is not possible to rule out the effects of social variables (or subjective states) on any given experience, and therefore it is not possible to assess the relative weights of internal and external variables, respectively. But perhaps more important, the very existence of a truly all-internal sphere is questionable. As soon as a second person enters the room, social responding commences for both parties. It is conditioned by the endless intersections of individual history and social signifiers that all of us perforce convey: clothing, gestures, speech, styles on innumerable dimensions. To speak of experience that is "uniquely private and personal" (when the subject is not physically alone) is to speak of an autonomous asociality that, for good or ill, is impossible to have. Language permits us to name a concept of full interiority, but how it could be constituted in human life is a mystery. It seems likely that when individuals who are currently in the company of an other believe they are having a "private" moment, they are deceiving themselves. When analysts imagine they have furnished such privacy through silence or radically limiting their responses, they, too, are deceiving themselves.

With no method to address it and its existence in doubt, the idea of the "uniquely private and personal" begins to seem more of a political or cultural regulator than a descriptor. But more on that below.[11]

2. *Desire on the part of the analyst is bad for therapy. Its role in a therapeutic process should be minimized. This is difficult but doable.* Here Green-

berg has articulated in remarkably stark language the assumption that underlies a central tenet of classical psychoanalytic theory and technique: the principle of therapeutic abstinence. It is an assumption and recommendation as deeply antithetical to postmodernism as any. It imagines that desire is something we understand, that its mechanisms or rules are known, and that its allegedly negative effects are relatively avoidable. If we think about the concept of desire epistemologically—from the point of view of what we can know about it—the problematic nature of this vision becomes clear. In contrast to the sources of experience, which, as discussed above, can be conceptualized as including some (albeit undifferentiatable) combination of internal and external factors, desire, an aspect of experience itself, is, by definition, private. Desire is something inside me about which you can only imperfectly know to the extent that my behavior is presumably marked by it. Its unknowability and unsuitability for empirical generalization are guaranteed by these aspects of its definition and usage—that is, by its logical and semantic nature. In light of this it is not surprising that in pressing for a recognition of the danger of the analyst's desire in psychoanalysis Greenberg invokes authorities, Bion and Gandhi in particular. Any argument from observation would amount to the overvalued conjecture and polemicizing to which Greenberg does not want to consciously succumb. Should we analysts try to minimize this thing that is only indirectly graspable and of disputable value? The postmodernist sensibility (and perhaps common sense, too) suggests our energy would be better spent trying to simply know when it is present, and, depending on its meaning in a particular case, to act in a way that is likely to allow that meaning to be understood in the analytic encounter. To aim for something more, for example to influence the actual intensity of desire, as I will elaborate below, is to advocate a particular political stance vis-à-vis desire.

3. *The essence of psychoanalysis continues to be found in Freud. He is our disciplinary father, the alpha-analyst and progenitor of true psychoanalysis.* In ascribing this view to Greenberg, in contrast to the two previous assertions, I am venturing beyond his explicit text and making an inference at some logical distance from it. This is warranted because in the present essay Greenberg engages a rhetorical practice that, appearing in a relatively consistent format, has been widespread in psychoanalytic writing and thus possesses something of the commu-

nity meaning that I have emphasized above. I call the practice *strategic Freud-referencing*.[12] It is most prominently to be seen in papers that comment on other papers, but not exclusively. It works as follows: In discussing a topic in clinical psychoanalysis the author locates a text by Freud (usually an early text, preferably before 1924) that can be understood as having some relevance to the topic of the paper. The Freud text is then described admiringly, noting its presumed innovation for its time. Some attention may then be given to how Freud arrived at this innovation through struggling with a particular clinical dilemma, emphasizing his curiosity and creativity. Then Freud's revision of his thinking is illustrated by adverting to a later text. In this sequence Freud is made to appear, by turns, innovative, guided chiefly by clinical data, and intelligently flexible.[13] Returns to Freud's text then mark the rest of the paper, increasingly building the impression that he got it right from the beginning and that straying from the wisdom contained in the Freudian text amounts to a kind of failure of recognition or respect for the true origination of an insight. A significant aspect of strategic Freud-referencing is that the Freud text selected may not principally address the question with which the original writer was concerned. Rather the Freud text represents what that writer *should* have been concerned with, which is to say, what Freud correctly focused on when he encountered what is presumed to be the same problem.

Now Greenberg's references to Freud in the present essay do not correspond in all details to the stereotype sketched above, but they match enough and are enough used in behalf of pejoratively creating a contrast with Hoffman's "excesses" so that a resonance with this rhetorical practice is audible, as is its meaning. Rightly or wrongly, Freud enjoys the status of "father of psychoanalysis." When his name and one of his texts are (with some reverence) inserted into a discussion of contemporary theory and technique, a range of psychological and discursive processes are triggered, intentionally or not and consciously or not. A full consideration of the depth and breadth of those processes is beyond the scope of this essay, but permit me to offer a sampling of what I have in mind: The reader is signaled as to the likely allegiances of the writer, and, perhaps more important, informed of the writer's partisanship. He or she feels pressured to accord a particular kind of attention to Freud's words. Depending on the allegiances of the reader, some inner conflict follows, probably some sort of interplay of guilt, admiration, and defiance. In other words, a deeply felt debate is instigated in which a powerfully valenced historical figure (not a living participant) is central. Each time this is done, Freud is re-established and grows as the ambivalently loved father, as does the notion of psychoanalysis as derived from and organically linked to him. An old debate is refueled at its shallowest point; a definition of psychoanalysis that emphasizes a particular historical figure instead of a general practice is implied.

From my postmodern point of view, the process described above constitutes a deadening epistemology that tends to constrict the psychoanalytic imagination and fetter the psychoanalytic process via the superego of the analyst. If, as I maintain, psychoanalysis is the dialectical exploration of experience, including unconscious experience, then it existed before Freud and before the coining of the word *psychoanalysis*. Understood in this way, the presence of psychoanalysis can be seen in philosophy, literature, theater, and even in theological writing, long before it became conflated with the modern practices of psychology and psychiatry. The arbitrary identification of psychoanalysis with Freud and his epoch has been so powerful that its very existence outside that historical and disciplinary framework has become less and less visible. The particular development of psychoanalysis (including its naming) in the work of Freud is just that: particular. Repeatedly tilting back toward the work of one prodigious practitioner and his followers distorts the general process of dialectically analyzing human experience. The at times gratuitous injecting of Freud's texts into contemporary discussions, and thus the de-contextualizing of those texts, is part of the way that tilt is accomplished.

Among the rewards of keeping psychoanalysis centered on Freud is the experience of having a stable textual corpus and a minimally varying theoretical framework from which to derive psychoanalytic technique. In addition, of course, there is the ambiguous pleasure of having a specific idealized father sempiternally present in one's work and in one's debates. But the most fundamental mandate of psychoanalysis—to seek the idiosyncratic particulars of individuals' experience—argues in favor of abstaining from such rewards. Probably more than the analyst's private ideation or desire, they threaten to distract attention from the uniqueness of each patient's experience. For the idealization of Freud, however ambivalent, reflects something created in a time and place apart from the present patient, unlike the analyst's present experience, which arises *with* that patient.

These three tropes—the primacy of the patient alone, the danger of desire, and the Freudian genesis—weave their way through Greenberg's text as he builds his argument that relational case reports tend to promote certain excesses in psychoanalytic practice. His initial observation of an inappropriately moralistic rhetoric in those case reports becomes less and less audible as his own essay's moralism increases in volume. Greenberg's moralism, devoid as it is of the heroic cadence that he identified as a significant presence in many relational clinical narratives, is not obvious. But his explicit and indirect remonstrances to the analyst not to overemphasize the analyst–patient transactions, to avoid desire, and to respect Freud's thinking certainly do constitute a moralism, a positivist moralism that tells us that the best way to explore human experience is known and can be generalized, and that we ignore it at the peril of doing bad analysis. Moreover, Greenberg's presuming to have discovered in Hoffman's text the unsuspected (and iatrogenic) source of the patient's behavior has the distinct ring of a knowing "gotcha" if not the self-congratulatory tone to be found in relational narratives.

But to discover that one writer has subtly reproduced something that he has criticized in another writer's work has only the very limited interest of pointing to a common human process. Something more significant is happening in Greenberg's essay that has implications both for psychoanalysis and for its larger cultural context. I will explain:

Psychoanalysis is especially vulnerable to the temptations of positivism, the promise of knowledge through the proper application of method. Patients, who are, after all, participants in modern culture persistently press for closure and an end to ambiguity. Apparent correspondences between what they seem to be saying and the analyst's pre-existing theoretical framework (coupled with the analyst's own need for certainty) can produce the seductive "aha!" that may halt the continuous questioning that is the psychoanalytic mandate. In addition, the unfortunate historical coincidence of the rise of psychoanalysis with the rapid development of biomedical science has encouraged some psychoanalysts to unreflectively import the language and trappings of science. But when we have the language and trappings of science, which is to say the rhetorical format of etiological claims and generalizations, but not its methodology, the narrative produced is largely a reflection of a currently popular cultural framework, which is to say contemporary prejudices. In other words, the dialectical exploration of human experience is intrinsically and irreparably fraught with ambiguity and the impossibility of verification. To the extent that psychoanalysts cannot accept the anxiety associated therewith, they, like other would-be knowers of human experience, may resort to claims that will reflect and promote current ideologies as though they were empirically derived.

Claims about the method of psychoanalysis, the topic of both Greenberg's and Hoffman's papers, are no less susceptible to ideological colonization than are other psychoanalytic claims. Outside general principles built into the purpose of analysis (focus on the patient, receptivity to most ideation, confidentiality), there is very little basis for arguing that one technical recommendation is superior to another. So when analysts do argue for their favorite technical recommendations, as do Greenberg *and* Hoffman, it is very likely that their texts will wind up representing particular cultural themes, themes that are remote from the authors' conscious intent but deeply woven into the fabric of modern life. Indeed, Greenberg's essay illustrates this, for it shows, subtly but unmistakably, the mark of a major contemporary cultural theme: the virtue of masculinity. This, no doubt, seems out of left field. But consider: Greenberg is first of all concerned that "the [interpersonal] transactions that are . . . created . . . in analysis [may] become too much the focus of inquiry." He suggests that it would be "more important or more useful [to allow] whatever is happening to develop further and to deepen," but that "to get to this, both participants would have to be . . . willing to dwell in an experience that was becoming grim and . . . terrifying for patient and analyst alike." Second, he warns against texts that might "inflame the analyst's desire to be a good analyst or . . . a good person" and weighs in as against "even the desire to help." Third, Greenberg organizes his cautions and recommendations around an admired text of Freud. So what image of a good analyst emerges out of these cautions? What are the personality traits associated with these recommendations? They are stoicism, self-sufficiency, valorization of pain endurance, the struggle for self-control and against desire, and loyalty to the father. They speak for themselves, both with respect to the gender stereotype they conjure and their likely utility as therapeutic agents. And I will admit that I am especially distressed about the prospect of supplying additional validation within psychoanalysis for this particular cultural structure, but that is far from my principal reason for wanting to identify its concealed presence in Greenberg's text. The larger and more important point is that the unanalyzed invasion of psychoanalysis by contemporary cultural regulators is made more likely and more difficult to detect whenever we try to argue for one method (or vision of human nature) over another. This is because of the epistemological situation in which all explorers of human experience find themselves, namely that of uncontrolled and unmanipulable experimental variables. Advocacy under these conditions leads to cultural prescriptions replacing the facts that are out of reach, overwriting ambiguity with claims and sentiments that are familiar, if unconvincing. The very same argument I am making against Greenberg's essay could be made against Hoffman's, and Greenberg was on the brink of making it before he displaced it with a modernist supervisory rhetoric. The cultural morality play that Greenberg uncovers in Hoffman's text is one of antiauthoritarian heroism, in which humanist iconoclasm is elevated to the spot that classical theorists reserve for abstinence. Personally, I like its rebelliousness better, but to suggest that the terrible ambiguity of madness can be penetrated by[14] goodness is no truer than Greenberg's more ascetic recommendations.

It is no doubt true that there are better and worse ways to make an analysis more successful or resilient, but the logic of knowledge prohibits us from using the psychoanalytic situation (and most imaginable experimental situations) to learn which are which. That is the psychoanalyst's dilemma: to be obliged to foster treatment without much in the way of a documented road map. The postmodern perspective does not offer a way out of this dilemma; it only insists that we are stuck with it, and that we should write accordingly. When I say that both Greenberg and Hoffman are only transmitting different cultural imperatives, and not offering factually debatable assertions about how best to do psychoanalysis, I am not suggesting that there is a way other than theirs that makes it possible to escape culture and thus to really do psychoanalysis right. Postmodernism and deconstruction are themselves cultural, historically contingent phenomena that will no doubt shift over time: there is no escaping culture. But if we speak and argue as though the truth about people and about doing psychoanalysis is discoverable, then we act as though we psychoanalysts have *already* escaped culture and that our patients can, too, if only they follow the latest rules of psychoanalysis. We then contribute to the obfuscation of what might be our most important message to the patient and to society: that the rules are made up, that if you must pay attention to the man behind the curtain, remember that he is having as hard a time as you are.

## NOTES

1. Freud and Foucault have been selected as icons of their respective intellectual frameworks, not as representing themselves.

2. And if Freud was ambivalent about science, Hartmann and the ego psychologists were in love with it, so we must concede that there is at least a significant vein in the history of psychoanalysis, if not in its fundamental principles, that truly runs counter to the postmodern critique.

3. I have chosen to use the narrowest possible sense of "postmodern," avoiding any reference to ontology or history. My intent is to be inclusive and ask the least of anyone who is considering classifying his or her thinking as postmodern.

4. I do not intend here to make any judgment with respect to whether or not Hoffman's paper exemplifies this practice.

5. It is worth mentioning at this point that this formulation of the underlying function of such relational clinical narratives is quite debatable and probably would not be agreed to by many relational writers.

6. This conceptualization of what psychoanalysis offers patients seems to me antiquated.

7. This way of describing relational technical recommendations bears an interesting resemblance to the "corrective emotional experience" of other psychoanalytic debates. Curiously, Greenberg attributes its source solely to the work of Ferenczi.

8. Incidentally, in another context, that is, one that grants that *virtually always* the human idiosyncrasies present in an analysis are what determine its outcome, a statement such as this might not constitute a negative assessment of the analyst's work; but that is not Greenberg's point of view and his sharp disapproval is unmistakable.

9. Indeed, it seems to me that it is on the occasions when interchanges between psychoanalysts of differing theoretical persuasions are marked by etiological claims that the least mutual listening takes place; one can easily anticipate Hoffman's retort as he chafes under Greenberg's criticism.

10. Of course this view is known in philosophy as Cartesian dualism, and it was challenged well before postmodernism began its work. The work of Brentano, Husserl, and the French phenomenologists springs most readily to mind. Interestingly, this work has yet to find its way into classical psychoanalysis.

11. I probably do not need to add that a critique of Cartesian dualism, briefly sketched above, is at the heart of relational theory. Contrariwise, belief in a differentiable reality of subject and object is at the heart of certain classical technical principles, particularly the principle of neutrality.

12. I doubt that I am the first to note this practice, but I am unaware of any published thoughts about it.

13. Lately, as in Greenberg's paper, some of Freud's personal faults may also be alluded to, such as his exclusionary efforts with respect to the inner circle of psychoanalysis. This strikes me as an effort to dispel the impression of an unrestrained idealization of Freud that the first part of the sequence may convey.

14. It may be that the virtual "masculine panic" (Mark Finn, personal communication 2000) that relational texts often set off in classical readers is due to their subliminal representation of a phallic mother as the best therapeutic agent.

## REFERENCE

Freud, S. (1933). The question of a *Weltanschauung*. (New introductory lectures on psycho-analysis.) *Standard Edition* 22:158–182.

# 9b

---

# Reply to Schwartz

## Jay Greenberg

In reviewing my paper through the lens of postmodern theory, David Schwartz presents me with a challenge that I did not expect to face when I first wrote it. The paper, as I see it, is primarily a clinical piece, and I thought that debate about what I wrote would focus on clinical rather than theoretical issues. Nevertheless, I find what Schwartz has to say thoughtful and interesting and am pleased to have a chance to respond to his critique. I also greatly appreciate his recognition that close examination of the innovations in relational technique that have been greeted with unequivocal enthusiasm by its proponents (including, at times, myself) is overdue.

But I will focus my discussion on the conceptual issues that Schwartz raises. Early on, he says that my paper "is one that eyes the arrival of postmodernism with some suspicion even while it seems to recognize some of its virtue." In this, he is largely correct, although I would add that it somewhat overemphasizes the extent to which post-modernism is my focus and greatly overstates my knowledge of and sophistication with it or any other philosophical system. Like psycho-analysis, postmodernism offers analytic tools (and terms to describe them) that can be appropriated by anybody who is inclined to do so, irrespective of how deeply one appreciates or even understands the underlying system. So yes, I take from the body of postmodern thought—more accurately, from postmodern theory as it has filtered into the atmosphere in which contemporary psychoanalytic discourse is conducted—what seems useful to me. And yes, I am skeptical of many of its assertions.

Schwartz is sufficiently enthusiastic both about the potential of postmodern theory to illuminate the shortcomings of psychoanalysis and about my use of it to open up some of the unexplored problems in contemporary relational practice. This leaves me free to focus on my skepticism, and I do have two central problems with postmodernism, especially as it is explicated and wielded in Schwartz's paper. First, I find the theory's central premise self-refuting; second, and more important from my perspective, I believe that if fully embraced it would eviscer-ate the power of the clinical encounter. I will address each of these concerns in turn.

Consider Schwartz's concise statement of the fundamental pre-mises of postmodern theory: "Assertions about human experience are almost always supported by data of ambiguous significance" and "Such claims generally reflect the interests of the claim-maker, or of the claim-subscriber, which interests often overshadow any rigor that might have accompanied the establishment of any given assertion." While these premises appear to suggest a kind of caution and an admirable philo-sophic humility, to me they betray a bedrock certainty that competes with the most extravagant claims of the logical positivists. And the certainty is not just epistemological; it extends to both psychological and moral propositions. Epistemologically, Schwartz is quite sure that the data are of ambiguous significance (almost always?). Psychologically, he is certain that the claim-maker has a hidden agenda (which, as the latter part of his essay demonstrates, he is quite sure he can discern, at least in my case). Morally, he is equally clear that the claim-maker has abandoned rigor in favor of other, presumably less laudable interests, an assertion that sounds remarkably close to saying that the claim-maker is acting in bad faith.

So the certainty that postmodern theory allows a commentator to bring to an analysis of what the other person claims to know, what causes the other person to claim to know it, and the compromises that the other has made in pursuing his or her agenda refutes the postmodern premises themselves.

I want quickly to add that I am particularly sensitive to the self-refuting potential of postmodern theory at the moment because Schwartz uses its premises to gore my ox. That is, before he has finished looking at my paper he has come up with some ideas about what I am up to that go far enough to make a Freudian analyst blush. Before he is through with his dissection of my meaning, he has me upholding "the virtue of masculinity," which he quickly ties to the possibility of a "virtual 'masculine panic' that relational texts often set off in classical readers." Can castration anxiety be far behind? Note that although he does acknowledge his own biases here and there, Schwartz claims to have discovered (*sic*) something in my text by virtue of a careful reading of it.

While in the area, I want to take note of one assertion about which I am quite sure that Schwartz is wrong. With some discreet disclaimers he ties me into the tradition of what he calls strategic Freud-referencing, a practice that perpetuates a veneration for the father (note the connection to the point I addressed immediately above) and for true thoughtfulness. Along with Schwartz and many others, I acknowledge that this has been both characteristic and problematic for psychoanalysis over the course of many years. But that is far from what I was doing in my paper. In fact, I instanced Freud as the originator of the propensity for excess that I addressed, and I took his work as a polar opposite of what I see as contemporary relational excess. Yes, I think there is a great deal in what Freud said that deserves consideration even in our very different time. But nobody who has read very much of what I have written (including this paper) should conclude that I am not at least as critical of Freud as I am of anybody else.

Let me turn to my second objection to a wholesale application of postmodern theory to the clinical psychoanalytic enterprise. Schwartz is correct in saying that my paper has two parts, written in somewhat different voices. The first part is, roughly speaking, deconstructive; the second builds a point of view about a particular clinical vignette and so is constructive or, in Schwartz's term, "supervisory." Schwartz approves of my deconstructive efforts, but his "postmodern heart sank" when I started to talk about what I thought might be going on between Hoffman and his analysand. I disappointed Schwartz, he tells us, because "[l]ike many analysts before him, Greenberg was claiming to be able to determine the etiological sequence of an analysis from having read the analyst's report of it."

It sounds a bit sinister in Schwartz's phrasing, but isn't this what analysts do? We listen (or read), we reflect, we come up with our own theories, we talk about what we have come up with. We do, in short, what I did with respect to Hoffman's presentation and what Schwartz did with respect to my paper. And, perhaps most importantly, I believe this is what our analysands count on us to do. They come to us with the hope and expectation that an encounter with another person—with another mind—will help them to find aspects of themselves and of their experience that they have lost and that haunt them in crippling ways. Different analysts have stressed the workings of very different modes of engagement: empathy, explanation, recognition, confrontation, support, benign skepticism, and so on. I suspect that this reflects the hopes and perhaps the needs of various analysands, and the strengths and weaknesses of various analysts. What each of these formulations has in common is that they assume that analysis is a meeting between two people, each of whom is opinionated, passionate, biased, fallible, and free to speak in a way that he or she believes most genuine at any given moment.

So yes, I suggested an etiological hypothesis. In doing so I seem to have offended Schwartz, because he goes on to say that "given the data available, a determination of the mechanism that produced 'what happened' in the analysis that Hoffman reports is out of human reach." If this is a guiding premise of postmodernism, the theory seriously misunderstands the clinical enterprise, and if taken seriously enough could undermine it. The misunderstanding involves what analysts think they are doing when they say something. From my point of view, at least, I judge etiological hypotheses according to whether they are helpful or not. And being helpful depends on whether what I have to say generates self-reflection and dialogue.

I suspect that most (not all) contemporary analysts judge their clinical hypotheses on the basis of whether they are facilitative, and that they care little about whether they are "true" in any sweeping way. Even those who continue to focus on the analysis of resistance are thinking more about resistance to being touched by the analytic process and by the person of the analyst than about resistance to knowing the truth. In this respect Schwartz is, unexpectedly, a fellow traveler with Adolf Grünbaum; they both overestimate how concerned analysts are about the truth value of their propositions.

So I think that while the postmodern critique (like psychoanalysis itself) does an important service by reminding us of how necessary humility about our own ideas always is, it addresses a problem that is less prevalent than one might imagine it to be (and is perhaps less prevalent than it once was). And, pushed to its conclusion, the theory runs the risk of silencing us, leading us away from our responsibility to make judgments and from the human inevitability of judging. That holds true for our engagement with patients and for our engagement with the ideas of others. We say what we think to be true, we try to stay open to biases (hidden agendas, countertransferences) that we can never hope to know fully, we understand that whatever we have to say can be deconstructed, and we hope that nevertheless it will be useful. This is what makes both clinical psychoanalysis and discourse about psychoanalytic ideas worth doing.

In his analysis of my rhetorical strategy and the ideas I have come up with, Schwartz has given me a great deal to think about. So has Hoffman, and I hope I have done the same for each of them. But as to whether Schwartz is on to something about me or merely doggedly pursuing his own agenda—allow me to respond to this admittedly modernist question with an appropriately postmodern answer: Who knows?

# Index